W9-BCL-735

and Other Essays

Geoffrey H.
Hartman

University of Chicago Press
Chicago and London

GEOFFREY H. HARTMAN is professor of English and comparative literature at Yale University. He has received the Christian Gauss prize, and he is the author of *The Unmediated Vision*, *André Malraux*, *Wordsworth's Poetry*, and *Beyond Formalism*.

The University of Chicago Press, Chicago 60637
The University of Chicago Press, Ltd., London

Printed in the United States of America
79 78 77 76 75 987654321

Library of Congress Cataloging in Publication Data

Hartman, Geoffrey H.
The fate of reading and other essays.

Includes index.
1. Literature—History and criticism—Theory, etc.
I. Title
PN441.H35 801'.95 74-11624
ISBN 0-226-31844-3
ISBN 0-226-31845-1 pbk.

For René Wellek and
William K. Wimsatt

praesentia numina

Contents

Preface

"He who has raised himself above the alms-basket, and, not content to live lazily on scraps of begged opinions, sets his own thoughts on work, to find and follow truth, will (whatever he lights on) not miss the hunter's satisfaction; every moment of his pursuit will reward his pains with some delight; and he will have reason to think his time not ill spent, even when he cannot much boast of any great acquisition."

John Locke

The essays in this book were written during the last five years and extend the concerns of *Beyond Formalism* (1970). It seems to me as important as ever to study art from within, to respect the rigor of its code and the expressiveness of its traditions; and I am more rather than less impressed now by how hard it is to advance "beyond formalism" in the understanding of literature.

This does not mean the attempt should not be made. I have not found, however, a method to distinguish clearly what is formal and what is not, or what is figurative and what is not, or what is the reader's and what the author's share in "producing" the complex understanding which surrounds a literary work. Another difficulty is that whoever thinks about our "confusion of tongues" does not know whether to rejoice in it or to seek its reduction to a genuinely communal and purified language. It is no accident, surely, that our time has produced such Fables for the Critic as Nabokov's *Pale Fire*, Borges's *The Aleph*, and Pynchon's *The Crying of Lot 49*. In flight from Babel, they suggest that our obsessive concern with language is more than formalistic or self-regarding.

There is no need to exaggerate the present situation. What is happening may be a repetition, for the Grub Street of scribbling to which Alexander Pope and Christopher Smart reacted, each in his own way, was probably no different from today's print-plenitude. Nor has the status of the critic changed radically.

"Criticism," Oliver Goldsmith wrote, "may properly be called the natural destroyer of polite learning. We have seen that critics, or those whose only business is to write books upon other books, are always more numerous as learning is more diffused; and experience has shown that, instead of promoting its interest, which they profess to do, they generally injure it. This decay which criticism produced may be deplored, but can scarcely be remedied, as the man who writes against the critics is obliged to add himself to the number. . . ." (*An Enquiry into the Present State of Polite Learning in Europe*, 1774.)

The critic today is as necessary and ineffectual as ever. His text is simply another text added to the heap. Many interpreters, therefore, become alchemists and puff every work as if it were potentially a treasure, while others seek a philosopher's (or scientist's) stone which would achieve this redemptive transformation by changing our point of view and reconstituting art as "productive"—in a social or semiotic way. There is also a group which justifies everything by the pragmatic test of the classroom, as if the world had to pass through that needle's eye, or as if a pedagogy accommodated to the pressures of a particular community were the best we could hope for.

My essays tend to be descriptive rather than prescriptive, but they do have certain aims. One is to broaden literary interpretation without leaving literature behind for any reason: scientific truth, social productivity, evangelism. A second aim is to look inward toward the discipline of literary study itself. In "The Interpreter: A Self-Analysis" I question, for example, my tendency to stick with the text, to be voluntarily dependent on it. A critic should be scrupulous in dealing with particular texts and tonalities, yet how magnanimous a scrupling is this? Are we trapped in minute criticism, end-stopping it, as it were, making it a value in itself rather than a procedural means to some greater end? My feeling is that in literary studies the whole is always vaguer than its parts, however important it may be to raise oneself from particular to general or from case study to the erection of a supreme, synoptic law.

If two titles had been allowed this book, the other might have been *For Interpretation.* To interpret is a creative, and at times willful, act, as everyone knows who has considered the history of a discipline far wider and deeper than "criticism." We are still in a reactionary or neoclassical mood when it comes to interpreting texts: behind us is the dark age, the fearful and colorful chaos of rabbinical, gnostic, patristic, kabbalistic, and other sorts of interpretation. Here and there, with Freud, and now with "French Freud," one glimpses the text-abysses we have somehow crossed but which our forefathers brooded on with such a various, powerful, and chimerical imagination. Yet there is a thinking-back still to be done, even if there is no going back, and even if it is no comfort to recall the story of the four Rabbis who entered *Pardes*, the "paradise" of Biblical exegesis. One, the story says, died; one went mad; one damaged it; and only Rabbi Akiba returned safe and sound.

Psychoanalysis may seem to future critics a *Pardes* of this kind. If we must enter it, let us not do it like most psychoanalysts. Instead of pretending to save literature for psychoanalysis, and showing a Pygmalion condescension toward all those dumb if beautiful works of art, let us rather claim to save psychoanalysis for literary studies. The essays in the first part of this book seek to lay the ground for a field of inquiry that might be called psychoesthetics. But in other essays too, such as "Wordsworth and Goethe in Literary History," I comment on the dangerous liaison between literary studies and psychoanalysis.

Equally dangerous is the liaison between rhetorical studies and literature. It is newly imported from France, via Lacan and Derrida, though the work of Kenneth Burke, as well as that of Empson, Richards, Frye, and even the academic revival of rhetorical studies in the period between roughly 1930 and 1960 (Curtius, Wallerstein, Tuve, Ong) resembles it. Anthropology plays an important if different role in both revivals. In England and America the literary archeology of the Cambridge Anthropologists provided the impetus for a genetic structuralism comparing ritual, myth, and art. In France, the structural anthropology of Lévi-Strauss discarded the genetic method, considering it not only a methodological, but also an ideological, error. The primitive mind never existed, or if it did, its thought-processes were not unlike those of the civilized mind. It was, in fact, the civilized mind which created the "myth" of the primitive mind as a kind of pseudo-history glorifying its own status and justifying its repressions. The French School, therefore, uses structuralism as a way to modify or even transcend the historical study of art which it considers infected by a self-idealizing, political humanism. It calls for a study of art whose context would be anthropological or structural rather than European and Humanist; and for the general removal of privileged points of view from history writing and all formal discourse.

I am under no illusion that my essay on Valéry, and my comments in "The Fate of Reading", engage this school in a sustained or consistent way. They merely insist on the historicity of even the most purified kinds of thinking. Hence my periodization of Derrida's philosophical antimasque: he remains in the line of Mallarmé, and is willy-nilly a cousin of Borges. Derrida, of course, has made it clear that he is not opposed to historical reflection (in which he immerses himself while "deconstructing" it). Like Lévi-Strauss he is only against the "history of the historians." Indeed I sometimes feel I am attempting a similar thing, but in a tentative and critical, rather than transcendently reductive, way. Some will accuse me, no doubt, of deconstructing without a license.

Is literary history a genuine discipline: does it have a real bearing on literary interpretation? This concern motivates the second part of the present book. The most cogent objection to writing literary history is not that it coerces accidents, making schemes and causal systems out of adventitious happenings. Accidents have themselves something coercive in them, so why shouldn't we respond with a "violence from within"? That literary history may be a *fable convenue* makes it all the more important for the historian to be conscious of his debt to fiction and rhetorical configuration.

Hayden White's recent *Metahistory*, in exposing the mastertropes of historiography, de-realizes a discipline which had barely demythologized itself. Yet White, I believe, is no more subversive of history writing than Derrida is of philosophizing. To their disciplines, which have sought to become a science, and so to demystify other activities, they seem to say: Physician (historian, philosopher . . .), cure thyself. But the only way history writing can cure itself is through more history writing.

Even the simplest sort of positivistic history can serve a purpose. It is good to be reminded of the *fait divers*—that George Eliot, for instance, was in Berlin at a certain date, sitting in a certain café, reading Macaulay and munching Pfefferkuchen; that Wordsworth and his sister, shortly after their arrival in Hamburg in the winter of 1798, went to a bookstore and purchased copies of two books: Percy's *Reliques* and Bürger's *Ballads*. "Another emblem there!" Yeats might say, but for us it is a question rather than an exclamation.

The *fait divers* now relieves and now intensifies the "burden of history," and so does tropological (rhetorical) analysis. The latter also raises the particular question of the role of tradition and shared assumptions. The burden of history is that we must make sense of our lives by assimilating them to a greater life; and we do this principally by sharing words, or values implied by them. These words, however, can seem curiously empty: they are too often official commonplaces, or a monument to curious beliefs. Yet we need their social cement, the privileged commonplaces of Rhetoric; and that is why Vico distinguished between the *certum* (received or established truth) and the *verum* (absolute or philosophical truth). Rhetoric is part of the *certum*; and we have to learn to defend it without confusing it with the *verum*, as propaganda and ideology tend to do. One wonders, in fact, whether in the era of mass propaganda, which may have begun with Napoleon, there exists any defense for independent thought except through this insistence on the problematics of narrative historiography, or through our respect for what Schiller called "aesthetic education"—which includes an awareness of the playful, even illusionist, element in all speculative thought. The levity of fiction is as important as the burden of history.

The "open society," for all its intimist and liberal media of communication, is no less vulnerable to the ideological appropriation of historical knowledge. Now, however, this appropriation may take the form of expropriation. Historical thinking is attacked as a relativizing procedure, or as an overburdening of contemporary life. The question of what *use* historical thinking is (so sharply formulated by Nietzsche in his well known attack on its abuse) arises for all those who have seen the "canon" explode into an open "curriculum" and books decline from fetish to codable fiche. The death of the past, as it has been named, is accompanied by an aggressive study of contemporaneity; and many fugitive works, on tomorrow's remainder shelf, compete with or displace the once-and-future classics.

Such reflections lead specifically to the third part of this book, which explores changes in the canon and in conventions or habits of reading. *Habent sua fata libelli*: that "fate" includes the type of reading they get. Our best readers use poetry up in a desperate effort to save a sublime discipline: they see it as secular scripture and surround it with a minute, religious, self-institutionalizing body of commentary. Others despoil the works of the past, lumping together old and new, contaminating by inspired bricolage personal and esoteric notions—in an equally desperate effort not to lose their hold on a felt but prior greatness. To put it plainly: what analytic or projective device (if any) allows a poem like Keats's *Hyperion* to compete in terms of "intellectual sensation" with a Bergman movie?

There are no answers in the essays that follow, but I do try to gain an intrinsic mode of historical analysis—intrinsic to literature. While some doubt always accompanies such dichotomies as intrinsic-extrinsic, it remains true that till now historical analysis has been considered an extrinsic approach with respect to art. The latest fashion, for example, is to devalue it as "thematic" in contradistinction to "semiotic," semiotic analysis claiming to be scientifically concerned with how meaning is produced and coded. In Roland Barthes the semiotic approach is generous enough, since "sense" is as plural for him as the codes which determine readability; but the phenomenon of tradition or canon-formation or (inter-) textuality has not, I think, found a sufficient rationale except in the line of thinking which derives from Husserl. I experiment therefore with a *phenomenological thematics* ("Evening Star and Evening Land"); with expanding a historical poetics founded by Aristotle until it becomes more aware of, for example, the category of "voice" as distinct from "character"; and with reinvigorating the theory of art as mimesis or representation.

Even if, in terms of theory, the intrinsic mode of historical analysis proves to be fallacious, it does reveal the impact of the historical (ruins-and-riches) consciousness on the poets, how they faced it, how their poetry participated in it. The sense of nationality is itself a historical achievement as well as a liability; and I am not the first to suggest that the rise of the vernacular arts was accompanied by an ideology which produced, for instance, a "Theory of English Literature." In America this quest for national characteristics was especially patent because the American writer considered himself at once a latecomer and a newborn; but so did, if in a different way, the writer in the European Renaissance. The "westering" of the poetical spirit, and similar notions of belatedness, are certainly grand—now inspiring and now depressive—ideas haunting the literary mind; and in such pieces as "Evening Star and Evening Land" and "Poem and Ideology" the artist is shown formulating or fighting them in his concrete poetics, the elaborated work of art.

As for the critic, belated or transcendent, my argument runs that he owes the great poem or novel an "answerable style"; and that through a genuinely reflective history writing he protects the very concept of art from the twin dangers of ideological appropriation and formalistic devaluation. The demand for contemporaneity on the one hand, and endlessly competing formal options on the other, pressure the reader as much as the artist. A hygienic response, deflating every speculation, and doubting by some impossible criterion of verifiability every play of the mind, is not enough. It makes us the zealots of a plain-style criticism shrinking our ability to read intelligently and generously. Even system-making is preferable. System-makers are still makers: the unacknowledged poets of our time. They are mistaken if they think they can legislate rules for criticism, but at least they do not feed the inferiority complex so endemic to a profession which writes books about books. If we live by impossible aims, let the interpreter be at once critical and speculative.

Acknowledgments

I am grateful to Christine Schulze and to Christine and Brainard Cowan for their help in preparing the manuscript. Of the many who have challenged and directed my ideas I want to mention Harold Bloom, Paul de Man, J. Hillis Miller, and Hayden White. Also Ralph Cohen, friend and editor, who kept me writing. My wife tolerated my absences and occasionally tried to chasten my style.

Most of these papers were first drafted as talks or lectures. I owe a real debt to students and faculty at Yale and elsewhere. I am especially grateful to universities which allowed debate to extend over several days: let me cite, for their patience and intellectual hospitality, Wesleyan, Stanford, Virginia, Pittsburgh, Indiana, Toronto, and Southern Methodist.

The following journals have kindly granted permission to reprint essays which appeared in their pages. *New Literary History*: "History Writing as Answerable Style"; "The Interpreter: A Self-Analysis"; "Wordsworth and Goethe in Literary History." *ELH*: "Christopher Smart's *Magnificat*: Toward a Theory of Representation" (Fall 1974 issue), © The Johns Hopkins University Press. *Essays in Criticism* (Oxford): "Spectral Symbolism and Authorial Self in Keats's *Hyperion*." *Diacritics*: "War in Heaven." *The Wordsworth Circle*: "On the Theory of Romanticism." *The American Scholar*: "Signs of the Times." *The New York Times Sunday Book Review*: "Lionel Trilling as Man in the Middle" (© 1973 by The New York Times Company, reprinted by permission). I also thank the following publishing houses for permission to reprint: Columbia University Press and The English Institute: "Evening Star and Evening Land," from *New Perspectives on Coleridge and Wordsworth.* Yale University Press: "Poem and Ideology: A Study of Keats's 'To Autumn,'" from *Literary Theory and Structure*, F. Brady, J. Palmer, and M. Price, eds. José Corti (Paris): "From the Sublime to the Hermeneutic." Oxford University Press (New York): "I. A. Richards and the Dream of Communication," from *I. A. Richards: Essays in his Honor*, edited by Reuben Brower, Helen Vendler, and John Hollander (copyright © 1973 by Oxford University Press, Inc.; reprinted by permission).

The essays found in part 3 are published here for the first time. Several paragraphs of "Literature High and Low: The Case of the Mystery Story" are adapted from a review originally written for the *New York Review of Books*. Reprinted with permission from *The New York Review of Books* (copyright © 1972 Nyrev, Inc.).

Part One

The Interpreter: A Self-Analysis

"Critics have as yet hardly begun to ask themselves what they are doing or under what conditions they work."

I. A. Richards

Confession. I have a superiority complex vis-à-vis other critics, and an inferiority complex vis-à-vis art. The interpreter, molded on me, is an overgoer with pen-envy strong enough to compel him into the foolishness of print. His self-disgust is merely that of the artist, intensified. "Joe, throw my book away." Sometimes his discontent with the "secondary" act of writing—with living in the reflective or imitative sphere—makes him privilege some primary act at the expense of art or commentary on art. He turns into Mystic or Vitalist. But, more often, he compromises by establishing a special relationship to what transcends him. Having discounted other critics, and reduced art to its greatest exemplars, he feels naked enough to say: "Myself and Art." Like Emerson, who said that ultimately there was "I and the Abyss."

The more books multiply, or knowledge about them—the more secondariness—the greater the Protestantism of this stance. Each man his own interpreter; to each his own thing. No man is an island (except some Englishmen) yet it becomes increasingly necessary to insulate oneself from the flood. "Ich wäre im Material ertrunken," Erich Auerbach wrote at the end of *Mimesis*, retrospectively calling his Turkish exile fortunate. Out of scarcity salvation: given the Library, and his scholarly scruples, the materials would have drowned him.

Epigraph from I. A. Richards, *Principles of Literary Criticism* (London, 1924). My emphasis in what follows is as much on "what critics are" (interpreters) as on "what they are doing" (interpretation). I take Richards' "conditions" as meaning something broader than "rules."

Each of us finds his own exile, but with less of a good conscience. To be creative, to recover through exile a paradise within or a fruitful solitude, one needs the sense of being moved by some *force majeure*, whether that be Politics, Art, or Destiny. "I and the Abyss"—*that* is bracing. The anthropologist recording a dying culture, or Auerbach the decline of the Western historical consciousness—*that* is gloomily inspiriting. What is my saving paranoia? What will justify that discourse of the dead (*Phaedrus*, 276) called Writing?

A strange case. When I was young (real young) what came in through the senses was so profuse and arbitrary I had no need of heaven and hell. I lived instead in chaos: "Es regnet mir in die Augen."[1] Perception was enough, and too much. The human (i.e., other people) seemed a type of closure, and at best a false mediation that, as Virginia Woolf remarked, shut out the view. I was already overpopulated.

The "unmediated vision" I sought then, seems, in retrospect, not a solution but a form of heroism. I wanted to make the eyeball even more transparent. I wrote because I was too alive and unwilling to die even symbolically. Concentration not dissemination was my ideal. I didn't realize that the chaos I lived in was already a chaos of *forms*, not the abyss God sat brooding on at first creation but the bric-a-brac of centuries. Though I talked about mediation—its need, its impossibility—what I showed happening in art, and identified with symbolic process as such, was more analogous to religious or ritual purification. In short, I was an Ancient without knowing it. Even so . . . I felt that the burden of such purification had now fallen entirely on the individual, or on the artist. Was I right, at least, in this?

I was wrong, certainly, in thinking that because the authority of sacred or canonical writing had been removed, the artist's only "text" was nature, the body, consciousness. I forgot—with that fortunate forgetting honored by Nietzsche—that proliferating texts were part of the chaos. I suppose I didn't really forget; but as the unique text dissolved into variant interpretations, my allegory turned the artist into a purifying hero who suffered this fragmentation in the flesh: with primary rather than secondary materials. Perseus, I said, now went against the Medusa with naked eye.

Man on the Dump. "Christ, thief of energies," according to Rimbaud. For a while he was a different kind of sacred monster. He stole texts or eased the burden of the letter. With him interpretation seems so assured. Verily, verily. I say unto you. Take comfort . . . His immediacy to events is fatal to no one but himself. He establishes the relevance of what is already written, erases our *Kulturschuld*, and then, obligingly, self-destructs.

His death proves too fertile, however. Culture-guilt returns, shame what hands or words have done. *He words me,* Shakespeare's Cleopatra cries in disgust, and every writer hears that reproach coming from life. Those heavy terms "history" and "secularization" put us back on the *fumier philosophique.*[2] What sacred monster can we believe in now? In a thousand years, perhaps the vacuum-machine monster in *The Yellow Submarine* will seem to new Fathers of the Church a perverted glimpse of divine truth. It sweeps away the "sweeping meanings" we add to things; all the detritus or waste-materials of the process of interpretation. It also self-destructs.

Dejection as disjection. Doubles and plurals everywhere. *Elohim,* the sexes, two trees in paradise. Nothing hits the mark, or the right mark in *Hamlet*—except the play. Construct, then, a mousetrap that will catch a sublimer evidence. I see the angel struggling ("you must bless me before dawn") but he has many wings and at cock-crow I find scattered feathers only, a barnyard token. What is it anyway, this fairy trace, but his snare to keep me interpreting? Like a dream we wake up with, fading into a half-life of minutes.

No defense is possible: his countermove works as in chess. Playing his game I scan the fairy-fetish like Kierkegaard the Story of Abraham and Isaac.[3] I who cried "No substitutes!" brood on the silences and articulate the missing portions. The constructivist illusion grows in me, like an archeologist's dream. Can I find my way to the mountain of sight-say through the thickets of exegesis? Sinai, both mountain and thornbush.

Brooding on the Abyss. More hawk than dove, I try to put myself in an original relation to my text. I won't be hood-winked by it. If too much seeing makes the author blind, his blindness makes me see. I will hunt this deluded hunter of god, this anthropologist after a virginal Nature; I will reveal his passion for immediacy; though he be Proteus, I will eye him (myself unseen) into shape and essence.

How strange, in any case, the role of the eyes, mine or his. In *The Unmediated Vision* the tyranny of sight in the domain of sensory organization is acknowledged, and symbol-making is understood as a kind of "therapeutic alliance" between the eye and other senses through the medium of art. I remember how easy it was to put a woman in the landscape, into every eyescape rather; and it struck me that in works of art there were similar centers, depicted or inferred: a *Thou*, or "master folded in his fire" or, in the older painters, Christ's passion used as a formal device to justify the pictorial riches gathered by the artist. The ever-libidinous eye: was that what the book was really about?

It talks, however, only of "ideal blindness" and not of "guilty eyes." It acknowledges that Acteon's *cur aliquid vidi* points to a "deeper" perplexity, but then interprets it in metaphysical terms. "Why did I see *any* thing? What is sight fragmented by objects each of which, in isolation, appears to me as an arbitrary focus or solicitation?" Freud and Karl Abraham classify such intellectual (and unresolvable) perplexity as a defense mechanism. It is just another form of *Schaulust* or scoptophilia. The compulsive brooding masks a displaced infantile and sexual curiosity: "Where did I come from? Can I see that secret place? Can I see or envision my own birth?" Then, "Can I see the origin (source) of my own thoughts?" How much philosophy is a search for origins, and how much poetry an evocation of mythical births: of divine beds that become mortal battlefields. The visionary as voyeur: so much for my central emphasis not only on the eyes but also on recovering an "image of original creation" and "seeing the body in the act of waking."[4]

A Poison Pawn. Why am I not shocked at the Freudian reduction? I say to myself that I knew it all along but practiced a phenomenological "reticence," even perhaps Meister Eckhardt's "unerkennendes Erkennen." Psychoanalysis might explain that too as a defense mechanism or a type of dissociated thinking. It could give as evidence the Perseus and Medusa myth which organized my last chapter where tradition is seen as the mirror of Perseus that helped subdue the monster.

Yet to use these kinds of defenses is to survive, or even to brave life. I don't steal fire like Prometheus: I steal me some cool. Sublimation is dissociated thinking as a positive force. Perseus-Freud himself, by his clarified brooding on coital and oedipal fantasies, supplements the mirror of art.

Waiting for the down. My formula "pure representation" or "perception without percepts" was a temporary escape from eye-idol into ideal. Though filled with images I was determined not to succumb to the image (especially not to the "concrete image" of modern poetics). I was haunted after all not by particular visibles but rather by the power of visibility: the ghost was my own strength of sense perception.

Irreducible, in that I could not analyze it into practical ends: it remained perception, an impersonal power personally exerted, which stood against all ideas or figures except "shap'd and palpable Gods" direct from the senses. I did not know what it meant, and did not seem to need to know. The nearest analogue to what I felt was jubilation, breath becoming praise as in the Psalms.

In that too happy state my only perplexity was how to "represent" it. I did not wish to assign priorities, to give the palm to the mind or the mind to the palm; nor did I wish to unify forcibly (that is, artificially) the luminous opera of sense perception. What plot, then, what symbolism might be devised for it? Might not any image, in this state of creative impatience, take over and become a fixation? *In hoc signo vinces.* . . . Unless I renounced the passion of mimesis—my impatience to be actively creative—I could go nowhere but down.

Thou shalt tell. Can representation become "pure"? Can the artist or the interpreter consider himself simply a witness? Consider the lilies of the field. Virginity here is the absence of labor, or not to distort the given.

Yet "lilies that fester smell far worse than weeds" (Shakespeare). Wise passiveness or indolence becomes oppressive, and the endless pregnancy of artistic maturation moves inexorably toward a deutero-creation. "Herr: es ist Zeit. Der Sommer war sehr gross" (Rilke). Even as witnesses that "give the glory" to God, we still "represent":

Let man and beast appear before him and magnify his name together.
Let Abraham present a Ram, and worship the God of his Redemption.
Let Isaac, the Bridegroom, kneel with his Camels, and bless the hope of his pilgrimage.[5]

The point is not to present the self without atoning (at-one-ing) it.

Representation, in short, is Coming Out. The self makes its début (*Beyond Formalism*, pp. 367-70) with or without "animal forms of wisdom" that lessen separation anxiety. There is in the artist, perhaps in everyone, a representation-compulsion inseparable from coming-of-age. Hence the clear link between Smart's perpetual praying and the free-associating encouraged by psychoanalysis. The representation-compulsion is now allowed to express itself innocently, or without fear of retribution. The artist is no longer God's rival.[6] The interpreter too, from this perspective, "presents" himself together with the work of art, "representing" both it and himself at the same time. He is always, like Smart's figures, *au pair*.

For interpretation. Sometimes the interpreter, unlike the artist, does not want to "come out." He becomes a pedagogue, or what Blake calls a "horse of instruction"; and horses are beautiful. In the mythic landscape of education, centaurs are necessary shapes, and no one will make them scapegoats. But there is also the critic who judges only in order not to be judged. Whose relation to art is like that of Man, in Blake, to the Divine Vision from which he has shrunk into his present, Rumpelstiltskin form. His professional demeanor is the result of self-astonishment followed by self-retreat: he turns into a bundle of defensive reactions, into a scaly creature of the rock who conserves himself against the promptings of a diviner imagination. If nothing arrests his retreat, go look for him in the *Satyricon*. Trimalchus belches and the interpreter-priest haruspicates the sound.

A Vision of Judgment. Outside those pearly gates I see a mob eddying about and shouting confusedly, Shakespeare! Milton! Emerson! Mailer! Nietzsche! Rousseau! Mallarmé! Like children they alternately cover their faces with their hands and open them expectantly. What is St. Peter to do with them? They don't have faces: each time they uncover where their face is supposed to be he seems to glimpse something associated with their cry. But the more they whirl the more they look alike, and eventually they form a limbo of their own, a new circle neither in heaven nor hell, the Circle of the Interpreters.

The interpreter is methodically humble. ("Bescheidenheit ist sein beschieden Teil.")[7] He subdues himself to commentary on work or writer, is effusive about the *integrity of the text*, and feels exalted by exhibiting art's controlled, fully organized energy of imagination. What passion yet what objectivity! What range yet what unity! What consistency of theme and style! His essays, called articles, merchandized in the depressed market place of academic periodicals, conform strictly to the cool element of scholarly prose. They are sober, literate, literal, pointed. Leave behind all fantasy, you who read these pages.

He is writing, after all, criticism not fiction. He will not violate the work of art by imposing on it his own, subjective flights of fancy, however intriguing these may be. He has put off personality except for the precise amount it needs to animate his prose. Who can fault him? Is anyone against objectivity, integrity, and the scrupulous distinction of functions?

The interpreter knows there are those who consider him a parasite. He is said to live off his authors like a pimp or to cannibalize them with affection. All the more reason, then, to insist on the objectivity of the interpreter and the integrity of the text.

The interpreter knows also that he is a teacher. And that it has taken centuries to separate teaching and evangelism, to establish the academy on a secular basis. He is not willing to make his discipline the handmaiden of ideologies once more, or of some dazzling private light.

The interpreter, of course, is also a critic. He compares authors, and judges them by their conformity (nonconformity) to tradition, school, or internalized norms. Interpretation has its wars. Under their pressure a real personality may sometimes form, and a critic-interpreter appear to astonish the scholarly community by his wild-man nature. Burke, Fiedler, Leavis, Empson have a face—yet not one to live with when we see its caricature dawning on every student who wants to reform English studies.

The specter of personalism is a real one when it appears in a discipline so antagonistic to it. In this atmosphere, personalism is almost bound to become extremist. Many succumb to the old heresy that it is better to act—fantasize—whatever the consequences. Is it possible for the critic-interpreter to be himself and faithful to the text? To genuinely interpret himself as well as the work of art?

We do not ask for personality in the critic any more than in the artist. Nor do we ask him to suppress it. We ask him not to hide behind his text. The writer of fiction has a persona, a face wrought from life to look at life with, and often more than one face. Should the interpreter not have personae? Is it not his strength to be as deeply moved by works of imagination as by life itself? Interpreter: define thyself.

Every item in the interpreter's ethos should be submitted to a methodical suspicion. If he stresses objectivity, one should ask whether he is not overreacting to his fear of private compulsions, and using textual study as self-discipline. Nothing wrong with that, but let it be thought. If he stresses too much the integrity of the text, one should wonder about the streaminess or pseudocontinuity of his mental life. The text-fetichist may be deeply concerned with excluding the influence of strange ideas—usurpations from within him as well as from anthropology, psychology, etc. Similarly, if we find too great an emphasis on unity, we can suspect a fear of ambivalence, or of split states of consciousness. The unitive or reconciling critic often harbors a love-hate of literature: his devotion to "unity" may become a demand for "totality" and turn against art in the name of a more comprehensive (religious or political) vision. The greatest advances in interpretation have occurred, moreover, by showing that a false unity has been imposed on an author: in his work there may be another work trying to get out.

The bearing of self-criticism on the critic is quite simple. He can no longer be tacitly schizoid in the way he separates his activity from that of art. It is strange how those who insist on respecting the fine print of a *literary* text, words within words, its subtlest tone, are often incapable of discriminating them in a *literary-critical* text: there they allow no figurative play, no fantasia. They divide mental life sanely into the energies of art, on the one hand, and the incompetency of all but a self-denying criticism on the other.

Of course criticism is not fiction. It is sometimes more—call it fantasia—and sometimes less—grammar, explication, ancillary comment (*Hilfswissenschaft*). This does not alter the fact that criticism deals, essentially, with that impressively impure and very complex "formal calculus" we call language: that it discriminates between the modes, and evaluates the claims, of language. What is literal and what is figurative? What continuum is there between them? The critic cannot afford to be Lear whose mistake, according to Sigurd Burckhardt, "is the regal one of taking people *at their word* in the most radical and literal sense." The interpreter, in short, cannot appoint himself exclusively a guardian of the letter (the "integrity of the text") or as its emancipator (the latest depth-analysis that restores it to life). He alternates between these according to his best sense of what is needed at a particular time and for a particular work.

Act and Shadow. Such terms as "literal" and "figurative" are convenient rather than definitive. They are useful holdovers from religious hermeneutics. Nothing, strictly considered, is literal, since nothing can coincide with itself. Each letter casts a shadowy type, each word implies a whole both greater and vaguer than it. Hegel's analysis of Writing near the beginning of the *Phenome-*

nology, Derrida's valorization of *écriture* in terms of "différance," and current semiotics converge on this observation. One cannot step twice into the same language-stream.

Art does not coincide with itself either. It is continually being displaced into new forms of art, or into commentary. Let us think, for a moment, of interpretation as a shadowy double of the work of art. There are two related ways this shadow can be understood: as cast by the individual work onto the interpretive consciousness, or as a "form" that makes art-understanding possible—that allows us to connect art with other concerns through "interpretation." A difference between shadow and act remains in each case, for interpretation is either like a repetition of the work in a finer or paler mode or like a genre-conception which could be insatiably abstract. There is a danger, in both instances, of the prey being relinquished for the shadow—of the work being exchanged for its anatomy.

For those who acknowledge strongly the priority of the individual work of art, interpretation becomes a matter of extending its charm or memorability. Yet not indulgently so. Interpretation *interrupts* a spell which has made us too enjoyably passive. We allow the spell only by touching back—through the critical or interpretive process—to our sense of reality. If the imagination that held us is great enough, that sense is delighted rather than offended, and, deeply touched now, cooperates actively with the spell.[8]

Interruption has its dangers. Certain types of discourse, for example solipsistic ones like that of Cardenio in *Don Quixote*, may not be interrupted. Yet *Don Quixote* itself is full of interruptions, story displacing story in Romance fashion. Art, like Romance, teaches us to interrupt. Only, like a hero in Romance, the interpreter must ask the right question. If he asks it wrongly, or at the wrong time, he wakes into emptiness.

The alternate theory tends to stress the *déjà lu* character of our response to the individual work. We do not "encounter" but rather "recognize."[9] The interpreter here is initially less passive: he tests the work against an ideal he also shares. Philosophically speaking, the shadow is as much "before" as "after," a *Vor-Ver-*

ständniss which makes both art and its interpretation possible, and implies thus a virtual *community of interpreters.*[10]

The advantage of the alternate theory is that act and shadow are considered of equal dignity. Both, that is, reflect the possibility of a Heavenly City of Mutual Discourse. At the same time, the reactive or *a posteriori* character of interpretation, which includes its dependence on source texts, is questioned. The hermeneutic universe now envisaged is no longer a closed system, with Classics at the center, spin-off works as satellites, and the critic-interpreter either encouraging such spin-offs by denying exhaustive centrality to certain books (and so keeping the system expanding) or discouraging them (and inviting closure). "The stubborn center must / Be scattered . . ." (Shelley).

There are disadvantages too, in terms of literary-critical *praxis.* (I do not try to judge the theory except in this light.) By diminishing the book-centeredness of literary discourse you bring it closer to philosophical discourse and run the risk of homogenizing it. True, you may still have "texts" rather than "books"—but what constitutes a text is a slippery thing to define, and the tendency of Heidegger to excerpt freely, of Derrida to use a highly repetitive or snippety canon, and of Lacan to meld everything into his prose by inner quotation, produces an intensely frustrating *clair-obscur.* Theology also fragmented scripture into proof-texts, yet the literal text remained, and the discrepancy between letter and figurative development was the very space of revisionary shock or "hermeneutic reversal." Now, however, the *facticity* of a book or the *force* of a "dialectical lyric" like Hölderlin's "Der Rhein" or Shelley's "Mont Blanc" or Kierkegaard's *Fear and Trembling* may be lost. The perpetually self-displacing, decentering movement of the new philosophical style shows that value is not dependent on the idea of some primary or privileged text-moment: value is intrinsically in the domain of the secondary, of *écriture.* Writing is a "second navigation," as Derrida has finely said. With this foregrounding of secondariness I am in agreement. I want to examine it, however, from a somewhat different angle.

Interpretation as theft. The secondary character of interpretation is a dangerous if perfectly commonsensical notion. How could I lose sight of the fact that I am belated in some way vis-à-vis the thing interpreted? Or less than it? How difficult, for instance, I find it right now to think about interpretation without touching back, like Anteus, to the "ground" of a specific work, which would illustrate or support my remarks, or simply let me *lean.* Interpretation is always, at some point, anaclitic: the art of leaning, of falling back, on something given.

My metaphor suggests that though interpretation can't stand by itself, it fuses with the art-work or helps it to integrate (compare the function of enclitic particle or "bound" morpheme) with other structures. This implies, in turn, that a work becomes detached from its original context or that criticism actually helps to detach (decontextualize) it, and so make it available for another purpose, generation, or place.

However, with the idea of an "original" context, the interpreter begins to appear as a thief, or a purveyor of stolen goods. He is like the little foxes in the *Song of Solomon* that spoil the vines. Or, occasionally, like the one big fox. In short, he is Reynard-Hermes.[11] This patron of thieves knows the language of men as well as of gods; and even the Bible, the rabbis said, must speak "in the language of men." Hermes moves among all classes and can accommodate his speech to them. While literary criticism is not commerce, it does make works of art negotiable from generation to generation, or affects their value.

You can hold, of course, that art has no "original" context. This leads to an ecstatic rather than enclitic form of interpretation, for art is now seen to stand outside time or for all time: it is only a prisoner or pensioner of its age. The critic's function would then be to make that clear: if art is property, he "liberates" it; if the artist's genius has sacrificed to the genius loci, he purifies it of that bond.

Yet art, whatever it may be in itself, is "earlier" than the interpreter. It preempts him in some way; it has influenced, for example, the very language he speaks as well as his sense of national identity. Though philosophical reflection keeps worrying the distinction between primary and secondary process, nature and art, natural and positive law, the *belatedness thesis,* as I want to call it, retains its psychological power.

Interpretation as preposterous. Belatedness seems at first a modern kind of feeling. It helps to inspire, certainly, the Battle of Ancients and Moderns that follows on the Revival of Antiquity. Most Renaissance writers are quite lighthearted vis-à-vis the Classics: they steal or adapt to their heart's content. But some are grave and burdened like Gabriel Harvey, who complains of Spenser's *Faerie Queene* that it is "hobgoblin run away with the crown from Apollo."

This hobgoblin, as Classicists know, is the infant Hermes who is no sooner born than he challenges Apollo by stealing his cattle, brazening this out by sheer denial, and inventing the lyre from a tortoise shell.[12] The Hermes-myth of the mighty imp counters an author's sense of being preempted by Classical authority. Yet Apollo is not always a heavy father. He is also "golden" Apollo, a "rich-hair'd youth of morn" who shakes his dewey locks as if the accumulated riches of antiquity will disperse through him into the effulgence of a new literary day. The success of the Renaissance in opening the storehouse of Antiquity and converting its treasure into native coin produces an "embarrassment of riches" for the poets that follow, many of whom admire intensely if ambivalently native Originals in addition to Classical patriarchs.[13]

From the Renaissance through the Romantics and perhaps the contemporary poets, belatedness is a complex and tricky notion. Only recently, in Harold Bloom's theory of poetic influence, has this notion been psychoanalyzed and applied to the understanding of English authors in their historical sequence. Bloom argues that "The Child is Father of the Man" is true, if anywhere, in *literary* kinship relations. These relations show "a compromise between the competition with and the submission to the father-figure.[14] Meditating on the rivalry between later and earlier poets, Bloom concludes that the ephebe can only survive his precursors by a complex and ambivalent act of identification. Like Hermes, the cunning literary imp attempts to "snatch his share away" from Phoebus. He can never be more than a child, given the weight of literary authority, but he is always more than a child in the way he creates room (legitimacy) for himself by manipulating tradition and claiming to make it reality minded. Thus, by a "preposterous" act of interpretation the new artist sees himself as his own father redeemed of error. The father, one might say, becomes a prefiguration of the son.

Bloom considers these complexities indistinguishable from everyday psychopathology—from oedipal rivalry and its fantasies. He demystifies in this way the sources of literary or creative talent. He uncovers the nakedness of the poets, and lo, it is our own: the so-called autonomy of art is based on a wish for omnipotence, on a deep revolt against *influence* which makes us desire to beget ourselves, to be our own fathers.

Here one must remark that just as the idea of interpretation as theft depends on strongly valuing the original text or context, so the idea of interpretation as "preposterously" putting the later before depends on the psychology of belatedness—which is not unconnected, of course, with a vivid interest in what came first. Other dramatic instances of preposterous thinking are found in eschatologies where the "last becomes the first" or in the Kantian critique where the belatedness of thought to experience is overturned by thought making experience possible; or in instances of hermeneutic reversal which show that an earlier author (Milton) is better understood through a later (Blake), or an "illegitimate" point of view (Satan's in *Paradise Lost*, the eroticism of the *Song of Solomon*) is redeemed.

Beyond belatedness. Belatedness, then, is hardly the special curse of the interpreter: it is, rather, the psychological position we most naturally find ourselves in. We methodically question or "discount" it, as we do other "natural" prejudices that seem to obstruct or limit our horizon. We try and see beyond them, as Copernicus did, when he challenged common sense and saw earth circling the sun.

Even as interpreters, then, we must set interpretation *against* hermeneutics. For the distinction between a primary source and secondary literature, or between a "great Original" and its imitations, is the space in which traditional hermeneutics works. It seeks to reconstruct, or get back to, an origin in the form of sacred text, archetypal unity or authentic story. To apply hermeneutics to fiction is to treat it as lapsed scripture; just as to apply interpretation to scripture is to consider it a mode, among others, of fiction. Both points of view, it can be argued, involve a category mistake.

Yet Blake could view the Bible as lapsed scripture, and seek the Original Vision it displaced. The thesis of a divorce between a great Original and its derivatives can lead to the impasse where the Bible itself is a fiction. The obverse of this is to open the canon and multiply the Books of God. "Who declared the Bible closed?" Novalis asked. Since the Renaissance it had become a commonplace to say that nature (or history) was the *other* Book of God; but such extensions of the canon raise difficult questions about the status of the various supplements—for they do not always harmonize.

The decline of hermeneutics is related to a critique of *any* description of life which divides it into "original" and "secondary" components—vision and mediation, experience and rationalization, Bible and books. Concepts of organic form evolve at this point; they combine often with incarnationist notions of the Word (Logos) considered as—in poetry at least—the *res* itself, rather than "about" it. But because of a new confusion between the concept of word and voice, and a privileging of speech over writing (in anthropology, of ritual and myth over literature), we find ourselves questioning again every theory that posits a more than heuristic "beginning"—an "In the beginning" rather than a "starting point."

I think that is where we are now. We have entered an era that can challenge even the priority of literary to literary-critical texts. Longinus is studied as seriously as the sublime texts he comments on; Jacques Derrida on Rousseau almost as interestingly as Rousseau. This is not as perverse as it sounds: most of us know Milton better than the Bible, or have read the latter again by way of Milton.

The fading distinction between primary and secondary texts argues a renewed loss of innocence, like eating once more from the tree of knowledge. By now that loss must be associated with Writing. I don't mean that the fall is from oral into print culture but that book-bearing, like child-bearing, is as much a curse as a blessing to us. And again, I don't mean by that the discomfort of living in Academia where so many feel they must choose between two kinds of perdition, publish or perish. I mean that Writing is living in the secondary, knowing it is the secondary. To be conscious is already to be writing. That is the curse, or the blessing.

Book and Body. Bertram Lewin, a famous psychoanalyst, surmised that the "screen" onto which we project our dreams is not a blank (a "table rase") but a body image. He had a patient who would say to the analyst, I have a dream for you, then claimed that the dream had rolled up or away. The understandably frustrated analyst rose to the occasion. He had nothing much to go on, but that nothing was still something, it had features. He decided that what the patient was seeing or dreaming about was the dream screen itself; and he identified it as the mother's breast withdrawing, rolling away like globe or cup.[15]

I find this at once bemusing and exemplary. On several counts: first as expressive of the interpreter's situation. He interprets nature, whether nature wants it or not. One might almost say, paraphrasing Dilthey, he understands nature better than nature understands itself.

Secondly, it is brilliant in its own right, suggesting what interpretation should always be. Interpretation is a feast, not a fast. It imposes an obligatory excess. The only hypotheses that count are those "which may seem fantastic," as Freud remarked in *Totem and Taboo*. Even those—pace Popper and Hirsch—which may seem unverifiable.

But lastly, as a solution to a particular problem, it throws light on it and contains larger implications. Lewin's thought is that the screen, in this instance, is the breast, or its mnemic trace. Now it is clear what this hypothesis, generalizable or not, does. It makes word or image flesh again. Being projected on such a screen, they put us once more in "touch" with the mother, or lost body-feelings. In addition, the hypothesis is an example of "hermeneutic reversal," where something forgotten or inert proves to be central. We had forgotten the breast; we *must* forget it to develop maturely; but we had also forgotten something about the act of writing or dreaming; and perhaps we must forget (subsume) it to dream on. Or dream upon: what is forgotten becomes the subtlest ground, a magic medium now empty and now full. Surely, if we collapse the differential space between the blankness of the screen and the "whiteness" of the breast, if we enter too much into fantasies of incorporation (so that everything becomes body or part of a body) we close the book we are writing. Till then, I cleave to you, o doublebreasted book.

The Last Word.

Interpreter: Who's there?
Book: Nay, answer me; stand, and unfold yourself.

Things get crossed up in this jittery situation. It should be the interpreter who unfolds the text. But the book begins to question the questioner, its *qui vive* challenges him to prove he's not a ghost. What is he then?

Imagine yourself on those parapets in the dark.
Watchful, you're guarding something, yourself perhaps.
A ghost comes and says, you're guarding a ghost.
He is the real. You turn green, or whiter than green.
Does one argue with a majestical ghost?
Or does one, like a scholar, stay it with words?

I. A. Richards and the Dream of Communication

why hath not the mind
Some element to stamp her image on,
In nature somewhat nearer
to her own?

Wordsworth

1

Aesthetics has long been linked to a study of the affective properties of art. It should really be called *psychoesthetics*, for it investigates the relation of art to the life of the mind, and particularly the affections.

Following I. A. Richards' *Principles of Literary Criticism* (1924) new interest was generated in psychoesthetics. Richards envisaged the possibility of raising our "standard of response" not only *to* art but also *through* art to experience in general. Indeed, the arts entered the picture so strongly because they were the chief instrument by which the standard of response could be raised. Or lowered—"An improvement of response is the only benefit which anyone can receive, and the degradation, the lowering of a response, is the only calamity."[1]

Eloquent and onerous words. They reflect Richards' utilitarianism and suggest that the *Principles* are implicitly a Defense of Poetry. The situation was different, of course, from that inspiring Sidney or Shelley. It was (and remains) what F. R. Leavis described five years later as "Mass Civilization and Minority Culture."[2] Richards is not frightened into aestheticism by this growing contradiction between "civilization" and "culture"; he does not restrict the name and nature of art. On the contrary, he attacks the "phantom aesthetic state"—the separation of aesthetic from ordinary patterns of experience—and he extends this way the responsibilities of both artist and critic. If art is a normal part of experience (a "criticism of life," Arnold had said), then art is capable of exerting its influence on "mass civilization"; but if art has influence, art can corrupt, and criticism must be more alive and discriminating than ever.

The sense of art's corruptibility is unusually vivid in Richards. Indeed, it is almost Puritan. He is not concerned, of course, with its challenge to religion or morality but rather with its substitutability for experience. Artists can become vicars of vicariousness and erode the capacity for direct and critical response. Art should not become, any more than religion, a popular narcotic.

> No one can intensely and wholeheartedly enjoy and enter into experience whose fabric is as crude as that of the average superfilm without a disorganization which has its effects in everyday life. The extent to which second-hand experience of a crass and inchoate type is replacing ordinary life offers a threat which has not yet been realized.[3]

We recognize the immediate context because it is still ours. Bad popular art was contributing to that "stimulus flooding" and "psychic numbing"—as modern sociologists call it—already combated by Wordsworth in his *Lyrical Ballads:*

> . . . the human mind is capable of being excited without the application of gross and violent stimulants, and he must have a very faint perception of its beauty and dignity who does not know this, and who does not further know that one being is elevated above another in proportion as he possesses this capability.[4]

The undramatic subject matter of a Wordsworth ballad was intended to wean contemporary minds from their dependence on the novel-making and news-mongering of urbanized society.

The situation has intensified but not changed since 1800. The journalistic economy of plenty which is ours seems more frightening than the preceding economy of scarcity. How does one respond to sensationalism? For both Wordsworth and Richards, responsibility begins with the ability to respond. It is easy to see, then, why Richards wrote his most seminal book on the critic's function rather than continuing directly his work on aesthetics and semantics. If art is the instrument which might improve or re-enable our response to experience, what improves our response to art? How does art become experience, to echo John Dewey? According to Richards, the principled critic's understanding of his task should lead not only to a more competent account of how art communicates but also to a more active discrimination between the communicated responses, and so to a "premillenial" perfectibility of the whole stimulus-response relation.

2

Richards maintains, therefore, an ideal of rightness but formulates it in terms of the adequation (however complex) of stimulus and response. Among the wealth of assumptions which support his book is the classicist's belief in benevolent normativeness. His emphasis on the possibility of reconciling opposed, or stabilizing extreme, impulses (it superimposes Coleridge's definition of imagination on Wordsworth's sensibility) is only the strongest and best-known instance of this romantic classicism. The Ricardian ideal of "balanced poise, stable through its power of inclusion, not through the force of its exclusions,"[5] has been as influential in our era as Winckelmann's "edle Einfalt und stille Grösse" in his.

We do not have an English Winckelmann, but we have a Dr. Johnson, and Richards' comments on the normality of art can sound like pronouncements of the great Cham, colored by the abstract vocabulary of their time:

> So much must be alike in the nature of all men, their situation in the world so much the same, and organization building upon this basis must depend upon such similar processes, that variation both wide and successful is most unlikely.[6]

This tenacious principle of uniformity supports both "pillars" of Richards' theory: his account of literary communication, and his account of literary value.

To start with the former. "The arts," says Richards, "are the supreme form of the communicative activity." Moreover, though "an experience has to be formed, no doubt, before it is communicated . . . it takes the form it does largely because it may have to be communicated." In fact, "a large part of the distinctive features of the mind are due to its being an instrument for communication." If we add to this that the "priority of formal elements to content" in the arts, their most distinctive feature, is explained in terms of a communications rationale, one wonders whether the medium is not becoming the message: the phantom ideal of a perfect response to a perfect input. "What communication requires is responses which are uniform, sufficiently varied, and capable of being set off by stimuli which are physically manageable. These three requisites explain why the number of the arts are limited and why formal elements have such importance."[7]

Richards will not give up the dream of reason. Its newest version seems to be the dream of communication—of total, controllable communication. It would be foolish, of course, to try and draw a straight line from Richards to Marshall McLuhan or B. F. Skinner. For all their apparent rigor the *Principles* are, in Harry Levin's perceptive phrase, a "methodology of doubts."[8] Yet to turn to Richards' theory of value is not only to find it merging, despite disclaimers, with that of communication but also to find this merger strangely consecrated by classical ideas of order.

Richards on value sounds, at first, purely cautionary. Like certain commercials, he warns us against accepting substitutes. With imitations and inferior goods all around, he recalls the possibility of firsthand experience and the need for discrimination. But has not the spread of technical knowledge, with craft-secrets becoming available to so many, made it easier to fake the genuine "fecit"? The problem of the counterfeit troubles Richards far less than it does some of the great artists of his time, notably Borges, Gide and Mann. He always presupposes something that, if it may not be called "authority," comes through as "standard or normal criticism" based on "a class of more or less similar experiences." What kind of criterion is this?

It can be argued that Richards aims at a convergence of judgment rather than its uniformity; and that what he calls a "normal" range of response does not involve a belief in authority. Convergence implies a coming-together of empirical acts of evaluation; and *Practical Criticism* will show more precisely what is entailed. Yet the same book also shows how much is dependent on our being exposed to a certain "class" of experiences—in this case poetry and its traditions. The notion of a "class of similar experiences" is more complex than appears, for it may involve forcible or planned exposures (as in scientific experiments) which in turn depend for evaluation on accepted notions of what is probative. If this is so, the difference between an appeal to authority and to empirically founded judgment dissolves into a difference between what, at any time, is considered scientific or probative.

Once upon a time "authority" was considered so. It is likely, then, that the categories of probative and persuasive mingle insidiously, and that all values or standards must pass also a *rhetorical test.* Yet who is to devise, evaluate or improve this test? The question not posed by Richards—yet imposing itself on the life work of F. R. Leavis—is how to determine the "class" of communicants (respondents) which would, in effect, set the standard and so become an authoritative group—if not an elite, then a clerisy.

Perhaps the reason all this is not a problem for Richards is that his account of values is deeply influenced by the managerial model of the behavioral sciences. It helps him to give a scientific updating to classicist norms. The principle of uniformity modulates into that of an ideal conformation of stimulus and response, to be achieved by a scientific type of training. As in so many thinkers of the period, a "blessed rage for order" coexists with a residual trust in nature. Science and education are still Nature methodized.

3

If there is, however, a rhetorical test which affirmations of value must pass, this should lead us beyond a renewed appreciation of literary criticism (its role in the scrutiny of the link between value and rhetoric) to a meditation on authority. Empson and

Leavis, who are closest to Richards, bring this out; so does Kenneth Burke in America. Richards, instead of confronting the base-superstructure split in society (Marxist terms respected by Empson) or the potential conflict between popular and high art (Leavis), concentrates on a methodological rather than sociological dichotomy: that of poetry and science, or of the two uses (poetic and scientific) of language.[9]

What a founder omits is often what his followers find most crucial. All the more so, in the case of Richards, since the evaded meditation on authority in his theory of value tends to distort his theory of the affective structure of art. To define the poetic use of language as "pseudostatement"[10] acknowledges the special power of a discourse that does not share the referential precision of science, and so draws a *concordat* between science (or philosophy) and figurative speech; but it fails to "value" precisely enough the character of non-reference in poetic speech. While increased precision or verifiability of reference justifies, and so authorizes, scientific discourse, what can justify literary discourse?

The two paths not taken by Richards, and which are being explored today, are a theory of symbolic action, inspired in good part by Freudian psychology; and a theory of speech-acts, inspired by post-Saussurian semiology as well as by a theory of institutions that winds its way from the work on authoritarianism done at the Frankfort School of Social Research in the 1930s (Horkheimer, Adorno, Erich Fromm, Marcuse) to Gadamer's and Habermas' reflections on the relation between interest and inter-esse, or community and interpretability.[11] A further enriching complication is Wittgenstein, and the theory of convention implicit in language rules, especially on the level of illocutionary acts.[12] Yet if there is a shared problem centering on *literary authority*, or on the philosophy of rhetoric, there is as yet little awareness of the fact. Harry Levin's "Literature as an Institution" (1946) and Richard Ohmann's recent attempts to expose the ideological content of literature by means of speech-act theory could not be more different in their intellectual debts or teaching programme. Yet both reveal, and to a degree supply, the same defect in our "Principles" of literary criticism.

That there is an evasion of the sociological issue in Richards is also suggested by the verbal style of his *Principles.* They are written in a kind of Basic Philosophical English. Everyone with a certain level of culture can understand the terms and follow the argument. Elements are repeated till the mind behind them becomes clear through iteration and aggregation rather than absolute logical schemes on the one hand or artistic inventiveness on the other. At no point is ordinary, commonsensical experience threatened. We have entered a Normal School of discourse; and this would be all right if it were not accompanied by an artificial dignity that "levels" us in quite another way.

I mean that Richards' language of description, in this early work, takes what dignity it has from a highly managerial scientific model, one that is born in the laboratory or is sustained by the ideal of controlled experimentation. Propositional sentences and impersonal forms of diction are its staple, as they are in bureaucratic "organization building." The book's excessively serial structure, moreover—which promises to treat things not "now" but "later," under their proper heading—though methodologically justified[13] also greatly impedes that integration or interanimation of words and impulses which the actual literary theory seeks to strengthen as a whole. In short, the base is English but the superstructure is the managerial imperative of what is now called Social Science.

What I say is meant to qualify and not to diminish our debt to Richards. The dis-suasion of his style is something that reflects his criticism of contemporary criticism. He helped to rescue literary studies for our time by raising its ante, by rejecting less strenuous conceptions. Literary study was to be neither a "soothing piece of manners" (the alleged forte of Oxford dons from Raleigh to Garrod) nor ersatz politics.[14] But what was it then? After what social acts of larger design and disinterested application could it model itself?

The answer is deceptively simple, and by no means obsolete. Richards' Defense of Poetry became intertwined with a Defense of Reading, not only because of his psychological bias but also because a science of the "behavior of words" seemed to him a social act of great, even redemptive urgency. How could criticism afford to be a luxury trade, and the preserve of amateurs, when the disappearance of a homogenous intellectual tradition endangered interpretive reading as a transmitted skill? "Intellectual tradition tells us, among other things, *how literally* to read a passage. It guides us in our metaphorical, allegorical, symbolical modes of interpretation. The hierarchy of these modes is elaborate and variable; and to read aright we need to shift with an at present indescribable adroitness and celerity from one mode to another." Modern heterogeneous growth—it includes the rise of other media—has "disordered" our ability to read: that which was second nature is no longer to be relied on. It is time, therefore, to begin "the reflective inquiry which may lead to a theory by which the skill may be regained—this time as a less vulnerable and more deeply grounded, because more consciously recognized, endowment."[15]

There is no need to recall how consistently Richards pursued this project for a theory, from *Practical Criticism* (1927) to *Design for Escape: World Education Through Modern Media* (1968). It is clear, at the same time, that the necessity for theory arises when a skill disintegrates or must be reintegrated on a wider, more conscious basis. The wound nurtures the bow. Richards discerns a "general drift" in Western interests that has strengthened "the aptitude of the average mind for self-dissolving introspection . . . awareness of the goings on of our own minds, merely *as goings on*, not as transitions from one well-known and linguistically recognized moral or intellectual condition to another."[16] Like Pater, in his famous essay "Style" (1888), Beckett in his study of *Proust* (1931), and Erich Auerbach in *Mimesis* (1945), Richards values fully modernist advances in the descriptive potential of prose, though he characteristically wishes to exploit this potential for the benefit of the greatest number. The theoretical study of language (which Coleridge is said to have initiated in its modern form) should be made "capable of opening to us new powers over our minds comparable to those which systematic physical inquiries are giving us over our environment."[17] The optimistic turn in his conception of science emerges once again; the dream of communication is the dream of reason made practicable.

4

Language, says Coleridge in a high-flown allusion, is "the medium by which spirits communicate with one another." Richards seeks to envision this medium, for there is still something of the quest-hero in him. Yet, to adapt Browning's *Childe Roland*, "What in the midst lay but language itself?"

The envisioning is aided, as well as impeded, by associationist psychology. Wordsworth had already made it the base of a new, more scientific classicism which aimed at saner relations between thoughts or feelings and their objects. He can be as scrupulously abstract (if more long-winded) than Richards.

> our continued influxes of feeling are modified and directed by our thoughts, which are indeed the representatives of all our past feelings; and as by contemplating the relation of these general representatives to each other, we discover what is really important to men, so by the repetition and continuance of this act feelings connected with important subjects will be nourished, till at length, if we be originally possessed of much organic sensibility, such habits of mind will be produced that by obeying blindly and mechanically the impulses of those habits we shall describe objects and utter sentiments of such a nature and in such connection with each other, that the understanding of the being to whom we address ourselves, if he be in a healthful state of association, must necessarily be in some degree enlightened, his taste exalted, and his affections ameliorated.[18]

Yet Wordsworth's over-qualifying of the associationist thesis shows his uneasiness with the doctrine. He saw that associationism, as a model influencing self-interpretation, unbalanced the relation between psyche and environment in favor of the latter. It gave the developing mind too strong an image of its passivity, or of the complex web of relations it had to thread to be genuinely creative. Coleridge, of course, made the intellectual struggle with associationism ("Matter has no *Inward*") a major focus of his *Biographia Literaria*. He followed Leibnitz in postulating a *vis representativa*, and so anticipates (without influencing) a development also found in Schopenhauer and Nietzsche.[19] Despite its defects, however, associationist psychology emphasized several aspects of mental life which made it survive to Richards' day.

The first of these was its realistic acknowledgement that we are indeed in a basically responsive position, or strongly pressed in upon by our environment. Not nature alone determines us, but more inextricably a second nature: associations established early, or constructions put on experience; in short, mental habits. Mind, in these forms, surrounds us like matter; it may be, in fact, a material medium of a subtler kind. How to imagine this materiality is the challenge; and Hartley's crude explanatory schemes only kept this challenge alive.

Associationism, moreover, was *structural* (though insufficiently *dynamic*) in its understanding of growth. The web of habit being so complex, and originating so far in the past, one cannot change the single element. The whole system must be affected: not "world" or "mind" but the stimulus-response relation the ecology or interanimation of mind and world.

Much depends, therefore, on the quality of therapeutic intervention, another important aspect of this psychology for Richards. He displays prudent respect for old habits and a knowledge that new ones require lengthy formation. Reconstruction rather than upheaval is called for. The idea of simples (for example, religious conversion) is discounted; indeed, recourse to simples merely continues the problem. The therapy which art—the *work* of art—suggests is de-obstruction rather than a destructive conversion-experience. The artist outwits the stock response or qualifies the immediate reflex, and so allows a new and fuller working out of experiences, a more plastic and less impulsive reaction.

Thus the main emphasis in Richards falls on the *medium of response*. Art brings the whole soul of man into activity, said Coleridge; Richards prefers to talk of this wholeness in terms of the nervous system. It is more empirical, and affords the image of an extremely sensitive "material," constituted by "stresses, preponderances, conflicts, resolutions and interanimations . . . remote relationships between different systems of impulses . . . before unapprehended and inexecutable connections."[20]

It is his vision (one can call it no less) of such a medium that invigorates Richards' quest. So responsive, so deeply interactive, and yet so powerfully if inscrutably self-unifying: what medium can this be except language itself in its ideal form? Richards tends to think of it by analogy to the nervous system, developing this way the materialist emphasis in associationism. Not the analogy is important but what it helps him to envision. Bachelard believed that the human imagination was deeply material—that always, whatever its apparent content, it was also meditating air, earth, water, fire. Richards' imagination is meditating a fifth element, more visionary and more material than these: the element of language. Its workings or the "unimaginable touch" that makes it ideally responsive can be described in terms borrowed from Wordsworth:

There is a dark
Inscrutable workmanship that reconciles
Discordant elements, makes them cling together
In one society . . .[21]

5

The early Richards was a classicist of the nervous system. Freud also sought a neurological model for mental processes. The neurotic escaped neurology, however; indeed, it seemed to many as if abnormal psychology were discontinuous with normal psychology. Richards himself remained firmly committed to the latter, for several reasons. One was the scientific stress on verifiability. "The mental processes of the poet . . . offer far too happy a hunting-ground for uncontrollable conjecture."[22] More important was the evident sanity of the work of art, its victory over disturbances that may be psychogenic but can only be guessed at. As Richards stated simply and eloquently: "One thing only perhaps is certain; what happens is the exact opposite to deadlock, for compared to the experience of great poetry every other state of mind is one of bafflement."[23] Most important, though, was his resistance to ideological impositions from any sphere, whether religion or politics or science itself.

Richards, that is, feared the violence of ideas—the violence ideas could lead to when men enforced "spiritual laws by carnal power."[24] There is something in the crude structure of most ideas that can violate minds even less finicky than that of Henry James. Psychoanalysis must have seemed full of ideas, and crudely interventionist. What Richards may not have realized is that Freud and Breuer began with the thesis that the hysteric essentially suffered from an idea.[25] The hysteric symptom was diagnosed as a "carnal" reaction to an intolerable, because intolerant, truth. Richards, in any case, preferred an "impulse" to a "compulsion" model of psychic activity. The nervous system, that brilliant ultimate, that responsive *deus in machina*, made all other explanations superfluous.[26]

This combination in him of idealism and skepticism, a strong feature of modern British thought, resisted the science of psychoanalysis as long as possible. Richards sought a critical-scientific point of view uncorrosive of art, as of all normal experience. He even subdued the troubled genius of Coleridge to his approach, as if to normalize the psychology of art. To advance beyond Richards means, therefore, to respect the findings of psychoanalysis without abandoning normal psychology or the integrity of the work of art.

Something has already been done toward such an end: insights are provided by Kenneth Burke, or similar analyses of the reader's share, by phenomenological models of the process of reading or by Jungian studies of art's affective structure (Bodkin, Werblowski, Shumaker) and the Freudian applications of Kris, Gombrich, Fletcher and Holland. Gombrich, particularly eclectic, knows that a cogent psychoesthetics would have to comprise both Freud and Richards:

> It is the ego that acquires the capacity to transmute and canalize the impulses from the id, and to unite them in these multiform crystals of miraculous complexity we call works of art. They are symbols, not symptoms, of such control. It is *our* ego which, in resonance, receives from these configurations the certainty that the resolution of conflict, the achievement of freedom without threat to our inner security, is not wholly beyond the grasp of the aspiring human mind.[27]

But this, to quote Shakespeare, "makes mouths at the invisible event." No assured general theory has yet emerged.

6

What will be at issue in a psychoesthetics of literary representation? It should result in analyses that are neither reductionist nor crude. The discussion of the oral or anal character of the artist's impulses has continued long enough. I admire E. Kris on Messerschmidt and N. O. Brown on Swift; and I am intrigued by Norman Holland on Arnold's *Dover Beach*. But their conceptual apparatus remains strangely fixated and the interpreter's attitude resembles, inevitably, that of a methodized voyeur. The "defensive mastery" (Holland) of the artist harmonizes with that of a critic always trying to keep his cool. Representation, moreover, is considered simply as a displaced mimesis, or even mimicry: there is as yet no convincing psychogenetic theory of figurative thinking.[28]

Besides a psychogenesis of figurative (at least, of autoplastic) thinking, we would need to resolve a question raised by Kenneth Burke about the communicative (public-affective) qualities of art. He quite rightly insists on them against the Freudian analogy of art to dream, but underestimates the difficulty of elaborating a general theory of affective structures that would comprise, without falsely dichotomizing, private and public, dream and ritual, elements. "Freud's co-ordinates," writes Burke, "in stressing the poem as dream, understress the poem as a communicative structure and as a realistic gauging of human situations. Communication, rather than wish fulfillment, is the key term for literary analysis."[29]

Communication, however, is not so easily ranged on the side of the reality principle. There is, as we have suggested, a dream of communication; this dream can influence science as well as art; so that wishing returns as a visionariness shared by sister-arts. Obversely, wish fulfillment is a tricky term, for usually the only fulfillment a wish can have is to communicate itself. The wishing studied by Freud remains a craving that cannot be satisfied—a wishing unto death. It is a reality-hunger that tests reality, again and again. So in religious thought the falsified apocalyptic prediction revives; so in art reader-expectations are aroused, defeated and renewed by an indefinite series of mock closures; so in fairy tales magical wishing often returns the hero to the *status quo ante*; so dreaming cannot merge with the daylight world but must begin again each night. Wishing can lead to as much reality testing as communication; and communication is a dream that cannot find its truth.

The paradox is strengthened by the persistence of idealism. Despite Marxism, scientific empiricism, and other critiques, it is a type of thought that has not been dislodged, either in Richards' day or in ours. And as a kind of realism—the realism of the solipsist—it will never be dislodged but will continue to nourish our skepticism vis-à-vis a true or decisive contact with "reality."[30] From the idealist's point of view all "communication" is from within a prison. The verses toward the end of *The Waste Land*,

We think of the key, each in his prison
Thinking of the key, each confirms a prison . . .

are annotated by Eliot with a reference to F. H. Bradley's *Appearance and Reality*, an important revaluation of idealist philosophy. An equally appropriate gloss, however, and less esoteric, might have been a famous passage from Anatole France's *La Vie littéraire*. It rejects "objective criticism" with the assertion that the good critic "relates the adventures of his soul among masterpieces," and continues:

The truth is that one never gets out of oneself. That is one of our greatest miseries. . . . We cannot, like Tiresias, be men and remember having been women. We are locked into our persons as into a lasting prison. The best we can do, it seems to me, is gracefully to recognize this terrible situation and to admit that we speak of ourselves every time that we have not the strength to be silent.[31]

In this exacerbated version of Pater, idealism shows its power as a form of skeptical and realistic thought.

Nature, said Mallarmé, who never doubted its existence, is an "idée tangible pour intimer quelque réalité aux sens frustes." That is true idealism, a reality-hunger that knows it must be frustrated. In Freud the reality-hunger of the libido is even more radically imprisoned. Our capacity for love is basically self-love, and when it turns to others it does so only so as not to die of self. "Ultimately man must begin to love in order not to get ill." Idealism here is degraded into narcissism, yet remains so constitutive that the turn to others or "reality" always appears as if superimposed: a vulnerable conversion, a heroic and alien superstructure. Is there really a *discours de l'autre* or only an interrupted monologue? The analytic situation plays that drama out: it exposes the hidden wishes of the analysand, it brings to consciousness his resistances toward or projections upon others. In so doing it reveals not only the particular (repressed) thoughts that make the attempt to communicate difficult, but also the curious link between wishing and communicating.

The therapeutic alliance of patient and doctor in clinical analysis could not work if the patient were wholly passive, if he did not "wish" for dialogue or communication of some sort. More precisely, his symptoms or dreams force him to seek help or expose him to others in such a way that they seek help for him. This shows that the repressed wish not only persists in the Unconscious but continues to seek expression. Why is this? Why can't the repressed wish simply "give up"?

The early Freud views wishing as essentially libidinous, generated by a sexual energy that, *qua* energy, must discharge. The libido can be repressed but not eliminated: Freud's epigraph to *The Interpretation of Dreams* and his reference to the fallen Titans who continue to lead a subterranean and volcanic existence, indicate that the energic wish is always there, pressing against consciousness, waiting to reemerge. There is no problem about why the wish "wishes" to express itself, because, precisely, that is its nature. Freud proposes an explanatory model based on an intelligible, if mechanistic, understanding of neurological events.

Yet *The Interpretation of Dreams* is devoted chiefly to what Freud calls the "dream-work": a description of the *cunning* of dream or repressed wish. There is nothing very mechanistic about either the manifest form of dreams or the hermeneutic task of the analyst. Freud shows, for instance, that the dream often casts thoughts into a visual (rather than verbal) form to disguise their meaning or charm the mind into admitting them. He calls this the dream-work's "regard for representability."[32] Yet he does not draw from this one of two possible conclusions that would modify his mechanistic model of the libido. The wish that "wishes" to express itself shows a *vis representativa* that should be acknowledged in addition to (in place of?) the *vis libido*. Or similarly, we could posit a desire for communication which is so strong, so idealistic and hence so frustrated, that it becomes inevitably a dream-state.

Even if the primary character of the dream-wish is sexual, its passage from latency into the content of the dream can only be explained in terms of a *communication-compulsion*. The dream aspect of this compulsion, moreover, or the autoplastic character of symptom formation, would suggest an "organic" idealism that is the beginning of the cure. By substituting action upon self for action upon others, it limits the *demand* placed upon others. That demand may be described as exacting from the world a defining (accepting or accusatory) response to oneself. If this is so, the idealism of art can likewise be seen as a therapeutic modification of this demand for a defining response: for achieving self-presence despite or through the presence of others.

Describing the *vis representativa* as a communication-compulsion allows us to bring in reader or audience—the social factor. Freudian psychoesthetics fails to connect the drive for representability with the drive for presentability. This social (perhaps "phenomenological") factor of presentability, even if often noted in the case histories, does not enter the basic theory because Freud considers the sexual or criminal nature of the dream-wish sufficient to account for the latter's difficulty in presenting itself directly. Yet to talk of the dream-work's "regard" for representability subtly merges two notions: the social-ethical one of presentability ("Vorstellen") and the expressive-aesthetic one of representability ("Darstellen"). It is surely because the dream-wish cannot be admitted into our presence that explains why it must be "represented." As in legal or ritual "representation" a subject needs a "representative" because it cannot be present in its own right. It requires advocacy or seconding.

There is, then, on the one hand, an excess of (semiotic and social) demand which I have called a communication-compulsion; and, on the other, a feared defect of (semiotic and social) status which leads to oneiric or symbolic "representation." Yet whatever the reason for the defect which makes representation necessary, we cannot assume that art exists simply to compensate us for that defect. The situation, in this regard, is even more complex in art than in law or religion. The analogy between the various concepts of representation breaks down because in art "representability" is precisely the thing being questioned. For what is sought "beyond representability" is an *unmediated presence* (which raises religious problems) or an *immediate presentability* (which goes against societal or even anthropological ideas of order).

By way of illustration, let me apply these notions briefly to Coleridge's *Ancient Mariner*. Could it be a desire for "presence" which incites the Mariner to kill the albatross? What follows this self-inaugural act certainly heightens the presence of otherness. The new distance between self and other, which the self experiences in "coming out," is part of a separation anxiety which exaggerates the other into a quasi-supernatural or spectral otherness. The spectral happenings test the victim-hero in a way which takes us beyond the obvious moral frame of the story. There is, of course, as the poem makes clear, no fully achieved presence of self or other, but rather a necessary and compulsive repetition as the self realizes its difference and deepens its sense of isolation.

O Wedding-Guest! this soul hath been
Alone on a wide wide sea:
So lonely 'twas, that God himself
Scarce seemèd there to be.

We lay ourselves under contribution until a test is found strong enough to make us feel truly present, "sufficient to have stood." "The Daemon," says Yeats, "by using his mediatorial shades, brings man again and again to the place of choice, heightening temptation that the choice may be as final as possible." Art "represents" a self which is either insufficiently "present" or feels itself as not "presentable."

Basically, then, the proposed psychoesthetics would use an unbalanced "excess" (of demand) and "defect" (of response) model, rather than an idealized stimulus and response pattern. It is not by chance that art is a formal activity whose metaphors (trial, court, judgment, initiation) converge on the idea of a place of heightened demand or intensified consciousness. Whatever the historical circumstances that color these metaphors or affect the nature of the unbalancing demand, there is always the invariant quest to get beyond "representation" to "presence." A psychoesthetics of *literary* representation, moreover, would have to associate the demand we put on ourselves or others with an anxiety for language. Words commonly help to "present" us, and should we feel that they are defective, or else that we are defective vis-à-vis them (words then becoming the "other," as is not unusual in poets who have a magnified regard for a great precursor or tradition), a complex psychological situation arises. In every case, however, art's psychic function would be seen as either limiting a demand or reenforcing a potentiality of response.

7

A final glance at these two "therapies." I have already suggested that the idealism inherent to art (as to any autoplastic shaping) is not, as the early Freud thought, the sign of virtually limitless narcissism but rather a precarious limitation of the demand placed by the self on others. Freud, of course, respects this fact more in his later writings, which develop the concepts of introjection and super-ego. Yet the problem of the demand placed by the self on itself (via the super-ego) remains; as does the problem of the anguish involved in turning away from a mourned object toward its substitute, or the mourning self.[33] Psychoesthetic theory, as I have sketched it out, does throw a possible light on this kind of pain. It suggests that the limitation of demand we call introjection (internalization) may raise the specter of a *further* limitation: of something more properly called a *sacrifice*. This sacrifice is not the self, even if, in some way, it is the self that is being "overcome." For those who seek to overcome the self do it in the hope of a magical transformation: self-conquest is assumed to be the key step toward conquering others—that is, toward fostering a corresponding achievement in this world or the next. The sacrifice feared by one who has internalized demand is simply that of the whole principle of *mimesis:* of a magical correspondence of internal action and external effect, of a mimetic aiming at "The Real Thing." In semiotic terms, of wishing to convert symbols into signs with real, immediate reference.[34]

What of the other solution, that of strengthening adequacy of response? Both mimetic and semiotic functions of art can contribute to this, insofar as they show that the source on which the demand falls is resourceful, i.e. capable of being animated (animation is an important figurative device) or made as inexhaustibly responsive to demand as the Well of Life. There is an important link between representation and recreation. Art restores the sense of powers we feared were used up, or renews images associated with them. "Imagination and taste, how impaired and restored," is the title of Books 12–13 of Wordsworth's *Prelude.* The mimetic-restorative function, moreover, may not be all that different from the semiotic, since language can be that on which the demand falls.

No complete harmony between demand and response is really possible. One reason is that though art can temper demand or strengthen the responsiveness of the (language) source, it must itself enter the cycle of demand and response. It becomes a demand as well as responding to one. Moreover, insofar as we can generalize psychoanalytically on the nature of the demand put by art on us, or to which art responds, it connects representation with reality testing. Symbols or figures point to a lack: to something used up or lost or not sufficiently "present." They do not, in short, imitate so much as test (feel out) a desired mode of being. As Freud remarks: "The first and immediate aim . . . of reality testing is not to *find* an object in real perception which corresponds to the one presented, but to *refind* such an object, to convince oneself it is still there."[35] The *one presented* points, paradoxically, to the *one absent;* the substitute or figure to the phantasm. There is a kind of harmony, a correspondence of lack with lack; but it is easy to see how this testing could incite an indefinite series of figurative substitutions. All we need suppose is, with Freud and the poets, the persistence of wishing or the endlessness of imaginative demand.

A last complication that should be mentioned, and which carries us furthest into psychoanalysis, is the *anxiety of demand* itself. I mean an anxiety generated by the very pressure of the demand we put on things, and the resultant fear that they cannot "bear" us, that what loving-patience there is must turn to resentment and even hate. This feeling is, of course, very closely allied to that of trespass—of over-stepping a limit preventatively defined in religious or moral law (the "you shall not eat" of Genesis 2:17), or not clearly defined at all, as is the case in most "existential" situations. A radical perspective could even suggest that mankind is always *hyper moron*, or its imagination always *hyperbolic*. We are doomed to disturb God's peace.

The anxiety of demand can be studied in developmental terms. As a child grows up he feels more rather than less exposed. To be in the world involves a "sowing of needs" (Traherne): we multiply, consciously or not, our bonds, though generally we call them interests rather than bonds. Part of such self-dissemination is due to anxieties that follow the feared loss of first or parental love; but it is equally due to the realization that no love-object is inexhaustible. We can't eat the breast and have it too. "The child's relationships to his first object, as primitive man's relationship to a totemic animal, is fundamentally ambivalent. The object that is eaten is 'all gone': it needs to be recreated." [36]

Thus the anxiety of demand is deeply rooted in the fear that everything that can be used can be used up: that demand creates the danger of depletion; and whether or not this danger is actual, it is always there in the form of anxiousness. The moralist is anxious about waste, the neurotic about castration or death or money; the narcissist about "Am I still beautiful and loved?" Given this basic anxiety, in whatever form, the question is obviously not whether we can scientifically determine what is in danger of being destroyed by use but rather how we can *recreate* what is being used—the usables including, of course, our feelings.

It is generally acknowledged that art is an effective mode of recreation. The artist may be as prone (or more so) to depletion anxiety. He may be unsure as to where his next inspiration will come from; and he may be tempted to use all sorts of magical, compulsive tricks to summon it. Yet the new object he creates answers him in some way: it reassures him, he feels a reciprocity there, a reality he can master somehow though he cannot shake it off. In Wordsworth's utopian formula, if the mind is "insatiate," then nature should be "inexhaustible." [37]

At the end of this propaedeutic essay, I return therefore to the "psychoesthetic" ideal of perfect reciprocity, of giving and taking humanely balanced, and even of a psychic development that overcomes death, repression and discord by a "mighty working" able to subdue all things to itself. Here Richards, Freud and Wordsworth are of the same company. For invulnerability is the other side of pressure of demand. There should be something "from all internal injury exempt." [38] Such anxiety myths as Balzac's *peau de chagrin*, a skin which magically shrinks itself and its owner's life every time a wish is consummated, is balanced by the dream the rabbis had of the righteous eating Leviathan in the world to come, without fear or satiety. A "consummation" devoutly to be wished! The word is useful here, in its ambiguity: Wordsworth calls his poems a "spousal verse" to anticipate a great and blissful "consummation"—a universally shared vision of Nature as re-created rather than consumed by the demands of consciousness.[39] A consuming that does not consume but consummates: this is indeed the feast of the blessed.

War in Heaven

A Review of Harold Bloom's "The Anxiety of Influence: A Theory of Poetry"

Dies ist kein Buch: Was liegt an Büchern!
Was liegt an Särgen und Leichentüchern!
Dies ist ein Wille, dies ist ein Versprechen,
Dies ist ein letztes Brücken-Zerbrechen.

["This is no book: what good are books! what good are coffins and winding-sheets! This is a will, this is a promise, this is a final burning of bridges."]

Nietzsche, "The Gay Science"

Six essays emerge from this dense, eloquent and experiential brooding, flanked by two prose poems and accompanied by a synoptic introduction and an interchapter on "Antithetical Criticism." Each essay defines what is called a "revisionary ratio," that is, a specific type of "misreading" which helps poets to overcome the influence of previous poets. Influence is understood as dangerously preemptive (hence the anxiety), as an in-flowing that tends to become a flooding, so that for the later poet to survive means to wilfully revise (euphemistically, "correct") his precursor. That precursor may be a composite (Keats, in the *Hyperion*, struggles with the influence of Wordsworth as well as Milton), but there is always a "numinous shadow," "ancestor-god," "Covering Cherub" of this kind—in short, a blocking-agent. Bloom seeks a "wholly different practical criticism" which would transfigure source-study by revealing in each poem, or in the poet's corpus as a whole, echoings of a precursor, imitations as complex as those by which the child wrests his life-space from parents. "Battle between strong equals, father and son as mighty opposites, Laius and Oedipus at the crossroads: only this is my subject here" (p. 11).

The mention of Oedipus is, of course, more than illustrative. Bloom seems to accept Freud's statement that "the beginnings of religion, morals, society and art converge in the Oedipus com-

The Anxiety of Influence was published by Oxford University Press, New York, in 1973.

plex" (*Totem and Taboo*). Moreover, the later poet's apparent victory over the "mighty dead" remains a sublimation and diminishment. His revisionary and deviant imitations of precursors always end in defeat; the latecomer or ephebe can only survive as a shadow of himself. "An enormous curtailment," writes Bloom, "made Wordsworth the inventor of modern poetry, which at last we can recognize as the diminished thing it is, or more plainly: modern poetry (Romanticism) is the result of a more prodigious sublimation of imagination than Western poetry from Homer through Milton had to undergo" (p. 125).[1]

With an audacity and pathos hard to parallel in modern scholarship, Bloom apprehends English literary history from Milton to the present as a single movement, calls it Romanticism, and, even while making it exemplary of the burdens of Freudian or psychological man, dooms it to a precession which looks toward the death of poetry more firmly than Hegel does. For there is, in his augury, no compensation arising from the side of Science, Religion or Criticism. "The strong imagination comes to its painful birth through savagery and misrepresentation. The only humane virtue we can hope to teach through a more advanced study of literature than we have now is the social virtue of detachment from one's own imagination, recognizing always that such detachment made absolute destroys any individual imagination" (p. 86). Bloom's embrace of Western poetry since the Renaissance is a final, desperate hug in the knowledge that there is nothing else.

The result is not as disheartening as it might seem. To make so many poets available to us in a new light, even if that proves to be a twilight—"O joy! that in our embers/Is something that doth live" (Wordsworth)—tells us that the "quickening power" of creative verse is still recognized among us. Bloom's resolute pessimism, in fact, is the shade from which he sees beauties that many of his contemporaries overlook. The valetudinarian perspective is so intense that each artist appears in turn as a new and splendid farewell, "a great shadow's last embellishment" (Wallace Stevens, "The Auroras of Autumn"). Wordsworth is less than Milton, Keats than Wordsworth, Stevens than Keats, but we never reach the "And then there was none." For lo, Ammons and Ashbery rise to the startled view as brave "revisions" of Emerson and Stevens.

There are, in this "brief epic," many assumptions. They are not made explicit so that we don't know what hits us until it hits. The fundamental assumption is, strangely enough, not dissimilar from something that haunted Marx. "Le mort saisit le vif!" Or, as Freud puts it, "the dead father becomes stronger than the living had been." The reality of personal or collective action is usurped by this *danse macabre* or "dramatic mimesis" [2] which alienates person into persona, self into role, and every intended revolution into a degraded repetition of the past. The Marxist reply, therefore, to the basic perspective of *The Anxiety of Influence* might sound like the primitive Christian: Let the dead bury the dead. Yet as long as human nature is dependent on mimesis (imitation), or as long as mimesis itself is dependent on the biological family, it is hard to see how one can more than either exploit or temporarily outwit this principle. Bloom's revisionary ratios are heroic ruses or witticisms that affirm the mimetic passion as ambivalently as Don Juan the sexual.

Other assumptions seem more superficial. First, that there was a "giant age before the flood," i.e., "before the anxiety of influence became central to poetic consciousness." Shakespeare still belongs to this age; some later giants too, like Goethe and Victor Hugo. Bloom's theory of poetry covers therefore not the literary cosmos as a whole but only that portion of it in which influence becomes an anxiety and even a disease of consciousness.

This era is identified in philosophy as post-Cartesian, and in literature as post-Miltonic. A second assumption is that in this era (the only one we really know from within) it is a condition of strength that we recognize prior strength and struggle with it. "That Tennyson triumphed in his long, hidden contest with Keats, no one can assert absolutely, but his clear superiority over Arnold, Hopkins and Rossetti is due to his relative victory or at least holding his own in contrast to their partial defeats" (p. 12). The archetype of such hidden contest between the modern poet and prior greatness is Milton's Satan.

> Why call Satan a modern poet? Because he shadows forth gigantically a trouble at the core of Milton and of Pope, a sorrow that purifies by isolation in Collins and Gray, in Smart and Cowper, emerging fully to stand clear in Wordsworth, who is the exemplary Modern Poet, the Poet proper. The incarnation of the Poetic character in Satan begins when Milton's story truly begins, with the Incarnation of God's Son and Satan's rejection of *that* incarnation. (p. 20)

Is Satan all that modern, however? Is he not as old as the dispute between the "allegory of the poets" and the "allegory of the theologians"? Bloom certainly sharpens our perception of the opposition between Poetry and Divinity. Yet what he calls the "incarnation of the Poetic Character" seems to imply a countertheology. M. H. Abrams' *Natural Supernaturalism* is also unclear as to what secularization (or the "swerve" from a religious into a poetical sphere) implies. The effect of Bloom's poeticotheological tractate may well be to stand Matthew Arnold on his head. Arnold thought that what would remain of religion is its poetry. After reading Bloom one feels that what remains of poetry is its enormously creative theology. Milton and Blake who exploded the Trinitarian bias are important here; but one can foresee, not without anxiety, a post-Bloomian era in which Theology itself, like Jung's Alchemy, is studied as fallen poetry—as a vast, intricate domain of psychopoetic events.

Nor am I sure that Bloom really admires those Antediluvians who are said to have escaped the anxiety of influence. The age that follows—our own—is still one of heroes, if not of giants or gods; and is it not better to be a hero than a god? A Prometheus, though bound, than a Jupiter? To admit that one does not know what made Shakespeare or Goethe strong (they seem to have no strong precursors) is tantamount to saying one has not found what makes them interesting.

Thus the *Anxiety of Influence* moves squarely in the realm of "heroic argument." It is neither a pastoral work which treats poets as friendly competitors for the makebelieve favors of woman or muse; nor a georgic work full of pedagogical care for the reader, and instructing him how to bear burdens lightly. It is revelatory and apodictic, a "severe poem" ("all criticism," affirms Bloom, "is prose poetry"), a *Paradise Lost* transformed into satanic scholarship. "The Eternal Hell revives."

Bloom reveals a War in Heaven: the war of poet with poet, or of artists with the "dark riddle of imaginative priority." This riddle, best expressed in the myth of Covering Cherub and Oedipal Sphinx, had been veiled by a platitudinous and benign understanding of literary influence. After reading Bloom the innocence of influence is lost. We enter a realm of psychic assault, spiritual imposition and quasi-astrological fatality. Nietzschean insights into the "guilt of indebtedness" combine with Freud's vision of mediated man to show that all influence is daemonic and the resistance to it heroic. Bloom's six "revisionary ratios," with their exuberantly eclectic names (Clinamen, Tessera, Kenosis, Daemonization, Askesis, Apophrades), begin to sound like an apotropaic litany. They suggest that *The Anxiety of Influence* is a War Game Manual in the tradition of allegorical psychomachia, and a "tessera" (antithetical completion) of that other amazing codification of the war within the psyche, Anna Freud's *The Ego and its Mechanisms of Defense.*

"Enough, or Too Much," as Blake said. To humanize the poets, or de-idealize the concept of influence, must we make the poets into daemons? To admit that their relations, as manifest in the actual, written poetry, are exploitative and full of envious manipulation, must there be so heroic-prophetic a point of view? "Rintrah roars & shakes his fires in the burden'd air."

The heroic perspective removes the odium of *otium* from art. But the war of critic with critic also enters here. Blake contended with Angels and Swedenborgians, Bloom engages the sky-gods of Modern Criticism and Romantic Scholarship.

Since the deviousness of the critic matches that of the poets he admires, there is little direct polemics. One should compare, however, Bloom's first chapter on "Clinamen, or Poetic Misprision," which contains "an allegory of the modern poet," with W. J. Bate's "The Emergence of a Modern Poet" in his fine biography of *Keats* (chapter 13) or with the full relation of that thesis in *The Burden of the Past and the English Poet.* Though

Bloom stands close to Bate's general view he expunges from it the residual idealism of believing, like Keats, in a "freemasonry" of great spirits.

More deeply uneasy is the relationship between his dark vision of influence and M. H. Abrams's cheerful tracing of the significant and enormous debt the Romantics owed to Judeo-Christian tradition. There is nothing even faintly evangelistic in Bloom: he is totally a kaka-angelist, a bearer of bad news. For him the dynamic of history is governed by a necessary demon rather than a necessary angel—the "demon of continuity." Not fear and trembling and salvation but cunning and wrath and survival are what make history move on.

But the intensest struggle (because of the greatest debt) is with Northrop Frye. To overturn Frye means to re-introduce the "sour myth" of Time into criticism. It is to show that the continuity of literary history, or the magnanimity of its patterns, reposes on a "lie against time" which every strong artist commits when he denies or recreates his origins. *Not myth but the lie as a principle of structure.* "The history of fruitful poetic influence, which is to say the main tradition of Western poetry since the Renaissance, is a history of anxiety and self-saving caricature, of distortion, of perverse wilful revisionism without which modern poetry as such could not exist" (p. 30). As critics, both Frye and Bloom (Borges is a third) lead us back to Oscar Wilde's *Decay of Lying.* But where Frye develops Wilde's eulogy of artifice into a full-scale vision of the debt art owes to art, Bloom will not let us forget that art is based on that six-fold, ecstatic lie he calls the revisionary ratios.

Farewell happy fields
Where joy for ever dwells: Hail,
horrors, hail
Infernal world.

Milton, Paradise Lost

Let me pursue, in an interchapter of my own, the difference between Frye and Bloom. Frye proposes a clear and simple theory of cultural assimilation. It holds that both as artists and critics we join ourselves necessarily to a larger body of thought without which we could not think. The *de facto* continuum is stressed rather than the anxiety for continuity; the communicable grammar or categories rather than the psychomachia of ephebe and ghostly father. Accepting T. S. Eliot's dictum that literature exists as a simultaneous order which the truly new work changes, it posits a diagrammatic and specious present curiously like the view of space as a Hall of Fame—the abode of human stars. This understanding of how art "repeats" the past, affects our idea of the past, but strangely enough not of the present. The history of art, projected to stellar distance (though everything can star) moves beyond temporality on a plane where art is no burden and genealogy no problem. Frye would understand immediately, reading the Biblical story of Abraham and Isaac, that it is a covenant story with a symbolic or ritual substitution which exorcises fear and orders all things well by a Happy End committing God to a Community. This ordering toward the idea of order is what is clearest in Frye: the postponed death, like every mythic substitution, is the very basis of integration.

Moreover the critic, for Frye, is always late. He cannot be where art was. Art has already "substituted" itself for experience; it is impossible to go back; and Frye refuses to get excited about this. He is not, like Alice's rabbit, frantic about Time. "I'm late, I'm late, for a very important date." The very act of systematic criticism is based on the accepted loss of art's temporal immediacy, its power to make us a provincial of its world (Ortega), to subdue us to its influence. He is not Kierkegaard's "insomniac reader" who compulsively scans the story of Isaac seeking beyond the "ingenious web of imagination" the "shudder of thought" (*Fear and Trembling*, "Prelude"). Kierkegaard, that is, fastens on the moment of recognition and how men bear it. The narrative line exists in view of that moment: it is drawn toward an encounter in which death means discontinuity—the death of a child (Isaac) but also of a race, of something barely out of history's womb. Death, for Frye, like loss in general, is a formal moment rather than an existential problem.

Frye is not Kierkegaard nor was he meant to be. His faith in continuity is intellectual and pragmatic rather than personal and religious. He knows that critics continue, whether or not art will. One feels sometimes that he shifts to another category merely to maintain his discourse, or that if great art failed he would accept the genius of popular art. Hagar's son will do as well as Sarah's.

Harold Bloom does not accept substitution as a principle of order. In Bloom genealogy counts, not in the racial sense, but in the strong sense of priority. Art contends with, but cannot escape, a natural order in which fathers precede sons, and where priority combined with strength of presence makes genius a hard act to follow. Bloom refuses to be late. The anxiety about the continuity of art—of great art—raised by Collins and the Romantics, is also his anxiety. He recalls how exposed to *internal* injury art is; how the main threat is not from the outside—science, religion, politics—but from the negative or shadow-side of greatness. Post-Miltonic verse has so clear a history because it is haunted by the preemptions of its father, Milton.

In one sense, therefore, literary history is no problem: it is always "family history" and comes out of what Otto Rank called "the struggle of the artist with art." Its character is determined by strategies for survival devised by the strong sons of strong fathers. Yet strength here is chiefly cunning: more Jacob's strength than Esau's, more Odyssean than Achillean. The revisionary ratios are a "typology of evasions" that do not simply "displace" an archetype, but grapple with a spiritual form, an imposing literary presence. For Bloom "displacement" is more like a trespass: creative envy is not the nicest of emotions. His "misprision" makes sense only in a world with family dimensions of gothic intensity, where the individual is bounded by others, all motion is accountable, and we can scarcely stir because of the protective or oppressive air.

This recovery of the dark side of "displacement" revises Frye and is a true if exploitative return to Freud. Freud noted that children go through a stage in which they deny that their parents are their parents and "quest" for new ones ("Family Romances"). They think of themselves as changelings; and life bears them out when they exchange father for husband, mother for wife. The blood-parent (Nature) is eventually denied in favor of an imaginative adoption. The ephebe-quester does the same. He myth-takes his parents or "creates his own precursors," as Borges would say. For, in the realm of art, where no natural fathers are, greatness begins by choosing a worthy obstacle. If there were no precursor he would have to be invented. The imagination needs a blocking-agent to raise itself, or not to fall into solipsism. We become great, Kierkegaard said, in proportion to striven-with greatness.

Yet Bloom revises Freud as well as Frye. Freud sees life as possessing a binary structure through the mercy of time: childhood/adolescence, mother/wife, father/husband. This repetition, or second chance, is essential for development; to collapse the binary poles (and subtler oppositions) is fatal. Through this repetition we can redirect our needs by substitution or sublimation. Family Romance, in the child, his quest for new or the real parents, is a "figurative" prophecy of the loss to come and of the imaginative capacity for substitutes. The imagination is like Adam's dream: the child awakes, in adolescence, and finds it truth (Compare *Paradise Lost*, Book VIII, lines 478–82.)

In Bloom, however, there is only the awakening into failure as if the quest could never be fulfilled. Time is a deception, a mere, endless repetition revealed by art's anti-naturalism. The creative mind no more accepts the second family (wife, husband, etc.) than the first (parents). It remains a Blakean Infant Sorrow, "struggling in my father's hands/Striving against my swaddling bands."

There is something overcondensed in this account. Bloom's theory is vulnerable because *priority* (a concept from the natural order) and *authority* (from the spiritual order) are not clearly distinguished; in fact, they merge and become a single, overwhelming *proton pseudos.* By seeking to overcome priority, art fights nature on nature's own ground, and is bound to lose. Nothing *could* grow in the shadow of this first principle except by delusion or misrepresentation. The awareness of a prior greatness is unanswerably strong, and the argument that art—or its survival—is based on misprision looks suspiciously like one which holds that blasphemy is an acknowledgment of God. Disconnection proves to be impossible: each slap is an antithetical embrace. Where is the joyous franchise of art? Hermeneutic freedom becomes misinterpretation, the wit of poetry a compulsive "swerving" from identity, and family romance the nightmare of always walking into parents.

Now it may be that in *life* we don't ever get far—no farther than Oedipus—from our parents. Yet even in strict Freudian terms Nature tends toward the "hermeneutic freedom" of art by allowing a second chance; and this is expressed by categories common to psychoanalysis and literary analysis. Repetition, substitution, projection, transference are not unlike imitation, symbolism, metonymy, metaphor. Freud's analysis of maturation into the binary forms already mentioned resembles, moreover, the linguistic and structuralist principle of binary opposition. These categories allow the fullest development of the important concept of *error* which Bloom narrows to misprision. Error formally separates a beginning and an end: it determines the narratable line, or process of discovery, as a wonder-wandering that is valuable in itself rather than being merely a delayed, catastrophic closure. Bloom's overcondensing takes away the second chance: literary history is for him like human life, a polymorphous quest-romance collapsing always into one tragic recognition. Flight from the precursor leads to him by fatal prolepsis, nature always defeats imagination, history is the repetition of "one story and one story only."

In that case we must indeed fear for the survival of art. As the consciousness of defeat grows, artists will have to think of art as necromancy, or a perpetual, desperate gamble—a "yet once more." Such knowledge would depress the creative motive as thoroughly as Dr. Johnson's theology. One wonders whether Bloom's version of literary history is not a new Johnsonianism, or a dark version of the neoclassical "What is there left to do?" W. J. Bate has called "the remorseless deepening of self-consciousness before the rich and intimidating legacy of the past" the great problem of modern art. Before Bate we tended to think that the *tout est dit* oppressed only the neoclassical writer, but he has shown it as an anxiety accumulating since Milton. "The arts stutter, stagger, pull pack into paralysis and indecision."

Bloom is equally puritan in his conception of greatness and not less pessimistic about the future. He also implies a diminished succession of the great ages of English poetry: Renaissance, Romanticism, Modernism. The emasculating burden of the past or an effeminate embarrassment of riches take their toll. *Someone was there before us.*

To understand the "before" in a chronological sense is not wrong but also not sufficient. The presence of greatness is what matters, a beforeness which makes readers, like poets, see for a moment nothing but one master-spirit. A "shudder of thought" collapses the narrative web, and deprives us of all historicizing. It is a moment of the unmediated and not of the comparable—of purity and even reversal, in which all sundries are sundered. In Bloom's sublime yet sour myth, time refuses time. Xronos-Chronos emerges blatant, ready to eat his children once again.

> What though not through the sin of Pierre, but through his father's sin, that father's fair fame now lay at the mercy of the son, and could only be kept inviolate by the son's free sacrifice of all earthly felicity;—what if this were so? It but struck a still loftier chord in the bosom of the son, and filled him with infinite magnanimities.
>
> *Melville,* Pierre

It makes us realize, this book, that we are only near the beginning of a psychoanalysis of literary representation. Happy conjecture in this field remains, to use Christopher Smart's phrase, a "miraculous cast." Every sentence of Bloom's wagers itself: whether epigrammatically concise or prophetically burdened it tends to move forward by analogies and is precariously assimilative. Unlike Freud, who also relies on the analogical method,[3] Bloom cannot always make the rich and echoing thoughts his own; but then Freud is one who had no genuine precursor and whose theory of sexuality turns us even now into "wonder-wounded hearers." The *Anxiety of Influence*, original as it is, is a latecomer in terms of the basic theory of psychoanalysis.

An advantage of coming late is that Bloom can link Freud to a moralist tradition that stretches from Pascal ("A poet, and not an honest man" is a maxim he quotes) to Nietzsche and Oscar Wilde. The theory of sexuality is seen as corrosive of idealistic meanings. So the force of Bloom's book depends greatly on the wedge it drives between meaning (especially literary meaning) and sublimation. A poem, we read, is not "an overcoming of anxiety" but an "achieved anxiety." The hurt itself must be the meaning.

This proposition, unfortunately, can be reversed. A disadvantage of coming late is that by now the relations between sexuality and meaning seem very complicated indeed. So one can argue that meaning, or rather what Freud calls *Bedeutungswandel* (tropism of meaning? wandering signification?) is itself the hurtful. Freud appears as Ovid *dé-moralisé:* his "metamorphoses" tells us not only that nothing is stable (that meanings change even as relationships do) but that what is most stable is most reversible, and so fullest of potential hurt. Meanings or persons betray us in the same way: what we thought real proves to be a delusive figure, what we thought a figure becomes truth.

The *Anxiety of Influence* stops short of this area where "word representation" is problematized. It is interested in types of ambivalence rather than types of ambiguity. Yet as an antiformalistic theory it should have gone further and argued that there is an anxiety attaching to representation itself. Strong symbols like the Covering Cherub together with strong dicta like the Second Commandment ("You shall not make yourself any graven image") point to an acute sense of violation or trespass that often accompanies what Jacques Derrida has aptly named the *Scene of Writing* ("Freud et la scène de l'écriture" in *L'Ecriture et la différence*).

Derrida, of course, develops an antimimetic theory which identifies Writing itself as primal, rather than as a compulsive sublimation of something in the past. In Bloom, however, a primal scene, or the impossible return to it, motivates that "repetition and commemoration" for which his own poetic Prologue and Epilogue quest. Derrida's semiotic turn, which does not turn from anything but is a kind of free fall, is very different from Bloom's *clinamen* or *swerve* avoiding (as well as voiding) an unbearable presence. The Writer, in Bloom, is strong because he is supermimetic—because he faces and overcomes a primal influence—not because he is antimimetic.

I do not know who is ultimately truer to *Bedeutungswandel:* Bloom or Derrida. For Bloom's theory of the relation of literary sons and fathers, while a significant contribution, is a strangely literal transfer to art of one strain in Freud's thinking. Freud had carefully traced the *Bedeutungswandel* leading from the oedipal situation to the child's wish to rescue the beloved (mother) from the father, or the beloved (father) from imagined dangers. In both cases the child-hero is really seeking a reversal of identity, whereby it would take its father's place, or give itself to the mother—that is, seek to be its parents. "All instinctual drives," Freud wrote, "the tender, grateful, lascivious, stubborn, self-exalting, are satisfied in this one wish: to be the father of oneself."[4] Or as Bloom restates it: "Freud thought all men unconsciously wished to beget themselves, to be their own fathers in place of their phallic fathers, and so 'rescue' their mothers from erotic degradation. It may not be true of all men, but it seems to be definitive of poets as *poets.* The poet, if he could, would be his own precursor, and so rescue the Muse from her degradation."[5]

A bewildering and powerful transfer, which Bloom could defend by claiming he is reinterpreting Freud by means of the second revisionary ratio, the *tessera:* "A poet antithetically 'completes' his precursor, by so reading the parent poem as to retain its terms but to mean them in another sense, as though the precursor had failed to go far enough" (p. 14). What Lacan and others in France are doing to Father Freud is here seen to be a special case of a vital revisionist principle. Bloom's subversive technique makes Freud's work into a "parent poem" and so diminishes the difference between figurative and scientific writing. At the same time it may be overliteralizing the Freudian metaphor of the child who "saves" his parents.

What, finally speaking, is being "saved" by Bloom or Freud? The very existence of a *Bedeutungswandel*—intra- or inter-textual, from image to image or author to author—must eventually entropy all positive knowledge and make it seem a blind (i.e. literal) elaboration of this or that metaphor.

Let us propose, for example, that Bloom is saving the phenomenon of poetry and Freud the phantasm that underlies it.

Yet Bloom can call poetry an "illusory therapy" as if there were a real illness or possible cure, instead of a phantasm to be laid again and again. As to Freud, he insists on the reality not only of a primal scene ("Urszene") but also of a primal history scene ("Urgeschichte") which saw the removal of the primal father ("Urvater") by his cohort of sons. In *Totem and Taboo*, after some vacillation, he asserts that the neurotic is defending himself against a historical reality (however far-engendered) as well as a psychical reality. "In the beginning was the Deed," runs the last sentence of *Totem and Taboo*, quoting Goethe who quotes (revisionistically) Scripture; yet the "Deed" is clearly not any act whatsoever but "this memorable and criminal deed" which, stripped of mythic or pseudohistorical trappings, reduces to Coming into the World, or coming into the Presence of Others as a Person (Poet) in one's own right.

I would prefer a phenomenological to a psychoanalytic view of this "deed" of self-presence. Yet the daring of Bloom's thesis and the importance of its transfer to literary studies are clear. The coincidence of Satan's boast in *Paradise Lost,*

Who saw
When this creation was? Remember'st thou
Thy making, while the maker gave thee being?
We know no time when we were not as now;
Know none before us, self-begot, self-rais'd
By our own quick'ning power

with Freud's "All instinctual drives [. . .] are satisfied in this one wish: to be the father of oneself," allows Bloom to make Milton the *literary* Founder who not only anticipates Freud but exerts a decisive textual and imaginative pressure on English poetry. Such questions as to what difference it would make if we substituted Shakespeare for Milton (and, say, MacDuff's legend for Satan's) as the "beginning" of a theory of English poetry will not disqualify but rather deepen the relevance of Bloom's pioneering work. We may eventually decide that his preference of Milton to Shakespeare is prejudicial, and reflects a swerve from the haunting image of female Generation into the Gnostic view that Regeneration (or all true creativity) is a second birth, "of the Father." Yet in doing so we will only have continued Bloom's mode of analysis and begun to make sense of the perplexing yet persistent link between poetry and negative theology, or fiction and the liberties of myth.

Post-script: a note on "ratio." Blake associates "ratio" with Newtonian science, and uses it to denote a proportionate (rational) and yet—in his view—reductive or uncreative relation between two or more terms of similar magnitude. ("But in Milton, the Father is Destiny, the Son a Ratio of the five senses, & the Holy-ghost Vacuum!") For Bloom, since the two terms are always precursor-source and later poet, or literary "father" and "son," the revisionist relation is basically a tricky attempt to establish commensurability between incommensurables. The "ratio" turns out to be a false and, ultimately, "fearful" attempt at "symmetry."

It may be worthwhile pointing out that "fearful symmetry"—the famous phrase from "The Tyger"—should be read as meaning "fearful ratio." A ratio-nal view of the world, identified by Blake with Natural Religion or Natural Philosophy,[6] is deeply perplexed by the creator:creature relation the tiger seems to pose. For Blake, moreover, a reduced (ration-al) power of perception is bound to raise a "spectre" which terrifies and so humbles the very "reason" that dared frame it. It is extravagant yet not exaggerated to suggest that the precursor is, in Bloom's system, a spectre or tiger of this kind, imposed by the imagination on itself in its desperate attempts to gain parity (commensurability).

Bloom does not stop with the psychological truth of this but affirms the real superiority of giant precursor to rival ephebe. He now seems opposed, therefore, to Blake's view that a strong but later poet can genuinely revise an earlier master. His claim is rather that the new poet or "container"[7] is necessarily less than the "contained" source. Though *The Anxiety of Influence* honors Blake as the greatest revisionist of the Enlightenment, he does not play as central a role as in Bloom's previous work. For the anagogical-progressive model of history, to which Blake is indebted, leads us back to the Pauline "revision" of the Old Testament, and its powerful device of the *figura* that eventually reached a literary highpoint in Dante's *Commedia*. Bloom exposes this model (at least by inference) as a psychic necessity that compensates for the overwhelming strength of the Old Testament. It is the Old, not the New, Testament which is the scandal. Blake's revisionism[8] remains indebted to a superficial anagogy.

Yet Bloom also criticizes the analogical-progressive model which secularizes the *figura* and makes it into a purely metaphoric equivalence. His insistence on origin and source upsets a sentence of that other Blake scholar, Northrop Frye, who evokes the ultimate commensurability or "unfearful symmetry" of all great art. "In the study of Blake [viz. literature] it is the analogue that is important, not the source."[9] Like structuralism this too can free us prematurely from art's burden of anagogy—from its sublime and shaming "load of immortality" (Keats).

The connection of Bloom's "ratios" with those of Kenneth Burke's "dramatistic pentad" in *The Grammar of Motives* is interesting rather than essential—interesting because of the "competitive" and "strategic" motives underlying them also. Yet Burke's theory, as a whole, elaborates a principle of catharsis ("ad bellum purificandum" is his motto for *The Grammar*), while Bloom's work, however cathartic in itself, emphasizes in point of theory the necessity of an "endless imitation" motivated compulsively by creative jealousy or emulation, and so forever instigating "Mental Fight" and "War in Heaven."

Spectral Symbolism and Authorial Self in Keats's "Hyperion"

These are death's own supremest images,
The pure perfections of parental space.

Wallace Stevens,
"The Owl in the Sarcophagus"

Of Keats's two versions of the *Hyperion*, the first was begun in the autumn of 1818, and the second (the *Fall of Hyperion*) in the summer of 1819, and both were abandoned close to September 1819,[1] as a letter suggests which also mentions that the poet had just composed "To Autumn." I will consider the two versions of *Hyperion* as a single, though unfinished, project.

Spectral symbolism may be defined as episodes in which beings appear that are not human, or not entirely so, yet have intentions involving us. It features ghosts or gods or creatures of disproportionate size: incredibly large (giants) or small (fairies). The word "spectral" has, in addition, an ominous edge: it suggests a particular group of these figures, apparitions endowed with such intensity vis-a-vis us that we feel anxiety or terror. *They mean us*, in some curious way.

That this terror may be no more than an imaginative thrill is not important. As the unmasked Magician says in Bergman's movie: *I merely gave you what you wanted.* For the more we think about these "forms, that do not live/Like living men" (Wordsworth), the less sure we are what they mean. It is just this absence of a precise referent together with the heightened sense of self they produce, which makes them ominous.

The relation of the *Hyperion* to spectral symbolism is particularly intriguing. The poem suggests a link between the presence of spectral symbols and the artist's quest for identity. The heightened sense of self is here that of the *authorial* self which must abide the demand of sublime yet "questionable" shapes. These shapes, like the ghost in *Hamlet*, are parental or ancestral—if only in the sense that they are the "supreme fictions" which have always haunted poetry. Reanimating the ancient fictions is almost a way of describing Keats's program in the *Hyperion*.

Yet Keats, at the same time, resolutely excludes the gothic-spooky and, to an extent, psychic-spectral side of these symbols. His sublime personifications—Saturn, Hyperion, Mnemosyne-Moneta—are images of an enlightened mind: the products of a "fine spell of words" and not of a "dumb enchantment." He thought of them as an English or "natural sculpture" rivaling the Greek ideal confirmed in him by the Elgin Marbles. If gods at all, they were to be of the Northern sky, "the color of ice and fire and solitude."[2]

The reason for this was not (or not only) a nostalgic Hellenism. Keats, intensely aware of himself as a modern artist, sought to share in the "grand march" of the intellect which Enlightenment philosophies of progress were propounding. For him too the era between Classical antiquity and the European renaissance was a "middle" age of "superstition." His quest for authorial identity, therefore, touches at this point the vexed question of a modern or "northern" equivalent to Greek objectivity.

It is well known how this (supposedly) Grecian character of sublime simplicity haunted the mind of artists from Winckelmann on, and determined the course of art in Germany. Keats waged his own fight with the Greek ideal, with those marvelous marbles that enter the first *Hyperion* in ruder and nativist form as "a Stonehenge of reverberance" (W. M. Rossetti). Yet the tyranny of Greece over England has not been described, though Keats begat Tennyson who begat Stevens. A comparison of Keats with Stevens can illuminate it.

The auroral poems of Stevens, written in the very twilight of the gods, are "Greek" in refusing to accept the "world of the dead" as a land of unlikeness. They insist that even the spectral world must satisfy our desire for resemblances and become "parental space." Owlish or macabre symbolism disappears from a verse in which ghosts wear colored nightgowns or where we are granted the "floreate flare" of gods dissolving. And the music left in the wake of their demise is a great poetry, though limited by its very power to console:

It is a child that sings itself to sleep,
The mind, among the creatures that it makes,
The people, those by which it lives and dies.[3]

For this self-haunted child, however, the floreate often turns back into a spectral flare. "On he flared" (*FH*, 2, 61)[4] is what we could say also of the poetic mind. It moves from pleasure garden to haunted temple, as in the *Fall of Hyperion*. So, when Stevens writes of the northern heavens,

The stars are putting on their glittering belts,
They throw around their shoulders cloaks that flash
Like a great shadow's last embellishment[5]

it should indeed be a last embellishment, a sign from the sky itself that the sublime "may come tomorrow in the simplest word." But tomorrow is not today, and we understand that Stevens will not give up the figure, that he tropes the simple word, and that his poetry is a farewell to the gods which intends to linger.

Keats's "adieu" to the gods also remains an à-dieu. He aspires to enlightenment, yet parental space, in his epic, does not triumph except as spectral space.[6] The living and troubled development of the *Hyperion* sequence will allow us to see gods become ghosts despite themselves, and a consciously modern and objective poet a shade nourishing their darkness like a dying flame. The *Fall of Hyperion* has a greater affinity to the gothic novel than to so-called Greek or epic objectivity.

War in Heaven. Perhaps the oldest theme of myth. It is the subject of Hesiod's *Theogony*; it is basic to the *Gilgamesh* epic and the *Eddas*; and though censored from the Bible, it occasionally finds its way back through hints in Genesis (Blake makes a great deal of the plural ending of "Elohim"), Isaiah, the Book of Job, the Psalms, and, of course, the Satan-Lucifer myth in Revelations. It may even enter the Jewish prayer for the Dead:

"He who makes peace in the high heavens. . . ." For English poetry the theme is triumphantly revived in Milton's *Paradise Lost.*

The subject of *Hyperion* is War in Heaven. One generation of gods has displaced another. Yet we see no battles; we are not even told what happened. Saturn, the deposed Titan, does not himself seem to know what befell. He is presented to us in a state of plaintive ignorance. As if a god, or a whole generation of gods, had suffered a stroke.

I do not mean to complicate Keats needlessly. It is quite proper for an artist to choose his starting-point as he wishes. In this "transcendental cosmopolitics," as Leigh Hunt called it, Keats begins with the physical action over; and we can easily speculate on the rightness of his plan. He avoids the kind of heavy, mock-heroic effect that both intrigues and disturbs us in *Paradise Lost*, Books V and VI, where angel wars with angel in a predetermined war-game. Moreover, he can now throw all the emphasis on the psychological state of the fallen Titans. If Wordsworth wrote "lyrical ballads," that is, ballads that interest us not because of thrilling adventure or spooky episodes but because of the character or psyche of the persons they depict, Keats can write "lyrical epics." Perhaps, too, had he finished this fragmentary narrative, the actions that led to the fall of the old gods, or produced the new, might have been clarified.

Yet there is something too peculiar and definitive about the *Hyperion* to make such reflections persuasive. *Hyperion* is a strange epic in that it deals only with gods, rather than with gods and men. The closest to a subject matter so relentlessly divine is the *Prometheus* of Aeschylus, which Shelley revives in his long drama published about this time; but there mankind, without appearing, is the very center, the *casus belli.*[7] In Keats's *Hyperion*, not only are we in an atmosphere where mankind plays no formal role, but the poet, almost without exception, excludes himself till the third book. The style of that book constitutes a clear break and anticipates the *Fall of Hyperion*, where the poet enters immediately in his own person as a Dantesque dream-voyager. Here too, though, the other figures remain exclusively divine, as in the first *Hyperion*.

Yet, paradoxically, the effect on us of these divinities is a deeply human one. They tempt us to a question similar to that inspired by the Grecian Urn, "What gods, or men, are these?" This humanization is a curious achievement, and one is puzzled as to what it intends. For why choose a super-objective mythic form, which excludes even the person of the poet, if the end is subjective? In wishing to escape an adolescent style, that of *Endymion*, was Keats duped into an obsolescent one?

Certain realia of literary and personal history enter here, not so much to explain why Keats chose the objective mode but why its possibility caught him up. He was, first of all, in flight from the Wordsworthian "egotistical sublime." He felt that poetry should not be made of personal moods heightened or intensified. Poetry should surprise the reader by "fine excess and not by singularity," so that it "appears almost a Remembrance." It should be "great & unobtrusive, a thing which enters into one's soul, and does not startle it or amaze it with itself but with its subject."[8]

Reinforcing this classicist poetics, though subtly changing its character, was his experience of the death of his brother Tom, whom he nursed during the fall of 1818, when he was actively composing the *Hyperion*. Tom was dying of tuberculosis, and his "identity"—an important word, repeated by Keats a month later in his famous letter on the "poetical character" ("A Poet has no Identity—he is continually in for—& filling some other Body . . . the identity of every one in the room begins to press upon me that I am in a very little time annihilated")[9]—Tom's identity, he writes, so presses on him all day "that I am obliged to go out. . . . I am obliged to write, and plunge into abstract images to ease myself of his countenance, his voice and feebleness—so that I live now in a continual fever. . . ." And he adds, referring to the fever, "it must be poisonous to life although I feel well. . . ." A day or so later, what he names by a strange transfer "the feverous relief of poetry" enters again:

> This morning poetry has conquered—I have relapsed into those abstractions which are my only life—I feel escaped from a new strange and threatening sorrow. . . . There is an awful warmth about my heart like a load of Immortality.[10]

We understand almost instinctively the complex psychological act taking place. There is Tom's fever and there is the poet's "fever." One cannot rule out the thought of physical contagion in "it must be poisonous to life," but the main sense is surely the reproach Moneta flings at the personalized dream-visionary in the *Fall of Hyperion*:

What benefit canst thou do, or all thy tribe
To the great world? Thou are a dreaming thing,
A fever of thyself.

(1, 167–69)

Keats, even had he studied medicine more, could hardly have altered the course of his brother's illness; but in the second *Hyperion* Moneta seems to suggest that his failure in the practical sphere is due to an aspiration in the poetical, which is itself in doubt of success. Trying to fathom for once the intimate link between personal psychology and the psychology of art, one can speculate that Keats's "plunge" or "relapse" into mythic "abstractions" through the "fever" of poetry is a *counter-identification* which, at one and the same time, associates him deeply with his dying brother and translates the mortal facts into the sublimity and impersonality of myth.

By this counter-identification, then, Keats produces images that are—at least in theory—*immortal*: they are poetic images, and they are images of gods. When Keats talks of a "load of Immortality," he is referring quite literally to Saturn, Thea, Hyperion, Mnemosyne, and so forth. These sublime figures are imaginative antibodies that correspond to the compound fever—Tom's and poetry's—consuming him. Yet to claim they are as cool as he is hot, or as eternal as he feels mortal (in a word, not only sublime but sublimating) would belie a complex situation.

For the gods clearly feel the contagion of mortality. Consciousness, our "burden of the mystery," is also their burden. It is, in fact, their very immortality that weighs on them now and becomes a "load." They have not changed utterly; they may not even have changed; but they have the intense consciousness of a change. Since, as among men, "thinking is sorrow," their sublimity begins to be deeply human, and their sorrow indistinguishable from an obscure brooding. "Even here, into my center of repose," Hyperion cries, "The shady visions come to domineer." (*Hyperion* 1, 243–44.) A night-world has come into being, or more precisely a gothic world in which there is no evidence except by way of omens and ambiguous symbols. But this is simply our own human world, where things need interpretation. The thunderbolt or primal trauma—whatever caused their change into this kind of conscious being—exists only as a phantasm with an extraordinary imaginative hold on the psyche.

There is, moreover, a second, very important kind of contagion. Even where Keats is successful, where he is sublime and impersonal in mode, the poetry freezes his fever into so majestic and enigmatic a form that a new sense of what is unbearable erupts. The "load of Immortality," in short, becomes an overload, and obliges the mortal or humanizing strain to reenter a realm from which it had been banished—to reenter it, indeed, with redeeming force.

This reentry of the mortal into a sacred or separated sphere, this redemptive humanization of the concepts of imagination, has many phases, and is the only genuine "progress" among all the pseudo-progressions of the poem. It can be a mere reflux, as in Saturn's first, pathos-laden speech; it can be a dramatic and desperate intrusion, as in Book 3 of the first *Hyperion*; and it can be a formal and sustained decision as when Keats, in the revised poem, chooses to bring himself (in Dante's manner) directly into the presence of the divine. But it is never complete, no more than the *Hyperion* is; and I do not want to give the impression that there is an absolute progress between the earlier and later poem.

In the first *Hyperion*, this psychological and humanizing underplot never quite achieves the status of plot. Though the real action lies between Keats's psyche and the abstract weight of those grand conceptions—between the poet, in short, and the demands of sublime poetry—the action unfolds as if it were autonomous. It is no real action, of course; it is a passion rather than an action; but it retains, at least, the enigmatic substantiality of myth.

Things are quite different in the *Fall of Hyperion.* Consider its culminating episode: Keats' reenvisioning of the frieze of Saturn and Thea, with which the original poem opened. In the earlier version there is no mediating frame or voice. There is the direct, objective presentation of a mysterious scene with the stillness of a picture. Now this picture is framed both by Moneta's voice and the poet's explicit presence. As in a movie we hear a voice that begins to speak: "So Saturn sat/When he had lost his realms." This voice, Moneta's, induces the poet's vision of Saturn and Thea: "the lofty theme/Of those few words hung vast before my mind. . . ." (1, 306–7.) The double mediation, it is true, fades back into the picture, for the prophetess speaks only once more (1, 332–35), and the poet's presence remains unobtrusive. This renewed moment of objectivity proves, however, highly deceptive, for Moneta's mediation is every bit as treacherous as that which the gods can exert on the Homeric heroes, and which leaves Hector suddenly alone with Achilles. All at once the poet's absorbed looking (he forgets himself to marble, or to the still life before him) changes into a spectral confrontation as profound as the ghostly calms which befall Coleridge's Ancient Mariner. But Moneta, at this crucial point, remains silent, and so adds herself to what must be borne:

A long awful time
I look'd upon them: still they were the same;
The frozen God still bending to the Earth,
And the sad Goddess weeping at his feet.
Moneta silent. Without stay or prop,
But my own weak mortality, I bore
The load of this eternal quietude,
The unchanging gloom and the three fixed shapes
Ponderous upon my senses, a whole moon.
For by my burning brain I measured sure
Her silver seasons shedded on the night,
And ever day by day methought I grew
More gaunt and ghostly. Oftentimes I pray'd
Intense, that Death would take me from the vale
And all its burthens—Gasping with despair
Of change, hour after hour I curs'd myself;
Until old Saturn rais'd his faded eyes,

And look'd around, and saw his kingdom gone,
And all the gloom and sorrow of the place,
And that fair kneeling Goddess at his feet.

(1, 384–403)

Here the reentry of the mortal into a "lunar" realm, or the surfacing of the poet in the world of myth, is most dramatic. We see the man who sees the vision: the "invisible poet" discovers his presence. Yet is it a moment of humanization, or the reverse?

The poet still stands *under* rather than *beside* his visions. Indeed, though Moneta is as changeable as the moon to which she is compared—a moon traditionally the symbol of the border between higher and lower, mortal and immortal realms—her presence now intensifies only the pressure of immortality. When Keats says that the three fixed shapes, the haunting trinity of Saturn, Thea, and Moneta, converging here for the first time in the *Hyperion* sequence, were borne up by his unaided senses "a whole moon," we feel licensed to take the phrase as an appositive which could be interpreted in more than the obvious temporal sense: they (Saturn, Thea, and Moneta) collectively *are* the moon. So that the poet, who had been tacitly "under Saturn" at the beginning of the first *Hyperion*, bearing or bearing up that "load of Immortality," is now literally the "burning brain" whose "fever" must endure this "frozen." If this vision, this poem, is his creation, he must take responsibility for it: he must assume the status of creator and overcome, somehow, that ingrained sense of trespass or intrusion which may have caused him to conceal his person in the first place. Lemprière, one of Keats's mythographical guides, tells us that Latium, where Saturn lived after his fall, is derived from *lateo*, to conceal. Poetry may not be Keats's Latium.

I am tempted to engage, at this point, in a digression on the artist's sense of trespass, and how it is linked to some of our major myths. The act of writing can be deeply expressive of feelings of violation, ancestor-profanation, forgery, self-exposure. These feelings, extricated by depth-psychology, are also a matter of public record, since our myths are so often about confidence men, rebels or thiefs: cunning liars like Odysseus, amorous gangsters like Don Juan, robinhoods like Satan-Prometheus. The psychotic sculptor Messerschmidt, about whom Ernst Kris has written, felt he was being punished for his art which had uncovered the divine secret of proportion. Freud, similarly, creates his own myth of the band of brothers who "steal" their women from a tyrannous father. This myth is the exact counterpart of all that posit the existence in prehistory of sacred or inalienable property and date our troubles from its forbidden consumption. The action of the *Iliad* and *Odyssey*, as well as that of the Old Testament, is kindled or rekindled by such an act. So Coleridge's *Ancient Mariner*, with its spectral sense of place, its invisible yet fatal lines of demarcation, and its isolation and exposure of the dream-voyager, uses the killing of a sacred bird (associated with the Polar spirit) to justify the visionary bother.

What of Keats's trespass? The *still* with which the first *Hyperion* opens is not devoid of a threshold sense of possible profanation, and when, in the *Fall of Hyperion*, the *still* becomes a movie that will not move on, it exposes the poet-souffleur who has played god, or concealed his own image.[11] Keats is now forced into the light; obliged to recognize his presence in a moment that is so searingly self-conscious that instead of humanizing him it suggests the impossibility of bringing the human into so strong a light, of placing it under so heavy a burden. The poet here fails to move his images; or simply to move—animate—them: this Pastoral is colder than that of the Grecian Urn, these figures will never be fully humanized. Indeed, they begin to vamp him. Instead of the *myth* becoming more human, the *poet* becomes less human: "ever day by day methought I grew/More gaunt and ghostly." (*Fall of Hyperion*, 1, 395–96.) The renewed loss of identity he suffers may indicate that the psychological quest, which we have ranged on the side of humanization, cannot genuinely prevail against the sublime—even vampiristic—force of myth or tradition.

I have passed from personal psychology, Keats at the deathbed of his brother, to the psychology of art: a poet saving the grand, moribund symbols of the sublime mode. The two psychologies are not without connection, if we think of Keats as deeply engaged in a sympathetic, even magical, *nursing* The mortal presence of Tom and the giant agony of the Titans may seem to be incommensurable things, yet the poet's "identity" is tested by both. What a soul-making, to have to sustain symbols which should have sustained him! They may not—cannot—reconcile him to "The weariness, the fever, and the fret," the death of Tom or the fact that "women have cancers." Those dying forms add themselves to his suffering as if they too had to be nursed. Poetry here is not a mediation supporting the poet. The opposite seems to be the case, for poetry now stands in dire need of Keats:

Without stay or prop,
But my own weak mortality, I bore
The load . . .

Like Dante or Wordsworth, Keats once more includes in the vision "the transitory Being that beheld/ This vision."[12] He polarizes, however, his mortal psyche and the conceptions it endures. The result is a more dramatic poetry than Wordsworth's, and perhaps a more radical one. For the *Hyperions* not only depict, vividly, the "fear and awe" that befall us when we consider the human mind as a "haunt"[13]; they also seek, by that depiction, to become a soul-making or *gradus ad psychem.* Their subject matter is therefore akin to the labors of Psyche. Keats' authorial identity was, in a sense, still to be born—or justified by these poetic labors. The two *Hyperions*, consequently, are linked by a birth-scene (*Hyperion*, 2, 113ff.) which might have revealed the psyche of the poet in manifest or justified form: perhaps as the goddess Keats "discovers" in his "Ode to Psyche" of April 1819,[14] perhaps as the figure or persona of the Poet—probably as both of these together, a finer-toned repetition of the Thea-Saturn, Apollo-Mnemosyne group. Keats wants to envisage his soul as a "shaped and palpable god."

He was bound to fail in the first *Hyperion*, because those terminal figures (Psyche and Poet) are not terminal at all, but quietly present all the time, sustaining an action which should not have to legitimate them in this falsely narrative, genealogical manner. But when, in the *Fall of Hyperion*, the last becomes the first, and the poet's psyche enters visibly (as a *persona dramatis*) from the beginning, the narrative also runs into an impasse. The poem punishes Keats's assumption of an identity, or his presumption that he can endure visions as of old.[15] The poetic psyche is forced to undergo a paralyzing test of its inner strength: a moment both temporal and timeless, mortalizing and immortalizing. Temporality and vision become a single sufferance, an unmediated burden.

In neither poem, of course, is there an easy progression: the sculptures barely move under the Pygmalion touch of the poet. We await an enlightenment or transformation which does not come. "Deathwards progressing/To no death was that visage." (*Fall of Hyperion*, 1, 260f.) Instead of the continuous, transfigurative thrust of a Spenser or a Blake there is at most a perpetually delayed metamorphosis. Nothing lightens the sufferance of temporality, except that it is the gods themselves who are subjected to time, and the poet suffers their suffering rather than his own.

If this curious perspective limits realistic detail, it also serves to place Keats under the double burden already mentioned: temporality is experienced in an abstract or figurative way, but visionariness in a very concrete, literal way. The poet "bears" the gods like the consciousness of the Greeks, which Hegel describes as "the womb that conceived the gods, the breast that suckled them, the spiritual to which their grandeur and purity is owing. Thus it feels itself calm in contemplating them, and not only free in itself, but possessing the consciousness of its freedom."[16] Yet Keats's psyche, of course, is not emancipated by this self-knowledge. The fact that "All deities reside in the Human Breast" (Blake) can lead to nightmare as well as enlightenment. The at once daring and grotesque thought of a human being *nursing* these giant forms moves toward a literal representation in Keats who wishes to save the phenomenon (or perhaps phantasm) of visionary poetry. The *Hyperions* call Hegel's bluff.

Keats feels the burden of authorship. He is not relieved but shamed by the knowledge that the gods are born once more of him, that great poetry must survive, if at all, in a cockney's breast. He is the Way. He also, occasionally, seeks the Way Out. Is there a mode which would escape this overload of authorial consciousness? Could he turn frivolous (as in parts of *Lamia*) and imitate that elegant, erotic trifling with fable which the line of wit, from Marlowe to Byron, learnt of Ovid?

Most of the time, however, his shame at self-assertion, whether or not social in origin, leads to genuine moral perplexity. He knows that the desire for vision can be a private compulsion rather than a prophetic and justifiable gift. His flight from subjectivity and striving for Epic should be seen in this light.

Thus the *Hyperion* sequence reveals from within—and more powerfully than anything in Mallarmé or Yeats—the problems besetting a modernist art-morality: its claim for a new kind of classical poetics, objective and impersonal. Keats's halted epics expose the ideology of impersonal narration even as they honor it. They show an artist concerned with effacing the self both as subject and mediator of the fiction; and they then show him, by poetic justice, compelled to enter his own fiction in a form that seems to be him but is increasingly empty. By the time the second *Hyperion* breaks off, Keats is more of an ephebe than ever: a spectator surrounded by divine cartoons, a child-poet in epic Wonderland. The objective artist—we can also think of novelists like Flaubert and Henry James—tries to find an *image* rather than *himself*,[17] and comes to rest with neither. Though he flirts with magic or myth—though, as Yeats puts it, he walks in the moon (*per amica silentia Moneta*)—he cannot find a true self-objectification.

In conclusion, then, let us watch the suppressed self of the poet already breaking through at the high-point of his impersonal art, the opening of the first *Hyperion*:

Deep in the shady sadness of a vale
Far sunken from the healthy breath of morn,
Far from the fiery noon, and eve's one star,
Sat gray-hair'd Saturn, quiet as a stone,
Still as the silence round about his lair;
Forest on forest hung above his head
Like cloud on cloud. No stir of air was there,

Not so much life as on a summer's day
Robs not one light seed from the feather'd grass,
But where the dead leaf fell, there did it rest.
A stream went voiceless by, still deadened more
By reason of his fallen divinity
Spreading a shade: the Naiad 'mid her reeds
Press'd her cold finger closer to her lips.

Along the margin-sand large foot-marks went,
No further than to where his feet had stray'd,
And slept there since. Upon the sodden ground
His old right hand lay nerveless, listless, dead,
Unsceptered; and his realmless eyes were closed;
While his bow'd head seem'd list'ning to the Earth,
His ancient mother, for some comfort yet.

These twenty-one lines are divided into a passage we hardly recognize as a blank verse sonnet, followed by what is proportionately half a sonnet. We do not recognize it as a sonnet because usually sonnets are rhymed as well as personal in their sentiment. The sonnet resemblance may be accidental but the poet's careful effacing of his personality would be remarkable even if we overlooked the sonnet form. For whereas the epic poet traditionally allows himself a call to the Muse or to inspiration—a personal cheer of some kind—Keats here subdues his spirit totally to description of place.

It is a mood, of course, as well as a place: a "weather of the mind," an inward landscape. Yet words descriptive of mood are surprisingly few. In the first paragraph only "sadness" refers specifically to the emotions, and even it is qualified by "shady" and tends to fade into sound: "sadness . . . sat . . . Saturn." To say that the passage depicts a mood of withdrawal or dejection may be the best way out, yet to do so means that we amplify a single metaphor, that of "far sunken."

Before we agree that Keats has accomplished the modernist miracle and made the subjective thinker disappear into a grand yet naive fiction—if not a Greek-Apollonian then, at least, a Saturnian radiance of form—let us look more closely at this adequate landscape. Its stillness is intensified, by lines 7-10, into windlessness. But is this not strange when we consider that these are the verses which normally contain a call for *in-spiration*? The theme of windlessness modulates quite naturally (lines 11–14) into voicelessness; and the Naiad's emblematic gesture not only strengthens the theme of stillness but suggests an action that is the opposite of *feeding* (nursing). The god who sleeps on the sodden "margin-sand" near the stream, dispersed into his members, has gone away, surely, not only from his own bosom ("I am gone away from my own bosom," says Saturn later, "I have left my strong identity, my real self. . . .") but also from that maternal comfort mentioned in the last line. So near the feeding source, he cannot take nourishment.

A giant world, and yet an "infant world." (*Hyperion*, 1, 25.) The reversal is surprising, yet what is symbolism—especially spectral symbolism—but the scene of such reversals? Even writing as such retains a *micromegas* quality, eliciting great inferences from tiny marks, and returning them to that closet. Semiotics has its psychology too.

The Keatsian landscape, then, moves by what seems a pure logic of the senses toward touch, mouth, and a maternal presence. There is a hidden specter after all. When Thea appears we are made conscious of this, though not satisfied: a stronger figure than Thea was expected. To quote Stevens once more: "The mother's face, the purpose of the poem, fills the room." Or does not fill it, here. The sublime forms we meet are the host-symbols of an imaginative demand that becomes an anxiety because it does not know if the "Shade of Memory" (*Fall of Hyperion*, 1, 282) it seeks will in truth nourish or inspire. Where are the *lymphae loquaces*, the nymphs of the springs and speech-nourishing waters? We think instead of "La Belle Dame sans Merci" and its quester's "starved lips in the gloam."

We also recall that shortly after the "Shade of Memory" does appear as Mnemosyne in Book 3, the poem breaks off. And that it breaks off, speechless a second time, when she has clearly taken over in the *Fall of Hyperion*. The psychogenesis of womanly figures is always remarkable in Keats—in April 1819, right in between the two *Hyperions*, he discovers Psyche—but so is the connection of their appearance with aphasia (in-fancy). It may be the high aphasia suggested by Psyche's "wide quietness" or the "tuneless" numbers he addresses to her; or one that comes from despair at reaching "the large utterance of the early Gods" or even that enjoined by the Naiad whose gesture (an ancient one) warns the profane not to pollute a sacred source. It is, in any case, equivalent to that strange return to infancy which makes of Keats a "marvelous boy" in Mnemosyne's myth-museum.

Have I gone too far? The poem, it is true, begins in a deep sense of loss, yet can it be tied so specifically to loss of the mother, or to the poet's anxiety as to whether any womanly presence can nurture (rather than vamp) his identity?[18] Now the *Hyperions* are obviously not a wild, regressive quest for the absent mother or the trustworthy breast. Not even if we use some saving formula like "regression in the service of the ego" (E. Kris). The literary aspect is essential here and is provided for by Keats. He himself connects for us the spectral mother, the idea of nurture and a concept of language.

The link is made explicit through the notion of "mother tongue" which opens the *Fall of Hyperion*. "Every man whose soul is not a clod/Hath visions, and would speak, if he had loved . . ." (1, 13ff.) At this point in the verse the thought is conventional, yet Keats goes on: "would speak, if he had loved/And been well nurtured. . . ." Speech now appears as a natural fulfillment, the fruit of previous stages in the developing life of the affections. But the poet, of course, wrote: "And been well nurtured in his mother tongue." Even when the sentence is read as a whole, it is impossible to tell whether being a poet depends on two conditions or only on one: on having loved (1) and having been well nurtured in the mother tongue (2), or on having loved the mother tongue which has nurtured us well. Love, speech, and nurture are woven together by the verse.

It would do the poet wrong to inventory here lip, palate, and breast, to make us "drunk" with Endymion "from pleasure's nipple," or to follow now his delight in pictures of feasting and now his macabre inversion of the nursing situation in the *Pot of Basil* (where Basil and Isabel are *labial* rimes). Better, perhaps, to note the metaphors in "That full draught is parent of my theme," a line which together with "All the dead whose names are in our lips" (*Fall of Hyperion*, 1, 45-46) associates so finely the parental quest with nourishment and necromancy. It is also an interesting fact, perhaps to be seen in the light of Keats's relation to Boccaccio and then to Dante, that one of Dante's books defending the mother tongue is entitled the *Convito* or *Banquet*.[19] Even the vernacular banquet offered in such casual verses as "Lines on the Mermaid Tavern" appears then as a jovial exorcism of all poetic food of a "Lamian" or spectral kind.[20]

This may seem highly speculative, but one thing is not. Keats's explanation for abandoning the *Hyperion* was that Milton's diction was getting the better of his English, and "English must be kept up." We know what he means, for Mnemosyne, in the *Fall of Hyperion*, though she attempts to "soften" "an immortal's sphered words . . . to a mother's" (1, 249f.), ultimately turns into a Male Mother or Miltonic Muse—one who starves the poet in the midst of her sublime lushness. "Instead of sweets, his ample palate takes/ Savor of poisonous brass and metals sick." (2, 32f.) To write the nurturing English of "To Autumn," a poem flowing with native sounds and food, was the relief Keats found. "To Autumn" is a *Convito*.

The contrast of "To Autumn" with the opening of *Hyperion* reveals once more the latter's repressed and spectral side. How different the stasis of a Saturn, withdrawn from time (*Hyperion*, 1, 2-3), from his identity as C(h)ronos, and the "ripe progress" of the figure of Autumn, who is only as unmoving as she is watchful of the "press" of things that satisfy time into peace. Her food, surely, will not "turn to poison as the bee-mouth sips" ("Ode on Melancholy"). The granary is full, and a poet feels nourished—stilled—at last.

Christopher Smart's "Magnificat"
Toward a Theory of Representation

What is the consummation of perfect freedom? Not to be ashamed of one's self.

Nietzsche

For when men get their horns again, they will delight to go uncovered.

C. Smart

Theory as Prologue

When we present one person to another, a feeling of formality persists. It may be a residual awe, relating to exceptional presentations (of the child to elders in early or ritual circumstances) or it may be a more general sense of the distance between persons. The latter feeling would still have a psychological component, for the distance between persons is like that between self and other.

What if someone cannot be presented? The sense of distance has been thrown out of balance: either the self feels defective vis-a-vis the other, or the other appears magnified, unapproachable. The someone can be a something: certain subjects may not be introduced into discourse, certain taboos restrict or delimit the kinds of words used.

I introduce the example of words early, because words commonly help to present us.[1] Should we feel that words are defective, or else that we are defective vis-a-vis them (words becoming the other, as is not unusual in poets who have a magnified regard for a great precursor or tradition), then a complex psychic situation arises. It is fair to assume, however, that the distance between self and other is always disturbed, or being disturbed; that there is always some difficulty of self-presentation in us; and that, therefore, we are obliged to fall back on a form of "representation."

Representation implies that the subject cannot be adequately "present" in his own person or substance, so that advocacy is called for. The reason for this "absence," compensated for by "representation," can be various. In legal or ritual matters, the subject may not be of age or not competent. But even when he is competent, of age, fully presentable, situations arise which produce a fiction of his having to be "seconded": in presentation at court (and sometimes in courts of law) he does not appear by himself but needs the support of someone already admitted into the superior presence.

The self does not, of course, disappear into its representative, for then the means would defeat the end, which remains self-presentation. Even in visionary poetry, which so clearly sublimes the self into the other, or exalts the other into quasi-supernatural otherness, the self persists in selfhood. Though Charles Lamb is right in remarking that Coleridge's Ancient Mariner "undergoes such trials as overwhelm and bury all individuality or memory of what he was—like the state of a man in a bad dream, one terrible peculiarity of which is that all consciousness of personality is gone," the spectral happenings in the poem actually doom the Mariner to survival. He is unable to die, or find release from his experience except in the "punctual agony" of storytelling.

Whether or not this doom of deathlessness is preferable to nothingness—"Who would lose," says Milton's Belial, "Though full of pain, this intellectual being,/ Those thoughts that wander through Eternity,/ To perish rather, swallow'd up and lost/ In the wide womb of uncreated night . . ."—the self can never be so sublimated or so objectified, that only its representative is left. Even granted that self desires an absolute escape from self, what would be satisfied by that escape: indeed would anything of self be left to register the satisfaction? To urge questions of this kind is to approach psychoanalysis, but at the same time to link it with speculations on the sublime going back at least to Edmund Burke. These speculations ponder the vertiginous relation between self-loss and self-aggrandizement.

Let me return briefly to Coleridge's poem. Why does the Mariner kill the albatross? A fascinating question; but even the simplest answer, that it was willfulness, implies a drive on the

Mariner's part for self-presence. The killing is a shadow of the Mariner's own casting.[2] What follows his self-determining, self-inaugural act is, paradoxically, the presence of otherness. In seeking to "emerge," the self experiences separation anxieties, and these express themselves in motions akin to the defense mechanism of "beautiful indifference" (noted by Charcot in patients suffering from hysteria) as well as to the terror which may accompany isolation.

At the same time, there is a movement toward atonement (at-one-ment, reconciliation) in Coleridge's poem. "Representation" cannot be divorced from advocacy. You justify either the self or that which stands greatly against it: perhaps both at once. The situation could be likened to a trial, though not to one resulting in a definite verdict. The trouble with this line of inquiry is that too many metaphors come into play until one begins to move within art's own richness of thematic variation. Yet such metaphors as trial, court, theater, debut and so on, converge on the idea of a place of heightened demand and intensified consciousness. "The daemon," says Yeats, " . . . brings man again and again to the place of choice, heightening temptation that the choice may be as final as possible . . ." Let us consider the nature of this "place," imagined or real.

When Christopher Smart writes in *Jubilate Agno*, "For I pray the Lord Jesus to translate my MAGNIFICAT into verse and represent it,"[3] the pun (magnifi-cat) alluding to the "magnification" of the cat Jeoffrey and of the animal kingdom generally, corroborates what Freud says about wit both submitting to and escaping the censor. To compare a hymn (the Magnificat) associated with the Virgin Mary to the gambols of Jeoffrey is blasphemous—except that the pun remains unexplicit and the poet, in any case, "gives the glory" to God by asking Christ to make his verses acceptable. Yet the anxiety, I believe, or the pressure resulting in this kind of wit, goes deeper. It is not one outrageously smart comparison which is at stake, but the legitimacy of artistic representation as a whole. The magnifi-cat theme expresses, in its marvelous mixture of humility and daring, the artist's sense that he is disturbing the "holy Sabbath" of creation by his recreation; that he is trespassing on sacred property or stealing an image of it or even exalting himself as a maker—in short, that he is magnifying mankind instead of "giving the glory" to God. Smart therefore atones the exposed, self-conscious self by "at-one-ing" it with the creature. He shows mankind "presenting" before God the animal creation it has exploited. And, in return, he asks that his verse-representation be "represented" before God by a mediator who enters the first line of his poem as "Lord, and Lamb." The opening of *Jubilate Agno* sets the pattern by compounding man and animal into ritual pairs:

Let man and beast appear before him, and magnify his name together.
Let Noah and his company approach the throne of Grace, and do homage to the Ark of their Salvation.
Let Abraham present a Ram, and worship the God of his Redemption.
Let Isaac, the Bridegroom, kneel with his Camels, and bless the hope of his pilgrimage.

(A, 3-6)

Inspired by *Revelations*, Smart begins with a judgment scene: it envisages an ark that might survive a second flood. We find ourselves in a place of demand where everything must be "presented." The precise nature of the demand is not absolutely clear, and need not be the same in all works of art: perhaps it varies with historical circumstances, and perhaps it is the interpreter's task to make the relation between demand and response (demand and inner capability) perfectly clear. But artistic representation does seem to mediate a demand of this kind: one, moreover, not to be thought of as coming from outside, but rather, or also, from within. Again, whether "within" means the unconscious, or refers to a self-realizing instinct, may not be possible to determine generally but only in each case.

There is no way of being precise about this without engaging in considered acts of textual interpretation. We have to identify the nature of the challenge met by Smart and the "place" or "situation" he is in. It would be inadequate, for instance, to say of his "representation" of the animal creation that it springs from the same anxiety for the survival of the physical species that, according to Gertrude Levy's *The Gate of Horn* (1948), inspired the Cro-Magnon cave paintings at Lascaux. They may have had an apotropaic function, for they gather the essential traits of the hunted species into totemic sketches that intend to placate the Spirit of the hunted creature and so assure its fertile continuance. The creature is graphically "represented" by man to a Spirit in order for both human kind and the creature to survive.

Such recreative or reparative magic *is* relevant to Smart's poem; the analogy is too strong, and the theme of generation haunts too many of his verses. Yet it is only a beginning to specific interpretation. For we must add that in Smart the very *medium* of representation—visionary language itself—has become questionable, or subject to a demand which it cannot meet except by being renewed. His recreation of visionary categories is literally a re-creation: the source of vision is not exhausted but still operative through him. That, at least, is the claim he seems to make, or the test he puts himself to. The anxiety for survival has associated itself with an anxiety for language-source, liturgy, and the entire process of representation.

Enthusiasm and Entropy

The fear that visionary language has lost its effectiveness may not be very different from the fear that nature grows old. Such "depletion anxieties" are linked to the not unrational feeling in us that our appetites—including that for presence—put a demand on the order of things which that order may not be able to satisfy; which, indeed, it may resent and reject.[4] The "economy" of language use arising from depletion anxiety ranges from such devices of conservation as double-entendre, hermeticism, and classical restraint, to the complementary if opposite ones of revivalist forgery, radical innovation, and homeopathic promiscuity. You can write as sparse a hymn as Addison's famous "The spatious firmament on high" (1712), which, in spite of its source in Psalm 19, reflects Pascal's fright at the silence of the starry spaces; or you can fill the vacuum with the "clang expressions" of *Jubilate Agno*, till "barrenness becomes a thousand things" (Wallace Stevens).

Smart's aberrant verses would have been classified in their time as a product of "enthusiasm"; and this widespread and loosely knit religious movement was also a kind of counter-entropy. Affecting principally Puritans and Dissenters, it claimed to have uncovered a new source of truth, that of the individual in his privacy, who would know from "internal" grounds what revelation there was; but if that was all there was, then we were abandoned to individuality, and prone to the hell of unrelieved, sterile selfhood. The blessing proved to be the curse; the precious was also the accused object. "My selfhood, Satan, arm'd in Gold" (Blake). The danger in enthusiasm, moreover, was its inevitable closeness to fanaticism, for the enthusiast found it difficult not to impose his "internal" evidences on others, not to exhibit his "antitheatrical" truth. He sought out or compelled a like-minded community.[5]

Enthusiasm in literature took many forms: it attacked, for example, the scientific "Religion of Nature" which affirmed the stability of the cosmos (nature would *not* grow old) at the cost of dehumanizing it and "untenanting Creation of its God" (Coleridge); and it overrode the pessimism of the neoclassic artist who felt he had come too late in history. The visionary or even the poet was felt to be superfluous in an Age of Reason; but the wish for originality, which enthusiasm abetted, increased in direct proportion to one's distance from the possibility. Yet the dilemma, even for the enthusiasts, was that originality and Original Sin were hard to tell apart.

Smart had to find, therefore, not only a well of visionary English but also an undefiled well. Every attempt to replenish, or imitate directly, the great source-books of secular and religious culture was open to the charge of false testimony—of giving glory to God as a cover for "representing" one's own passions. Today we have no problem with the first person singular, and fiction is inconceivable without a semblance of self-exposure. Enthusiasm in art has gone public and taken the name of confessionalism. Consequently, it is hard for us to appreciate Pascal's notorious maxim, "Le moi est haïssable," and the fact that he was so sensitive to the liaison between egotism and enthusiasm that he condemned even Montaigne:

The stupid plan he has to depict himself, and this not incidentally and against his better judgment as it may happen to all us mortals, but by design and as a matter of principle. For to say foolish things by chance or weakness is an ordinary fault; but to say them intentionally, that is not tolerable, and moreover his kind of stuff.[6]

Yet Pascal is protesting too much, for the lines of confession (his *Mémorial*) found hemmed in his garments at his death showed how close he was to what his time, and the next century, castigated as enthusiasm:

The year of grace 1654. Monday 23rd November. Feast of St. Clement, Pope and Martyr, and of others in the martyrology. Eve of Chrysogonous. Martyr and others. From about half past 10 in the evening until half past midnight. Fire. God of Abraham, God of Isaac, God of Jacob, not of philosophers and scholars. Certainty, certainty, heart-felt, joy, peace. God of Jesus Christ. God of Jesus Christ. *My God and your God.* Thy God shall be my God. The world forgotten and everything except God . . . Joy, joy, joy, tears of joy.[7]

Apocalyptic visions, trances, egomania, or what Dr. Johnson was to call, memorably, the "hunger" and "dangerous prevalence" of imagination, were the diseases of enthusiasm against which Pascal and others erected their ideal of the "honnête homme," with his good sense, moderation, reasonable language. England, after the Puritan Revolution, imported this neoclassical ideal of correcting and improving not only the understanding but also speech itself, since an erroneous or corrupt language encourages intellectual and religious error. Swift's *Proposal for Correcting, Improving and Ascertaining the English Tongue* (1712) denounced the "Enthusiastick Jargon" of "Fanatick Times" (the Puritan Revolution and its epigones); and as Professor Wimsatt has noted in a remarkable essay on the "laughter" of the Augustans, behind all these calls for decorum there lurked a heightened sense of unreality, which was not dissimilar, perhaps, to experiences of spiritual vastation.[8] The nearness of *flatus* and *afflatus*, of wind and inspiration, the manic-depressive cycle which all these doctors were seeking to cure, kept reasserting itself in epidemics of wit and farfetched conceits, in the incurable prevalence of the mock-heroic mode, in the hysterical style of the sublime ode, and the laughing, biting speech that joins Swift to a late Augustan poet called William Blake.

The wars of religion against enthusiasm are an old story. But why should so irreligious a poet as Keats complain of Wordsworth's *egotistical sublime*? Why is he so defensive with Moneta, denouncing to her "all mock lyrists, large self-worshipers,/ And careless Hectorers in proud bad verse" (*The Fall of Hyperion*, I, 207-8)? The reason is that he could not give up the sublime. He feared that poetry without enthusiasm was no longer poetry; and he was all the more sensitive to the charge of self-inflation because he knew that to create a sublime mode not based on personal experience was to revert to a vacuous archaism, to that impersonation of impersonality which MacPherson and Chatterton succumbed to. The sublime had to be associated with personal experience: there was no other way. Something drives fiction to that recognition in the two hundred years which comprise *Paradise Lost*, the neoclassical reaction, the emergence of Romanticism, and that renewed valediction to the sublime which fails so gloriously in Browning's "Childe Roland" and Tennyson's "Morte D'Artur."

Let me add, before returning to Smart, that Freud also treats enthusiasm. He is our latest "doctor of the sublime," the twentieth century facing the gods or the pathology of ecstasy. A modern analytics of the sublime must begin with Boileau's remarks on Longinus, study Vico on the way to Burke, Kant, and Schopenhauer, and then admit that Freud is the inheritor of all these in his canny knowledge of the fortress against enthusiasm which polite society, or the soul itself, builds in the soul. Defense mechanisms cannot blossom when there is nothing—no fire or flood—to defend against.

Smart's poetic career is emblematic of the fate of enthusiasm. It divides neatly into two parts. Before 1756 he was "the ingenious Mr. Smart," a facile and brilliant practitioner of neoclassic modes of verse. But recovering from a serious fever he began "confessing God openly" by praying aloud whenever the impulse came. "I blessed God in St James's Park till I routed all the company" (B 1, 89). He was confined for insanity in 1757-58 and again from 1759-63. During his "illness" he produced two long poems as daring and personal as any the Romantics were to write. The *Song to David* (1763) was dismissed in its time as a "fine piece of ruins," while the *Jubilate Agno* was not published till 1939. Smart's contemporaries saw him as an excellent versifier misled by religious mania, and though he reverted to such modest tasks as translating Horace and composing hymns for children, he never reestablished himself in their eyes.

What is one to do, even today, with verses like "Let Lapidoth with Percnos the Lord is the builder of the wall of CHINA—REJOICE" (B 1, 97)? The marvelous thing here is not, despite appearances, "Enthusiasm, Spiritual Operations, and pretences to the Gifts of the Spirit, with the whole train of New Lights, Raptures, Experiences, and the like."[9] It is the poet's total, consistent, critical rather than crazy, attack on the attenuated religious language of his day. "Percnos" is a bird of prey, like the Persian "Roc," punningly associated with the "Rock of Israel" in a previous line (B 1, 94), while "Lapidoth" (Judges 4:4) is linked to "Percnos-Roc" by an etymological pun which gives the Hebrew name a Latin root that means "stone" (*lapis, lapidis*). Add the "Wall of China" as the greatest stonework in the world, and the line as a whole is seen to "give the glory to the Lord." It says, in effect, "Let Rock with Rock, the Lord is the Rock of Rocks, rejoice."

"In this plenty," to quote Stevens once more, "the poem makes meanings of the rock." Visionary language knows itself as superfluous, redundant; yet its very breaking against the rock reveals a more than gratuitous splendor. The disparity between the sustained base (the unvarying ROCK or REJOICE) and Smart's ever-shifting, eclectic play of fancy, discloses a twofold problem of representation: the traditional one of ineffability, related to the belief that God is "dark with excessive bright," or not attainable through mortal speech; and the somewhat rarer view, that the fault lies with language, which has lost yet may regain its representational power. To the crisis which stresses the inattainability of the signified, Smart adds the impressively impotent splendor of the signifier.

This is too cold a description, however, of the agony of the signifier. The question is less whether language can represent than whether by doing so it seconds or comforts the creature. Representation, I have argued, contains the idea of advocacy; and in Christian theology it is Christ who preeminently acts as comforter and advocate. To rejoice in the "Lord, and the Lamb" is to rejoice in the hope that the Judge (Lord) will turn out to be the Comforter (Lamb).

Yet the premise of that comfort, hidden away for the most part in the "Songs of Innocence" of Smart's time—in children's poetry or catechistical emblem books—was that the creation (*res creatae*, Romans 1:20 and 8:19) would help the tormented or doubting spirit to be instructed. By a proliferation of types, emblems, analogies, and the like, the Christian was encouraged to "suck Divinity from the flowers of Nature," in Sir Thomas Browne's words. As long as instruction could be drawn from flower or beast, then "Man and Earth suffer together" (C, 155) while waiting to be redeemed. Smart's poetry serves to strengthen their bond, even if it is one of suffering. But in doing so, in seeking to "represent" the creature, the poet discovers that language too is a creature in need of reparation.

For Smart's animated diction is the other side of his feeling for the lost animal spirits of a language "amerced" of its "horn" (C, 118-62). His poem, therefore, blends theriomorphic and theomorphic as the animals named by Adam in the first act of divinely instituted speech are now named again, restitutively. Language is the rib taken from Adam's tongue to "helpmate" his solitude before Eve. And it is interesting that in *Jubilate Agno* Eve does not formally appear. Even Mary's "Magnificat," when mentioned in B 1, 43, exalts not the woman and mother but rather language in its creature-naming and creature-presenting function. So close is the bondage of language and the bondage of the creature that both are one for a poet who is their male comforter, their *logos*. His Magnificat consoles what originally was to console Adam, by "translating" and "representing" it.

Cat and Bat

By magnifying Jeoffrey, Smart is training the telescope of wit on an ordinary creature instead of on the heavens or a certifiably divine subject. The meditation on the creature (that is, on anything created, which included the heavens) was not uncommon; and a contemporary of Smart's, James Hervey, Methodist Rector of Weston-Favell, had popularized the genre by his *Meditations Among the Tombs* and *Contemplations of the Starry Heavens* (1746-47). Hervey provides his readers with a flattering humiliation of the spirit, a Urizenic (so Blake will call it) calculus of apparent human power and actual limitation. Hervey, in short, is second-rate Sir Thomas Browne and third-rate Book of Job. "I have often been charmed and awed," he writes, "at the sight of the nocturnal Heavens; even before I knew how to consider them in their proper circumstances of majesty and beauty. Something like magic, has struck my mind, on a transient and unthinking survey of the aethereal vault, tinged throughout with the purest azure, and decorated with innumerable starry lamps. I have felt, I know not what powerful and aggrandizing impulse; which seemed to snatch me from the low entanglements of vanity, and prompted an ardent sigh for sublimer objects. Methought I heard, even from the silent spheres, a commanding call, to spurn the abject earth, and pant after unseen delights.—Henceforward, I hope to imbibe more copiously this moral emanation of the skies, when, in some such manner as the preceding, they are rationally seen, and the sight is duly improved. The stars, I trust, will teach me as well as shine; and help to dispel, both Nature's gloom, and my intellectual darkness . . . .

"I gaze, I ponder. I ponder, I gaze; and think ineffable things. —I roll an eye of awe and admiration. Again and again I repeat my ravished views, and can never satiate my immense field, till even Fancy tires upon her wing. I find wonders ever new; wonders more and more amazing.—Yet, after all my present inquiries, what a mere nothing do I know; by all my future searches, how little shall I be able to learn, of those vastly distant suns, and their circling retinue of worlds! Could I pry with Newton's piercing sagacity, or launch into his extensive surveys; even then my apprehensions would be little better, than those dim and scanty images, which the mole, just emerged from her cavern, receives on her feeble optic . . . . To fathom the depths of the Divine Essence, or to scan universal Nature with a critical exactness, is an attempt which sets the acutest philosopher very nearly on a level with the ideot."[10]

This is also the period of Robert Blair's *The Grave* (1743) and Edward Young's *Night Thoughts* (1742–45). Smart's meditation on Jeoffrey is surely a criticism of such effusions. It replaces their self-regarding, didactic gloom with real observation, empathy, and a spirit as playful as that of the creature portrayed. The cat is the style; and the style, as a sustained song of innocence, is totally unchary. It leaps; it is prankish; not only in its "mixture of gravity and waggery," as when Smart avers "For the Lord commanded Moses concerning the cats at the departure of the Children of Israel from Egypt," but also in its semblance of plot.

The opening of the passage shows Jeoffrey at his "exercises." These ordinary gambols turn into a ritual calisthenics curiously like the "Spiritual Exercises" of Ignatius of Loyola. When the poet "considers" his cat, the word "considers," which seems to have the Latin root for "star" in it, is a technical term from the tradition of the Spiritual Exercises (Compare "I have often been charmed and awed at the sight of the nocturnal Heavens; even before I knew how to consider them in their proper circumstances," and so forth). Here the term is applied *à rebours* to an uncelestial object; yet Jeoffrey *is* a solar creature, worshipping at "the first glance of the glory of God in the East" and counteracting the powers of darkness "by his electrical skin and glaring eyes." The poet's consideration of Jeoffrey is reinforced when Jeoffrey "begins to consider himself" (B 2, 703) "in ten degrees" —"degrees" are also a term common to the genre of the Spiritual Exercises. In the argument prefaced to Smart's *A Song to David*, stanzas 65–71 constitute "An exercise upon the senses, and how to subdue them . . . . [with] An amplification in five degrees."

It is not my intent to turn Jeoffrey the cat into a Christian soldier marching with Loyola. What the poem conveys is a spreading *consideration* from which nothing will eventually be excluded: Smart opens the covenant so that every creature—"The cat does not appear in the Bible," W.F. Stead, Smart's editor, notes drily—or at least the *names* of all created things may enter. "Let the Levites of the Lord take the Beavers of ye Brook alive into the Ark of the Testimony" (A, 16): the Beavers do not appear in the Bible either, but here they enter alive into an Ark which could have proved as deadly as in Exodus 25:9.

At this moment in time the covenant is merely the rainbow language before us, revived by Smart. But perhaps language is the only covenant. Smart renews the responsive prayer of the psalms and of the liturgy as if to provide the Church with a Book of Common Prayer genuinely "common." More and more of creation enters the Ark of Testimony as not only the verses pair ("Let . . . For") but also different orders of creation; and it becomes vain to distinguish in Smart responsive poetry and resurrected wit. Both deal with strange conjunctions, hidden echoes, powerful yokings together, the "grappling of the words upon one another" (B 2, 632). This principle of "clapperclaw," with its residual sexuality, sometimes extends itself into the phonation of single verses, which then seem built, like "clapperclaw" itself, out of the competing responsiveness of mutual parts.[11] "Let Ross, house of Ross rejoice with the Great Flabber Dabber Flat Clapping Fish with hands" (D, 11).

Imagine the House of Ahab rejoicing with Moby Dick . . . We hear the voice of the hands, in this applause; indeed the animal body itself grows to be all voice and enters the language. "For the power of some animal is predominant in every language" (B 2, 627), writes Smart; and he exemplifies this by an outrageous onomatopoeic punning. "For the pleasantry of a cat at pranks is in the language ten thousand times over./ For JACK UPON PRANCK is in the performance of *peri* together or seperate" (B 2, 630–31). (Read *purr* for *pr* or *per*.) This covenant-language is quite literally the Ark where man and animal pair in amity, and the "Cherub Cat is a term of the Angel Tiger" (B 2, 725).

All creatures in Smart become flaming creatures, and the Great Chain of Being a Great Chain of Language. To characterize Smart as a late or parodic meditationist is not adequate, therefore. It does not clarify the nature of the demand on him or the burden of his response. "Gird up thy loins now, like a man, I will demand of thee and answer thou me," God thunders at Job. And Job is finally persuaded to put his finger on his mouth. James Hervey, and other pseudo-enthusiast worshippers of the whirlwind, put their deflating finger of inflated moralistic prose on our mouths. They make us kiss the rod. But Smart is not put out by Newton, Nature, or Nature's God. He escapes the stupor induced by Natural Religion—by the contemplation of Leviathan, Tiger, or the System of the World. And he does so by answering its "cunning alphabet" with his own force of language. I will demand of thee and answer thou me, means for Smart, girding up the loins of language and meeting the challenge of a divine text. The Bible is less a proof text than a shame text; and to escape this shame which affects, preeminently, the tongue, he must become David again and restore the Chain of Inspiration. "Rejoice in God, O ye Tongues . . ." The Great Chain of Being is honored not on account of order and hierarchy but only as it continues to electrify the tongue and represent the creature. In Smart's "consideration" everything stars; and the elation, or jubilation, of speech seems to sustain a demand put on it by the Book of God or the "cunning alphabet" of the Book of Nature.

Yet Bethlehem is not far from Bedlam. The madhouses of Smart's time had more than one King David in them, not to mention King Solomons and Queens of Sheba. The pressure on Smart of the divine text or of the need to respond to it by the creation of a New Song, that is, by a language covenant embracing the creature which had fallen with and away from man, heaps this Christopher as thoroughly as Melville's white whale "heaped" Ahab. When we read Smart's boast, "I am the Reviver of Adoration amongst English Men," we do not feel the tension of a pun that mounts up in stanzas 50 and following of the *Song to David*:

Praise above all—for praise prevails,
Heap up the measure, load the scales . . .

This is followed by twenty stanzas centering on the repeated word "adoration." The method is indeed accumulative, additive, rather than calculating and accounting. Double the "d" in "adoration" and the pun becomes visible.

A "Song to David" means dedicated to, or spoken toward, David, but also *add*ing itself by *ad*oration until measure and scale break and the account is closed. Smart's ad libitum at once acknowledges and destroys the Johnsonian morality of style; the Doctor's reservation, for instance, that "Sublimity is by aggregation" yet that it is impossible to add to the divine glory:

> The ideas of Christian theology are too simple for eloquence, too sacred for fiction, and too majestick for ornament. To recommend them by tropes and figures is to magnify by a concave mirror the sidereal universe.
>
> Omnipotence cannot be exalted; infinity cannot be amplified; perfection cannot be improved.[12]

Smart might have enjoyed William Blake's joshing of Dr. Johnson in *An Island in the Moon*:

> I say this evening we'll all get drunk. I say dash, an Anthem, an Anthem, said Suction
>
> *Lo the Bat with Leathern Wing*
> *Winking & blinking*
> *Winking & blinking*
> *Winking & blinking*
> *Like Doctor Johnson*

I quote only the more decent part. Compare cat and bat.

A Speckled Language

Our delight in Smart is not a constant thing. Even in controlled sequences, like that on Jeoffrey, where the catalogue (no pun intended) is less chaotic than usual, the poet's exuberance may fall into a near-infantile strain:

> *For he rolls upon prank to work it in.*
> *For having done duty and received blessing he begins to consider himself.*
>
> (B 1, 702–3)

"Having done duty" may refer to Jeoffrey's sunrise worship, but it could also be a euphemism, especially when followed by a lengthy description of a cat cleaning itself.

For first he looks upon his fore-paws to see if they are clean.
For secondly he kicks up behind to clear away there.
For thirdly he works it upon stretch with fore paws extended.
(B 2, 705–7)

As every child knows, cleanliness is next to godliness, and Jeoffrey provides an emblematic and charming illustration. Yet since Smart seems more wary of mentioning excrement than of mentioning the devil (B 2, 720ff.), and Jeoffrey's ritual exorcism of dirt is continuous with his "dutiful" worship of God, the thought may arise as to what is being euphemistically "pranked" or "worked in" at the higher level of godliness, benevolence, or jubilant verse-making.

One could try to find that "foundation on slander" (or "on the devil") which Smart mentions in B 1, 170. "The furnace itself shall come up at the last" (B 1, 293) he also writes, alluding to Abraham's fearful vision. Whether at the bottom of it all is a lie or evil or detritus, a redemptive poet like Smart has to extend his *contrafactum* to embrace even the excrementitious. The "soil" needed to fertilize the soil works on language too. Yet Smart's consciousness that when the deep opens, or the foundation rises up, it is the "Adversary" who may appear—indeed the shadow-thought, perhaps there from the beginning, that the tongues invoked in the very first line of the poem might be used for the opposite of glorification—for slander or blasphemy or accusation—could help explain the *Jubilate's* ritual or litany-like character, that apotropaic iteration which limits an otherwise emancipated verse line. Smart's verses are, as he implies, a "conjecture" (B 1, 173), a "cast" of the line or tongue whose outcome is uncertain enough to be the object of a wager like that between God and the Accuser (Satan) in the Book of Job.

The nature of Smart's anxiety about "slander" may never be clear to us. It may not have been clear to himself. It is an anxiety about the foundation, about origins, about genealogy;[13] and so about the truth issuing from his own tongue:

Let Ziba rejoice with Glottis whose tongue is wreathed in his throat.
For I am the seed of the WELCH WOMAN and speak the truth from my heart.
Let Micah rejoice with the spotted Spider, who counterfeits death to effect his purposes.
For they lay wagers touching my life.—God be gracious to the winners.

(B 1, 91–92)

Yet Smart's anxiety about "tongues" may have produced too good a poetic defense mechanism. It is not immediately obvious that the animals here are cited for *their* defense mechanisms. "Let Abiezer, the Anethothite, rejoice with Phrynos who is the scaled frog. For I am like a frog in the brambles, but the Lord hath put his whole armour upon me" (B 1, 95). Euphemism and benediction feed the perpetual motion machine of Smart's poetry. "Let" and "For," and such punnable morphemes as "cat" and "ble" (bull), are linguistic simples, easily combined into phrases and sentences. They support the poet's run-on, combinatory technique, his compulsion to perpetual benevolence.

This may turn, also, by a momentum of its own, into a cat-and-mouse game with language, to see how much life can be eked out before the spirit fails and an adversary consciousness, or melancholia,[14] penetrates:

For the power of some animal is predominant in every language.
For the power and spirit of a CAT is in the Greek.
For the sound of a cat is in the most useful preposition κατ' εὐχήν
For the pleasantry of a cat at pranks is in the language ten thousand times over.
For JACK UPON PRANCK is in the performance of περί *together or seperate.*
For Clapperclaw is in the grappling of the words upon one another in all the modes of versification.
For the sleekness of a Cat is in his ἀγλαίηφι.
For the Greek is thrown from heaven and falls upon its feet.
For the Greek when distracted from the line is sooner restored to rank & rallied into some form than any other.
For the purring of a Cat is his own τρύζει.

For his cry is in ουαι which I am sorry for.
For the Mouse (Mus) prevails in the Latin.
For Edi-mus, bibi-mus, vivi-mus—ore-mus.

(B 2, 627–39)

In brief, the overdetermination of simples like "cat" or "mus" keeps us within a sphere of childlike instruction. Smart's poem, at these points, is not so much a renovated liturgy as a marvelously inflated hornbook: a spiritual grammar rock ("Conjunction Junction, What's your function?") which averts discontinuity or catastrophic thoughts. However serious the content, the form remains propaedeutic; however dangerous Smart's insight, the verse recovers into business ("benevolence") as usual.

Despite Smart's delightful and outrageous wordplay, then, his resourcefulness may be a testing of the source, and his witty, promiscuous conjunctions may point to the fear of being cut off, by his family, or eternally by Satanic accusation. How else are we to understand that long fragment which is but a variation of "Let X, house of X, rejoice with creature Y"?

Let Westbrooke, house of Westbrooke rejoice with the Quail of
Bengal. God be gracious to the people of Maidstone.
Let Allcock, house of Allcock rejoice with The King of the
Wavows a strange fowl. I pray for the whole University of
Cambridge especially Jesus College this blessed day.
Let Audley, house of Audley rejoice with The Green Crown
Bird. The Lord help on with the hymns.
Let Bloom, house of Bloom rejoice with Hecatompus a fish
with an hundred feet.
Let Beacon, house of Beacon rejoice with Amadavad a fine
bird in the East Indies.
Let Blomer, house of Blomer rejoice with Halimus a Shrub to
hedge with. Lord have mercy upon poor labourers this
bitter frost Decr. 29 N.S. 1762.

(D, 197–202)

Here the themes of house, foundation, fertility and rejoicing are interlaced with cries for help and mercy. The contiguity of "Maidstone" and "Allcock" is a parallel puzzle. "Without contraries," Blake wrote, "no progression," but what is progressive here except a verse that somehow keeps renewing itself?

I want to explore further the "wreathed" way in which Smart builds his verse. Take his basic words "Let" and "For." Though they "generate" sentences, they are really a *stutterance*: a verbal compromise-formation which at once "lets" (hinders) and forwards his song ("Let Forward, house of Forward rejoice with Immussulus a kind of bird the Lord forward my translation of the psalms this year" D, 220). "Let" is close to being a primal word with antithetical meanings; and the tension between these meanings—whether identified as control and permissiveness or contraction and expansiveness or chastity and promiscuity—can give an extraordinary twist effect to the verse. Sometimes the contraries are almost too close to be spotted ("*Let Forward* . . ."); sometimes they seem apposites rather than opposites because of their position in the paired pattern of the verse ("Let . . . For . . ."); and sometimes they form a crisscross pattern varying in distance (how far is it from "Maidstone" to "Allcock"?).

Smart has left us hints of a poetics of pairing, opposition and distancing:

For the relations of words are in pairs first.
For the relations of words are sometimes in oppositions.
For the relations of words are according to their distances from the pair.

(B 2, 600–602)

It could roughly summarize the actual unfolding of verse sentences in Smart: words are in pairs first, "Let Jubal rejoice with Caecilia"; this pairing may also introduce a contrast, "the woman and the slow-worm" (B 1, 43). The contrast may be more pathetic as when "Let Jorim rejoice with the Roach" is followed by "God bless my throat & keep me from things stranggled" (B 1, 179). The oppositions Smart mentions can also be that of the "Let" verse and the "For" response. Relations of distance, finally, are clearest in a group of iterative or antiphonal verses. In

Let Jubal rejoice with Caecilia, the woman and the slow-worm praise the name of the Lord.
For I pray the Lord Jesus to translate my MAGNIFICAT into verse and represent it.

(B 1, 43)

the first, relatively easy relation of words (Jubal and Caecilia being well-known patrons of music) becomes progressively more allusive and distant. Caecilia and the worm are linked by an etymological play on the Latin for the slow- or blind-worm (Caecilian, from *caecus*), but it needs more than curious learning to connect woman and worm with Mary's Magnificat through (1) the identification of Jesus as the seed of the woman who bruised the serpent's head (slow-worm/ Caecilia; serpent/ Eve); (2) the idea of "translation," that is, transformation, as from low to high, or from one species to another, and (3) the pun on Magnificat which turns the word into a compound (Magnifi-cat) and so establishes fully the relation between the "Let" and "For" verses through the paired opposition of lowly worm and magnified creature.[15]

To refine this kind of analysis is to come ultimately on the *hendiadys* in covert or open form. Puns are condensed or covert two-in-one structures, while Smart's synthetic "compounding" of nouns or nounlike words provides a more open form of the hendiadys. Allcock and Maidstone, when interpreted as two-folds, are simply hendiadys; Magnificat is a somewhat more complex instance; Jorim seems atomic until we notice its Hebrew plural ending (creating, once again, uncertainty as to whether a creature is to be thought of as one or more than one); and "the woman and the slow-worm," as it emerges from the name "Caecilia," is an especially characteristic hendiadys. One begins to suspect every name, in this name-freighted poetry, of being potentially emanative: other parts of speech too seem often like the attributes or derived sounds of some magical noun. Smart composes as if he had a choice between analytic and synthetic language formation, as if he were writing a Hebrew-English or Hebrew-Greek-Latin-English. Something of this is certainly in his mind, since he shares in the pentecostal aim to reconcile Babel into a universal code of worship. But whatever it is he wishes to achieve, the hendiadys is indispensable. There are remarkable moments in which his verses "reproduce" or "replicate" by drawing two or even three words out of one, yet remain one-ly:

Let Jorim rejoice with the Roach—God bless
my throat & keep me from things stranggled.
Let Addi rejoice with the Dace—It is good
to angle with meditation.
Let Luke rejoice with the Trout—Blessed be
Jesus in Aa, in Dee and in Isis.
(B 1, 179–81)

In the first verse above, Roach, a monosyllable, if read on the analogy of Jorim, becomes disyllabic, with an aspirated ending (Ro-ach),[16] so that the "stranggled" is not only thematically sustained by the image of the caught fish but equally by the throaty sound. In the following verses we see a proper noun, Addi, breaking up into three components that are sounds or rivers or both: Aa, Dee, Isis (A-D-I). Strictly speaking, we need only the "i" of Isis to complete Addi (itself a pun on the additive process?). But even the -sis may be accounted for if we read Isis as I-c's, and by a bit of scrabbling involve the second proper noun, Dace, also composed of the letter-sounds, A, D, and—this time—C. One name is A,D, plus I; the other A,D, plus C; so that Jesus (that famous fish, almost rhyming here with Isis, considering the closeness of I and J) comprehends both names, being blessed in A, in D, and in I, C's.

It is almost impossible to summarize Smart's poetic method. It is not, or not only, a "mad, philological vision of reality."[17] It does not, or not merely, subvert the referential aspect of words like Isis by deconstructing them as acoustic images or magical sounds. It is best seen as a sacred poetics driving to astonishing extremes the principle of antiphony or "parallelism of members" (Is-is!) discovered by Bishop Lowth in the Psalms. So, Jorim goes with the Roach and is paralleled by Addi with the Dace, and even by angle "with" meditation; while Addi and Dace and Isis can be shown to be "members" of Jesus. But how do you fit in Hecatompus with an hundred feet? "Why, then, I'le fit you!" And, indeed, there is a mad attempt to speak with tongues and write with all those feet, to re-member or re-present every last creature by a "pairing" that will exclude nothing from the "Ark" of testimony.

In society the simplest form of representation (in the sense of a normative presentation of the self) is by one's personal name. Names are a compromise, of course; for no name is unique; and Smart's use of single names (Abraham, Jorim, Dace, Hecatompus) makes them ambiguously individual and generic.[18] Names, moreover, like all proper nouns, are curiously split in their semantic character. They tend to be both subsemantic (so conventional as to be meaningless, semantically neutral) and supersemantic (they can be analyzed or pseudoanalyzed into richly meaningful parts). The idea of naming, therefore, recapitulates the drama played out in Smart's verse. Names individualize and socialize: they are always a kind of two-in-one. "Christopher Smart" names a single person whose Christ-bearing (Christopher) wit and wound (Smart) are one like the "Lord, and the Lamb" (A, 1) are one.

Every individual is *impair*. He sticks out or should stick out. Yet selfhood is both a demand to be met and subject to accusation. Analysis could go from here in many directions: religious, sociological, or what I have called psychoesthetic. Smart invariably connects representability of the self (*by* language, *with* the creature, and *to* God) and the treatment of the impair (also the impaired). He first reduces the impair to an infantile charm or a linguistic simple (cat, mus, the opaque proper noun, and so forth). By this method he both acknowledges and comforts the isolation of each creature. The linguistic simple, at the same time, is given the chance to multiply or replicate, but the match that results also escapes divine assessment. It cannot be judged. Will you frown at "Rehob" because he "rejoices with Caucalis Bastard Parsley"? Or at the Wild Cucumber with which "Nebai" is asked to rejoice (C, 152, 160)? Such matchmakings are beyond good and evil.

It may be useful to summarize the ways of Smart with language because his comforting of creatureliness extends to language—to sounds and words, large and small. He delights in (1) morphemes which can be individualized as words (cat, Dee); (2) words that are reduplicative in structure and remain simples because quasi-reversible (Aa, David, Amadavad, Wavow, Immussulus); (3) self-replicating or redundant phrases which can expand into a whole verse, as in the following (D, 175) inspired by the very idea of "re": "Let Ready, house of Ready" (redundancy) "rejoice" (Re . . . Re . . . re . . .) "with Junco The Reed Sparrow" (Ready . . . Reed); (4) the categorical hendiadys, which brings together, not as in the story of Noah, pairs of the same species but unmatable *res creatae*.

If the ark into which these pairs enter cannot be that of generation, it must be that of regeneration. But does regeneration involve or exclude generation? The new order here invoked, at once linguistic and ontic, coexists ambivalently with an older order which it neither subsumes nor yet suppresses. Smart's poetics of relation never quite turns into a poetics of translation. The name "Jesus" embraces the name "Isis" and the result is a speckled language. In the opening scene of the *Jubilate*, when Abraham presents a ram and Jacob his speckled drove, we cannot tell whether sexual generation is being sacrificed or consecrated.

Theory as Epilogue

A swallow is an emancipated owl, and a glorified bat . . . an owl that has been trained by the Graces . . . a bat that loves the morning light.

J. Ruskin, Love's Meinie

Let Shephatiah rejoice with the little Owl, which is the wingged Cat.

C. Smart

The newest movement in philosophy, which extends into literary studies, questions the idea of presence. It is said to be an illusion fostered by our tendency to privilege voice over the written word. Voice, for Jacques Derrida, is the egotistical sublime, and our desire for the proper name (*mot propre, nom unique*) a metaphysical comfort. The best voice can do is to become literature; that is, to subvert its referential or representational function by bruising itself on the limits of language.

Derrida moves within a philosophical context of his own, and it is confusing to juxtapose his theory and Smart's poetics. I apologize for this "perspective by incongruity," as Kenneth Burke would call it, but I see no better way of suggesting how complex yet empty the concept of representation may become. Even if one acknowledges that Derrida's very aim is to empty this concept, at least of its psychologistic and metaphysical pathos, the "nature" of representation remains a puzzle.[19]

I have argued that representation supports the ideal of self-presence in its psychic and social aspects. "Vilest things become themselves in her," Shakespeare's Enobarbus says of Cleopatra. She is "beautiful in corruption," like Smart's "Eyed Moth" (B 1, 93); and Enobarbus may indeed be playing on the idea of life engendered by Nilotic slime. Yet toward this "becoming," this triumph over the shame of creaturely origin, artistic representation also aspires. It may turn out, of course, that representation is all there is, and that we will never experience a self-presence in which we see—and are seen—not as in a glass darkly but face to face. Yet who can decide how ultimate the category of substitution is, and in particular the substitution of representation for presence?

The tropes of literature, or similar kinds of imaginative substitution, could as easily be said to pursue that "presence" which "identifies" all creatures, as to defer it. Perhaps it does not matter which, since both pursuit and deferment are endless. That the identifying moment, like a snapshot, is too deathlike or ecstatic; that movement or troping must begin again; that the acute self-consciousness must be transcended by an act of what is commonly called imagination—all this is part of the psychopathology of ordinary life, or of that principle of "clapperclaw" which "joyces" language in Shakespeare, Smart, and even in Derrida.

It may be that the theory of representation finds a less problematic exponent in an intermediate figure, more congruous with Smart, and exerting through Proust some influence on French thought. Let me conclude, then, with a note on John Ruskin. His prose may be the best nature poetry in the language. Ruskin also "represents" the creature, though to his fellow-man rather than God. How sane he appears when placed beside Smart, even if touched by a madness and childishness similar to Smart's. There is probably no better antidote to the *Jubilate Agno* than Ruskin's celebration of robin and swallow in *Love's Meinie*.[20]

These lectures, given by him as Slade Professor of Fine Art before the University of Oxford, are clearly acts of reparation toward robin and swallow and, indeed, all "lower classes" exploited by the Victorian combination of Wealth and Science. "That, then, is the utmost which the lords of land, and masters of science, do for us in their watch upon our feathered suppliants. One kills them, the other writes classifying epitaphs." The painters and monks, lumped together by Ruskin, do us no good either. "They have plucked the wings from birds, to make angels of men, and the claws from birds, to make devils of men." The emphasis on genetic development in Darwinian science seems equally pernicious to Ruskin, who fears that all such speculation on origins will distract us from the present, from the endangered beauty and aptness of the *living* creature.

But it is not the common creatures alone, the swallows, fissirostres, or split-beaks, which must be saved. The common words too must be "represented": English names in their vernacular being, winged expressions which lead Ruskin to reflect on the troubadours, Chaucer and the *Romance of the Rose.* The habitat of the creature is in literature and art as well as in wood and field. Nature and art are both endangered by the deadly Latin of modern anatomical analysis.[21] We should not see the things of this world under the species of a false objectivity, or of its killing nomenclature, but through the medium of their own natures and the *lingua franca et jocundissima* of vernacular perception. Reading *Love's Meinie* I repent me for not being able to "translate" such words as "representation." "All of you who care for life as well as literature," Ruskin advises, "and for spirit,—even the poor souls of birds,—as well as lettering of their classes in books,—you, with all care, should cherish the old Saxon, English and Norman-French names of birds, and ascertain them with the most affectionate research."

Part Two

History Writing as Answerable Style

O quam te memorem . . .
Virgil, The Aeneid

Bussoftlhee mememormee
Joyce, Finnegans Wake

The Style of the Historian and the Style of Art

*A*ll men desire knowledge; but not the knowledge explosion. Knowledge may always have had a "mortal taste" yet it used to contain the promise of a better position in the scale of being and a surer sense of one's true or effective identity. But what if earth becomes "an earth of ideas"? The sea "a metaphor for the multiplication of facts and sensations"? What *can* soul desire, sitting unhappily "on superstructures of explanation, poor bird, not knowing which way to fly"?[1]

The ease with which earth, sea and bird become symbolic counters is part of the problem. Their lapsed value is felt, if only in passing. Marvell's image of the soul, gliding into the boughs, waving in its plumes the "various light" while it waits to be released from earthliness, is appropriate as a counter-reminiscence: that image has a *reserve* of resonances which the mind can explore at leisure, while as a whole it evokes that very restraint of ecstasy which makes leisure possible. It does not matter, of course, that such images are, or seem to be, from nature; what matters is the quality of our association with them—the decorum of use. "It is a great Pity that People should by associating themselves with the finest things spoil them," Keats complains, "[Leigh] Hunt has damned Hampstead and Masks and Sonnets and italian tales." Hunt's fault is at once moral and aesthetic. "Instead of giving other minds credit for the same degree of perception as he himself possesses—he begins an explanation in such a curious manner that our taste and self-love is offended continually."[2]

Keats's sensitivity to "palpable design," to the knowing or self-assertive mind, is only as significant as his understanding of the morality of art. The figures on his Grecian Urn resist the explainer-ravisher. The poet's crescendoing questions (see stanza I) are like the ecstasy they project onto the mute dancers: their very intensity of speculation seems to animate the urn until its mystery is in danger of being dissolved, its form broken for the sake of a message. We behold, as in a primal scene, the ravishments of truth, the identifying—and over-identifying—mind. The poem itself, however, by various, finely graded stages—part of art's ritual coldness—tempers an intellectual questing not unlike love-madness.

As the eye cannot choose but see, the soul cannot but desire truths; and art engages this lust for knowing or merging. To conceptualize art's relation to it is difficult. Aristotle's *Poetics* evolved the key notions of "recognition" and "catharsis," but even interpretations not clarified by precise concepts can do much to illumine the decorum of art by the intelligence of their despair. It is no *ultimate* objection to an interpretation that it merges partly with its object, "too much the syllables" of art itself; or lets artifacts, like Keats's urn, tease and evade our meditation.

What of histories of art? While not excluded from studying the "reserve" of a work of art, the style of its resistance to ideas, they remain histories, and a function of the historical consciousness. Beyond describing the form of art they seek to link it to the quality of the artist's historical awareness. Walter Benjamin, for example, connects the disappearance of the art of storytelling to our psychological and urban restlessness:

> There is nothing that commends a story to memory more effectively than that chaste compactness which precludes psychological analysis. And the more natural the process by which the storyteller forgoes psychological shading, the greater becomes the story's claim to a place in the memory of the listener, the more completely is it integrated into his own experience. . . . This process of assimilation, which takes place

> in depth, requires a state of relaxation becoming ever more rare. If sleep is the apogee of physical relaxation, boredom is the apogee of mental relaxation. Boredom is the dream bird that hatches the egg of experience. A rustling in the leaves drives him away. His nesting places—the activities intimately associated with boredom—are already extinct in the cities and are declining in the country as well. With this the gift of listening is lost and the community of listeners disappears. . . . It is lost because there is no more weaving and spinning to go on while they are being listened to. The more self-forgetful the listener is, the more deeply is what he listens to impressed upon his memory. When the rhythm of work has seized him, he listens to the tales in such a way that the gift of retelling then comes to him all by itself.[3]

Erich Auerbach undertakes a fuller analysis of this kind in the opening chapter of *Mimesis*, where two influential narrative styles, of the Book of Genesis and the *Odyssey*, are radically distinguished by the charm they exert on the communal listener, or conversely by the limits of their interpretability. Such an approach leads historically from the mythical way of storytelling to its difficulty in Wordsworth or Henry James—even to the difficulty of history-writing itself, which has reduced the role of fabulation in favor of psychological and sociological shading. Yet, in modern art at least, a new non-fabulous "reserve" is forged, so that Eliot remarks of James's mind that it was too fine to be violated by ideas.

Critics are right to worry about the proper relation of ideas (explanations, truths, beliefs) to art. The problem has outrun Wordsworth, Keats or James. The very word "idea" has now become problematic. It embraces things with very different status: organizing ideas or models, and truths imperatively held. It is one thing to say that certain beliefs or their symbols (pagan gods, for example) are essential to literature; another that they are true. This difference is being eroded by the historical consciousness. We live in an era of convergence where all truths, outmoded or not, seem to enjoy a "formal" value. The growth of the historical consciousness, its multiplying of disparate models all of which press their claim, amounts to a peculiarly modern burden, an overhead weighing on the individual like a new theology. To be aware of the past is to be surrounded by abstract potentialities, imperatives that cannot all be heeded, options exhausting the power of choice. One need not be a historian to suffer this state of *surnomie*. A liberation, not of men and women, but of images, has created a *theatrum mundi* in which the distance between past and present, culture and culture, truth and superstition is suspended by a quasi-divine synchronism. A living cinema surrounds us, a Plato's cave full of colored shadows.[4]

If art is to retain a certain purity—that "cunning stroke," as Emerson called it, which separates out the precise symbol or the one adequate form—it must triumph over this synchronic pressure of abstract knowledge. But the crisis is not solved by bringing, once again, order out of variety and discovering new forms. There are too many forms already: they now debouch into life directly, without the special mediation of masterworks. Our hearts are sad at the culture supermarket; packaged historical reminiscences meet us everywhere; the Beatles' *Yellow Submarine* is a moving toyshop of topoi. Purity in art? It is no longer achieved by new forms but rather by new media that allow existing forms to survive the contamination of meaning—of historical or ideological accretions.

In the Renaissance the translation of Classical riches into the "new medium" of the vernacular must have been a purification of this kind, making things new and concrete at the same time. And within the vernacular itself the pastoral mode was not so much a new form as the creation of a new reserve evoking the "silence and slow time" of a fading latinity. Today we translate into the "language" of the cinema: frames speak by sheer juxtaposition (montage) or generally by the disassociation and then remixing of images and their meanings. It is far, yet not so far, from Keats's pictorialism in the Ode on the Grecian Urn—the way each frame in the turned object repeats a questionable shape or mysterious defilade, a mute picture dubbed by the poet—and the purification of "contaminated" images in Wallace Stevens or the scenarios of Robbe-Grillet. It is far, yet not so far, from the obsessively detailed inspections of one spot in Wordsworth's "The Thorn" to the narrative *retours* of the same, itemized scene in a *nouveau roman*. One difference, of course, is that images have now to survive explicitly sexual or vulgar attributions. But whether the "mensonge sémantique" is of a noble or vulgar kind seems less important than that structured negation by which images reject meanings they save in the end. The image is always *anathematic* in David Jones's sense, always a "Lady of silences/ Torn and most whole":

> La jeune femme se figera parfois, comme une statue de cire du musée Grévin, ou comme une déesse, une prostituée de convention, voire une photo érotique dans le style le plus traditionnel, le plus naif. De même pour la ville. Toute contaminée dans l'esprit de l'homme par un mélange de Pierre Loti, de Guide Bleu et de Mille-et-une-Nuits, elle passera sans cesse de la carte postale touristique au "symbolisme" affiché des chaînes et de grilles de fer, mais sans cesser pour cela d'être pleine de la rumeur vivante des bateaux, des ports et des foules.[5]

Can history-writing, or interpretation in touch with it, become a new medium—a supreme fiction which does not reduce being to meaning but defines a thing sharply in "the difficulty of what it is to be"? We have stressed only the moral obstacle: wrong hypotheses may "spoil the finest things" by their kind of slander. But the present situation takes us beyond questions of decorum into an ontological perplexity. The hypothesis-making mood we are in—with its variorum of perspectives or "superstructures of explanation"—threatens artifacts in a peculiar way. It endows them with a *false* reserve created by the very pressure of interpretations brought to bear. As interpretability becomes more important than historicity, and the prey is relinquished for the shadow, art-objects seem to split into, on the one hand, a *gegenstand*, the artifact as indeterminable, mere ob-stance of the interpreting mind; and, on the other, a prehensile corpus of explanations incited by art's ipseity. The very openness of symbols to several, even opposed, kinds of meaning assures their impregnable reserve in the midst of explanatory assaults. This ontic stubbornness, however, is hardly sufficient to characterize the reserve of art, which should be a reservoir of resonances rather than a mystifying void. Modern theories attempting to distinguish between the being and meaning of art ("a poem must not mean/But be") are trapped into too empty an understanding of art's reserve. They reduce art to objects that cry, "I am dark but beautiful."

Such thoughts bear, however, on the structure of all interpretation, rather than specifically on historical kinds. To some extent this is inevitable. History, as reflected in histories, is both a series of acts and a series of intentions—acts whose intention was falsified or at least modified. A later knowledge sees they were based on myths or imperfect assumptions. History-writing, therefore, while inherently "critical" is not inherently "judgmental": it is judgmental only by the claim that human beings could act without blindness, without that which makes them finite enough to act. But this claim is not made when history is told by historians, by critics rather than gods. Men act by overlooking certain possibilities or delimiting speculation, so that history appears as an illuminating progress of errors. Though we may differ over the cause of the "blindness" which precipitates men into action or maintains them in it, central error of this kind lies in the nature of action whether or not described as "historical." Interpretation, which makes that error appear, or gives it its dignity, is always historical to this extent.

A systematic view of the problem would have to consider our greatest philosophers of existential error: Nietzsche and Heidegger. I will content myself with an eloquence of Emerson's. Emerson, seeing error of this kind as basic to the crystallization of passion or to symbol-making generally, places it under "the mystery of form":

> Love and all the passions concentrate all existence around a single form. It is the habit of certain minds to give an all-excluding fulness to the object, the thought, the word, they alight upon, and to make that for the time the deputy of the world. These are the artists, the orators, the leaders of society. The power to detach, and to magnify by detaching, is the essence of rhetoric in the hands of the orator and the poet. This rhetoric, or power to fix the momentary eminency of an object . . . depends on the depth of the artist's insight of that object he contemplates. For every object has its roots in central nature, and may of course be so exhibited to us as to represent

the world. . . . Presently we pass to some other object, which rounds itself into a whole, as did the first. . . . From this succession of excellent objects learn we at last the immensity of the world, the opulence of human nature.[6]

Perhaps Nietzsche is, after all, the proper antidote to this astonishing optimism. Yet it is true that we constantly seek to master the accidents of life: to roll up our fortunes into a ball, to find religious, artistic or technological means of self-concentration. By such fatal centering we become conscious, then over-conscious, then flee what is desired. History is, as it were, the wake of a mobile mind falling in and out of love with things it detaches by its attachment. Its centering and decentering path leaves a chaos of forms behind. By negative transcendence it produces something as deep as a tragedy or as opulent as Emerson's view of Nature.

An updated—more realistic—Emerson would have to acknowledge a new stage, with men increasingly divided into two camps. A nihilistic period has begun in which one camp wishes to live "without reserve"—without role-models, or squandering them as a rich son his inheritance; while the other, fearing a debilitating loss of binding forms, deliberately espouses the crudest social myths. There is no "mystery of form" when forms lose their representativeness or mediating virtue: when men, distorting rather than exploring art's common-wealth, its link with an interpretable fund of roles, fall back on narrow concepts of manliness and reenact those tragedies of revenge which society was founded to control. "Greatness without models? Inconceivable. One could not be the thing itself—Reality. . . . Make peace therefore with intermediacy and representation."[7] Is it too late, or can our age, like every previous one, protect the concept of art?

The Reserve of Art and the Social Reserve

Art history presupposes that creation comes out of a "chaos of forms" rather than simply out of chaos or miraculously out of nothing. This chaos, with which the historical consciousness begins, has had many depictions, from the Rabbinical *Pardes* and that reservoir of perplexing images Yeats associated with the secrets of an *anima mundi*, to Dürer's *Melencholia I, The Wasteland's* "heap of broken images" and David Jones's "anathémata." When institutionalized this chaos becomes a *thesaurus* or *museum*, and expands with the historical consciousness. Hegel's observation that the Roman pantheon relativized the gods it brought together anticipates Malraux's universal "musée imaginaire" in which the gods are pictures.

Were that museum, however, truly imaginary or "without walls," it would mean the end of art as we know it. A secular sparagmos would "carry art up into the kingdom of nature, and destroy its separated and contrasted existence."[8] Our chaos of forms would move, in other words, from a beginning to an end position, one characterized by Hegel as a *revel* of forms, the sober bacchanalia of the human spirit reconciled with all its incarnations.[9] That revel might be compared to the formal dance which ends certain comedies, except that it erases rather than affirms the art-reality distinction. The reconciliation is to be real, not formal.

What lies between the "chaos" and the "revel" of forms? Conventions or institutions which are familiar, and sometimes too familiar. There exists a highly structured *reserve* of forms which claims to represent for each generation the genius of a nation, class or culture. Here are found the official commonplaces; the symbols and passwords that bind a community together or identify members to each other. It may be that the artist, at present, is tempted to pass from the chaos to the revel of forms without respecting this more structured realm. But since he cannot avoid it entirely, he violates its "reserve" by various kinds of self-exhausting parody—as in Woodstock's feast of tongues.

The image of society resulting from a century of progress in social anthropology may help to clarify these concepts. Society is built up of tribes, communities and special interests. To bind them together needs places, myths and heroes in common. The idea of a "commonplace" is more concrete here than in the History of Ideas or Topoi. There is first an official, highly organized *mythology*, a state religion, for example; but underlying it, or not quite reducible, a pervasive, unofficial *ideology* or complex of beliefs. The difference between written and oral culture connects with this division; the latter shows, in any case, that what we have called the reserve is not totally rigid but contains two systems of expression more or less conscious of each other. Sometimes, no doubt, the one will not know what the other is doing; but a strong relationship is necessary if the "higher" language is to retain its resonance and be more than superstructure.

In addition to the reserve we find an area which corresponds quite closely to the "chaos of forms" Van Gennep saw that there was a phase of aggregation rituals (*rites de passage*) in which the candidate is "betwixt and between" and which allows him a degree of self-determination in the choice of a social identity. During this *liminal* or *marginal* phase the candidate is segregated and exposed to spirit-powers directly, without forms or mediations available to men in society. He discovers in this way both his individuality and his isolation, both selfhood and the meaning of society.[10]

If we reflect that marginality is dangerous not because it is empty but because the absence of conventional social structuring allows room for an irruption of energies society has not integrated, then we see how similar this state is to the "chaos of forms" which art explores. The artist is surely the liminal or threshold person par excellence, while art provides society with a "chaos of roles" strengthening the individual's sense of unstructured community yet offering him ideal parts to try. Only the concept of liminality, moreover, as developed by Turner from Van Gennep[11] explains why art is statusless despite its civilizing role. Art is not reality; the relation of the one to the other is essentially liminal; between art and its translation into immediate relevance a threshold intervenes which cannot be crossed without destroying art's very place in society. The modern university is characterized by a similar kind of marginality, one basic to the development of man as a citizen yet an individual.

The liminal state is not restricted to puberty rites. It plays a significant role in initiations generally. Here is where the patience ("negative capability") of the candidate may be tested, where symbolic sights and acts reverse his status or question his integrity. The mature man, after all, may need more "restructuring" than the ephebe. Or his responsibilities may be heavier. He is therefore disoriented (disaggregated) under test-conditions imposed by the group, before being accepted in (aggregated) once more. An artist, of course, is a group of one and has little or no ritual authority. Yet art does submit us to a ritual and controlled experience of this kind. We are not compelled to participate in it, yet there are those who abide its question. It is no mean test to view what Aristotle calls a scene of pathos without being traumatized by it or distancing it into symbolic meaning—to let oneself be confronted by an ambiguity that, when it occurs in real life, splits the soul.

The ritual process leads, of course, beyond liminality. A new identity, or reidentification, should emerge. This is not so clear in art because art extends the liminal moment. There the identity quest is a formal device and always something of a deception. In fact, whereas in the primitive rite there is probably no such thing as *failing* the process of aggregation[12] (except for special cases in which "the king must die"), in art there is no such thing as fully succeeding in it. Art interests us less in the outcome of an ethical or vocational crisis than in the passion that attends, and the vision from passion. The hero, by suffering the chaos of forms, by descending into that hades, glimpses the point where "All Human Forms are Identified."[13] A Redeemed City emerges from Ancestral Chaos. Yet to bring the vision back is greater than to attain it. The return, which corresponds socially to reaggregation and psychologically to reintegration, is the moment of art itself—the opus. *Facilis descensus Averno . . . sed revocare gradum superasque evadere ad auras, hoc opus, hic labor est.*

Goethe's Faust is an exceptionally clear instance of the work of art conceived as a socializing *rite de passage.* It shows, at the same time, the danger of confusing art with the production of new identities or role-models. Faust moves from a spiritual acedia reflecting the burden of culture to the illusory revel of the Walpurgisnacht and the more sophisticated dream of a reconciliation between those mighty cultural opposites: classic and gothic,

Greece and Germany. When the quest collapses and Faust adopts the pragmatic role of bridge-builder, Goethe's myriad-minded play is unmasked as a ponderous ritual *embourgeoisement*. We have entered the era of the well-made rite of passage.

But how else can we emerge from the chaos of forms? What can art create if not a reconciling social myth or an ideal personal role? Is art's truth merely in its obsessive consumption or negative transcendence of historical models?

We recall the contemporary situation. While primitive ritual makes room for the living by ceremonies that both propitiate and separate the dead—"the dead, if not separated from the living, bring madness on them"[14]—the growth of the historical sense makes clean, ritual separations difficult. If the dead are less dangerous when viewed as historically transcended, or sublimated, forces, they are also more insinuating. They do not fall easily into pure and impure, malevolent and beneficent, tribal and alien. The time spent in the marginal state, the submission to visions of the night, lengthens. We feel more strongly than ever that the past pollutes *and* that it saves. "Nothing human alienates me"—for the historical consciousness exotic or irrational are simply estranged potentialities of the human spirit. "All Human Forms are Identified" in Blake's redeemed city.

In these circumstances art both accepts and rejects more: it resists the spirits it calls up and absorbs conflicting traditions by a movement more eccentric than Miltonic similes. The new myth that kills the old, the new form that separates what is dead from what is living, has the value of a purification rather than of truth. The chaos of form aspires to become a revel: in the sublimities of a Milton, Blake or Shelley there is a high laughter as well as high seriousness. There remains, of course, the shadow of the false or premature revel: promiscuous acceptance (as in the Walpurgisnacht) of the chaos of forms, or such fickle at-one-ments as Blake places into Beulah. The unitive vision of art is not a spiritual cannibalism or triumph of death.

Consider Goethe once more. His Faust enters the chaos of the past but rejects its abstract promises. He wants participation, mastery, universality. Yet Faust's progress in that direction gives renewed birth to sacrificial abstractions. The more universal his vision, the more blatant his disregard of parochial dignities and individual suffering. And Goethe, too, pays a price in his art for a clarity superior to that of contemporaries like Hölderlin and Blake. He stylizes the dynamic character of the vast cultural reserve embodied in his poems. The conflict of classes and tongues becomes matter for a virtuoso display. Art has now acquired its own reserve, a backlog of forms which Goethe *applies* perfectly, mixing types of verse and transcending national boundaries through a deployment of inherited topoi. This art-reserve has advantages over both the chaos of forms and the social reserve: it is better organized than the first and broader than the second. Its disadvantage, however, is that charted still further by humanists like Northrop Frye it could substitute itself for the ritual process. Then art becomes a technique and culture-grammar rather than a genuine mediation: a wrestling with, and separating of, the dead.[15]

Afterthought

In the 1930s Ernst Robert Curtius began the studies that led to *European Literature and the Latin Middle Ages* (1948). For that work Goethe was the central man: through his art the great body of formal (and formative) commonplaces elaborated since Homer is said to have reached the threshold of modern German literature. Through him they were saved from becoming a dead language.

At our distance from the 1930s (which saw a parallel though less literary development in America, A. O. Lovejoy's *Great Chain of Being*, also concerned with continuity) this type of literary history seems faulty. It tends to be a courtesy book for scholars, an exercise in the urbane diffusion of knowledge. Histories of topical ideas, literary or philosophical, remain in the domain of *memoria technica* rather than serving the living, ancestor-haunted consciousness. Histories should tell us what made a person or a group historical: what marked them and passed into mind with the force of the Biblical injunction: "Remember, Thou shalt not forget." Or what helped them learn to forget, to remit the burden of the past. This individuating, and often delimiting cycle, disappears from histories of topoi. Their humanistic kind of monism sees little that is new under the sun.

Yet scholarship has its own historical context, and we easily overlook the call it answered. Faulty or not, Curtius's great commonplace book is the protest of Mnemosyne against Germania. It enlarged the memory of a nation when political pressures had reduced art to a narrow, racialist canon. Curtius appealed to Memory not for the sake of the past but for the sake of Romania, which he viewed as more than a country of the mind: it was a wronged spirit, a *genius loci* expelled from Germania by fascism. Like Blake, therefore, but in a darker time, he engaged in mental fight to restore his country's genius to its memorable form.

From the Sublime to the Hermeneutic

*I*nfluence is a word that points to the stars; and literary history, as a history of the influence of artist on artist or culture on culture, often involves those theogonic bodies. Literature always contends with a star-system of some kind: with foreign inheritances, native debts, or an overhead of great works whose light still pulses though they existed long ago. It is no accident that the Book of Genesis begins by putting the stars in their place and making them signs rather than powers. Recent scholarship has shown how radical a displacement of the surrounding Canaanite belief that account is. The Bible of one nation can be the systematic dismembering, or disremembering, of another.

It is no accident, similarly, that toward the beginning of the modern era of historical speculation, Hegel addresses a poem to Hölderlin in which the thought-annihilating stars (*Gestirn*) become through the meditation of "Phantasie" the sublime brow (*Stirne*) of monitory spirits:

Mein Aug erhebt sich zu des ewgen Himmels Wölbung,
zu dir, o glänzendes Gestirn der Nacht,
und aller Wünsche, aller Hoffnungen
Vergessen strömt aus deiner Ewigkeit herab,
der Sinn verliert sich in dem Anschaun,
was mein ich nannte schwindet
ich gebe mich dem unermesslichen dahin,
ich bin in ihm, bin alles, bin nur es.
Dem wiederkehrenden Gedanken fremdet,
ihm graut vor dem unendlichen, und staunend fasst

er dieses Anschauns Tiefe nicht.
Dem Sinne nähert Phantasie das Ewige,
vermählt es mit Gestalt—Willkommen ihr
erhabne Geister, hohe Schatten,
von deren Stirne die Vollendung strahlt!
Er schrecket nicht,—ich fühl': es ist auch meiner Heimat Aether,
der Ernst, der Glanz, der euch umfliesst.[1]

Hegel's experience of the sublime—for so an eighteenth century writer would have called it—is essentially of a dazzlement which draws the mind into a self-forgetful vortex, then leaves the thoughts that struggle back alienated ("Dem wiederkehrenden Gedanken fremdet . . .") until imagination intervenes. This return from apocalyptic feelings to mortifying thoughts, this vacillation between nothingness and nothingness, becomes sufferable and even strengthening when it elicits, as here, a counter-assertive, inward, humanizing power. "So feeling comes in aid/ Of feeling, and diversity of strength/ Attends us if but once we have been strong" (Wordsworth, *Prelude* XII). It is, in fact, this assurance given by the sublime experience to the survivor—that is, to imaginative man—which allows Hegel to approach the mysteries of the historical past without taking leave of his mind. The element in which the greats live is his element too. "Es ist auch meiner Heimat Aether." He breathes the same spiritual air as they.

The eighteenth century had distinguished the sublime of art and the sublime of nature: Hegel added the sublime of history. The development was, I believe, inherent in general neoclassic doctrine which, by a strange dialectic, by an apotheosis that kicked genius upstairs, at once acknowledged and negated the influence of greatness. Genius could be admired but not imitated. The neoclassical writers knew that it contained otherness: an unacculturated and even demonic element. But Hegel, after *his* experience of the sublime almost dissolves the distance between him and the mysterious heavens of Eleusis:

Begeistrung trunken fühlt' ich jetzt
Die Schauer deiner Nähe,
verstände deiner Offenbarungen,
ich deutete der Bilder hohen Sinn . . .

The historical space between him and Greece is less the space of mystery than of interpretation: it is hermeneutic as well as pneumatic. Hegel stands here on the threshold of the passage from *Geistergeschichte* to *Geistesgeschichte.*

In fact, the mediating "imagination" of 1796 becomes in the *Phenomenology* of 1807 and the lectures on the *Philosophy of History* of 1818 and after a pivotal phase of human consciousness assigned to the time of the Greeks. It is said to have enabled the Eastern world, where mind tended to be lost in the sublime of nature, to evolve as a western consciousness, where mind knows its own sublimity. Hegel's poem remains, however, like the mystery it is drawn to, a night-piece; it does not move in the open field of consciousness like the *Geistesgeschichte* to come. Starlight, not the "great Day's work of Spirit" is its symbol.

I am not insisting that the sublime of nature as described by neoclassical writers, and deepened by Kant, is at the base of Hegel's dialectic. But the dialectic does contain a strong recognition of otherness, at first attractively antimnemonic—like Eastern nature-astonishment or Hegel's starry ecstasy—then repellent as the sense of mortality flows back with antithetical vigor. There is, finally, a kind of synthesis as imagination enters to humanize the stars or remove their taint of absoluteness.

The stars are put in their place. In Hegel, of course, this is not a religious but a hermeneutic degrading which follows from the tacit principle that man is the measure of all things. It is not unusual by the 1790s that the distinction between the sublime and the beautiful fades, or that sublimer nature gives way to a complex valuing of vestiges rather than of powers, of "absences," as it were, that permit the imaginative spirit a freer, more reflective response. Though the sublime survives, and all the more strongly at times ("Jetzt komme, Feuer" is the opening of Hölderlin's *Ister*), it is there to be overcome or mastered into mind. A small poem by Friederike Brun can illustrate this new, increasingly reflective verse:

Leise, wie Wellen des Bachs, kamen Gedanken mir—
Schwanden Gedanken dahin, welche, Erinnerung! du
Holde Schwester des Tiefsinns,
Stets im wechselnden Reigen führst!

This "Empfindung am Ufer" is deeply indebted to a conception of the Classical sensibility as individuality (here individual grief) conditioned by beauty, that is, restrained by the form-giving principle in beauty. The measured verses, like the waves themselves, are anti-mnemonic without denying memory: they are soothers of an absence whose depth (*Tiefsinn*) we do not appreciate till we learn they mourn the drowning of Friederike's brother. The personal circumstances of loss are muted together with its intensity: loss remains only as nature-feeling. Indeed, the personifications (*Erinnerung* which stands to *Tiefsinn* as Friederike to her brother) are indistinguishable from nature-spirits, so that the very form of feeling merges with that of the Greek numina which are traces rather than powers, things half-felt and half-imagined. "The immortal songs of the Muses are not that which is heard in the murmuring fountains," writes Hegel of the Greek sensibility, "they are the productions of the thoughtfully listening spirit (*sinnig lauschenden Geistes*)—creative while observant. The muse into which the fountain turns is human imagination itself." And again: "The Greek mind regards Nature as, at first, foreign to it yet not without presentiment that in it lodges something friendly. . . . Wonder and Presentiment are its fundamental categories, though the Greeks did not take these moods as ends but represented them as a distinct, if still veiled, form of consciousness." Friederike's comfort lies in a presentiment, an intimation of immortality which absorbs death into a form resembling nymph or naiad—those curiously deft deities who hardly bend that over which they pass.

The spirits that flit through so much poetry of the time are clearly second-class or degraded (*déclassé*) deities; and the manner called poetic diction helped to make them linguistic rather than divine beings. To compare their status to interpretable script is merely to compare one kind of trace or print (*vestigium*) to another. Both kinds traditionally lament the shadow they are. For Hegel such seeming poverty of being is a characteristic of all thought that has broken with immediacy and passed into the realm of what he calls the "negative." This realm, however, becomes the very basis of human freedom: it is the aether in which consciousness expands its hermeneutic powers.

The inherently degraded character of poetic diction is a curious phenomenon. I have no wish to justify neoclassic "godkins and goddesslings" (Coleridge), but the Enlightenment *was* enlightening: it eased certain burdens weighing on the human spirit, and especially the "burden of the mystery." Those multiplying personifications, at once linguistic and divine, mental and grammatical, hide what Hegel reveals: how dependent we moderns are on reflective forms that have replaced the sublimer forms of religious self-consciousness. Hegel makes us face the omnipresence of consciousness and so, in one sense, increases our burden—but it is no longer the "burden of mystery." He does not ask us to shoulder a set of absurdities called history which is mystifyingly explained by another set called religion, but the power of thought in all its modes: from the simple break with sensuous immediacy to the abstractions of science. Allow me to quote his famous passage on hermeneutic heroism, that is, on the capacity of the mind to stay with negative data, with forms so abstract or contrary that no one could plead, "Verweile doch, du bist so schön":

> The spirit gains its true identity only by discovering itself in dismemberment. Its power does not come from taking a positive stance that averts its face from everything negative—as when we say of something, this is nonsense, or wrong, and then, finished with it, turn to another matter. The spirit is power only by looking the negative in the face and abiding with it. This abiding (*Verweilen*) is the magic charm (*Zauberkraft*) which converts the negative into Being. (Preface, *Phenomenology of Mind.*)

An element of fairy-tale remains in this appeal (however light) to magic metamorphosis. But it must be so if Hegel is truly a humanist. The humanist is concerned with defining the powers of man, with detaching the being called man from a divine or overshadowing matrix. Humanism sees man as a cosmic alien engaged in what ultimately is a form of ideological warfare. "Soldier, there is a war between the mind and the sky" (Wallace Stevens). He is asked to bow down: to influences from the sky or nature or the prevailing *Realpolitik*. But his mind is his manhood; and the concern with influence, now seeing a revival, is a humanistic attempt to save art from those who would eliminate mind in favor of structure or who would sink it into the mechanical operation of the spirit. To save it from both structuralist and spiritualist, in other words. For influence, *in art*, is always personal, seductive, perverse, imposing. "And what am I that I am here?" Matthew Arnold cries when the shadow of his mentors falls on him.[2] To which the only answer is the creative blasphemy, "I am that I am."

Georges Poulet too is a humanist, haunted by the divine matrix he evades. He discerns where the objective form of art becomes pseudo-objective, where the spirit breaks through and establishes its "Here I am." This point, at once human and transcendent ("subjective"), cannot always be formalistically established; the where in a sense is everywhere; the point is not punctual. Hence there is a "critique d'identification," and the reader's sense of presence merges with that conveyed by the text. This double act of presence, though different from the sharp presence/absence structure of sublime experience, is perhaps a way of overcoming it. Poulet's conception of the artist's *cogito* also implies double presence and a virtual harmony: the genetic or palingenetic "Here I am" is not taken to be an actual response to some prior call but a moment of co-naissance that links mind and world, or restores their fragile continuity. It is, like the Bible's "in the beginning," a limiting concept, which tells us not to think about what went before. Whatever the nature of our origin, we begin as beings conscious of this power for correspondence, for capable dialogue. The positing of a *cogito*, although it seems to reintroduce a dubious first term or "valeur d'origine," functions really as a narrative or constructivist device which allows the self to remain present—to tell its story. It is the Archimedean point by which a reader stabilizes his relation to an author or makes the latter's inner world available.

One problem with this view of reading as identification, or as leading to a double, harmonic act of presence (the ideal form of any understanding) is the mode of existence attributed to the text. Can it be more than a go-between? Are texts all that necessary? In Poulet's criticism, text does not call unto text, but conscience unto conscience. The eristics of interpretation are its eros;

we do not gain a new freedom, we gain ourselves once again. There is one story and one story only. Textuality may itself be the one form of otherness—the only estranging formalism—we should fear. There is, as Paul de Man has pointed out, the danger of a "self-consuming identity in which language is destroyed."[3] That is, the link between language and temporality, or the genuine inbetweenness (*Zwischenbereich*) of narrative. Must art be forgotten in the unifying kiss of Paolo and Francesca?

Whatever paradoxes beset the relation of self and literary language (where language is, self is not; where self is, language is not) the structure of the act of reading, as Poulet understands it, is the structure of sublime experience in a finer mode. His *cogito* is like the counterassertive, humanizing moment that rises out of the vortex of self-forgetfulness. The identification of reader with writer, similarly, is like that dangerous assimilation to a sublime which comes to eighteenth-century man via the stars, or vast, inhuman nature. The context of the experience is now the act of reading, and the emphasis shifts from the surprised to the methodically recreative mind. But a critic like Charles du Bos (in the exemplary description offered by Poulet) passes through a moment of influence strong enough to be characterized as an invasion: "I begin by letting the thought that invades me . . . reoriginate within my own mind, as if it were reborn out of my own annihilation." The sublime still shadows the hermeneutic. We remain in the hermeneutic turn (from *Geistergeschichte* to *Geistesgeschichte*) initiated by Hegel.

Let me go back, then, to the stars, and to the historical development of the link between humanism and hermeneutics. In Romantic poetry there are two conspicuous and intertwining themes: that of the fallen star, and of the star redeemed. They are not new, but their use in this period is far-reaching. We come so often on the star/flower theme that it seems to be the founding topos of nature poetry. The gods fall like stars into nature, and this is felt, on the whole, as a lightening as well as lightning. The sky seems now not so heavy; the earth somewhat more substantial. Yet by this fall the gods do not lose all their potency, for nature-poetry becomes a second heaven, numinous and mythopoetic. In fact, no sooner have they fallen and become astral flowers, than a contrary movement of redemption is felt. To degrade hermeneutically the sublime realm—and the imaginative response to nature even in so simple a poem as Wordsworth's "Daffodils" is related to this descent of the stars—activates an important theme from Romance, the quest of nature spirits for *soul*, as in the myth of Ondine or even, perhaps, Goethe's "Erl-king."

This quest, sometimes benign, mostly demonic, brings "nature-astonishment" closer to home. It shows that the ancient struggle between man and spirit-influences—that is, of man for self-dependence—is continuing in a more intimate way. What do the spirits want? Always the same: man's fall, his ontic degradation. How does humanism deal with that? By sending against them the thunderbolt of hermeneutic degradation. The airy struggle persists as a theme in Wallace Stevens' "L'Esthetique du Mal," which opens with reminiscences of the sublime in a Vesuvian landscape, reflects on the "capital negation" that destroyed the Satanic spirits for poetry, and ends punningly where it began: among "dark italics."

One can venture the thought that the—now vanishing—era of philology brought together hermeneutics and the historical sense through this feeling for "dark italics." Its great scholars, from Vico to Fr. Schlegel, from Nietzsche to Leo Spitzer, were well acquainted with the region of Vesuvius. When it comes to the resuscitation of texts, they are all Neapolitan sorcerers. Perhaps they have raised too many ghosts by now, burdened us with an infected past; and not allowed signs to remain signs. Perhaps our freedom is being restricted by their philological magic which turns words into psychic etymologies. Less interested in the sign than in its source or intention, they often destroy its ideality, its character as trace, or respect that trace only as something to be tracked down. But interpretation that reduces words to clues or symptoms is in danger of becoming *nosology* and making us spies, doctors, debunkers, archeologists.

The myth we need as interpreters, and do not have, is that the stars fell into language. They are the "dark italics," the "fitful-fangled darknesses." Mallarmé came closest to the myth: for him poetic words are asterisk. The distance between a luminous event and its verbal trace is not the distance of loss or mystery: it is hermeneutic. The hermeneutic degrading allows an inward and human response. We are not confused by the fact that the golden apples of the Hesperides were, as Thoreau notes, goats and sheep "by the ambiguity of the language," or that the stars bear the names of animals. To be named is to be interpretable; not to be named is to be lost in light.

Take, in conclusion, this starry passage—a classical dawn scene —from *Paradise Regained* (Book II).

Thus pass'd the night so foul till morning fair
Came forth with Pilgrim steps in amice gray;
Who with her radiant finger still'd the roar
Of thunder, chas'd the clouds, and laid the winds,
And grisly Spectres, which the Fiend had rais'd . . .

"The radiant finger," says Bishop Hurd,[4] "points at the potent wand of the Gothic magician . . ." A just observation, which recovers the "dark italics" of the image, or its romance etymon. But the image also points at itself, at its power to dispel the night of history. The hypothesis that dawn's finger replaces a sorcerer's wand allows us to glimpse an elided historical era, the "middle" age between Classics and their revival. That indeed was filled with specters and superstitions from which art, according to Milton, had only just emerged. But his image remains unaffected by the dark middle it throws off as lightly as dawn the illusions of the night. It eases the burden of the past by eliding what gothicism there is like a letter no longer voiced, and by reviving with so slight a modification the classical topos "rosy-fingered dawn." The modifications of the topos are so small that they appear as displacements in a sign-system rather than dramatic changes in consciousness or history. Great art closes upon itself.

Hegel would have understood this exorcism or "sublation." He too shows how mind labors to free itself from impositions: from the stars, from nature, from foreign ideas—above all, from the curse of secondariness. How do the Greeks, for example, transform inherited symbols? "Hercules," Hegel writes, "is that Spiritual Humanity which by its own strength of doing conquers Olympus with the twelve far-famed labors; but the foreign, underlying idea is the Sun, completing its revolution through the twelve signs of the Zodiac." All the themes of the *Philosophy of History* are here: the degrading of the stars, the emancipation from foreign models, the increasing humanity and concreteness of symbolic representation, the reflection, in those symbols, of history as a self-imposed labor—not a punishment but a quest, the quest for freedom.

I will not try to make Hegel into Milton. To bring such names together is the comparatist's temptation and folly. Yet Hegel shares with Milton a Protestant consciousness which linked freedom to freedom of interpretation—he also shares, more personally, an ambivalence concerning that freedom. Hegel flirted with conflating freedom and necessity; and whether Milton, in putting Satan down, degraded a star or his own free spirit, is still unclear. We know, however, where Satan's power lies: he denies history, not only as defeat but as a superior claim or influence of any kind. He denies, in fact, having an origin ("Who saw/ When this creation was? remember'st thou/ Thy making . . .?") and proclaims himself an unfathered angel: self-begot, self-raised. Yet without a greatness prior to our own there may be nothing to respond to. There may be no dialogue, let alone dialectic. Culture and tradition would be vain concepts. "Das leblose Einsame"[5] would remain, playing with skulls in the Golgotha of imagination.

Poem and Ideology
A Study of Keats's "To Autumn"

"Most English great poems have little or nothing to say."[1] Few do that nothing so perfectly, one is tempted to add, as Keats's "To Autumn." Our difficulty as interpreters is related to the way consciousness almost disappears into the poem: the mind, for once, is not what is left (a kind of sublime litter) after the show is over. "To Autumn" seems to absorb rather than extrovert that questing imagination whose breeding fancies, feverish overidentifications, and ambitious projects motivate the other odes.

It is not that we lack terms to describe the poem. On the contrary, as W. J. Bate has said, "for no other poem of the last two centuries does the classical critical vocabulary prove so satisfying." We can talk of its decorum, "the parts . . . contributing directly to the whole, with nothing left dangling or independent," of its lack of egotism, "the poet himself . . . completely absent; there is no 'I', no suggestion of the discursive language that we find in the other odes," and finally of a perfect concreteness or adequacy of symbol, the union in the poem of ideal and real, of the "greeting of the Spirit" and its object.[2]

Yet terms like these point to an abstract perfection, to something as pure of content as a certain kind of music. They bespeak a triumph of form that exists but not—or not sufficiently—the nature of that form: its power to illumine experience, to cast a new light, a new shadow maybe, on things. In what follows I suggest, daringly, that "To Autumn" has something to say: that it is an ideological poem whose very form expresses a national idea and a new stage in consciousness, or what Keats himself once called the "gregarious advance" and "grand march of intellect."

There are problems with *ideological*, a word whose meaning is more charged in Marxist than in general usage. Marxism thinks of ideology as a set of ideas that claim universality while serving a materialistic or class interest. "Ideology is untruth, false consciousness, lie. It shows up in failed works of art . . . and is vulnerable to criticism. . . . Art's greatness consists in allowing that to be uttered which ideology covers up." [8] The attack on ideology in Marxism resembles that on "unearned abstractions" in Anglo-American formalistic theory, except that it engages in "depth politics" to uncover these abstractions. Formalistic criticism can worry overt ideas or idealisms, Keats's "Beauty is Truth, Truth Beauty," for example, yet it accepts gladly the disappearance of ideas, or disinterestedness of form in "To Autumn." There is no attempt to demystify this form by discovering behind its decorum a hidden interest. In a low-risk theory of this kind the presence of ideas can be disturbing but not, obviously, their absence.

The great interpretive systems we know of have all been interest-centered, however; they have dug deep, mined, undermined, removed the veils. The Synagogue is blind to what it utters, the Church understands. The patient dreams, the doctor translates the dream. The distant city is really our city; the *unheimlich* the *heim-lich*; strange, uncanny, and exotic are brought home. Like those etymologies older scholars were so fond of, which showed us the fossilized stem of abstract words, so everything is slain, in interest-theories, on the stem of generational or class conflict.

Yet like nature itself, which has so far survived man's use of it, art is not polluted by such appropriations. Some works may be discredited, others deepened—the scandal of form remains. From Kant through Schopenhauer and Nietzsche, the aesthetic element proper is associated with disinterestedness, impersonality, and resistance to utilitarian concepts. Beauty of this undetermined kind becomes an itch: the mind, says Empson, wants to scratch it, to see what is really there, and this scratching we call interpretation. Most men, says Schopenhauer, seek in objects "only some relation to their will, and with everything that has not such a relation there sounds within them, like a ground-bass, the constant, inconsolable lament, 'It is of no use to me.' " Though the link between art and impersonality is often acknowledged—in New Criticism as well as Neoclassic theory—no very successful *interpretive* use of the principle exists. The notion of impersonality is vulnerable because so easily retranslated into unconscious interest or the masked presence of some *force majeure.*

I try to face this problem of the ideology of form by choosing a poem without explicit social context and exploring its involvement in social and historical vision. This would be harder, needless to say, if Keats had not elsewhere explicitly worried the opposition of dreamer and poet or poet and thinker. Even if "To Autumn" were a holiday of the spirit, some workday concerns of the poet would show through. My use of the concept of ideology, at the same time, will seem half-way or uncritical to the Marxist thinker. In uncovering Keats's ideology I remain as far as possible within terms provided by Keats himself, or furnished by the ongoing history of poetry. This is not, I hope, antiquarianism, but also not transvaluation. It should be possible to consider a poem's *geschichtlicher Stundenschlag* (Adorno)—how it tells the time of history—without accepting a historical determinism. Keats's poetry is indeed an event in history: not in world-history, however, but simply in the history of fiction, in our awareness of the power and poverty of fictions.

My argument runs that "To Autumn," an ode that is hardly an ode, is best defined as an English or Hesperian model which overcomes not only the traditional type of sublime poem but the "Eastern" or epiphanic consciousness essential to it. The traditional type was transmitted by both Greek and Hebrew religious poetry, and throughout the late Renaissance and eighteenth century, by debased versions of the Pindaric or cult hymn.[4] Only one thing about epiphanic structure need be said now: it evokes the presence of a god, or vacillates sharply between imagined presence and absence. Its rhetoric is therefore a crisis-rhetoric, with priest or votary, vastation or rapture, precarious nearness or hieratic distance ("Ah Fear! Ah frantic Fear! I see, I see thee near!"). As these verses by William Collins suggest, epiphanic structure proceeds by dramatic turns of mood and its language is ejaculative (Lo, Behold, O come, O see). Keats's "Hesperianism" triumphs, in "To Autumn," over this archaic style with its ingrained, superstitious attitude toward power—power seen as external and epochal. The new sublimity domesticates with the heart; the poet's imagination is neither imp nor incubus. Though recognizably sublime, "To Autumn" is a poem of *our* climate.

Climate is important. It ripens wits as well as fruits, as Milton said in another context.[5] The higher temperature and higher style of the other odes are purged away: we have entered a temperate zone. What is grown here, this "produce of the air," is like its ambience: Hesperian art rather than oriental ecstasy or unnatural flight of the imagination. Autumn is clearly a mood as well as a season, and Stevens would have talked about a weather of the mind. Yet "mood" and "weather" have an aura of changeableness, even of volatility, while the Autumn ode expresses something firmer: not, as so often in Stevens or in the "Beulah" moments of other poets, a note among notes but, as in Spenser, a vast cloud-region or capability. The very shape of the poem—firm and regular without fading edges but also no overdefined contours—suggests a slowly expanding constellation that moves as a whole, if it moves at all.

Its motion is, in fact, part of the magic. Time lapses so gently here; we pass from the fullness of the maturing harvest to the stubble plains without experiencing a cutting edge. If time comes to a point in "To Autumn" it is only at the end of the poem, which verges (more poignant than pointed) on a last "gathering." The scythe of time, the sense of mortality, the cutting of life into distinct, epochal phases is not felt. We do not even stumble into revelation, however softly—there is no moment which divides before and after as in the "Ode to Psyche" with its supersoft epiphany, its Spenserian and bowery moment which makes the poet Psyche's devotee despite her "shadowy thought" nature. The Autumn ode is nevertheless a *poesis*, a shaped segment of life coterminous with that templar "region of the mind" which the other poems seek, though they may honor more insistently the dichotomy of inside and out, fane and profane. Poetry, to change "the whole habit of the mind,"[6] changes also our view of the mind's habitat. To say that "To Autumn" is ideological and that its pressure of form is "English" has to do with that also.

I begin with what is directly observable, rather than with curious knowledge of archaic ode or hymn. In the odes of Keats there is a strong, clearly marked moment of disenchantment, or of illusion followed by disillusion. Fancy, that "Queen of shadows" (Charlotte Smith), becomes a "deceiving elf"—and although the deception remains stylized, and its shock releases pathos rather than starker sentiments, it is as pointed as the traditional turn of the Great Ode. (Compare the turn, for example, from one mode of music to another in Dryden's *Alexander's Feast* or the anastrophe "He is not dead, he lives" in pastoral elegy.) The transition leading from stanzas 7 to 8 in the Nightingale ode is such a turn, which results in calling imagination a "deceiving elf." An imaginative fancy that has sustained itself despite colder thoughts is farewelled.

There is, exceptionally, no such turn in "To Autumn." The poem starts on enchanted ground and never leaves it. This special quality becomes even clearer when we recall that "La Belle Dame sans Merci," with its harvest background and soft ritual progression, ends in desolation of spirit on the cold hillside. But because the final turn of the Nightingale ode, though clear as a bell, is not gross in its effect, not productive of coital sadness, a comparison with Autumn's finale is still possible. In "To Autumn" birds are preparing to fly to a warmer clime, a "visionary south," though we do not see them leave or the cold interrupt. In "To a Nightingale" the poet is allowed a call—adieu, adieu—which is birdlike still and colors the darker "forlorn," while his complete awakening is delayed ("Do I wake or sleep?") and verbal prolongations are felt. There is no complete disenchantment even here.

"To Autumn," moreover, can be said to have something approaching a strophic turn as we enter the last stanza. With "Where are the songs of Spring? Aye, where are they?" a plaintive anthem sounds. It is a case, nevertheless, where a premise is anticipated and absorbed.[7] The premise is that of transience, or the feel of winter, and the rest of the stanza approaches that cold threshold. The premise is absorbed because its reference is back to Spring instead of forward to Winter; by shifting from eye to ear, to the music-theme, Keats enriches Autumn with Spring. We remain within a magical circle where things repeat each other in a finer tone, as Autumn turns into a second Spring: "While barred clouds *bloom* the soft-dying day" [8] The music now heard is no dirge of the year but a mingling of lullaby and aubade. For the swallows a second summer is at hand (aubade). For us—if we cannot follow them any more than the elusive nightingale—what comes next is not winter but night (lullaby). We go gently off, in either case, on extended wings.

Thus "To Autumn," like Stevens's "Sunday Morning," becomes oddly an Ode to Evening. The full meaning of this will appear. But in terms of formal analysis we can say that the poem has no epiphany or decisive turn or any absence / presence dialectic. It has, instead, a *westerly drift* like the sun. Each stanza, at the same time, is so equal in its poetical weight, so loaded with its own harvest, that westering is less a natural than a poetic state—it is a mood matured by the poem itself. "To Autumn," in fact, does not explicitly evolve from sunrise to sunset but rather from a rich to a clarified dark. Closely read it starts and ends in twilight. "Season of mists and mellow fruitfulness"—though the mists are of the morning, the line links fertility and semidarkness in a way that might be a syntactical accident were it not for the more highly developed instance of "I cannot see what flowers are at my feet . . . ," that famous stanza from the Nightingale ode where darkened senses also produce a surmise of fruitfulness. The Autumn ode's twilight is something inherent, a condition not simply of growth but of imaginative growth. Westering here is a spiritual movement, one that tempers visionariness into surmise and the lust for epiphany into finer-toned repetitions. We do not find ourselves in a temple but rather in Tempe "twixt sleepe and wake."[9] We can observe the ode unfolding as a self-renewing surmise of fruitfulness: as waking dream or "widening speculation" rather than nature-poem and secularized hymn.

Concerning *surmise:* I have suggested elsewhere its importance for Romantic poetry, how it hovers between factual and fantastic.[10] Its presence is often marked by a "magic casement" effect: as in Wordsworth's "Solitary Reaper," a window opens unexpectedly on a secret or faraway scene.

No nightingale did ever chaunt
More welcome notes to weary bands
Of travellers in some shady haunt,
Among Arabian sands:

Keats has the interesting habit of interpreting pictures (usually imaginary) as scenes beheld from a magic window of this kind. Yet since the frame of the window is also the frame of the picture, he finds himself on an ambiguous threshold, intimately near yet infinitely removed from the desired place. Most of the odes are a feverish quest to enter the life of a pictured scene, to be totally where the imagination is. In the Autumn ode, however, there is no effort to cross a magic threshold: though its three stanzas are like a composite picture from some Book of Hours, we are placed so exactly at the bourn of the invisible picture window that the frame is not felt, nor the desperate haunting of imagination to get in. There is no precipitous "Already with thee" and no stylized dejection.

Something, perhaps, is lost by this: the sense of dangerous transition, of consciousness opening up, of a frozen power unsealing. But the ode remains resolutely meditative. When important images of transition occur they are fully *composed* and no more vibrant than metrical enjambments: "And sometimes like a gleaner thou dost keep / Steady thy laden head." Or, "Sometimes whoever seeks may find / Thee sitting careless." Strictly construed the "sometimes" goes here both with the seeking and with the finding: it is factored out and made prepositional. This is a framing device which further augments the feeling of surmise, of lighthearted questing. What reverberates throughout, and especially in this image of the gleaner, the most pictorial of the poem, is a light but steady pondering. It is not a pondering, of course, devoid of all tension: "keep / Steady," understood as a performative or "cozening imperative,"[11] suggests that the poet is not so much describing as urging the image on, in-feeling it. Let us follow this picture-pondering from verse to verse.

The opening stanza is so strongly descriptive, so loaded with told riches, that there seems to be no space for surmise. A desire to fill every rift with Autumn's gold produces as rich a banquet as Porphyro's heap of delicates in "The Eve of St. Agnes." Thesaurus stanzas of this kind are self-delighting in Keats; but they also have a deeper reason. Porphyro knows that Madeline will find reality poorer than her dream and enhances his value by serving himself up this way. The sumptuous ploy is to help him melt into his lady's waking thought. So Autumn's banquet, perhaps, intends to hold the awakening consciousness and allow the dream to linger. Not only the bees are deceived; the dream "Warm days will never cease" is not in them alone; it is already in Autumn, in her "conspiring." On this phrase all the rich, descriptive details depend; they are infinitives not indicatives, so that we remain in the field of mind. "Conspiring how to load and bless . . . To bend with apples . . . fill all fruit . . . To swell the gourd." As we move through Autumn's thought to the ripening of that thought, we cease to feel her as an external agent.

Thus, the descriptive fullness of the first stanza turns out to be thought-full as well: its pastoral furniture is a golden surmise, imagination in her most deliberate mood. By moving the point of view inward, Keats makes these riches mental riches, imaginative projects. He does not, at the same time, push the mental horizon to infinity: the mood remains infinitive, looking onto "something evermore about to be."

Once we see that what is being satisfied is empathy or in-feeling,[12] and that to satisfy it Keats (like Autumn) fills outside with more and more inside, the structure of the poem as a progressive surmise becomes clear. In-feeling, in Keats, is always on the point of overidentifying; and even here it demands more than the first stanza's dream of truth. However glowing a prospect Autumn paints, it must still, as it were, come alive. This happens in the second stanza where the drowsy ponderer meets us in person. Now we are in the landscape itself; the harvest is now. The figure of Autumn amid her store is a moving picture, or the dream personified. Yet the two stanzas are perfectly continuous; in-feeling is still being expressed as the filling-up of a space—a figure like Autumn's was needed to plump the poem.

Though we approach epiphanic personification in the figure of Autumn, the casualness of "sometimes" "sometimes," together with the easy mood of the opening question, gives us a sense of "widening speculation" and prevents a more than cornucopial view of the goddess.

But the dream is almost shattered at the end of the stanza. The word "oozings" extends itself phonically into "hours by hours," a chime that leads to the idea of transience in "Where are the songs of Spring?" Though immediately reabsorbed, this muted ubi sunt introduces the theme of mutability. Oozings—hours—ubi sunt . . . A single word, or its echoes, might have disenchanted Keats like the turn on "forlorn" in the Nightingale ode. Disenchantment, however, does not occur: there is no reverse epiphany as in "La Belle Dame sans Merci," no waking into emptiness.

We have reached, nevertheless, the airiest of the stanzas. Does a chill wind not brush us, an airiness close to emptiness? Do we not anticipate the "cold hill's side"? Even if the mood of surmise is sustained, it might well be a surmise of death rather than fruitfulness.

Here, at the consummate point of Keats's art, in-feeling achieves its subtlest act. Keats conspires with autumn to fill even the air. Air becomes a granary of sounds, a continuation of the harvest, or *Spätlese.* In this last and softest stanza, the ear of the ear is ripened.

More than a tour de force or finely sustained idea is involved. For at the end of other odes we find an explicit *cry,* which is part of their elegiac envoi. Here that cry is uttered, as it were, by the air itself, and can only be heard by an ear that knows how to glean such sounds. What is heard, to quote the modern poet closest to Keats,

> *is not a cry of divine attention,*
> *Nor the smoke-drift of puffed-out heroes, nor human cry.*
> *It is the cry of leaves that do not transcend themselves.*[13]

In lyric poetry the cry is a sign of subjective feelings breaking through and in the cult-hymn of being possessed by divine power. It signifies in both a transcendence absent from this "final finding of the air." Lyricism, in "To Autumn," frees itself for once of elegy and ecstasy: it is neither a frozen moment of passion nor the inscription that prolongs it.

The Grecian urn's "Beauty is Truth, Truth Beauty" remains an extroverted, lapidary cry. However appropriate its philosophy, its form is barely snatched from a defeat of the imagination. "To Autumn" has no defeat in it. It is the most negative capable of all of Keats's great poems. Even its so-called death-stanza[14] expresses no rush toward death, no clasping of darkness as a bride, or quasi-oriental ecstasy. Its word-consciousness, its mind's weather—all remains Hesperian. As its verses move toward an image of southerly flight (the poem's nearest analogue to transcendence), patterns emerge that delay the poet's "transport to summer." Perception dwells on the border and refuses to overdefine. So "fullgrown lambs" rather than "sheep." Add such verbal ponderings or reversing repetitions as "borne aloft . . . hilly bourn," a casual chiastic construction, playing on a mix of semantic and phonetic properties. Or the noun-adjective phrase "treble soft" which becomes an adjective-noun phrase when "treble" is resolved into the northern "triple." And consider the northernisms. The proportion of northern words increases perceptibly as if to pull the poem back from its southerly orientation. There is hardly a romance language phrase: sound-shapes like sallows, swallows, borne, bourn, crickets, croft, predominate.[15] And, finally, the poise of the stanza's ending, on the verge of flight like joy always bidding adieu. How easily, in comparison, Hölderlin turns eastward and converts wish into visionary transport on the wings of an older rhetoric:

These my words, when, rapt
faster than I could have known,
and far, to where I never
thought to come, a Genius
took me from my own house. They glimmered
in the twilight, as I went,
the shadowy wood
and the yearning brooks
of my country; I knew the fields no more;
Yet soon, brighter and fresher,

mysterious
under the golden smoke
flowering, rising fast before me
in the sun's steps
with a thousand fragrant hills
Asia dawned

("Patmos")

Less magnificent, equally magnanimous, "To Autumn" remains a poem "in the northwind sung." Its progress is merely that of repetitions "in a finer tone," of "widening speculation," of "treble soft" surmise. Yet in its Hesperian reach it does not give up but joins a south to itself.

Keats's respect for the sublime poem does not have to be argued. There is his irritation with the "egotistical sublime" of Wordsworth, his admiration for Milton who broke through "the clouds which envelope so deliciously the Elysian field of verse, and committed himself to the Extreme," his anguished attempt to write the *Hyperion*, and the testimony of lesser but affecting verses like those to the "God of the Meridian" in which he foresees madness:

when the soul is fled
To high above our head,
Afrighted do we gaze
After its airy maze,
As doth a mother wild,
When her young infant child
Is in an eagle's claws—
And is not this the cause
Of madness?—God of Song,
Thou bearest me along
Through sights I scarce can bear

The "bear . . . bear" pun shows well enough the tension of epic flight. I must now make clear what kind of problem, formal and spiritual, the sublime poem was.

A first difficulty centers on the relation of romance to sublime or epic. The romance mode, for Keats, is now presublime (and so to be "broken through") and now postsublime. Where, as in the first *Hyperion*, Keats wishes to sublimate the sublime he turns with relief to the "golden theme" of Apollo after the Saturnine theme of the first two books. In the *Fall of Hyperion*, however, romance is an Elysium or Pleasure-garden to be transcended. While in "La Belle Dame sans Merci" romance becomes sheer oxymoron, a "golden tongued" nightmare.

It is best to find a view beyond this special dialectic of romance and epic in Keats, all the more so as that is complicated by the dream-truth, or vision-reality split. No formal analysis will disentangle these rich contraries. It can only reduce them to the difference suggested in the *Fall of Hyperion* between "an immortal's sphered words" and the mother-tongue. This is the dichotomy on which Keats's epic voyage foundered: the opposition between Miltonic art-diction and the vernacular. "Life to him [Milton] would be death to me." "English must be kept up." Yet such a distinction is no more satisfying than one in terms of genre. Vernacular romance is perhaps more feasible than vernacular epic—but we get as mixed up as Keats himself when we define each genre in family terms and put romance under mother, epic under father. In the *Fall of Hyperion* Moneta is as patriarchal as she is womanly.

A solution is to consider both romance and epic—or the high-visionary style in general—as belonging to an older, "epiphanic" structuring of consciousness. Against it can be put a nonepiphanic structuring; and if the older type is primarily associated with the East, the modern would be with the West or, at its broadest, Hesperia.[16] It is possible to treat this distinction formally as one between two types of structuring rather than two types of consciousness. Eventually, however, Keats's charge of superstition or obsolescence against the earlier mode will move us into ideology and beyond formalism. A man who says, like Keats, that life to Milton is death to him is concerned with more than formal options.

Epiphanic structure implies, first of all, the possibility of categorical shifts: of crossing into *allo genere*, and even, I suppose, out of ordinary human consciousness into something else. Apotheosis (as at the end of *Hyperion*), metamorphosis, and transformation scenes are type instances of such a crossing. It is accompanied by a doctrine of states, a philosophy of transcendence, and a formulary for the "translation" of states. Epiphanic structure can bear as much sophistication as an author is capable of. Take the sequence, based on *Paradise Lost*, Book VIII, which haunted Keats: "The Imagination may be compared to Adam's Dream: He awoke and found it truth."[17] This refers chiefly to Adam seeing Eve first in dream and, upon waking, in the flesh. Keats will often use it ironically rather than not use it at all. So in the "Eve of St. Agnes" Madeline wakes into Imagination's truth and finds it—how pale, how diminished! She melts the reality—Porphyro—back into her dream in a moment of, presumably, sexual union.

A more complex instance is the dark epiphany in "La Belle Dame sans Merci" where the enchanted knight wakes, as it were, into the arms of the wrong dream and cannot find his way back to the right one. Whereas, in Milton, one cunning enjambment expresses the intensity of the quest springing from imaginative loss,

She [Eve] disappear'd, and left me dark, I wak'd
To find her

a moment Keats repeats faintly in the Autumn ode,

Sometimes whoever seeks abroad may find
Thee

in "La Belle Dame" there is nothing—no natural food—can satisfy the knight. He starves for his drug, like Keats so often for the heightened consciousness of epiphanic style.

In *Paradise Lost*, Adam's dream prepares him for the truth he is to meet. Truth is conceived of as a fuller, perhaps more difficult, dream; and God seeks to strengthen Adam's visionary powers by engaging him in these dream-corridors. Instead of a single dramatic or traumatic change there is to be a gradual tempering of the mind. This modification of epiphanic structure may have inspired a favorite speculation of Keats, that happiness on earth would be enjoyed hereafter "repeated in a finer tone and so repeated." Miltonic tenderness, by allowing Adam's consciousness to develop, by giving it time for growth, lightens the all-or-nothing (sometimes, all-and-nothing) character of epiphanic vision.[18] Though the end remains transport and deification, the means are based, at least in part, on a respect for natural process.

The naturalization of epiphanic form is less effective in "La Belle Dame" than in this prototypal sequence from Milton. The reason lies perhaps in the genre as much as in Keats himself. Quest-romance is a particularly resistant example of epiphanic form. Though Spenser helps to detumesce it he also throws its archaic lineaments into relief: his faërie remains a montage, a learned if light superposition. The dominant feature of quest-romance (as of fairy-tale) is the ever-present danger of trespass: of stepping all at once or unconsciously into a daemonic field of force. Often the quest is motivated by redeeming such a prior trespass; but even when it starts unburdened it cannot gain its diviner end without the danger of *allo genere* crossings. Keats's knight steps ritually, if unknowingly, into demonry. So also Coleridge's mariner, whose act of trespass is clear but who before it and after crosses also invisible demarcations. From this perspective the exile of Adam and Eve and the wanderings of Odysseus are both the result of a trespass against the divine, or of stepping willy-nilly into a daemonic sphere.[19]

This is not the place to work out the formal variations of quest-romance. But when a poet does succeed in subduing the form, the result is both remarkable and mistakable. In "Strange Fits of Passion" Wordsworth's rider is a becalmed knight from Romance whose rhythm parodies the chivalric gallop and who is always approaching yet never crossing a fatal border. The moon that drops and deflates the dreaming into a mortal thought is a pale metonymy of itself when considered against the backdrop of epiphanic romance. It alone belongs to the sphere of "strange fits"; and while it still divides before and after and even suggests that an imaginative or unconscious trespass has occurred, it cannot be drawn fully into the lunatic symbolism of romance. Keats, I think, did not manage to humanize this form: he feared too much that leaving Romance behind meant being exiled from great poetry. He was unable to "translate" the inherited code either into the Miltonic Extreme or into Wordsworth's fulfillment of Miltonic tenderness.

And yet: did he not humanize epiphanic form in the special case of the ode? Recent scholarship by Kurt Schlüter and others has established the basic form of the ancient cult-hymn as it impinged on European poetry.[20] The easiest division of the form is, as you might expect, into three: invocation, narrative or mythic portion, and renewed invocation. Sappho's "Ode to Aphrodite" is a clear example, so is Shelley's "Ode to the West Wind." Basically, however, the structure consists simply of a series of apostrophes or turns petitioning an absent god or attesting his presence. To the modern reader it may all seem somewhat hysterical: a succession of cries modulated by narrative or reflective interludes.

The sublime or greater or Pindaric ode flourished in the eighteenth century like a turgid weed, all pseudo-epiphany and point, bloat and prickles, feeding off an obsolescent style. Dr. Johnson vilified Gray's Pindaric experiments as "cucumbers." The best that can be said for the genre is that like contemporary opera it became a refuge for visionary themes: an exotic and irrational entertainment which reminded the indulgent consumer of the polite good sense of his society, and sent him back, all afflatus spent, to trifle with the lesser ode. It is not till Collins that a dialogue begins within the genre between its sublime origins and the English ground to which it is transplanted.

A brief notice of this dialogue in Collins's "Ode to Evening" prepares us for Keats. Collins uses all the features characterizing the sublime ode except one. His extended apostrophe suggests the hieratic distance between votary and the invoked power, anticipates at the same time its presence, and leads into a narrative second half describing in greater detail the coming of the divinity and its effect on the poet. This is followed by a renewed invocation which acts as the poem's coda. The one feature conspicuously absent is the epiphany proper. The invoked personification, evening, is a transitional state, a season of the day, whose advent is its presence. By addressing in epiphanic terms a subject intrinsically nonepiphanic, and adjusting his style subtly to it, Collins opens the way to a new, if still uneasy, nature-poetry.

What adjustments of style are there? The movement of the ode is highly mimetic, as Collins, suiting his numbers to the nature of evening, slows and draws out his musings.

If aught of oaten stop, or pastoral song,
May hope, chaste Eve, to soothe thy modest ear,
Like thy own solemn springs
Thy springs and dying gales
O nymph reserved, while now . . .

Instead of hastening some eclipsing power, or leaping into a fuller present, his verse becomes a programmatic accompaniment to the gradual fall of night. The form, in other words, is self-fulfilling: as the processional verse blends with processual nature, and an expanding shadow (a "gradual, dusky veil") is all of relevation there is, the poet's prayer results in what it asks for: "Now teach me, *Maid* compos'd / To breathe some soften'd Strain." This "now" is only in echo that of an ecstatic, annihilative present: it refers to an actual time of day, and perhaps to a belated cultural moment. With this drawn-out "now" nature-poetry is born:

and now with treble soft
The red-breast whistles from the garden-croft;
And gathering swallows twitter in the skies.

Collins's "soften'd strain," his conversion of epiphanic style, will find its culminating instance in Keats's poetry of process.

That Collins represents Evening as a god is more than a naturalized archaism. Evening, invoked as the source of a new music, stands for Hesperia, the evening-star land; and what the poet asks for, in these prelusive strains, is a genuinely western verse, an *Abendlandpoesie.* Like Keats's Psyche, Evening is a new goddess: the poetic pantheon of the East contained only Sun and Night, but Evening is peculiar to the Western hemisphere. In the courts of the East, as Coleridge noted in his *Ancient Mariner*, "At one stride comes the dark." The East, in its sudden dawn and sudden darkness, is epiphanic country. But the English climate, in weather or weather of the mind, has a more temperate, even, evening effect. Collins embraces the idea that his native country, or the cultural region to which it belonged, has a style and vision of its own.[21] He shows spirit of place as a felt influence, and gothic eeriness as eariness. That is, he uncovers a new sense for nature by uncovering a new sense: the natural ear. What the sublime ode had attempted by overwhelming the eye—or the "descriptive and allegoric style" which dominates the age—Collins achieves through this finer sense. The eye, as in Wordsworth's "Tintern Abbey," and in the last stanza of "To Autumn," is made quiet by "the power of harmony."

In the "Ode to Evening" the concept of a Hesperian poetry conditions even sensory mimesis or impels it into a new region. It is no accident that the last stanza of "To Autumn" contains an evening ode in small. That "Evening Ear," which Collins elsewhere attributes to Milton, is, to use a rare Wordsworthian pun, an *organ of vision*: responsive to a particular climate or "spiritual air" (*Endymion*, IV) in which poets feel themselves part of a belated and burdened culture yet find their own relation to the life of things. As the landscape darkens gently, the blind and distant ear notices tones—finer tones—that had escaped a dominant and picture-ridden eye: a weak-eyed bat flits by, curious emblem, and the beetle emerges winding its horn, as if even pastoral had its epic notes. There is still, in Collins, this airy faërie which has often dissolved in Keats—who, however, is never very far from it. What matters is that creatures jargon, like "To Autumn"'s parliament of birds; that the sounds are real sounds, a produce of the air; that the heard is not exclusively divine or human; and that within the sheltering dark of the ear other senses emerge: "I cannot see what flowers are at my feet, / Nor what soft incense hangs upon the bough, / But in embalmed darkness guess each sweet." Here absence is presence, though not by way of mystical or epiphanic reversal. In every temperate zone the air is full of noises.

This sensory ideology, if I may call it such,[22] must have affected Keats one early autumn day looking at stubble fields:

How beautiful the season is now—How fine the Air. A temperate sharpness about it. Really, without joking, chaste weather—Dian skies—I never lik'd stubble fields so much as now—Aye better than the chilly green of the spring. Somehow a stubble plain looks warm—in the same way that some pictures look warm—this struck me so much in my sunday's walk that I composed upon it.

That ideology is in the air is proven by what follows:

I always somehow associate Chatterton with Autumn. He is the purest writer in the English language. [Chatterton's language is entirely northern.] He has no French idiom, or particles like Chaucer—'tis genuine English idiom in English words. I have given up Hyperion. . . . English ought to be kept up.[23]

We have already commented on the northernisms in "To Autumn" 's last stanza: even romance language (let alone romance) is gently shunned. Nothing but "home-bred glory."

Can we see the gods die in "To Autumn," the epiphanic forms dissolve, as it were, before our eyes? Autumn is, by tradition, the right season for this dissolution, or dis-illusion.

Let Phoebus lie in umber harvest

Stevens writes in "Notes toward a Supreme Fiction,"

Let Phoebus slumber and die in autumn umber
Phoebus is dead, ephebe.

But, in tradition also, a new god treads on the heels of the old, and loss figures forth a stronger presence. In Hesperian poetry, from Collins to Keats to Stevens, this entire absence/presence vacillation does no more than manure the ground of the poem, its "sensible ecstasy."

Consider the invocation "Season of mists and mellow fruitfulness." The odic O is hardly felt though the verses immediately fill one's mouth with rich labials extended in a kind of chiastic middle between "Season" and "sun." Nothing remains of the cultic distance between votary and personified power: we have instead two such powers, autumn and sun, whose closeness is emphasized, while the moment of hailing or petitioning is replaced by a presumptive question ("Who hath not seen thee") suggesting availability rather than remoteness. The most interesting dissolve, however, comes with the grammatical shift, in the opening line, from mythic-genealogical to descriptive-partitive "of," which effectively diffuses autumn into its attributes. Compare "Season of mists and mellow fruitfulness" with the following apostrophes:

Thou foster-child of silence and slow time.

Here the poet uses clearly and finely a formula which alludes to the high descent of the apostrophized object. In our next example

Nymph of the downward smile, and side-long glance

the grammatical form is analogous, but the "of" has moved from genealogical toward partitive. The nymph is eminently characterized by these two attributes: they *are* her in this statuesque moment. The opening of "To the Nile":

Son of the old moon-mountains African
Stream of the pyramid and crocodile

actually brings mythic-genealogical and partitive-descriptive together. Against this background we see how beautifully dissolved into the ground of description is the mythical formula of "To Autumn" 's first line.

We do, of course, by what appears to be a regressive technique, meet Autumn personified in the second stanza. If the poem approaches a noon-point of stasis—of arrest or centered revelation—it is here. The emergence of myth serves, however, to ripen the pictorial quality of the poem rather than to evoke astonishment. The emphasis is on self-forgetful relaxation (at most on "forget thyself to marble") not on saturnine fixation. No more than in "To Evening" is nature epiphanic: Keats's autumn is not a specter but a spirit, one who steals over the landscape, or "amid her store" swellingly imbues it.[24] The poet's mind is not rapt or astonished and so forced back on itself by a sublime apparition.

It is essential, in fact, to note what happens to mind. In the cult hymn the invocation merges with, or is followed by, the god's *comos:* an enumeration of his acts and attributes.[25] But Keats's first stanza becomes simply the filling up of a form, a golden chain of infinitives hovering between prospect and fulfillment, until every syntactical space is loaded and the poet's mind like the bees', loses itself in the richness. The stanza, in fact, though full, and with its eleven lines, more than full, is not a grammatical whole but a drunk sentence. The poet's mind, one is tempted to say, has entered the imagined picture so thoroughly that when the apostrophe proper is sprung at the opening of stanza 2, and the grammatical looseness corrected, it simultaneously opens a new speculative movement. And when the generative figure of Autumn appears in the second stanza, it is self-harvesting like the poet's own thoughts. The last stanza, then, leaves us in a "luxury of twilight" rather than dropping us into a void where "no birds sing."

The demise of epiphanic forms in "To Autumn" raises a last question: is not the sequential movement of the whole poem inspired by a progressive idea with Enlightenment roots? There seems to be, on the level of sensation, something that parallels the first *Hyperion*'s progress from heavier to lighter, from Hyperion to Apollo, and from fixed burdens to a softer oppression. Several key phrases in Keats's letters suggest an "enlightenment" of this kind. The poet talks of "widening speculation," of "the regular stepping of Imagination toward a Truth," and of easing the "Burden of the Mystery." Magical moments like the fourth stanza of "Ode on a Grecian Urn"

Who are these coming to the sacrifice?
To what green altar, O mysterious priest

are surely related to this lightening. Mystery survives, but in a purged, airy, speculative form. The "overwrought" questions of the ode's beginning, which sought to penetrate or fix a symbol-essence, are purified into surmise and evoke a scene of "wide quietness" rather than bacchic enthusiasm.

There is a progress then; but is it toward a truth? We know what the conclusion to the Grecian Urn ode suggests. "Beauty is Truth, Truth Beauty" is a chiastic phrase, as self-rounding as the urn. No ultimate turn or final step toward a truth occurs. Though there are turns in the poem, they are more musical than epiphanic, and the very notion of "the turn" merges with that of the art-object: Keats turns the urn in his imagination until the urn is its turnings. The poet's speculation is circular.

Keats's rondure, his counterprogression, subverts without rejecting the received idea of "enlightenment." Poetry clearly has its own progress, its own lights. Formalistic or art-centered terms have, therefore, a certain propriety. But they cannot suffice for Keats any more than for Wordsworth, who also seeks to ease the "burthen of the mystery" ("Tintern Abbey," line 39). Consider the profound difference between these poets, who both believe in a dispersion of older—poetical or religious—superstitions. Such qualities as decorum, impersonality, symbolic adequacy are a function mainly of the concenteredness of "To Autumn": the poem turns around one image like a "leaf-fring'd legend." Though Wordsworth's poems may also have a center of this kind (Lucy's death, a peculiar landscape, a remembered scene), it rarely appears as picturesque symbol or image. Wordsworth's kernels are mysteries: charged spiritual places which confront and confuse a mental traveler who circles their enchanted ground—or who, like a policeman, tries to cordon off the disturbance. This too is an important "enlightenment" form, delimiting a romance apparition or sublime feelings—yet how different from Keats! In Wordsworth the spirit must find its own containment, and never quite finds it; those "spots of time" erupt from their hiding-places like the Hebraic God; the structure of his poems expresses various attempts at containment which accrete with difficulty into a personal history ("Tintern Abbey") or an eschatological and cultural one ("Hart-Leap Well"). But Keats's experience is limited from the outset by Greek or picturesque example. What perplexes his imagination is a mysterious picture rather than a mystery.

Keats's formal a priori takes us back to Greece and where, according to Hegel, modern consciousness began. Formal beauty mediates "between the loss of individuality . . . as in Asia, where spiritual and divine are totally subsumed under a natural form, and infinite subjectivity." Greek character is "individuality conditioned by beauty" and in its respect for divine images modern and free, rather than Asiatic and superstitious. "He [the human being] is the womb that conceived them, he the breast that suckled them, he the spiritual to which their grandeur and purity is owing. Thus he feels himself calm in contemplating them, and not only free in himself, but possessing the consciousness of his freedom." [26]

That Hegel's description can fit Keats makes one cautious about the whole enterprise of dividing consciousness into historically localized phases. All the more so as Hölderlin has his own myth of the Hesperian character, which is said to begin when Homer moderates oriental pathos or "fire from heaven." [27] I make no claim for the historical exactness of either Hegel or Hölderlin. Historical speculation and criticism stand, as Professor Wimsatt has observed, in a highly problematic relationship.[28]

Yet there is something like "Hesperian" freedom in "To Autumn," a poem which becomes—in Hegel's words—the womb for the rebirth of an astral or divine image. Such a divine image is certainly there; we should not exaggerate the absence of poetical superstition in Keats. Though his central figure is picturesque its star quality glimmers through.

Much has been written on Autumn's affinities to Demeter or other harvest deities.[29] The divinity, however, that haunts Keats early and late is Apollo: sun-god, god of song, and "fore-seeing god." [30] The difference between Hyperion and Apollo is in good part, that the former is now doomed to live under "the burden of the mystery." Hyperion cannot dawn any more; he remains darkling. But Apollo in *Hyperion*, even though that poem breaks off and leaves the young god's metamorphosis incomplete—even though he too must shoulder the mystery—should break forth like the sun to "shape his actions" like "a fore-seeing god." [31] In the Autumn ode the major theme of clairvoyance—at once foreseeing and deep-seeing (deep into the heart or maw of life)—is tempered.[32] Yet it is far from absent.

For Autumn's "conspiring" function is comparable to that of the guardian genius, the *natale comes qui temperat astrum.*[33] An idea of poetic or personal destiny enters, in however veiled a form. The poet who writes this ode stands under the pressure of an omen. As summer passes into autumn (season of the year or human season), his dreaming deepens into foresight:

When I have fears that I may cease to be
Before my pen has glean'd my teeming brain,
Before high-piled books, in charact'ry,
Hold like rich garners the full-ripen'd grain . . .

Herr: es ist Zeit. Der Sommer war sehr gross [34]

In fear of early death, and sensing riches his pen might never glean, Keats evokes a figure of genial harvests. Three times he renews his surmise of fruitfulness, three times he grasps the shadow without self-defeating empathy. Even fruitfulness is not a burden in "To Autumn." This, at last, is true impersonality.

Evening Star and Evening Land

to say of the evening star,
The most ancient light in the most ancient sky
That it is wholly an inner light, that it shines
From the sleepy bosom of the real, re-creates,
Searches a possible for its possibleness.

Wallace Stevens

The perished patterns murmur

Emily Dickinson

For most readers the charm of Akenside's "Ode to the Evening Star," a minorpiece of the 1740s,[1] resides in its first stanza, perhaps even in its first two lines:

To-night retir'd, the queen of heaven
With young Endymion stays:
And now to Hesper it is given
Awhile to rule the vacant sky,
Till she shall to her lamp supply
A stream of brighter rays.

The rising of the moon is delayed, in Akenside's version of the myth, because she is dallying with a human lover, the shepherd Endymion; there is something like a divine, erotic slowing of time, familiar from myths associated with Jove or the prevention of dawn; the theme of "staying" (l. 2) leads, moreover, into that of "supply" (l. 5), so that it is tempting to connect the moon's dalliance with her brightened lamp, her refurbished rising. Yet the myth does not flower into the form of an epyllion or little romance: it glimmers above the action like a distant star or constellated image. The poem remains a curious variant on addresses to the Evening Star. Hesper's brief reign suits perhaps the idea of the brief hymn whose prototype the eighteenth century found in a small poem attributed to Bion.[2]

Bion's influence can only be understood through some ideal of classic decorum, of silver mediocrity. His poem approximates the length of an epigram or what was considered as its modern form, the sonnet—and it is a juvenile sonnet Coleridge will hymn to *his* Evening Star in 1790.[3] But in Akenside a tension is felt between the compact form and its narrative elaboration. If his opening stanza is more condensed and suggestive than anything in Bion, the remainder of this poem of 78 lines (compared to Bion's eight) is devious and prolix. Akenside seems to have a problem with "development" or "manner of proceeding," not uncommon in eighteenth-century lyrics, and especially nature poems.

In the Romantic poets the nature lyric is as much about consciousness as about nature. Moreover, it is often about the *development* of consciousness; and this dynamic factor helps poets in the otherwise paradoxical task to plot, or narrate, nature. Akenside's problem may hinge, similarly, on finding a developmental pattern. Not for nature so much as for poetry: how can poetry, at this time in its life, be developed? Does it have a future or only a past? The course of the poem is so stylized that one thinks of the sorrows of the poet rather than of Olympia's mourning lover—the tears are tears of the muses, cultured pearls. The poet's concern seems to be with literary rather than personal continuity, or how the first bears on the second. Hesper is invoked as a link in a symbolic chain leading from loss to acceptance, and strongly suggesting the centrality of poetic sublimation.

New Lamps for Old

In its simple form, patterned on Bion, the Hymn to the Evening Star makes Hesper a surrogate moon, a night-light guiding lover to beloved. But Akenside has "herald Hesper" (Keats) light the way to loss rather than to the beloved, for the star leads him to a second symbolic agent, the nightingale, which wakes memories of loss under the very moon that is the traditional sign of consummated love or restored presence. Ben Jonson's famous lyric from *Cynthia's Revels* (1601) with the refrain "Hesperus entreats thy light/Goddess excellently bright" and Milton's "Now came still Ev'ning on" (*Paradise Lost*, VI. 598–609) follow the straight pattern and so illumine the deviousness of the later ode. Hesperus, in Milton, is to the absence of light as the nightingale is to that of sound: both are "wakeful" powers that bridge a dark moment and prepare hierarchically for the emergence of the moon as "Apparent Queen." Compared to the purity of Jonson's, Milton's, and Bion's sequence, Akenside's lyric is the night-ramble of a gloomy egotist.

The formal problem is made more intriguing by the fact that the first three stanzas of the hymn, though prelusive, are a detachable unit. Close in theme and length to Bion's lyric, they constitute a small hailing that sets the scene (first stanza), invokes the star (second stanza), and rounds the invocation with a vow (third stanza). Their internal structure is equally cohesive. What the moon is to Endymion, Hesper is to be for the poet: both condescend, the one for love-brightness, the other for the poet's sake. This descendentalism exists, however, within a vivid sense of hierarchy. The latinate diction, in fact, and the elaborate, even contrived syntax of lines 9 to 12

Oh listen to my suppliant song,
If haply now the vocal sphere
Can suffer thy delighted ear
To stoop to mortal sounds

sensitize the reader to the whole question of subordination.

The poem's formal development is closely linked to the tension that surrounds the concept of subordination. If the first three stanzas are contortedly archaic in their evocation of sidereal hierarchy and the last three a moralizing frame aiming at a similar kind of overview, the middle or narrative portion of the ode depicts a reversal of influence. Philomel gradually becomes a star-symbol replacing Hesper, as he the moon. Though we begin in heaven, and stars stoop to conquer, as we approach ritually the magic center or "green space" of the nightingale (a centering movement we meet often in this type of poem), power flows from earth to heaven. In stanza 7 the nightingale's song "holds" the moon above the lovers in a repetition of the "staying" which began the ode, and in stanza 10 the breezes that attend the path of the nightingale's song repeat the star's attendance on Hesper (ll. 6–7):

Hark, how through many a melting note
She now prolongs her lays:
How sweetly down the void they float!
The breeze their magic path attends:
The stars shine out: the forest bends:
The wakeful heifers gaze.

This transfer of power, or reversal of earthly and starry agents, was foreshadowed by syntactical and phonemic stresses in the opening stanzas.[4]

"Far other vows must I prefer . . ." With these words, and still paying formal tribute to Hesper, Akenside deviates from Bion. He converts the Evening Star poem into something psychic and strange, haunted by loss, memory, sublimation, and the influence of poetic song. He leads us to a symmetrical and cunning space:

See the green space: on either hand
Inlarg'd it spreads around:
See, in the midst she takes her stand . . .

both empty and full, natural yet ghostly. That narrow, clearly framed, yet open space is not unlike poetry, especially when based on the classical sense of centering. The very predominance of a prototype, the very fixation on theme or symbol, becomes the poet's way to a wilder symbolic action and an enlarged vision of continuity.

A Phenomenological Thematics

The Evening Star poem is a fickle and minor genre. But its brief span of life, mainly as an eighteenth-century idyllion, belies the interest of a theme which poets occasionally renew and which is constantly merging with the larger question of continuity—personal or historical. The dual name of the star, Hesper (Vesper) and Phosphor (Venus), evening and morning star, and its "genial" (Venus-y or procreative) aspect make it symbolic of a continuity that persists within apparent loss. The epigram attributed to Plato and rendered by Shelley as

Thou wert the morning star among the living
Ere thy fair light had fled;—
Now, having died, thou art as Hesperus, giving
New splendour to the dead [5]

is the very emblem of triumphant sublimation, of identity maintained in the realms of death.

In its broadest literary aspect, the starry theme becomes expressive of the problematics of *poesy* Is there a true literary-historical continuity, a great chain of great poets, or how much vision (sublime style) can be saved? By 1750 the starry theme was in doubt; and while Blake in his deep and virtuoso way talks once more of poets "appearing" to him in the "poetical heavens," their succession is generally felt to be uncertain. Gray's "Stanzas to Mr. Bentley" (1752) expresses the sense of his age that poetry is in eclipse.

But not to one in this benighted age
Is that diviner inspiration given,
That burns in Shakespear's or in Milton's page,
The pomp and prodigality of heav'n.

This "not to one" may well echo Collins's "Ode on the Poetical Character," which assumes that each age has "one only one" significant poet and that his own age has not even him:

Heav'n, and Fancy, kindred Pow'rs,
Have now o'erturned th' inspiring Bow'rs,
Or curtain'd close such Scene from ev'ry future View.

Despite this cultural pessimism, hope does not die. Blake realized that the poets' loss of confidence was related to a wrong understanding of poetry's high seriousness. The divine makers of the previous era had raised poetry to the skies. Their strength had shown that Poetry and Divinity were "kindred pow'rs." But this did not mean poetry could compete with religion on religion's ground—as Milton had "inimitably" done. To burden it with divinity, to raise it to a sky preempted by the frozen forms of national religion, was to sink it under a weight Dr. Johnson's obstinate bass unwearily reiterated: "The good and evil of Eternity are too ponderous for the wings of wit. The mind sinks under them in passive helplessness, content with calm belief and humble admiration." The sidereal universe of religion, as he also said, could not be magnified.

In these circumstances, to bring an angel down could be more important than to raise a mortal to the skies. I will call this harrowing of the skies the descendental theme. So Milton enters Blake's left foot, and was already shown by Collins (in a complex image that goes up and down simultaneously) in the Eden of his own invention, and raising an "Evening Ear" from its ethereal dews toward a sphery music.[6]

Yet *poesy* is by no means a direct subject of evening star poems. The larger historical pathos is simply part of their aura. We begin, rather, with "the nightes dread," [7] a power failure or dangerous interval, a moment when the light goes out. The evening star rises in that space, on that loss; and however strongly it rises there is often the fear of new withdrawal ("Soon, full soon, dost thou withdraw" [8]) and the dangerous sense that "sacred dew" or starry "influence" no longer prevails. To the descendental theme we can add, therefore, that of the dangerous, *interlunar* moment.

It is remarkable that in Blake's poem on the evening star the moon does not actually rise; but were it to rise it would just be a second star rather than a transcending presence. "Genius dies with its Possessor, and does not rise again until Another is born." There is a difference between Blake and Milton on this: Blake thinks of each great poet as a new and equal star.

Indeed, though Hesperus is traditionally the moon's precursor, it can be subversive of that "laboring" planet. As the most brilliant of the early stars it becomes for the expectant mind a singular mark. It seems absolute in its "steadfast" (if often brief) presence, and begins to stand for itself rather than for something to come. It expresses a power of feeling that is both solipsistic and unchanging, or so transcendently hopeful as not to be fulfilled by a temporal—chronologically easy—next stage. Its "intense lamp" does not die into another light: it narrows into itself, or sets unmodified in a kind of *liebestod*.[9]

With this we reach a difficult and subtle motif. As the moon of its own twilight zone, Hesperus tends to personify the threshold and evoke an enchanted spot of time in which a richly ominous signifier is all there is. The star-signifier appears as a sign accompanied by signs, or leading to other symbols rather than to a sign-transcending reality. Since man cannot live by signs alone, the evening star poem rouses our reality-hunger and perplexes the very idea of *development.*

In this it is like love itself, or desire The star cannot be more than a sign, given the intensity of the desire invoking it. The poem feeds the sign, even fattens it: it wants it to be, if not more than a sign, then more of a sign. Yet the most successful poetry is still, so Shelley knew, "as darkness to a dying flame." The symbol remains a threshold; and the idea of development, of a waxing and waning that is also a ripening, a movement beyond mutability, remains moot. Darkness reenters the progression of interlunar moment, evening star, moonrise, at any point.

Why then, one might ask, do we need a starry paradigm at all? Could not any pseudo-progression serve? The reason why there is a star-symbolism is clarified by Los's struggle with his Spectre:

Los reads the Stars of Albion! the Spectre reads the Voids
Between the Stars; among the Arches of Albion's Tomb
sublime. . . .

Plate 91 of *Jerusalem* shows Los decreating the sublime structures of traditional visionary poetry, which have been, in Blake's interpretation, a "Tomb sublime," that is, built upon, or in fearful reaction to, "the Voids." Los smites the Spectre, or his ingrained habits of perceiving, until

all his pyramids were grains
Of sand & his pillars: dust on the flys wing: & his starry
Heavens; a moth of gold & silver mocking his anxious grasp.

What is foreseen here, though not attained—for Los remains "anxious," trembling before his new-found mortality as previously before phantoms—is a sublimity not based on sublimation. The stars, therefore, remain, but become as mortal (or immortal) as men. They are "consumed" like erotic desire and reborn out of its satisfaction:

The stars consumd like a lamp blown out & in their stead behold
The Expanding Eyes of Man behold the depths of wondrous worlds
One Earth one sea beneath nor Erring Globes wander but Stars
Of fire rise up nightly from the Ocean & one Sun
Each morning like a New born Man issues with songs & Joy [10]

The most interesting Romantic lyrics do not begin in the sky. They begin, nevertheless, with an interlunar moment created by the descendental "smiting" so powerfully stylized in Blake. There is a downward displacement of the stars which gives the impression of (1) sidereal darkness and (2) new powers (stars) emerging from below. Poetry itself, at this point in history, is generically associated with this downward displacement of the sky's energies. Our phenomenological thematics, in other words, become poetical.

Let me give two examples of the starry theme no longer in its thematic form, or not purely so. We are, for instance, only subliminally aware on reading

Tyger Tyger, burning bright,
In the forests of the night

that usually stars burn this way and that this "descendental" constellation, Tyger, presides over the moment after Hesper has set, when "the lion glares thro' the dun forest." And while there might seem to be no relation whatsoever between Blake's lyric and Wordsworth's "Daffodils," the poet who wanders "lonely as a cloud/That floats on high o'er vales and hills," could collide with a star. And that is, more or less, what happens: a moment of withdrawal, of Wordsworthian inwardness, is suddenly filled with the shock of *earthly* stars:

When all at once I saw a crowd
A host of golden daffodils . . .

The "golden" hint of these lines is elaborated by "Continuous as the stars that shine/ And twinkle on the Milky Way," and the "flash" of the final stanza.[11]

The interlunar moment merges in Wordsworth with the themes of retirement, reflectiveness, and self-renewal. His flowery shock is the descendental obverse of the emotion of the sublime. In other poems, of course, up and down are more dizzyingly related—not only in the great passages from *The Prelude* (Mont Blanc, the Simplon Pass, Snowdon) but also in such evening poems as "Composed by the Side of Lake Grasmere" where the lake that yields a "vivid repetition of the stars" leads him into a curious surmise:

Is it [the lake] a mirror, or the nether Sphere
Opening to view the abyss in which she feeds
Her own calm fires?

But it is not only the content of the surmise which interests here. If we try to go beyond thematics to poetics, the surmise becomes significant as a surmise, as part of a larger act of the poetic mind.

Wordsworth: (1) Star and Surmise

The surmise comes from a sonnet composed when "clouds, lingering yet, extend in solid bars/ Through the grey west." This lingering, a moment of suspense or interregnum, points to the interlunar rising of Hesperus. The brightest stars are already visible, intensified by the "mirror" of the lake. "And lo! these waters, steeled/ By breezeless air to smoothest polish, yield/ A vivid repetition of the stars." The word "steeled," which continues the metaphor "solid bars," echoes in the mind as "stilled"—"Tranquillity is here" (l. 14). Deeply internal, it repeats the wishful progress of the whole poem from martial to pastoral.

Yet no thematic continuity in Wordsworth is as remarkable as the poet's mind "in the act of finding/ What will suffice." Stillness, for that mind, is never loss: life should appear within loss, presence within absence. The evening sight is analogous, therefore, to the poet's morning vision of London from Westminster Bridge. The "lo" (l. 2) and "list" (l. 11) converge as gestures that skirt a desired epiphany. Yet, even as the mind searches for the sufficient, the twilight nature of the moment is fully respected. The very formality of the sonnet prevents the moment from merging into a next stage—it does not "die" into light. Time is almost suspended, like the clouds of the opening lines. The poem becomes a little sphere, restless within (since neither cloudland nor the battle-scarred earth suffices) but turning on its own axis, and furnished with its twilight, and tutelary, voice.

The image of clouds as bars already betrays the poet's desire for something firmer than cloud, for a *grounding* of eye or imagination. His descendental movement from sky to earth and even into earth is a movement toward both stillness (peace) and that ground. The more human field he reaches is, however, the Napoleonic battlefield, "earth's groaning field." The imagination moves away again, trying the nether sphere just as it had previously stepped among the stars. But the image of "calm fires" is counter-volcanic, and shows how precarious each speculation ("fancy") is: the middle-ground sought by Wordsworth, the twilight moment he respects, is always about to fade into starlight or fire.[12] To call earth's fires "calm" (sated) only emphasizes in its very boldness the restless journeying of his imagination toward a fold. So that the surmise ("Is it a mirror, or the nether Sphere . . .") is a restraint on that epiphanic movement, a "lingering" comparable to that of the clouds. The Wordsworthian imagination remains unpastured: it hungers for calm and finds no shepherd. Except Pan, at the every end, in the form of a piped-in, reedy voice, the opposite of panic.

Wordsworth: (2) Star and Symbol

Before showing the deepest use, or displacement, of the evening star theme in Wordsworth, it is best to double back and consider poems where the theme is more explicitly present. Hesperus appears in two earlier poems, "Fair Star of Evening, Splendor of the West," written at Calais in August, 1802, and "It is No Spirit Which from Heaven Hath Flown," composed in 1803. Both exhibit that tension between *zoning* (the star seen as inhabiting its own zone separated by nature's or poetry's magic from various continua) and *zooming* (a sympathetic or ecstatic movement of identification) that we found in very subtle form in the Grasmere sonnet. The idea, for instance, of "the sky / He hath it to himself—'tis all his own" [13] so corresponds to Wordsworth's own homing instinct that his appropriation of an image he has helped to create threatens to destroy the separateness essential to it. The poet zooms in on the star as his (and England's) encompassing symbol.

Both poems begin in the feeling of distance or exile. The earlier verses are written from Calais, with the poet looking westward toward his country during the fragile Peace of Amiens. The idea of an interregnum enters—however discreetly—if the political situation is kept in mind.[14] The star is "hanging" on the horizon's brink above the dusky spot which is England; and Wordsworth, though he sees the star and his country as twofold —one being the crown or bosom-jewel of the other—merges them finally into "one hope, one lot, / One life, one glory."

The star seems to be a symbol yet participates so nearly in the imaginative essence of "real" England that symbol and reality converge. Wordsworth knows that his imagination needs a "star" but he also knows it must be a "native star." It should encompass his own, human destiny from birth to setting. There is, on the one hand, a finely graded if descendental transformation of Hesperus from "Star of Evening" to "Star of my Country," and, on the other, an identifying movement which collapses distances and degrades the star into an emblem ("my Country's emblem . . . with laughter on her banners").

Wordsworth's later poem expresses a deeper or more general sense of exile. The distance is not that from Calais to Dover but an undefinable one from "my natural race" [15] to "some ground not [presently] mine." The star has transcended its zone by dominating the sky in broad daylight. It is so simply, so startlingly "there" that it at once incites and repels descendental or metamorphic myths (ll. 1–4). Wordsworth's need for a center or zoom, felt in the previous poem, culminates now in an almost hypnotic moment of enchanted stasis.

There is a further difference between the poems as acts of mind. The lyric of 1803 is more akin to experiences familiar to us from the great *Prelude* passages. Something startles sight by anticipating itself. Though the star is hoped for—indeed, one of hope's emblems—it defeats the perceptual or mythic apparatus prepared for its coming. It is there so naturally that it appears to be already *in its place* (compare l. 13), that is, absolute, beyond temporal change. It has become a "fixed star" to imagination.

The poet, it is true, still talks of it as a sign or "admonition" (l. 5). But then the octave of this lengthened sonnet is clearly a sparring for time—for rebounding from a sublime or unexpected impression. The real "admonition" is to himself; and Wordsworth adverts to his own mind in the poem's second half, which no longer seeks to render the immediacy of an external image. It turns instead (note the tense change, from present to past) to what "wrought" within him. With "O most ambitious star" we reach, in fact, the symmetrical center (9–1–9) of the poem, its exact turning-point. This cry, star-oriented yet reflexive, turns us not from image to meaning—nowhere, and certainly not in Wordsworth, is imaging free of the interpretive consciousness—but from an objectifying mode that subsumes the subjective context, back to subjectivity. While Wordsworth's star-staring (ll. 1–8) elides the sense of time, now there is an "inquest"—an inward questing—into which time returns as time-for-reflection.

The final verses, presented as a "thought"—an illusion sustained consciously and *in* time—are actually an audacious return to first impressions, and quietly merge the idea of ground and heaven. Their subject is transcendence, but this is depicted as a *stepping*, and compared to the ghostly apparition of the soul in a place (that is, heaven) not its own. Yet Wordsworth preserves, this time, a sense of distance: the soul is not of the place but appropriates it "strong her strength above."

Wordsworth: (3) Death of a Star

Sieh, Sie erstand und schlief

Rilke

A signal transformation of the evening star theme is found in the Lucy poems. "Fair as a star when only one / Is shining in the sky" is not, of course, a stingy compliment, but an allusion to Hesper which carries with it the suggestion of brief if intense emergence. Throughout the poems which have Lucy for subject the thought of her death blends curiously with that of her presence: she is a twilight or threshold figure that gleams upon the sight, then disappears. There is, almost simultaneously, emergence and discontinuity. As in Rilke's "Starker Stern," and in the later *Sonnets to Orpheus*, an image of setting overtakes that of dawning life:

> *tausendfachen Aufgang überholend*
> *Mit dem reinen Untergang.*

Though the erotic connotations are much stronger in Rilke, where Hesper is clearly Venus, in Wordsworth too the lover appears together with love's star. The guiding planet of "Strange Fits" is the "evening moon" rather than the evening star, yet it is already "sinking," and there occurs a ritual stepping and zoning similar to what guided Akenside's lover to a ghostly center. At the end of the lyric, in a reverse play of a familiar theme, both moon and Lucy enter on an "interlunar" phase, and it is only then that "thought" rises. The poem's curious use of both centering and descendental movements links it clearly enough to the idylls of Hesperus.

But Wordsworth's poem is as much about symbol as about star: in a sense, the symbol stars. We have, this time, an act of the mind finding what exceeds. The lover goes out of himself into star or moon: it is a mild case of ecstasy in which the distance between lover and Lucy—that precarious or psychic distance Hesper traditionally lights—is overcome by a deep, "symbolic" association of her with the moon. Lucy, to use a Renaissance term, is eternized, but unconsciously so. The evening moon not only leads to her but she becomes the moon, love's absorbing center. The narrative progressions of the poem make us feel the slope of things toward her until she is seen as their infinite threshold—and sets. When the moon drops it is as if a fixed had become a falling star; the distance between lover and Lucy is restored; the symbol proves fallible.

This purgation of the star-symbol is perfected in "A Slumber Did My Spirit Seal." Here is neither Lucy by name nor the visible image of a star. But she who is described in the first stanza, who rises on the poet's "slumber," is immortal as a star. Poet becomes Astrophil. She, however, who is described in the second stanza is ground not sky, yet "heaven" and "ground" subtly meet because she has merged with the rolling planet. The descendental theme is so subtly realized that the passage from stanza to stanza, which coincides with that from state to state, is a "stepping" not accompanied by open shock or disillusion. Because the rise and fall of the star-symbol occurs at a level "too deep for tears," there is no such formal cry-ing as: "If Lucy should be dead!" or "The difference to me!"

The absence of rhetorical glitter does not mean, of course, absence of structure. It means that Wordsworth has purified *exclamation* even further than in "Strange Fits" and "She Dwelt": he has killed the exclamation mark, in fact. Instead of a reversal (↓) followed by point (.) to make (!) we have a star turned asterisk:

How went the Agile Kernel out
Contusion of the Husk
Nor Rip, nor wrinkle indicate
But just an Asterisk.[16]

Stanza 1 implies the star ("The whole of Immortality/Secreted in a star"), stanza 2 star as asterisk, or sign of an absence. Lucy's essence and that of language coincide. If she is part of a galaxy, it is Gutenberg's. Yet absence here has its own presence, so that asterisk balances star. At last a poem without artificial center, a poem which does not overcondense consciousness into symbol and symbol into star.

An Excursus on the Romantic Image

A voice, a mystery.

Wordsworth

Wordsworth's revolt against the star-symbol has various reasons: its trivialization in eighteenth-century poetry, a religiously inspired prudence, etc. To conventionalize it we can think of his distrust of personification, which it extends, or of English poetry's recurrent bouts of conscience vis-à-vis pagan myth. Yet we read Wordsworth unconscious much of the time of his place in the history of ideas or the polemical history of style. These histories, recovered, allow us to be articulate about his intentions but they describe his novelty rather than his originality. They remain external to his strong poetic presence.

Curiously strong, considering how little "glitter," or conventional texture, his poetry has. Many have suspected, therefore, that his imagery comes from a different loom. They have sought to discover the formula of its secret weave. It is equally inadequate, however—though far more interesting—to describe the diffusion of theme or image in Wordsworth, or the change from parallelistic to chiastic patterns in his metaphors. The only adequate rhetorical analysis is one that views his poems in terms of "mind in act," with the very temptation of symbolizing—that is, overcondensing, or turning contiguity (metonymy) into identity (metaphor)—as its subject.

This kind of rhetorical analysis does not deal with rhetoric but with rhetoricity, or word-consciousness. Speech, written or voiced, is only a special field within semiotics, defined as the study of signs in the context of signification generally. A poem may have a direct theme, subject, or reference, but it also contains, modifying these, an indication concerning the power and poverty of symbols. The older kind of rhetorical analysis (with its interest in stylistics or psycho-practical acts) was bound to emphasize the persuasive, quasi-visual figure, or such subliminal voicings as pseudo-morphemes. It can usefully point out, for example, a pun in line 11 of "It Is No Spirit" (the star "startles") or the pattern of reversal and transference in "A Slumber" (the speaker's slumber seems to have become the girl's as he wakes).

In poetry, however, we respond less to images or figures as such than through them to the *image of a voice*. The newer rhetorical analysis is caught up in this highly complex notion. It does not automatically privilege voice over "dead speech" though it can do so, as when F. R. Leavis attacks Milton. We know, however, that the nostalgia for an "inviolable voice" is based quite consciously on the fact that such a voice is a fiction. It is always associated with prior loss or violation, as the Philomel myth perfectly expresses.[17] Philomel sings in the interlunar moment, when there is silence—and silence is pleased. Through the "wakeful descant" of poetry we become conscious of the immensity of the detour leading from absence to presence, or from symbol to symbol rather than to "the real thing."

What is Wordsworth's image of a voice? It might be said that he seeks to avoid both "writing up"—the artifices of declamation, of raising speech to oratory; and "writing down"—the appearance that verse is mere reflection, the mimesis of a prior event, or speech-event. "Voicing" is clearly part of the subject of the Lucy poems, and thus an older type of rhetorical reading will not suffice. As we have shown, exclamation is more at issue than declamation. Voice becomes intratextual, in the sense of merging with the text rather than seeking to transcend textuality by "opening" into an underlying or originative emotion.

As one moves, therefore, from "Strange Fits" to "A Slumber," not only does quoted speech disappear but something happens to the intentionality of signs. In "Strange Fits" the moon-sign is an omen, that is, it presages something greater (lesser) to come. Voice enters as voice when the omen rides the poet. The relation to voice is even stronger in "Three Years" where Nature takes over in *proprio sermone* at the very point at which children begin to speak articulately.[18] So that we hear Nature, and never Lucy: her life is tied to Nature's narrative. When Nature has finished speaking Lucy too is "finished." Nature's logos ("So Nature spoke, the work was done . . .") betrays. It promises life but produces death. Is the deeper thought here that speech always betrays—even this gentle, if still prophetic, mother-tongue?

The fully internalized speech of "A Slumber" does not cease to evoke a death, or the thought of a death. A representational element persists. Yet the poet's words neither anticipate a betrayal nor vicariously compensate for it. Their "pointed" or ominous quality is barely felt. There is no moon, no path, no precipitate symbol. They do not even give voice a chance to emerge as Voice.

We still feel, of course, how close the "idyll" of the first stanza is to a blind sublimity and the "elegy" of the second to a false sublimation. Yet they are shadows of moods only, reached through a purified form. The issue of loss and gain—of psychic balancing—has deepened measurably. If poetry still rises from loss, it has no magical (sublimating) or guilty (proleptic) relation to it. "A Slumber," a poem of enlightenment—and of the Enlightenment—removes superstition from poetic speech in a much deeper sense than expelling gaudy phrases and mythic personifications.

The Melodious Plot

Akenside's evening star lights him not to Olympia but from her tomb to Philomel's bower. One might take this as representing symbolically the very process of sublimation. A girl dies, song is born. The myth of Philomel already founded song on sorrow. Voice is intrinsically elegiac: Philomel's bower a melodious bier.

But this would simplify both the myth and Akenside's poem. The myth deals with loss of voice, not only with loss. A mutilated tongue speaks again through the cunning of art. In Akenside, moreover, the theme of voice precedes that of loss: if the "suppliant song" should fail, there would be no light for the poet. Loss of voice would mean loss of light. The lyrist skirts that darkening of the voice. Philomel is a symbol, primarily, for restored song rather than for restored love.

A "melodious plot," consequently, is both the aspired-to center of the poet's quest and the form of its path. The star must "suffer" the poet's song before it can grant a petition that allows song and loss to merge in the "green space" of memory. What moves us toward that full yet empty space, that para-paradise, is what we find when we get there: voice, our sense of its power and impotence. A memory-fiction of its starry influence survives together with an awareness of its present absence. This poet's poem helps us understand the forces of nostalgic lyricism Wordsworth overcame.

Voice is the only epiphany in Akenside's ode, but it reverberates in the confines of an operatic set. We hear a frozen music; such phrases as "the wakeful heifers gaze" are stagy orphisms. Nothing remains of the logos-power of the word, of its mimetic or re-creative virtue. What is evoked is a little moony world far tighter it would seem than that generous intercourse of gods and men suggested by the opening verses. How sterile this templar space when compared to the "wide quietness" of "To Psyche" or "murmurous haunt" of "To a Nightingale"! It is illumined by gaslight rather than by "a light in sound."[19] Voice, or poetry in general, is worshipped only as a fiction, as the fetish of a fiction even.

The tension between prophetic voice and fictive word becomes acute after Milton.[20] Not only is paradise understood to be lost (that is, understood to have been, or now always to be, a fiction) but the great voice seems lost that knew itself as logos: as participating in real influence. The *philomel moment* of English poetry is therefore the postprophetic moment,[21] when the theme of loss merges with that of voice—when, in fact, a "lost voice" becomes the subject or moving force of poetic song. "Shall we not hear thee in the storm? In the noise of the mountain stream? When the feeble sons of the wind come forth, and scarcely seen pass over the desert?"[22]

The Ossianic poems overhear these wind-notes that try to swell into a supreme fiction but remain curiously successive and apart, wreaths in the Gaelic night. Macpherson's melic vaporizer turns what light there is into motes of sound. One voice spells another in a supposedly epic chain which remains a composite lyric. The chain has no real continuity because what memories pass over Ossian, as over a wind-harp, are not ghosts of heroes so much as "sons of song." Their essence is vocative; their strength a fading power of vociferation. By a typical sublimation they die into song, or rather into the spectral, ominously heightened voice of nature. "When night comes on the hill; when the loud winds arise, my ghost shall stand in the blast, and mourn the death of my friends. The hunter shall hear from his booth. He shall fear but love my voice!"[23]

This melic undermining of the theme of succession—this substitution of voice for blood—is especially remarkable in the *Songs of Selma.* A hero's life flourishes as briefly there as the evening star, and with strange delight in its setting. The poem begins with Ossian's address to Hesperus: the "fair-hair'd angel," as Blake will call it, lifts its "unshorn head" from the cloud, to observe the scene but a moment and to depart. "The waves come with joy around thee: they bathe thy lovely hair. Farewell, thou silent beam!" It goes, as it came, in strength; from this, perhaps, the poet's delight in its setting, and the upswing of the ensuing movement: "Let the light of Ossian's soul arise!"

That light is memory, matrix of epic art. Ossian's soul lights up with memories of dead friends, the heroes and bards who used to gather annually in Selma. The evening star has led us not to the moon, its bright epiphany, but to memory—these dying voices from the past. We become aware of a reversal and a twofold sequence. The star's "silent beam" leads to memory by distancing the raging sounds of day ("The murmur of the torrent comes from afar. Roaring waves climb the distant rock"); memory, however, recovers an inconsolable sound. "Colma left alone on the hill with all her voice of song!"

The interlunar moment now repeats itself as Ossianic lover-hero-bard invokes the silence, or the hidden moon, or absent friend. "Rise, moon! from behind thy clouds. Stars of the night arise! Lead me, some light, to the place, where my love rests. . . . But here I must sit alone, by the rock of the mossy stream. The stream and the wind roar aloud. I hear not the voice of my love." These voices are like ghosts, doomed to wander about ravening and unsatisfied. They cannot center on anything because nothing abides their question. "Thou dost smile, and depart," as Ossian says of the evening star. The questioning voice alone, in its manifold, frustrated music of apostrophe, invocation, and exclamation, remains. This voice is heard as if afar, a passion to be memorialized but no longer owned. There is a kind of elegy in space itself, in our distance from the sublime of sound:

> The sons of song are gone to rest. My voice remains, like a blast, that roars, lonely, on a sea-surrounded rock, after the winds are laid. The dark moss whistles there; the distant mariner sees the waving trees![24]

A voice without issue, a poetry without succession, is what meets us in the Ossianic fragments. They reflect the anxiety of

English poetry as a whole. Macpherson's forgery is strangely true because the original voice he claimed to discover is so lonely, so discontinuous with the origin it posits. The poetry of this new Homer discloses "the westwardness of everything."[25] Deep no longer responds to deep and each hill repeats a lonely sound. The pseudo-psalmodic landscape before us actually spells the end of that "responsive" poetry Christopher Smart sought to revive at exactly the same historical moment.

Now too the poet's self-image changes radically. He sees himself as an aeolian harp, "self-sounding in the night."[26] Macpherson is acclaimed as a Northern Homer, an autochthonous poet springing from the peculiar genius of his region. Or, more sophisticated, poets understand that all origins are forged origins. For Blake they are part of the "mystery" caricatured in his mock-Eastern style, which multiplies births and creates an extraordinary mélange of genealogical fictions. The impossibility of succession leads to a clearer facing of the burden of originality on all poets, which a return to pseudo-origins evades. Blake's evening star, therefore, rises upon the twilight of English and classicizing poetry with the energy of dawn: it is, already, the morning star:

Thou fair-hair'd angel of the evening,
Now, while the sun rests on the mountains, light
Thy bright torch of love; thy radiant crown
Put on . . .

Coleridge and the Morning Star

Tell also of the false Tongue!
vegetated
Beneath your land of shadows, of its
sacrifices and
Its offerings

Blake

My subject has not been a theme, or even thematics, but poetry—poetry as it impinges on those who seek to continue it. The drama begins, as always, in a darkling moment. There is the shadow of a prior greatness, or the discovery of a distance from a creating source. That shadow is always there, but the manifest voice of achievement from Spenser to Milton had made of England classic ground and put the glory on each successor poet.[27]

The burden of creativity became both ineluctable and as heavy as the pack Christian wore. After Milton, poetry joins or even rivals divinity in pressing its claim on the artist. Moreover, as soon as greatness is acknowledged, it raises the question of succession. A theological element enters; a reflection on who is—or could be—worthy to continue the line. In these circumstances literary criticism can take the form of a theologico-poetical examination of the pretender. Is he apostolic? The question need not be imposed from the outside: indeed, it generally comes from within the visionary poet, and leads to self-doubt as easily as to self-justification. The poet's struggle with his vocation is not always overt or dramatic; only with Collins, Smart, and the great Romantics does it become religious in intensity and direct their voice. What is at stake is, in fact, the erection of a voice. "Would to God all the Lord's people were prophets."[28]

Like drama generally, this one can have two endings: a happy and an unhappy. Keats's poetry is representative of the former. His "To a Nightingale," with its finely repeated darkling moment and green space, is a fulfillment of Akenside's "To the Evening Star." A belated poet rejoices in the symbols and accouterments of his tradition. They fill his verses with a presence rarely as frigid as Akenside's. But Coleridge is representative of the sadder ending. He is afflicted by secondariness as by a curse: his relation to writing of all kinds is more embarrassed than that of Keats and more devious than that of Akenside. His imagination sees itself as inherently "secondary"—not only because it follows great precursors in poetry or philosophy (though that is a factor) but chiefly because of the one precursor, the "primary Imagination . . . living power and prime agent of all human perception . . . repetition in the finite mind of the eternal act of creation in the infinite I AM." His religious sensibility, conspiring with a burdened personal situation, makes him feel at a hopeless remove from originality.

That Coleridge was deeply disturbed by the priority of others —and of the Other—is hardly in question. Too much in his life and writings reflects it. It can be argued that he was, in his way, as "counterfeit" a poet as Macpherson and Chatterton. He had done better, perhaps, to invent new origins, as they did, rather than to be echo and imitate imitations in a perverse sacrifice to divine primacy. His poetry shows to what extent he *shrinks* into creation, like Blake's Urizen.[29]

But we are not engaged here in a biography that would expose the *contre-faisant* to real creation Coleridge practiced. The one biographical detail relevant to this study is that he had to contend not only with an inherited sublime that "counterfeited infinity" (see "Religious Musings" and "The Destiny of Nations") but also with "sounds less deep and loud," with the new voice of feeling in Wordsworth. The latter meets him at the very threshold of his liberation from sublimity.

Some of his early poems—the "To the Nightingale" and "Aeolian Harp" of 1795 in particular—are clearly moving in a Wordsworthian direction, as is Southey in his "English Eclogues." But then "the giant Wordsworth—God bless him" preempts them all. Coleridge soon entails his portion of poetic genius on this contemporary giant. Though "Frost at Midnight" and "To the Nightingale" (the latter as revised for *Lyrical Ballads*) repay Wordsworth's influence by leading into "Tintern Abbey," such dialogue between the poets (Coleridge's truest "conversation") lasts but a year. It breaks off when the poets separate in Germany, with Coleridge going off to study at Göttingen. To the priority of Wordsworth, Germany eventually adds that of Kant, Schelling, and the Schlegels in philosophy and criticism.

Of course, such nova as "Kubla Khan" and "The Ancient Mariner" may make the question of originality seem a blind alley. It is true, nevertheless, that the "Ancyent Marinere" was written "in imitation of the *style* as well as of the spirit of the elder poets" and that the gloss added by Coleridge at a later date antiques the poem even more as well as putting its author at curious remove from his own work. The gloss—that cool, continuous trot—frames a precipitous rime. The burden of originality, in this original poem, is relieved by a (repeated) return to fake eld.

A psychological analysis of the conditions that removed Coleridge's literary impotence is not our concern, however. Enough if we understand how problematic imaginative writing was for him. It was, at once, inherently dependent or secondary, yet virtually primary or participating in the divine "I AM." His bravest poems tend to recant themselves. The pattern is obvious in "The Aeolian Harp," yet elsewhere too, if more subtly, he worships the whirlwind or puts a finger on his mouth like Job.

A test-case for this sacrificial or self-counterfeiting movement (when originality was in his reach) is the "Hymn before Sunrise, in the Vale of Chamouni." Coleridge falsifies his experience in two ways. He had been on Scafell, not in Chamouny. This transposition to a traditionally sublime spot occurred despite Wordsworth, or perhaps because of him. It is difficult to work out the relation, but Coleridge, in this poem, could have celebrated a native mountain in Wordsworthian style before Wordsworth (*The Prelude*'s account of Snowdon was unwritten or still in manuscript). There is also his notorious use of a minor German poetess, Frederike Brun. He quietly incorporates essential lines from her short "Chamonix beym Sonnenaufgang." This double shift, from England to France in locality, and from English to German (Klopstockian) verse in features of style and experience, is surely a kind of flight from native origins, or from whatever Wordsworth exemplified.[30]

Even were we to accept the Hymn's egregious sublimity, it would remain a strange production. The style, as Wordsworth charged, is "mock sublime," a turgid almost parodistic development of Miltonic hymns to Creation. The impression is that Klopstock has been the model rather than an English visionary. Add to this that the poem turns on the old conceit of making silence speak—that its essential subject is presence or absence of Voice—and you have a signal case of Coleridge speaking with a tongue not his own, or adopting a counterfeit logos. "Bowed low/ In adoration" he ventriloquizes nature, and sacrifices his genius and the *genius loci* to the tritest forms of sublime ejaculation.

This is not the whole story, however. The poem's first section (to about line 37) bears traces of inward record and a powerful grasp of myth-making. The only conventional thing about it is the desensualizing movement from visible to invisible. This is imposed on a remarkable *situation*. The poem begins with the near-mythic contrast of the "white" mountain (Blanc) shrouded in black, and the silent mountain rising from a sounding base. We feel the contending elements and approach Manichaeanism. For a moment only—but still for that moment —we understand Abel's cry in "The Wanderings of Cain": "The Lord is God of the living only, the dead have another God."

The Manichaean contrasts disappear into the conventional paradoxes of sublime rhetoric which characterize the later portions of the Hymn. (A "mighty voice" both calls the torrents "from night and utter death/ From dark and icy caverns" and stops them "at once amid their maddest plunge," reverting them to "silent cataracts.") What does not disappear is the horror of stasis implicit in the opening moments. "Hast thou a charm to stay the morning-star . . . ?" Dread of stillness combines with dread of blackness. The mountain, co-herald of the dawn because of its snowy height, seems to be in league with darkness. It is a passing impression; yet that there was this *charm*, this bewitchment of time, is conveyed by a pattern of stills that, as in "The Ancient Mariner," can suddenly freeze the image of motion. It is as if time were subject to sudden arrest—to an embolism felt in the poem's development as a whole, which is really a non-development, or a passionate rhetorical goad to make the soul "rise" together with obstructed dawn.

In *this* darkling and enchanted moment it is morning that almost fails to rise. "Nightes dread" is now associated with dawn's delay. As a slowing of time it is, moreover, the opposite of erotic;[31] the "bald awful head," the "dread mountain form," etc., suggest if anything a scene of sacrifice. It is also significant that when the mountain is linked to the morning star a second time (ll. 30 ff.), the diction swells distinctly toward the Miltonic and repeats the nightmare resonance of the opening verses. Is the mountain or the poet's soul the true subject of these lines?

And thou, O silent Mountain, sole and bare
O blacker than the darkness all the night

(original version)

Thou first and chief, sole sovereign of the Vale!
O struggling with the darkness all the night

(later version)

And who is being contended for in this cosmic battle?

And visited all night by troops of stars
Or when they climb the sky or when they sink . . .

This place, then, soul or mountain, is a virtual Prince of Darkness. The visiting "troops of stars" could be the Satanic "Stars of Night" (*Paradise Lost*, V. 745) or a sustaining, heavenly host.[32] We are on the verge of a "wild allegory"; [33] but nothing really is clear except that the soul, in trying to "wake" or "rise," meets quasi-demonic forces. "Rising" gets confused with "rising up"—perhaps through a montage of the image of the morning star with the myth of Lucifer.

What more can be said? In this deeply religious, or mythopoeic, situation, continuity of self (in time) is threatened, and there is need for a rite, and specifically a rite of passage.[34] The morning star must be freed to continue its rising course: a progress leading toward dawn must be restored. The mountain too must "rise," for the sable charm invests it as well. But to free mountain or morning star is tantamount to finding some lost intermediary between darkness and dawn, some symbolic form, at least a voice. The darkness is a darkness of mediations. And in this darkness, even constituting it, is the poet's struggle to extricate a religious rather than demonic mediation. The image of Lucifer as Prince of the Air, Prince of Darkness, has merged with that of the mountain as "great hierarch" and "dread ambassador"; yet the image of Lucifer as morning star is also there, and blends with a mountain described as "Companion of the morning-star at dawn." The poet's soul, in this hymn, tries to call the one and not the other. "O which one, is it each one?" [35]

At the end, it is unsure who prevails. The mountain's mediation seems to lift the weight of that "dark, substantial, black" which oppressed air and soul in the beginning, but the supposed upward lumbering of its voice ("tell thou the silent sky," etc.) merely differentiates a silence which reaches, as in Pascal, the stars. Coleridge leaves us with a depressing sense of hierarchy, measured by the contrast between his bowed head and the "bald awful head" of "stupendous" Blanc. His "Instructions to a Mountain" would sound ludicrous if they were not despairing. They suggest the opposite of Shelley's "Thou hast a voice, great Mountain, to repeal/ Large codes of fraud and woe," for they effectively make the mountain into the rock of institutionalized religion, complete with frigidly hieratic spheres. In a sense, then, the debased (Urizenic) Lucifer has triumphed because indistinguishable from the religious code. The true morning star never rises.[36]

Only at one point is there something like a genuine release from the "ebon mass." It is not unlike what the mariner feels after the spell begins to break and the albatross falls off; and it involves quiet gazing rather than rhetorical shouting. Struggling against the charm, the poet views the mountain as a wedge that pierces the surrounding blackness. Then, as if recanting, he thinks the blackness away as a "crystal shrine" which is the mountain's home. Finally he desubstantializes it completely when through rapt gazing Mont Blanc vanishes from consciousness only to reappear blending subliminally—like a "beguiling melody"—into thought. Several stills, then, or re-visions relax the hold of a spell that almost paralyzed the soul. This spell becomes the "trance" of prayer and a "beguiling" thought-music. Its power continues to echo as the stills move quasi-cinematically into the unitive swell of mountain and mind.

The most curious of these still ecstasies [37] in Coleridge is also one of the earliest. A sonnet of 1790 shows the lover absorbed in the evening star:

On thee full oft with fixed eye I gaze
Till I, methinks, all spirit seem to grow.

By a sacrificial sleight of mind he then identifies the star with the beloved woman, so that, in effect, gazing is all there is—until his spirit should join hers in the star's "kindred orb":

Must she not be, as is thy placid sphere
Serenely brilliant? Whilst to gaze a while
Be all my wish 'mid Fancy's high career
E'en till she quit this scene of earthly toil;
Then Hope perchance might fondly sigh to join
Her spirit in thy kindred orb, O Star benign!

I am not convinced of the star's benignity. Anti-erotic, it leads to death not love, or to a life beyond life. Nothing is lost by this sublimation except all. Having is replaced by hoping in a fatal movement that confirms Blake's "O Sunflower." Coleridge does not hope to have, he hopes that *then* he may hope. He does not seem to know his life has been stolen—as he knows, at least, in his mountain poem. There he recognizes the charm and tries to break a heliotropic (or melantropic) trance by recovering a sense of his own presence amid the ghostliness. But though he resists the charm it gets the better of him. The desire for sublimation is too strong and his soul passes into "the mighty Vision" and so "swells" to heaven. This dilation is sublimation still. The mountain's presence is no more benign than the star's.

"Ghost of a mountain—the forms seizing my Body as I passed & became realities—I, a Ghost, till I had reconquered my substance." This notebook entry, recorded first in November, 1799, is repeated in September, 1802, at the time, probably, of composing the "Hymn before Sunrise." The ghostliness he describes also befell the Ancient Mariner. It takes away the sense of easy personal presence while intensifying the presence of otherness. Emptied of personality he must stand on this very emptiness against impinging surreality. It is his only "ground" (the question of ground being further subverted by locating the action on a shifty sea). One can understand why the "coal-ridge" of this massive mountain became a place for Coleridge's struggle to ground the self. A late and beautiful letter recapitulates his whole spiritual history as it impinges on the Hymn:

from my very childhood I have been accustomed to *abstract* and as it were unrealize whatever of more than common interest my eyes dwelt on; and then by a sort of transfusion and transmission of my consciousness to identify myself with the Object—and I have often thought . . . that if ever I should feel once again the genial warmth and stir of the poetic impulse, and refer to my own experiences, I should venture on a yet stranger & wilder Allegory than of yore—that I would *allegorize* myself, as a Rock with it's summit just raised above the surface of some Bay or Strait in the Arctic Sea,

While yet the stern and solitary Night
Brook'd no alternate Sway—

all around me fixed and firm, methought as my own Substance, and near me lofty Masses, that might have seemed to "hold the Moon and Stars in fee" and often in such wild play with meteoric lights, or with the quiet Shine from above . . . that it was a pride and a place of Healing to lie, as in an Apostle's Shadow, within the Eclipse and deep substance-seeming Gloom of "these dread Ambassadors from Earth to Heaven, Great Hierarchs"! and tho' obscured yet to think myself obscured by consubstantial Forms, based in the same Foundation as my own. I grieved not to serve them—yea, lovingly and with gladsomeness I abased myself in their presence: for they are my Brothers, I said.[38]

So the Valley of Chamouny is truly a "Valley of Wonders." But does the poet succeed in "reconquering" his "substance" there? (How much play with that grounding word in the above letter!) It is hard to say, from the Hymn, whether loss of self or loss of voice was more important. Yet writing the Hymn meant recovering a voice. In the Hymn as in the Rime, release from the curse—that dread stillness, or paralysis of motion—is obtained by the ability to pray. And prayer is interpreted in both poems as praise:

O happy living things! no tongue
Their beauty might declare . . .

The weight of the Albatross (like the air's "ebon mass") is removed, together with the stone from the tongue.

Yet voice remains uneasy, both in the Hymn and in the Rime. Praise mutes itself in the act:

O happy living things! no tongue
Their beauty might declare:
A spring of love gushed from my heart
And I blessed them unaware

There is too great a contrast between the compulsive speech of the Mariner and this first, tongueless moment. The Hymn, similarly, is hardly an "unaware" blessing: its one moment of sweet unconsciousness (ll. 17–23) does not compensate us for the forced sublimity of the rest.

Praise, according to the Psalmist, is a "sacrifice of thanksgiving." It substitutes for, or sublimates, the rite of blood-sacrifice. The Hymn on Mont Blanc is written against this background of sublimation. The exact pressure put on Coleridge—the offering demanded of him by the dread form—we shall never know. Coleridge's "Sca'fell Letter" shows him as "overawed," but there was nothing necessarily mysterious. He felt, that much is certain, a loss of substance, a passivity both shaming and sublime[39]—and he recovers himself, at least in the Hymn, by the will of his voice; more precisely, by the willed imitation of a sublime voice.

I will not deny that the inferred human situation is more impressive than the Hymn produced by it. But that is because, in Coleridge, poetry remains so closely linked to sublimation. Sublimation always sacrifices to an origin stronger than itself. If it did not cherish or dread this origin—this "hiding-place" of power—it would not shroud it from sight by displacement or falsification:

Never mortal saw
The cradle of the strong one,
Never mortal heard
The gathering of his voices;
The deep-murmured charm . . .[40]

Such "wildly-silent" scenes [41] are not infrequent in Coleridge. He is often, in fancy, near an origin where a "great Spirit" with "plastic sweep"—the wind or voice of the opening of Genesis—moves on the still darkness. But he is, at the same time, so removed from this primal scene that it becomes a "stilly murmur" which "tells of silence." The voice redeeming that silence, or vexed into being by it, can be as cold as the eye of Ancient Mariner or moon. "Green vales and icy cliffs, all join my Hymn." Its "sunny domes" are accompanied by "caves of ice." In the end what predominates are the strange soteriological images, the "secret ministry of frost," the rock "in wild play . . . with the quiet Shine from above," or others calm yet glittering: the "mild splendor," for instance, of a "serenely brilliant" star, which summons the poet at evening to accept his death-in-life.

Afterthought

The Imagination is always at the end of an era.

Wallace Stevens

These reflections must finally turn back on themselves. Is their objective really "objective"? Are we, should we be, aiming at positive literary history? Or have we found a kind of history-writing compatible with its subject-matter: poetry?

The theme of the evening star, as a point of departure, is not objective, but neither is it arbitrary. I have described elsewhere the idea of a Westering of the poetical spirit, and the fear of a decline in poetical energy which accompanied it. Others too have put forward a thesis on the belatedness of English poetry.[42] While it is notoriously difficult to explain the birth or rebirth of a symbol, I suspect that, after the Renaissance, the complex evening-consciousness of English poets reached toward the Hesper/Lucifer theme as toward a limit.

What was limited by the theme? The fear of discontinuity, of a break in personal or cultural development; but also a vatic overestimation of poetry which, putting too great a burden on the artist, made this break more likely. Vaticination remains in evening star poetry, yet is diminished in a special way. Symbol or substitute (Hesper/Philomel in Akenside) tends to become more important than the epiphanic source (the moon). A prophetic background supports a purely symbolic foreground. The aura of the symbol is reduced even as its autonomy is strengthened. It is ironic that, by the time of Stevens, "the philosophy of symbols" (as Yeats called it) confronts the poet with a new discontinuity: the symbols, or romantic relics, are so attenuated by common use that their ground (sky?) is lost. They become starry junk, and the poem is a device to dump them, to let the moon rise as moon, free of

the moon and moon
The yellow moon of words about the nightingale
In measureless measures . . .[43]

Perhaps it was the masque, with its courtly center and operatic machinery, which first encouraged a translation of prophecy into "descendental" picture. Ben Jonson's masques, for instance, can be elaborate night-pieces converging on queen-moon or *roi-soleil*. Royal center, epiphanic allegory, and pictorial hinge go together.[44] A star-god or genius of some kind "descends" to point out his representative on earth, or do obeisance. In *Pleasure Reconciled to Virtue* (1619) the center explicitly descends westward: King James and Prince Charles are linked to the "bright race of Hesperus," which delimits their royal aura yet still discloses, epiphanically, an origin. To call James "the glory of the West" evokes a consciously Hesperian ideology with consequences for later English poetry.[45] In Hesperian verse, the epiphanic figure

Sitting like a goddess bright
In the center of her light[46]

diffuses into various, equally mortal or westering, presences:

The Rainbow comes and goes,
And lovely is the Rose,
The Moon doth with delight
Look round her when the heavens are bare;
Waters on a starry night
Are beautiful and fair;
The sunshine is a glorious birth. . . .[47]

From Ben Jonson to Wordsworth, and from masque to ode, is too abrupt a jump. But it illumines an important difference between epochs, bridged in part by our previous, historically oriented sketch: a difference in structure of sensibility or mode of representation. Wordsworth's mind, in the above stanza, loses itself only fractionally in the moon-moment. Its delight in other images is even more restrained: they remain as intransitive as the verbs, and alternate deliberately between sky and earth. Sight is segmented by them; and the serial impression they leave is of Wordsworth counting his blessings or storing them against the dying of all light. He is restrained because he is reflective; he is reflective because he is perplexed at nature's losing its immediacy. But the image of the moon challenges his restraint. With it the verses almost leap from perplexity into vision: the poet too would throw off all shadow, like heaven its clouds.

Yet the visionary personification that rises in him is simply the act of seeing—natural seeing—magnified. A personified moon makes the eyes of man personal again. Sight hovers on the edge of visionariness without passing over: "when the heavens are bare" is not an apocalyptic notation. Wordsworth's restraint is, as always, a restraint of vision. Though his eye leaps up, he subdues the star-symbol.

The evening star is, typically, like this Rainbow, Rose, Moon. A Hesperian image, it both rouses and chastens the prophetic soul. A fixed yet fugitive sign, its virtue is virtuality. It signals at most a continuation of the line. Through its binominal character, moreover, Hesper/Lucifer points at once beyond and toward itself. Always setting, yet always steadfast, it repeats in small the strange survival of poetry within the lights and shadows of historical circumstance.

Wordsworth and Goethe in Literary History

1

Whatever the sources of historicism, the Ossianic fragments and similar "Lieder der Wilden" were of decisive importance for the person we consider its principal founder. "I may soon persecute you with a Psychology drawn from the poems of Ossian," Herder warns the reader in his letters on German Art published in 1773.[1] The psychology he refers to is clearly what we now call historicism. "The human race is destined to undergo a procession of scenes, of types of culture and manners: woe to the man who does not like his part in the drama in which he must act out and consummate his life! Woe also to the humane or moral Philosopher for whom the scene he appears on is the only possible one, and who always misunderstands the first scene as the worst! If all participate in the totality of the ongoing drama, then each will evince a new and remarkable aspect of humanity." In explaining why these primitive songs had affected him, Herder adds a second strong metaphor, of shipwreck, or being lost at sea, to that of the theater of history. An amazing confessional passage recaptures in its very swell the sense of danger and disorientation in this cultural traveler, this German Sinbad, when exposed to a Northern version of the Arabian Nights: "To be ejected, all at once, from business activities, from the tumult and mimicry of rank prevailing in the bourgeois world, from the armchair of the scholar and the soft sofa of social life, to have no distractions, libraries, scholarly or unscholarly journals; exposed on the open, infinite sea . . . in the midst of a totally different theater of events, an alive and active Nature; hanging between sky and deep, encompassed daily by the repetitive, eternal play of the elements, except for glimpsing intermittently a new and distant shore or cloud or mental horizon—reading now the songs and deeds of the ancient Scalds, one's soul completely absorbed in them and the places where they were formed—here the cliffs of Norway . . . over there Iceland . . . passing at a distance the shores where Fingal wrought and Ossian sang his melancholy strains . . . then, believe me, Skalds and Bards were experienced differently than under the auspices of the Professors!" Even at the moment of writing his calmer mind is colored by that experience. "Und das Gefühl der Nacht ist noch in mir, da ich auf scheiterndem Schiffe, das kein Sturm und keine Flut mehr bewegte, mit Meer bespühlt und mit Mitternachtwind umschauert, Fingal lass und Morgen hoffte."[2]

Did that morning come? Though the transition was a stormy one in Germany, it took less than half a century to achieve. Under Herder's influence—reinforced, of course, by many currents, Klopstock's nordic phase, the reviving interest in Gothic architecture—Bürger began to flirt in the 1770s, with the daemonry of the ballads; while Goethe, in his programmatic imitation of older verse-forms, also helped to recover that "Fortgang von Szenen, von Bildung, von Sitten" which in Herder's vision of things comprised the destiny of mankind. Thirty years later, Arnim and Brentano dedicate their collection of old German songs, *Des Knaben Wunderhorn*, to his excellency, Geheimrat von Goethe; and in another twenty years, his Excellency actually pronounces himself glad that his passion for the Northern Muse is over. "Das Teufels- und Hexenwesen machte ich nur einmal; ich war froh mein nordisches Erbteil verzehrt zu haben, und wandte mich zu den Tischen der Griechen." [3]

To some extent, then, it was a false dawn. When the sun rose in Germany, it was still Homer's sun. "Und die Sonne Homers, siehe! sie lächelt auch uns." Yet Schiller's verse (the last of *Der Spaziergang*, 1795) may be echoing a book which had precipitated the interest in Northern Antiquities. "Time produces strange revolutions," P.H. Mallet (or one of his translators) wrote in the eloquent conclusion to the *History of Denmark and Monuments of the Celts.* "Who knows whether the Sun will not one day rise in the North?" [4] By the nineteenth century this Northern sun was shining with more than borrowed light. Wilhelm Grimm's introduction to *Altdänische Heldenlieder, Balladen und Märchen* (1811) shows that the Herderian view has triumphed, but in an image far removed from the stormy pathos of Herder. "Und doch hat die Sonne Homers auch über diese Eisberge ihren Glanz, und über die bereifte Thäler ihre Edelsteine ausgestreut." The sun shines on all alike; there is one creative spirit at work everywhere. But this no longer argues the supremacy of the Classical Muse, or the conformity with it of true genius. Rather, that each culture has its own classics or genius loci.

I propose to apply the historicist imagination to the age of historicism. In particular, I would like to explore the different impact on a German and an English ballad poem of the Northern Enchantment. It is well known that the idea of a characteristic literature of the North which Mme de Staël championed with late and efficient clarity, helped to break the tyranny of France over Germany, but what role did it play in England? I cannot give for England a sketch of the importance of the Northern Enchantment except to remind you that the success of Macpherson's Erse fragments made Thomas Percy consider publishing in 1761 (the year in which Gray wrote his odes "from the Norse tongue") *Five Pieces of Runic Poetry Translated from the Islandic Language,*[5] and that Percy's translation of Mallet's book under the title *Northern Antiquities* (1770) extended its influence to, among others, Blake.

Wordsworth, Burns, and Scott came from the North Country; and of these Wordsworth made the most determined effort not only to respect the Matter of the North but also to modernize it. Choosing two poems, one by Wordsworth and the other by Goethe, may be too selective a procedure, but it enables me to attempt in a short essay what E. R. Curtius characterized as an essential task of comparative literature: to study the relation between the historical development of a culture and its ideology or self-interpretation. There is a potential "Theory of English Literature" in Wordsworth's poetry as there is a "Theory of German Literature" in that of Goethe.

2

Let me begin, then, with an English poem written in Germany during the very last year of the eighteenth century. It was first called "A Fragment," because the author, immersed in the ballad revival which had moved from England to Germany, thought of it as the "prelude to a ballad-poem." The later title of this lyric also points to the impact of the ballads or Northern Enchantment. Wordsworth, for he is the author, eventually named the poem "The Danish Boy"; and it is clear that the shadowy harper he evokes, sitting solitary, and close to the sky, in a spot washed clean of all images except mountain flowers, rills, a tempest-stricken tree and the corner stone of a hut, would have sung us a ballad ghostlier, or at least more spiritual, than any found in M. G. Lewis's *Tales of Wonder* (1801)—a collection which contains such "Danish" morsels as "The Water King" and "The Erl-King's Daughter," following on a version of Goethe's "Erl-King."[6] What the Danish Boy in his sacred isolation sang to the flocks and mountain ponies on neighboring hills we shall never know, any more than what songs the sirens warbled to Odysseus; for the actual ballad, to which this portrait is a prelude, was left unwritten. Yet there was a voice out of silence, and the silence knew it, and was pleased.

I say this unmystically because elsewhere too, in epitaph-inscription, prelusive biography, or ballad proper, Wordsworth summons that voice out of the silence of a nature-buried past, out of the rocky, half-animate landscape of a region, which, Northern or English, is a no-man's-land between earth and sky, life and death, memory and oblivion, tautology and muteness. What is that other Boy doing, in a fragment also composed in Germany during this time, when he blows "mimic hootings to the silent owls/ That they might answer him"? The "Boy of Winander" fragment opens with a formula which does not differ from the "There was" or "It was" of the anonymous ballad; and despite nature's generous, wild, even frighteningly deep response to the Boy's call, everything returns to silence. The curious apostrophe which interrupts Wordsworth's opening formula, "ye knew him well, ye Cliffs/ And islands of Winander!" suggests not only that the Boy could wake the pastoral echoes but also how enclosed his life was, a mere interruption of nature's silence. Like Lucy he lived unknown, and few (perhaps only that rocky shore) could know when he ceased to be. His brief moment of vocal challenge—it cannot even be termed song—proves to be a deceptive mimicry, ending in muteness. "Oftentimes/ A full half-hour together I have stood/ Mute—looking at the grave in which he lies."[7] The vale that gave birth to the Boy also buries with him his potential songs; and however different those two Boys or fragments of destiny, both utter a strange or "forgotten" tongue and dwell in a "sacred" spot as close to silence and death as to life:

The lovely Danish Boy is blest
And happy in his flowery cove:
From bloody deeds his thoughts are far,
And yet he warbles songs of war;
They seem like songs of love,
For calm and gentle is his mien;
*Like a dead Boy he is serene.**

Wordsworth's poetry has many such figures, neither quite alive nor dead: Lucy and the Leechgatherer date from near this period. Yet in the case of the Danish Boy there is a literal reason for describing him as a visionary "shadow" or "spirit" who both "seems a Form of flesh and blood" and resembles the dead. For, according to a Cumberland superstition, he *is* dead: a ghost or revenant haunting that spot. Wordsworth identifies him in a later note as a "Danish Prince who had fled from Battle, and, for the sake of the valuables about him, was murdered by the Inhabitants of a Cottage in which he had taken refuge. The House fell under a curse, and the Spirit of the Youth . . . haunted the Valley where the crime had been committed."[8] The corner stone mentioned in the first stanza links up with this story of a cursed

* See end of chapter for the full text of "The Danish Boy."

place. The poem, therefore, belongs with "The Three Graves," the "Ancient Mariner," "Hart-Leap Well," and several other ballads in telling of a crime against nature which results in doer or place falling under a curse.

Yet Wordsworth spiritualizes the superstition of curse and revenant: he makes the ghostly harper into the genius of a landscape which is haunted only in the sense that it inspires the poet. The poet's mind is already the "haunt and the main region" of his song. The unwritten ballad might well have been, like "The Thorn," an invention serving to express the mysterious impact on Wordsworth of a spot in nature. That Wordsworth is haunted by the spot argues the truth, though not literally so, of the superstition he preserves. To put it another way: the superstition allows him to honor what omens and intimations flow from nature.

The strange persistence of the Danish Boy thus resembles the persistence, shadowy and residual, of the spirit of poetry itself. To envision the harper in that place means that he has survived from the time of the Danish invasions. No wonder, then, his flowery cove is also a grave, and that someone so young is already becalmed. He must be as old as the northern ballads which never grow old. The mystery of this "Old Boy" is resolved more easily than that of Lucy or other border figures.

We are dealing, of course, with the *idea* of the northern ballad, with its "burden" on the consciousness of a poet deeply concerned with the vocation and survival of imaginative power. The question facing Wordsworth is whether this power is dead or obsolete; and if not, how the enlightened mind can accommodate it. The encounter of old and young in his verse expresses this problem of transmission, or, to put it strongly, of succession. The poet creates scenes parallel to that in which Elijah's mantle passes to Elisha. In Wordsworth, of course, there is no open vision but hints, rather, of power failure and diminishment. This does not make our analogy of the poetic to the prophetic situation any more disproportionate than it must always be. Part of the problem, in fact, is that the analogy so vividly survives; that the prophetic ideal will not give up; even though Wordsworth meets neither Elijah nor Milton in those border regions but only this marvelous Boy or a poor man hunting leeches or a pedlar nurtured on, and perhaps hawking, the old ballads.

"The Danish Boy" is, actually, the closest Wordsworth comes to a supernatural or explicitly visionary poetry. Yet it seems just one more ballad suggesting the spell or curse which makes a ghost of all of Wordsworth's sufferers—including the narrator himself. Consider that Wordsworth does more than empty the traditional ballad of multiple dramatic incidents in favor of an emphasis on character: for, without admitting this, he also divests character of its palpability. What "character" can one ascribe to the Danish Boy or Lucy or Matthew or indeed the narrator himself? As elemental as nature-spirits, yet wandering far from their home-element, these ghostly yet human beings are characterized by no qualities other than persistence, imaginative fixation, and the sadness of incompletion. They do not escape a silence from which an anonymous or obsessive voice redeems them. The tone of narration fails to embody the narrator, to characterize him, to present him as authoritative author. It shuttles between over-intimacy and detachment, evidential claim and legend, classical and colloquial diction, personal and impersonal modes of rhetoric.[9]

Critics have puzzled over this narrative tone which is neither personal nor yet impersonal—just as the beings described are often neither alive nor dead. The style, clearly, is not, or not yet, the man: it evades impersonating the author. Wordsworth, one must conclude, has not found his own voice or else his character (identity). He can be, of course, natural and direct, when he allows the lyrical ballad to become a dramatic monologue and present a shepherd's or mother's complaint. But in his more peculiar productions, such poems as "Simon Lee," "The Thorn," "The Idiot Boy," and "The Danish Boy," the narrator's presence is both overstated (leading to Keats's charge of "palpable design") and understated—in short, embarrassed. Thus, with plot and character and even narrative voice attenuated, what remains is indeed

A tale of silent suffering, hardly clothed
In bodily form, and to the grosser sense
But ill adapted, scarcely palpable
To him who does not think.

("The Ruined Cottage")

3

One wonders what "thinking" meant for Wordsworth. The mind is his haunt, he informs us; and the "Boy of Winander" episode ends with an emblem of reflective man, looking mutely at a life fallen into muteness. If we had "such stores as silent thought can bring," the author of "Simon Lee" admonishes us, then we would find "A tale in everything."

A strange antinomy, that, of "silent store" and story ("tale"). It is remarkable how often in Wordsworth this reading of "silent characters" is referred to.[10] Perhaps his mind dislikes a vacuum and strives to convert absence into presence, or silence into restituted speech. Yet the ethos of storytelling is a complex thing: it involves, as "The Ruined Cottage" so finely shows, a respect for the compact silence being disturbed. Fiction treads as gently here as on the graves of people whose lives were unconsummated. It should not be a false completion but rather a requiem acknowledging the unsatisfied nature of their lives and the restlessness of their ghosts.

Given Wordsworth's scruples about fictionalizing the dead it is amazing he can write narrative at all, even in the minor form of the ballad. He does it, in effect, by exposing the ghostly interstices of narrative. If stories give events an afterlife, it is because they enable the dead to haunt the living; and if that is so, it is essential to understand the relation of life to afterlife, or of those "silent characters" to the poetic speech they nourish. Indeed, as Wordsworth enters the haunt of his mind, a powerful confusion about what is living and what is dead—what is past and what is present—often takes hold. This confusion usually comes in the form of a disturbing image from legend or personal history, an image which has such usurpatory power that the poet's time-sense is bewildered. He feels "lost," "stopped," "halted," split into separate beings. These heightened moments of self-awareness, mainly from the *Prelude*, are much better known than subtle but equally perplexing "fits" which phantomize his narrative elsewhere and bring it to a halt. After recalling, for example, a pathetic speech of Margaret's, the pedlar says to the listening poet:

Sir, I feel
The story linger in my heart. I fear
'Tis long and tedious, but my spirit clings
To that poor woman. So familiarly
Do I perceive her manner and her look
And presence, and so deeply do I feel
Her goodness, that not seldom in my walks
A momentary trance comes over me,
And to myself I seem to muse on one
By sorrow laid asleep or borne away,
A human being destined to awake
To human life, or something very near
To human life, when he shall come again
For whom she suffered.

(*"The Ruined Cottage"*)

Margaret, in this trance, is seen as a person who will awake from the sleep of death to an afterlife which is not more than human, but merely human. Her humanity was not able to realize itself during her life, so that if the narrator's spirit clings to her, her spirit also clings to him, still hoping for completion. Margaret's fictional presence is simply an extension of the consuming ghostliness of her desire. She dies into the pedlar's mind like Lucy into the poet's. The tale is her haunting.

Poetry thus becomes a commemorative rite, a ceremony to evoke and at the same time appease the perturbed spirit. At the end of the pedlar's tale, the poet is so deeply moved that, he confesses, "with a brother's love/ I blessed her [Margaret] in the impotence of grief." A difficult response, for the grief and love elicited are not unlike Margaret's own, which cursed rather than blessed the place in which he stands. Yet blessing and cursing are reactions appropriate to the appearance of spirits: Margaret's story, her passion here revived, is so strong and ambiguously spiritual, it exacts this kind of acknowledgment.

How well Coleridge knew the curse, whose Mariner is never fully released from it! Or Shelley, who prefaced *Alastor* (1815) with lines taken from "The Ruined Cottage" (Oh Sir! the good die first/ And those whose hearts are dry as summer dust/ Burn to the socket"), and who relates an even darker version of the loss of Margaret's garden in *The Sensitive Plant*. What of the narrator who spots the Danish Boy near that other ruined cottage? Or the poet who contemplates the Boy of Winander's grave? Are they seeing spirits too? "Vision as thou art," says Wordsworth of the Highland girl, "I bless thee with a human heart." Visionariness and human-heartedness are not easily reconciled. In the curse ballads, as even perhaps in the Lucy poems, the human element ("I had no human fears") is spirited away.

If imaginative power is to survive, this "curse" of the spirit—of the ever-unconsummated spirit—must be acknowledged. It dooms the boy to remain a boy because immemorially older than the philosophic mind into which he appears to die. The imagination outlives both boyhood and manhood, as if its imperishable restlessness, which links story to story in a rhapsode's chain, were the one form of immortality granted to human beings. The teller's touch makes all nature kin. It restores the "family," broken by desertion or death, at the level of imaginative sympathy.[11] Though the pitcher breaks, though the container is destroyed by what it contains, from the shards ("the useless fragments of a wooden bowl") a poet somewhere raises Margaret's story.

Wordsworth's new ballad, then, is still a ghost story, like so many traditional ballads or even Coleridge's *Ancient Mariner*. The poet is not interested, however, in the supernatural as such. He deals with a contagion of the mind by human materials that exert a supernatural effect. The phantomization which occurs is ultimately that of a person drawn into a deeply imaginative yet antinatural frame of mind. The story, or the ghostly idea it contains, wants to carry the narrator off: it is after his soul, and desires an incarnation as dangerous to him as consorting with nature-spirits.

Wordsworth must hold onto his mind, stand firm in it, gain a foothold on this treacherous realm where ecstasy and bathos alternate. "For I must tread on shadowy ground, must sink/ Deep—and, aloft ascending, breathe in worlds/ To which the heaven of heavens is but a veil." Even in "Tintern Abbey" that "shadowy ground" is felt. The poet's act of emplacing himself remains uncertain, precarious. His psyche is encircled by the psychic from which it draws its being.

All the more so in "The Danish Boy" where both observer and observed remain shadowy. To what sacred or daemonic ground are we being led so insistently? Who is speaking, who is directing us there? The narrator has no real "character": this voice out of silence can only be that of an eccentric guide or of some ghostly being. Follow that voice at your risk. We can think of the story as a local tradition retold, like "The Thorn," by a disordered or infected imagination; but we can also think of it as a visionary seduction, the poet-traveler waylaid by the spirit of the place, or the Mind of Man by an image out of balladry's *anima mundi.*

4

No one, so far as I know, has set "The Danish Boy" to music. But Goethe's "Erlkönig," first recited during a *Singspiel* at Weimar in 1782, has haunted the musical as well as literary interpreter. It, rather than Wordsworth's poem, should be called a *lyrical* ballad. The poem is in several distinct voices, which alternate, rise to a climax and cease.* To characterize those voices is relatively simple because of the lyric's dramatic structure: one voice is anonymous, that of the ballad narrator; the others are the personal voices of father, son, and Erl-King. If the poem evokes, like Wordsworth's ballad, the presence of the daemonic, or of a mind prey to the daemonic, this does not embarrass the narrative or lead us to puzzle about the "character" (psychology) of the narrator. However eerie a silence from which these voices arise, they are so clearly typed, so bonded to role, that when Goethe's spectacle of sound is over they seem to have fulfilled a destined play; and the ending, though it involves a child's death, curiously satisfies our imagination.

It might have been a more disquieting ballad. Its atmosphere, certainly, is visionary enough. We are reminded of Herder's "Gefühl der Nacht," his reading Fingal and hoping for sunrise "mit Mitternachtwind umschauert." It is as if some passage-trial

* See end of chapter for the text of "Der Erlkönig."

were taking place: the rider must run, with the boy in his arms, a gauntlet of ghostly trees. No doubt Gundolf exaggerates when he talks of "Locken, Raunen, Dämmern, und Weben des Wassers und der Luft, zu Elementargeistern verdichtend, aus dem Grauen heraus ballend."[12] Yet the boy's death is difficult to explain except as a victory of the *Elementargeister*: have they not succeeded in stealing him away, in kidnapping his imagination? As in "Der Fischer," the victim lives between two realms, nature and supernatural, reasonableness and ecstasy; and he fails to maintain his separateness. Two fathers struggle for Goethe's Danish Boy; and however we interpret the outcome—whether we accept the supernatural intimation or rationalize it as the product of a fearful or feverish mind—the natural father here is not powerful enough to save his child.

Both poems, then, Goethe's and Wordsworth's, evoke a border region or no-man's-land between natural and daemonic; both are mysterious rather than mystical. Let me emphasize this similarity a moment. It is clear that, unlike Bürger, neither poet yields up his naturalism to the ghostly ballad. So, Wordsworth's comment on "The Thorn" and Goethe's on "Der Fischer" can be harmonized. The origin of the English poem was a natural impression heightened by atmospheric circumstances. "Cannot I by some invention . . . make this Thorn permanently an impressive object as the storm has made it to my eyes this moment?"[13] Goethe, for his part, wished to express through his poem "das Gefühl des Wassers . . . das Anmutige, was uns im Sommer lockt, uns zu baden." Does not the Erl-King also depict "das Anmutige," or an ominous variation of it: the ghostly solicitation of trees on a windy night?[14]

Yet it is not really wind or trees which emanates the dangerous charm. It is voice. In Wordsworth, voice is ghostly because it is a wandering sound in search of character or completion. We are compelled to ask: what does voice want? What is the point or hidden intent of the supposed narrative? Why does it haunt this place? But in Goethe's ballad, voice is ghostly because overdefined—so essentialized, so voicelike, it does not require localization. We are as close to *seeing* voices as is possible. More is involved, however, than Goethe's plastic power, a classicist will-to-form that seeks to dominate even a romantic-ghostly situation. The impression conveyed by the minimal art of this great artist is of voices overheard in the dark, therefore at once clear and obscure, piano and forte, individuated yet merging back into night, nature, and wind. They create as they speak the world of which they speak, as if it were through voice we reached the concept of being. The two fathers become simply two voices in the ear of the child and reader. There is nothing else but this ghostly "Nachtmusik" in which difference of being is reduced to difference of voice.

Goethe's poem, thus, eliminates narrative by absorbing it into voice. The disappearance—classical, musical or dramatic—of the narrator into his voices evades the very issue haunting Wordsworth, that of the complicity of art and artist, or of the psychology of narration. Only at the end is Goethe forced to revert to narrative and so to raise the question as to what "voice" has mediated the other voices. The author's disappearance is modified by a "remainder" of which we are not aware till that last stanza; and even there it is so carefully managed that it betrays less the invisible author than a directorial skill of near magical proportions.

On analysis, Goethe's first stanza is already a play of voices, though we do not know precisely who asks or who replies, or whether it is one voice or two. The emphasis is clearly shifted by his prelude from narrative to voice; and within this from the expressive pathos of each voice to a question and answer, or cry and reply, structure. The division of voices, in short, is as impersonal or modal as that between tenor and bass or parts assigned different instruments. Only in the second stanza do we feel this musical partition becoming a real division; and even here an ideal symmetry or balance of tones modifies the impression of *Zwiespalt*. There is, momentarily, a sense of containment: the father's words, which begin and end the verse, hold the boy as firmly as do his arms.

But the next lines complicate the cry and reply pattern. The Erl-King's voice takes over a whole stanza: it is put in its own, uninterrupted vocal space, apart from that of father and child, yet ominously complete. The middle of the poem (stanzas 4–5) repeats this pattern of a divided stanza followed by a whole; the movement seems to begin again with stanza six, but in the climax of the seventh the Erl-King's threat is followed at once by the boy's cry, which is followed, instead of by the father's words, by no reply at all. It is the narrator who takes over in a final stanza, which is the only strictly narrative portion of the ballad.

How do we interpret this narrative "remainder"? It heightens the impersonal mood and seems to confirm the poem as a masterful development of the impersonal ballad. But we can insist, at the same time, on the movement from voice to voice, and ask what kind of voice might have followed the climax of the seventh stanza. Narrativity then appears as a voice-substitute: a speaking silence which takes over when a voice fails or a new voice is wanting. The author shows his hand but not his voice.

What makes one shudder like the father ("Dem Vater grausets") is the role of the author rather than the situation in itself. The author seems to be in control to the very end, to the last syllables of the poem, in suggesting that the child might come through. "In seinem Armen das Kind," still raises a glimmer of hope, "war tot," extinguishes it. The shudder comes when we realize that we knew from the start a sacrifice would be required: that the boy must die, and voice fail. Something in the form itself compels this awareness. "Wer reitet so spät durch Nacht und Wind?" is, in retrospect, more than a functional device allowing the narrative to unfold. It is as much a challenge as a question, a *qui vive* indicating a satisfaction to be exacted, if only in the form of an appropriate answer. And the answer we then hear is indeed strangely impersonal, cold, ritualistic. Does it imply a judgment that father and son are trespassing on ghostly ground? Or is it, potentially, an intercession: doom-words which might still turn into passwords?

All we hear is voices, as if the action were to be played out on that level—yet if that is so, the expectation of a transcendent voice, redeeming or resolving, is raised without being fulfilled. The middle of the poem does waver subtly between personal and impersonal constructions, but the concluding stanza returns to impersonality. The *er*, dominant in the first stanza, then receding uninflected into Vat*er*, or hiding in *Er*lkönig, is sharply obtruded once more: er reitet . . . Er hält . . . Er-reicht. No password or saving voice has appeared. The "remainder" is like the corpse brought home.

The withholding of personal voice is, therefore, a formal triumph or else the price Goethe pays to wrest this genre from the past. Perhaps both are one; perhaps what Henry James called "the coercive charm of form" has here become an *amor fati* related to Goethe's sense of artistic and historical vocation. Let us recall the context. Goethe is directing a "Wald- und Wasserdrama," and he opens it with the "Erlkönig." The form he revives is a *Singspiel* in small, performed at Weimar, where less than ten years before Wieland staged an *Alceste* inspired by Gluck. Is not Goethe enacting something Orphic himself in leading this form, these voices, out of the silence of the past? If so, his orphism belongs to art alone: the artist is the only magus; the show begins and ends according to his will. "May I be bold to think these spirits?" Ferdinand asks Prospero in *The Tempest*, when shown another kind of "harmonious" vision. And Prospero replies: "Spirits, which by mine art/ I have from their confines call'd to enact/ My present fancies." Goethe's art is equal to the spirits he conceives. The literary form itself is the magic formula.[15]

Let us reflect further on Goethe's orphism. By 1780 his program for the renewal of letters in Germany had outgrown its nationalistic or nordic phase. He engages in a ransacking of North, South, East, and West which will culminate in the great Helena episode of *Faust*. "Bildung" is all; history itself is but a "Bildungsroman"; William must become "Master." Yet in 1827, the year in which he sends the *Helena* to press, Goethe still complains: "Wir Deutschen sind von gestern." How can someone born yesterday be reborn through art, and become, like the French or English, "ein Stück Geschichte"?[16]

Hence there is something magical in Goethe's genius, in his orphic catabasis, even if he stresses, like Hegel, *Werden, Bildung, Meisterschaft*. Instant history is impossible; culture does not come out of the mouth of a gun;[17] yet the very need of it goads him like Faust into magic reanimations. What are ghosts but reanimated ideas, abstractions with a face, a void full of voices?

The difference, in this respect, between Goethe and Wordsworth is telling. Wordsworth did not have to call up ballads from the vasty deep: despite a hiatus usually blamed on the school of Waller or of Pope, the ballad was not only around him in popular and debased form but its spirit had been taken up into literature by Shakespeare. Many of the Renaissance poets, in fact, provided a pattern (as Herder remarked) for the symbiosis of popular and sophisticated fiction, a symbiosis which enabled Friederich Schlegel's famous definition of Romantic poetry as "progressively universal," and which was also one of the sources for Goethe's concept of *Bildung*.

Wordsworth feared above all the daemonism of an imagination that might leave us naked of nature or culture; but for Goethe whatever heritage might have existed is so alienated, so far in the dark backward and abysm of time, that scholarly effort and revivalist affirmation are insufficient to bring it to life.[18] Goethe must produce a culture twice-born from the start, for the historicist or antiquarian impulse can only evoke animated abstractions which he discounts under the name of *allegory*. What he dignifies by the antonym *symbol* is based not so much on history as on natural history, and suggests a productive or generative principle by which dead matter is made organic once more. This natural magic merges with the "mystery" of a craft called art which at once organizes and organicizes a past so discontinuous with the present, that, but for art, only a volcanic (storm-and-stress) historicism or a new religious incarnation could represent it.

Two conclusions from this. We see, first, why Goethe's ballad is not primarily an accommodated northern form. It cannot be assigned to one era, to nordic rather than romance stirrings, to German rather than French culture, or even to an inspired, superconscious syncretism. It arises out of all this historical experience, all this "enormous labour of the world-spirit," as Hegel called it, and yet out of nothing—out of nothing more, that is, than misty trees on a windy night.

We also understand why Goethe's attitude toward the daemonic is so much freer than Wordsworth's. The rebuilding of culture in Germany is a magian enterprise. Yet Goethe defines the daemonic as a magic inherent in nature. The daemonic is not ultimately distinguishable from the productive power of nature, and is called the daemonic simply because adversity and death may accompany its energic drive. So Goethe's admiration for Napoleon and Byron includes their ruin as well as their achievements. The daemonic enlarges character as fate: it is genius in its human form.

Compare the tradition that goes from Wordsworth to Keats. It is deeply uncertain of the "character" or "identity" of the poet. What kind of labor is imaginative labor? The charge that poetry is an ignoble or idle dreaming—"Thou art a dreaming thing;/ A fever of thyself"[19]—is never far from the English consciousness. But Goethe's labor is cut out for him. Could any one be more productive than this demiurge who works at catching culture up, who builds *Bildung* with devilish energy of purpose? What a supremely confident maker!

We must not simplify, however: in one respect he too is wary of all this dream-work. He knows that many persons of daemonic character are not interested in culture as such but exclusively in rejuvenation, or what we today would call youth culture; and his own ideal is almost the opposite of that. He wants the young person to be so in touch with the cultural heritage that he and it would be mutually renewed. A purely daemonic ideal, in contrast, tends to become eudaemonic: eternal youth is sought for its own sake, not for the sake of a productive life. What the Erl-King promises the child is not unlike what Faust bitterly requests of that other demon king, Mephistopheles. The phantom seems to say to the boy, "Verweile doch, du bist so schön." He is luring him into eudaemonia, or arrested youth.

If for Wordsworth voice is daemonic, for Goethe it is eudaemonic. Wordsworth's "still sad music of humanity" wants to chastize voice, to ground its ghostliness, to endow it with the reality of character. But Goethe wants to make voice more genuinely daemonic, orphic, productive. The Word must become Act. The daemonic in man must triumph over the eudaemonic. Musicality must become characteristic and voice release itself from the Italian charm.[20]

It has become customary to use "voice" as a metonymy for "character," but this may conceal more than it reveals. I have tried to uncover an opposition which goes deeper than that between lyric and narrative, though related to it. The daemonic or eudaemonic charm of voice should be linked, I believe, to the study of character formation as we pass, to use psychoanalytic terms, from the pre-oedipal to the oedipal phase.[21] The notion of character, in its link to the question of mimesis, then to the problem of the character or identity of the poet, may be the largest subject of a historical poetics.

To connect the psychology of art and the history of art in any methodical way is beset by the temptation of psychohistory. But just as we have used poetry to analyze the notions of "voice" and "character," so we could use it to analyze the notion of "psyche." A psychoanalysis should emerge from this more adequate to art than any so far devised; and these concepts of voice, character, and psyche may then allow us to explore the history of the poets: the relation between the works of an artist and the role he plays or desires to play in literary history.

In this light a final remark on Goethe's poem. Its source was Herder's version of a Danish ballad, "The Erl-King's (Elfking's) Daughter"; and in this ballad Sir Oluf, on the evening before his wedding, happens on the Erl-King's daughter dancing in a fairy circle—a meeting which costs him his life. Although there is a touch of motiveless malignancy in Sir Oluf's fate, we know why he has to die; just as we know why Goethe's fisherman is fished by his lorelei. The fairies are frigid: they envy human passionateness and destroy what they envy unless permitted to incorporate with it. In short, they cannot be redeemed except by securing that *soul* or *psyche* which they lack. Thus the Erl-King's daughter, like the mermaid in "Der Fischer," commits a *crime passionelle* precisely because she is passionless; and the vampire maiden, as in Goethe's "Bride of Corinth," is but a variant of this ghostly figure who seeks and cannot receive full earthly pleasure.[22]

But how do we understand, from within this logic of myth, the Erl-King's rape of the child? It strikes one as more brutal, more instinctive even, than those other fatal acts, which contain a clear hint of sexual jealousy. Whatever erotic motive exists is surely secondary to the daemon's sheer envy of the "human form divine." It is as if this daemon, all ego and no psyche, wanted to seize the psyche itself, to possess it in its purest, most pristine state. Thus by extending the myth Goethe may also have clarified it. My remark, of course, is not intended to link poetry to a pathology of incorporation, although the imaginative gift is obviously a troubled or triumphant form of empathy.

It is, in any case, Herder rather than Goethe who suffers from the ambitious need to really know the soul of every age. Recall how he threatened to persecute us with a "psychology" drawn from Ossian. The frenzy of historicist redemption which possesses him, and which remains, despite all those hyperbolic books, curiously abstract, is reduced by Goethe to humane proportions, that of actual poems. Goethe also wishes to catch up with the past; but he recognizes the quasi-erotic or daemonic nature of this quest. His art can be seen as a critique of historicism which at once honors and limits it. He knows the myth of Orpheus is shadowed by failure, as the parallel myth of Alcestis by human sacrifice; and this knowledge, this shadow, never leaves the author of *Faust*, who seeks, like his hero, an eternally youthful psyche which draws him ever on.

The Danish Boy: A Fragment

Between two sister moorland rills
There is a spot that seems to lie
Sacred to flowrets of the hills,
And sacred to the sky.
And in this smooth and open dell
There is a tempest-stricken tree;
A corner-stone by lightning cut,
The last stone of a cottage hut;
And in this dell you see
A thing no storm can e'er destroy,
The shadow of a Danish Boy.

In clouds above, the Lark is heard,
He sings his blithest and his best;
But in this lonesome nook the Bird
Did never build his nest.
No Beast, no Bird hath here his home;
The Bees borne on the breezy air
Pass high above those fragrant bells
To other flowers, to other dells,
Nor ever linger there.
The Danish Boy walks here alone:
The lovely dell is all his own.

A spirit of noon day is he,
He seems a Form of flesh and blood;
Nor piping Shepherd shall he be,
Nor herd-boy of the wood.
A regal vest of fur he wears,
In colour like a raven's wing;
It fears not rain, nor wind, nor dew;
But in the storm 'tis fresh and blue
As budding pines in Spring;
His helmet has a vernal grace,
Fresh as the bloom upon his face.

A harp is from his shoulder slung:
He rests the harp upon his knee;
And there in a forgotten tongue
He warbles melody.
Of flocks upon the neighboring hills
He is the darling and the joy;

And often, when no cause appears,
The mountain ponies prick their ears,
They hear the Danish Boy,
While in the dell he sits alone
*Beside the tree and corner-stone.**

There sits he: in his face you spy
No trace of a ferocious air,
Nor ever was a cloudless sky
So steady or so fair.
The lovely Danish Boy is blest
And happy in his flowery cove:
From bloody deeds his thoughts are far;
And yet he warbles songs of war;
They seem like songs of love,
For calm and gentle is his mien;
Like a dead Boy he is serene.

. . . .

* In the 1800 *Lyrical Ballads*, an additional stanza follows:
When near this blasted tree you pass,
Two sods are plainly to be seen
Close at its root, and each with grass
Is cover'd fresh and green.
Like turf upon a new-made grave
These two green sods together lie,
Nor heat, nor cold, nor rain, nor wind
Can these two sods together bind,
Nor sun, nor earth, nor sky,
But side by side the two are laid,
As if sever'd by the spade.

Der Erlkönig

Wer reitet so spät durch Nacht und Wind?
Es ist der Vater mit seinem Kind;
Er hat den Knaben wohl in dem Arm,
Er fasst ihn sicher, er hält ihn warm.–

Mein Sohn, was birgst du so bang dein Gesicht?–
Siehst, Vater, du den Erlkönig nicht?
Den Erlenkönig mit Kron' und Schweif?–
Mein Sohn, es ist ein Nebelstreif.–

"Du liebes Kind, komm, geh mit mir!
Gar schöne Spiele spiel' ich mit dir;
Manch' bunte Blumen sind an dem Strand;
Meine Mutter hat manch' gülden Gewand."

Mein Vater, mein Vater, und hörest du nicht,
Was Erlenkönig mir leise verspricht?–
Sei ruhig, bleibe ruhig, mein Kind!
In dürren Blättern säuselt der Wind.–

"Willst, feiner Knabe, du mit mir gehn?
Meine Töchter sollen dich warten schön;
Meine Töchter führen den nächtlichen Reihn
Und wiegen und tanzen und singen dich ein."

Mein Vater, mein Vater, und siehst du nicht dort
Erlkönigs Töchter am düstern Ort?–
Mein Sohn, mein Sohn, ich seh' es genau;
Es scheinen die alten Weiden so grau.–

"Ich liebe dich, mich reizt deine schöne Gestalt;
Und bist du nicht willig, so brauch' ich Gewalt."–
Mein Vater, mein Vater, jetzt fasst er mich an!
Erlkönig hat mir ein Leids getan!–

Dem Vater grausets, er reitet geschwind,
Er hält in Armen das ächzende Kind,
Erreicht den Hof mit Mühe und Not;
In seinen Armen das Kind war tot.

Part Three

Literature High and Low
The Case of the Mystery Story

The terms reversal (*peripeteia*) and recognition (*anagnorisis*) are well known. They name, according to Aristotle, the essential ingredients of complex plots in tragedy. Reversal he defines as a change which makes the action veer in a different direction to that expected, and he refers us to the messenger from Corinth who comes to cheer Oedipus and eventually produces the recognition leading to an opposite result. Recognition is often linked to this kind of reversal, and is defined as a change from ignorance to knowledge. "Then once more I must bring what is dark to light," Oedipus says in the prologue of the play—and does exactly that, however unforeseen to him the result. In most detective stories, clearly, there is both a reversal and a recognition, but they are not linked as powerfully as in tragedy. The reversal in detective stories is more like an unmasking; and the recognition that takes place when the mask falls is not prepared for by dramatic irony. It is a belated, almost last minute affair, subordinating the reader's intelligence to such hero-detectives as Ross Macdonald's Archer, who is no Apollo, but who does roam the California scene with cleansing or catalyzing effect.

I wish, however, to draw attention to a third term, left obscure in the *Poetics*. Aristotle calls it *tò pathos*, "The Suffering," or as Butcher translates it, the "Scene of Suffering." *Tò pathos*, he says—and it is all he says—"is a destructive or painful action, such as death on the stage, bodily agony, wounds and the like."[1]

Aristotle is probably referring to what happens at the conclusion of *Oedipus Rex*, though chiefly offstage: the suicide of

Jocasta and self-blinding of Oedipus. Or to the exhibition of the mangled head of Pentheus by his deluded mother, in Euripides' *Bacchae*. He may also be thinking of the premise on which the tragic plot is built, the blood deed from which all consequences flow, and which, though premised rather than shown, is the real point of reference.[2] I wish to suggest that some such "heart of darkness" scene, some such *pathos*, is the relentless center or focus of detective fiction, and that recognition and reversal are merely paths toward it—techniques which seek to evoke it as strongly and visually as possible.

I don't mean that we must have the scene of suffering—the actual murder, mutilation, or whatever—exhibited to us. In *The Chill*, and in Ross Macdonald's novels generally, violence is as offstage as in *Oedipus Rex*. (The real violence, in any case, is perpetrated on the psyche.) But to solve a crime in detective stories means to give it an exact location: to pinpoint not merely the murderer and his motives but also the very place, the room, the ingenious or brutal circumstance. We want not only proof but, like Othello, ocular proof. Crime induces a perverse kind of epiphany: it marks the spot, or curses it, or invests it with enough meaning to separate it from the ordinary space-time continuum. Thus, though a Robbe-Grillet may remove the scene of pathos, our eyes nervously inspect all those graphic details which continue to evoke the detective story's lust for evidence.

The example of Robbe-Grillet—I want to return to it later—suggests that sophisticated art is closer to being an antimystery rather than a mystery. It limits, even while expressing, this passion for ocular proof. Take the medieval carol, "Lully, lulley," and regard how carefully it frames the heart of darkness scene, how with a zooming motion at once tactful and satisfyingly ritual, it approaches a central mystery:

Lully, lulley,
The faucon hath born my mak away

He bare him up, he bare him down,
He bare him into an orchard brown.

In that orchard there was an halle
Which was hanged with purpill and pall.

And in that hall there was a bed,
It was hanged with gold so red.

And in that bed there lith a knight,
His wounds bleding day and night.

By that bed side kneleth a may,
And she wepeth both night and day.

And by that bed side there stondeth a stone,
Corpus Christi *wreten there on.*

Here we have a scene of pathos, "death on the stage, bodily agony, wounds and the like," but in the form of picture-and-inscription, a still-life we can contemplate without fear. It is a gentle falcon, even if it be a visionary one, that lifts us in this ballad from the ordinary world into that of romance. This is no bird of prey attracted to battlefield carnage. And though the heart of the romance is dark enough, it is also comforting rather than frightening because interpreted by the inscription. We do not have to overcome an arresting moment of pity or fear, we do not even have to ask, as in the Parsifal legends, "What does this mean?" in order to redeem the strange sight. Its redeeming virtue is made clear to everyone borne away on this ritual trip.

The relation of the ballad to the modern mystery story is a complicated one; and my purpose here is not historical genealogy. The ballad revival had its influence not only on the gothic novel with its mystifications but also on the tension between brevity and elaboration in Melville's *Billy Budd*, the tales of Henry James, and the Gaucho stories of Borges. The modern elliptical ballad as well as the "novel turned tale"[3] qualify the element of mystery in a definably new, even generic way.

Consider Wordsworth's "The Thorn," first published in a collection called *Lyrical Ballads* (1798). The movement of this ballad is so slow, the dramatic fact so attenuated, that we begin to sense the possibility of a plotless story. A line of descent could easily be established between pseudonarratives like "The Thorn," which converge obsessively on an ocular center of uncertain interest (has a crime been committed near the thorn, or is the crime an illusion to stimulate crude imaginations?) and lyrical movies like Antonioni's *Blow Up* or Resnais's *Marienbad.* The center they scan is an absence; the darkness they illumine has no heart. There is pathos here but no defined scene of pathos. Instead of a whodunit we get a whodonut, a story with a hole in it.[4]

Wordsworth's poem begins and ends with a thornbush seen by the poet "on the ridge of Quantock Hill, on a stormy day, a thorn which I had often passed in calm and bright weather without noticing it. I said to myself, 'Cannot I by some invention do as much to make this Thorn permanently an impressive object as the storm has made it to my eyes at this moment?' " The narrator's eye, therefore, remains on the thorn, or the thorn (if you wish) in his eye: as always in Wordsworth the path from thing to meaning via an act of imaginative perception (an "invention") is fully, almost painfully respected. Though consciousness moves toward what it fears to find, a scene of ballad sorrow and bloodiness, it never actually presents that beautiful and ominous "still" which the Corpus Christi poem composes for us. The corpse has vanished and will not be found. The strange spot is not approached on the wings of a falcon, nor does it ever become a burning bush. Instead we approach it from within a peculiar consciousness, whose repetitive, quasi-ritual stepping from one object to another, from thorn to pond to hill of moss, as well as spurts of topographical precision—"And to the left, three yards beyond,/ You see a little muddy pond"—suggests we are behind the camera-eye of a mad movie maker, or . . . on the way to Robbe-Grillet.

But what exactly are we on the way to? Robbe-Grillet, after hints in Henry James, Gide, Faulkner, and Camus, has killed the scene of pathos. We all know that a corpse implies a story; yet Robbe-Grillet's contention that a story kills, that a story is a corpse, may be news for the novel. In his fiction the statement "He has a past" is equivalent to "He is doomed" or "It is written." So Oedipus, or a Robbe-Grillet hero, is safe as long as he has no past. So the detective in *The Erasers* commits the crime he is sent to solve: he enacts the prefigurative or formalistic force of traditional story-making which insists on its corpse or scene of suffering. If, moreover, we identify that scene of suffering with what Freud calls the primal scene—the "mystery" of lovemaking which the child stumbles on—then we also understand why Robbe-Grillet is opposed to character or plot based on a psychoanalytic model. For him Freudianism is simply another form of mystery religion, one which insists on its myth of depth and hidden scene of passion. Robbe-Grillet formulates therefore, what might be called the modern script-tease, of which Antonioni's *Blow Up* and *L'Avventura*, Bergman's *A Passion*, and Norman Mailer's *Maidstone*,[5] are disparate examples. What they share is the perplexing absence of *tò pathos*: one definitively visualized scene to which everything else might be referred.

I have brought you, safely I hope, from ancient to modern mystery stories by following the fortunes of the scene of pathos. But one comment should be added concerning this scene, and its structure. Comparing the scene of suffering with Freud's primal scene we gain a clue as to why it is able to motivate entire novels or plays.

It resembles, first of all, a highly condensed, supersemantic event like riddle, oracle, or mime. Now whether or not the power of such scenes is linked to our stumbling as innocents on sexual secrets—on seeing or overhearing that riddling mime[6]—it is clear that life is always in some way too fast for us, that it is a spectacle we can't interpret or a dumbshow difficult to word. The detective novel allows us to catch up a little by involving us in the interpretation of a mystery that seems at first to have no direct bearing on our life. We soon realize, of course, that "mystery" means that something is happening too fast to be spotted. We are made to experience a consciousness (like Oedipa's in Thomas Pynchon's *Crying of Lot 49*) always behind and running; vulnerable therefore, perhaps imposed on. But we are also allowed to triumph (unlike Oedipa) over passivity when the detective effects a catharsis or purgation of consciousness, and sweeps away all the false leads planted in the course of the novel.

No wonder the detective's reconstitution of the scene of pathos has something phantasmagoric about it. So quick that it is always "out of sight," the primal scene's existence, real or imagined, can only be mediated by a fabulous structure in which coincidence and convergence play a determining role. Time and space condense in strange ways, like language itself, and produce absurdly packed puns of fate. What is a clue, for instance, but a symbolic or condensed corpse, a living trace or materialized shadow? It shrinks space into place (furniture, and so forth) exactly as a bullet potentially shrinks or sensitizes time. The underdetermined or quasi-invisible becomes, by a reversal, so overdetermined and sharply visible that it is once again hard on the eyes. Bullet, clue, and pun have a comparable phenomenological shape: they are as magical in their power to heighten or oppress imagination as Balzac's "oriental" device of the fatal skin in *La Peau de Chagrin*.

Is it less oriental, magical, or punning when, in a Ross Macdonald story, the same gun is used for killings 15 years apart or the murders of father and then son take place in the same spot also fifteen years apart (*The Underground Man*)? Or when, as in *The Chill*, a man's "mother" turns out to be his wife? Or when, in Mrs. Radcliffe's *Romance of the Forest*, a marriageable girl happens to be brought to the very castle chamber where her true father was killed while she was still an infant? Recall also the speed with which things move in *Oedipus Rex*, and how a messenger who on entry is simply a UPI runner from Corinth proves to be an essential link in Oedipus' past, part of the chain that preserved him from death and for a second death—the consciousness to befall him. There is nothing more fearfully condensed than the self-image Oedipus is left with: "A man who entered his father's bed, wet with his father's blood."

I am haunted therefore by André Breton's image of "le revolver aux cheveux blancs." There has always been something like this greyhaired gun, some magic weapon in the service of superrealism. The movie camera that "shoots" a scene is the latest version of this venerable gadget. Our reality-hunger, our desire to know the worst and the best, is hard to satisfy. In Sophocles' day it was oracular speech that prowled the streets and intensified the consciousness of men. "This day will show your birth *and* will destroy you." Try to imagine how Tiresias's prophecy can come to pass. A lifetime must depend on a moment, or on one traumatic recognition.

Tragedy as an art that makes us remember death is not unlike a memory vestige forcing us back to birth—to the knowledge that man is born of woman rather than self-born, that he is a dependent and mortal being. We become conscious of human time. The detective story, however, allows *place* to turn the tables on *time* by means of its decisive visual reanimations. The detective's successful pursuit of vestiges turns them into quasi-immortal spores; and while this resuscitation of the past partakes of the uncanny,[7] it also neatly confines the deadly deed or its consequences to a determinate, visualized, field.

This observation brings me to a central if puzzling feature of the popular mystery. Its plot idea tends to be stronger than anything the author can make of it. The *surnaturel* is *expliqué*, and the djinni returned to the bottle by a trick. For the mystery story has always been a genre in which appalling facts are made to fit into a rational or realistic pattern. The formula dominating it began to emerge with the first instance of the genre, Horace Walpole's *Castle of Otranto* (1764), which begins when a child who is the heir apparent of a noble house is killed by the enormous helmet of an ancestral statue which buries him alive. After this ghostly opening Walpole's novel moves, like its descendants, from sensation to simplification, from bloody riddle to quasi-solution, embracing as much "machinery" as possible on the way.

The conservative cast of the mystery story is a puzzle. Born in the Enlightenment, it has not much changed. As mechanical and manipulative as ever, it explains the irrational, after exploiting it, by the latest rational system: Macdonald, for instance, likes to invent characters whose lives have Freudian or Oedipal explanations. In *The Underground Man*, the murderer turns out to be a murderess, a possessive mother with an overprotected son. The real underground man is the underground woman. With a sense of family nightmare as vivid as it is in Walpole, the novel advances inward, from the discovery of the corpse to the frozen psyche of the murderess, Mrs. Snow. All the characters are efficiently, even beautifully sketched, but they are somehow too understandable. They seem to owe as much to formula as the plot itself, which moves deviously yet inexorably toward a solution of the mystery.

A good writer, of course, will make us feel the gap between a mystery and its laying to rest. He will always write in a way that resists the expected ending: not simply to keep us guessing (for, as Edmund Wilson remarked, "The secret is nothing at all") but to show us more about life—that is, about the way people die while living. What is uncovered is not death but death-in-life.[8]

Perhaps endings (resolutions) are always weaker than beginnings, and not only in the "explained mystery" kind of detective story. What entropy is involved? Pynchon's *The Crying of Lot 49*, more imaginative than Mailer's *Barbary Shore*, and one of the few genuinely comic treatments in America of the detective story formula, suggests an answer. It is not simply a matter of beginnings and endings but of two sorts of repetition, one of which is magical or uncanny, the other deadly to spirit. Magical repetition releases us into the symbol: a meaning that sustains us while we try to thread secondary causes, trivialities, middles-and-muddles—the rich wastings of life in pre-energy-conserving America. As Pynchon's novel unfolds, we are literally wasted by its riches; those cries and sights; that treasure of trash; and to redeem it all only the notion of anamnesis, which reintroduces the idea of a "first" cause, counterbalances the drag:

> *She was meant to remember*. . . . She touched the edge of its voluptuous field, knowing it would be lovely beyond dreams simply to submit to it; that not gravity's pull, laws of ballistics, feral ravening, promised more delight. She tested it, shivering: I am meant to remember. Each clue that comes is *supposed* to have its own clarity, its fine chances for permanence.
> But then she wondered if the gemlike "clues" were only some kind of compensation. To make up for her having lost the direct, epileptic Word, the cry that might abolish the night.

Oedipa's vision of being trapped in an "excluded middle," that is, having to desire always some first or last event that would resolve life in terms of something or nothing, meaning or meaninglessness, is reenforced, in the novel's last pages, by a haunting blend of metaphors:

> It was like walking among matrices of a great digital computer, the zeros and ones twinned above, hanging like balanced mobiles right and left, ahead, thick, maybe endless. Behind the hieroglyphic streets there would either be a transcendent meaning, or only the earth. . . . either an accommodation reached, in some kind of dignity, with the Angel of Death, or only death and the daily, tedious preparations for it.

If Pynchon's novel ends strongly, it is because it doesn't end. "It's time to start," says Genghis Cohen, of the auction, and by a kind of "honest forgery" (a sustained theme in the book) we find ourselves with Oedipa, absurdly, lyrically, at the threshold of yet another initiation.[9] This outwitting of "the direct, epileptic Word" is like purifying the imagination of *tò pathos*; for the ritual "crying" evoked but not rendered at the close of Pynchon's book is simply a version of that "long-distance" call which perhaps began everything.

The detective story structure—strong beginnings and endings, and a deceptively rich, counterfeit, "excludable" middle—resembles almost too much that of symbol or trope.[10] Yet the recent temptation of linguistic theorists to collapse narrative structure into this or that kind of metaphoricity becomes counterproductive if it remains blind to the writer's very struggle to outwit the epileptic Word. Take a less symbolic novel than Pynchon's, one in the European tradition of selfconscious realism. In Alfred Andersch's *Efraim's Book* the narrator generates an entire novel by writing *against* a final disclosure.[11] Efraim keeps interpolating new incidents although he knows the book will trump him in the end. A journalist shuttling between London, Berlin, and Rome, he is moved to write a book whose climax is the embarrassing secret he continually delays telling. Efraim is a post-Auschwitz Jew and uprooted intellectual who broods on the human condition, yet the secret obsessing him is simply that his wife is unfaithful. It is as if Andersch wants to reduce the dilemmas of moral existence in postwar Europe to a humiliating sexual disclosure.

We are not deceived by this deflation any more than by the inflated secret of detective stories. I prefer Andersch's novel, a work of political and artistic intelligence, to most mystery stories, but there is much in it that suggests it is in flight from the detective novel mood—from a "mystery" too great to face. What if Efraim, after Auschwitz, had assumed the role of hero-detective and investigated that crime in order to fix its guilt with moral and visual precision? An impossible project: there is no language for it. Efraim thinks he is writing to delay facing a painful ending but he is really writing against the terror and intractability of historical events which the mind cannot resolve or integrate. He chooses a substitute secret, the infidelity of his wife, to keep himself writing, and moving into ordinary life. *Efraim's Book* has no formal ending other than the decision of the writer to accept himself: to accept to survive, in spite of Auschwitz and the defiling reality of posthumous existence.

Most popular mysteries are devoted to solving rather than examining a problem. Their reasonings put reason to sleep, abolish darkness by elucidation, and bury the corpse for good. Few detective novels want the reader to exert his intelligence fully, to find gaps in the plot or the reasoning, to worry about the moral question of fixing the blame. They are exorcisms, stories with happy endings that could be classified with comedy because they settle the unsettling. As to the killer, he is often a bogeyman chosen by the "finger" of the writer after it has wavered suspensefully between this and that person for the right number of pages.

There exists, of course, a defense of the mystery story as art, whose principal document is Raymond Chandler's *The Simple Art of Murder*. In his moving last pages about the gritty life of the hero-detective, Chandler claims that mystery stories create a serious fictional world:

> It is not a fragrant world, but it is the world you live in, and certain writers with tough minds and a cool spirit of detachment can make very interesting and even amusing patterns out of it . . . . In everything that can be called art there is a quality of redemption. It may be pure tragedy, if it is high tragedy, and it may be pity and irony, and it may be the raucous laughter of the strong man. But down these mean streets a man must go who is not himself mean, who is neither tarnished nor afraid . . . . He is a common man or he would not go among common people. He has a sense of character, or he would not know his job. He will take no man's money dishonestly and no man's insolence without a due and dispassionate revenge . . . . He talks as the man of his age talks—that is, with rude wit, a lively sense for the grotesque, a disgust for sham, and a contempt for pettiness. The story is this man's adventure in search of hidden truth.

Ross Macdonald has also defended the social and psychological importance of the detective story and described it as rooted "in the popular and literary tradition of the American frontier." Neither writer puts much emphasis on problem solving, on finding out who killed Roger Ackroyd. But as the claims grow for the honesty, morality, and the authentic American qualities of the detective novel, one cannot overlook the ritual persistence of the problem-solving formula.

Only in France has the eye of the private eye been thoroughly questioned. I have mentioned Robbe-Grillet; his collaboration with Resnais on films like *Marienbad* is also significant in this respect. What is missing from *Marienbad*, yet endlessly suggested, is *tò pathos*. Nothing moves us so much as when the image on the screen tries to escape at certain points a voice that would pin it down to one room, one bed, one time, one identity. Yet the screen image cannot be "framed": by remaining a moving picture it defeats our wish to spot the flagrant act, or to have speech and spectacle coincide. The scene of pathos—call it "Hiroshima," "Marienbad," or "Auschwitz"—eludes the mind it haunts.

A danger, of course, is the closeness of all this not only to mobile dreaming but also to erotic fantasy. The inbuilt voyeurism of the camera eye makes love and death interchangeable subjects. It cannot distinguish between these "mysteries" because of the mind's hunger for reality, its restless need to spot, or give the lie to, one more secret. It seeks to arrest the eyes yet is never satisfied with the still or snapshot that reveals all.

After writers like Andersch and Robbe-Grillet, one turns with relief to Ross Macdonald and the naive reality-hunger of American detective fiction. In *The Underground Man* Macdonald keeps entirely within the problem-solving formula but broadens it by providing a great California fire as the background. This fire is an "ecological crisis" linked more than fortuitously to the cigarillo dropped by Stanley Broadhurst, the murdered son. Stanley belongs to a "generation whose elders had been poisoned, like the pelicans, with a kind of moral DDT that damaged the lives of their young." By combining ecological and moral contamination Macdonald creates a double plot that spreads the crime over the California landscape.

California becomes a kind of "open city" where everyone seems related to everyone else through, ironically, a breakdown in family relations that spawns adolescent gangs and other new groupings. The only personal detail we learn about the detective, Lew Archer, is that his wife has left him, which is what we might expect. Neither cynical nor eccentric, Archer resembles an ombudsman or public defender rather than a tough detective. He doesn't seem to have a private office, often being approached by his clients in public. One might say he doesn't have clients since anyone can engage his moral sympathy.

He is, then, as Chandler prescribed, a catalyst, not a Casanova, who sees more sharply than others do. It is curious how the detective, as a type, is at the same time an ingénue and a man of experience—his reasoning must take evil or criminal motives into account, but through his eyes we enjoy the colors of the familiar world. Like other realistic artists the good crime writer makes the familiar new, but he can do so only under the pressure of extreme situations. It is as if crime alone could make us see again, or imaginatively enough, to enter someone else's life.

Archer is not better than what he sees but rather a knowing part of it. His observations (acute, overdefined, "Her eyes met me and blurred like cold windows") are those of an isolated, exposed man with a fragmented life. He finds just what he expects, people like himself, reluctantly free or on the run, and others equally lonely but still living within the shrinking embrace of an overprotective family. Yet just because Archer is so mobile and homeless he can bring estranged people together and evoke, as in *The Underground Man*, a consoling myth of community where there is none.

It is a myth only for the time being, perhaps only for the time of the book. Down these polluted freeways goes a man with undimmed vision, cutting through sentimental fog and fiery smog to speak face to face in motel or squalid rental or suburban ranch with Mr. and Mrs. and Young America! Superb in snapshot portraiture of California life, Macdonald gives us a sense of the wildlife flushed out by the smoke, the way people lean on one another when they fear crime and fire. They are neatly described by Archer, who moves among them as erratically as the fire itself.

This panoramic realism has its advantages. It is outward and visual rather than introspective, and so tends to simplify character and motive. There is a terrible urge—in Raymond Chandler even more than in Ross Macdonald—to make the most of gross visual impressions. Hence Moose Molloy in Chandler's *Farewell, My Lovely*, "a big man but not more than six feet five inches tall and no wider than a beer truck" who "looked about as inconspicuous as a tarantula on a slice of angel food." The images flash all around us like guns, though we can't always tell to what end. Their overall aim is to make the world as deceptively conspicuous as Moose Molloy.

The detective (American style) tortures human nature until it reveals itself. People froth or lose their nerve or crumple up: the divine eye of the private eye fixes them until their bodies incriminate them. What can't be seen can't be judged; and even if what we get to see is a nasty array of protective maneuvers and defense mechanisms, the horror of the visible is clearly preferred to what is unknown or invisible.

There are, of course, differences of style among American mystery story writers. Macdonald's characters, for example, are more credible than Chandler's, because they are more ordinary, or less bizarre. Chandler is often on the verge of surrealism, of tragicomic slapstick: the first meeting between Marlowe and Carmen Sternwood in *The Big Sleep* goes immediately as far as a relation can go, short of complicity. The novels of Chandler and Macdonald have, nevertheless, the same basic flaw: the only person in them whose motives remain somewhat mysterious, or exempt from this relentless reduction to overt and vulnerable gestures, is the detective.

Yet Chandler's Marlowe is not really mysterious. Just as in his world punks are punks, old generals old generals, and the small guys remain small guys killed by small-time methods (liquor spiked with cyanide), so a detective is a detective:

"The first time we met I told you I was a detective. Get it through your lovely head. I work at it, lady. I don't play at it."

When Marlowe is asked why he doesn't marry, he answers "I don't like policemen's wives." To marry Mr. Detective means becoming Mrs. Detective. Nothing here is immune from specialization: you can hire killers or peekers or produce sex or sell friendliness. Identities are roles changed from time to time yet as physically clear as warts or fingerprints. Your only hope is not being trapped by your *role* into an *identity*. Once you are marked, or the bite is on you, fun is over. It is, consequently, a clownish world: grotesque, manic, evasive, hilariously sad. Chandleresque is not far from Chaplinesque.

The one apparent superiority of the detective is that although he can be hired, he doesn't care for money (even if he respects its power). We really don't know whether the other characters care for it either, but they are placed in situations where they *must* have it—to make a getaway, for instance—or where it is the visible sign of grace, of their power to dominate and so to survive. What Marlowe says to a beautiful woman who offers him money is puzzlingly accurate: "You don't owe me anything. I'm paid off." Puzzling because it is unclear where his real satisfaction comes from. He seems under no compulsion to dominate others and rarely gets pleasure from taking gambles. What is there in it for him? The money is only expense money. We don't ever learn who is paying off the inner Marlowe or Archer. Their motives are virtually the only things in these stories that are not visible.

We are forced to assume that the detective is in the service of no one—or of a higher power. Perhaps there is an idealism in these tough tales stronger than the idealisms they are out to destroy.

I sat down on a pink chair and hoped I wouldn't leave a mark on it. I lit a Camel, blew smoke through my nose and looked at a piece of black shiny metal on a stand. It showed a full, smooth curve with a small fold in it and two protuberances on the curve. I stared at it. Marriott saw me staring at it. "An interesting bit," he said negligently. "I picked it up the other day. Asta Dial's *Spirit of Dawn*." "I thought it was Klopstein's *Two Warts on a Fanny*," I said.

This is merely a sideshow, but behind other and comparable scenes big questions are being raised: of reality, justice, mercy and loyalty. When Lew Archer says, "I think it started before Nick was born, and that his part is fairly innocent," he begins to sound theological, especially when he continues, "I can't promise to get him off the hook entirely. But I hope to prove he's a victim, a patsy" (*The Goodbye Look*).

The moral issues, however, are no more genuinely explored than the murders. They too are corpses—or ghosts that haunt us in the face of intractable situations. So in *The Goodbye Look*, a man picks up an eight-year-old boy and makes a pass at him. Boy shoots man. But the man is the boy's estranged father and the seduction was only an act of sentiment and boozy affection. Grim mistakes of this kind belong to folklore or to high tragedy. The detective story, however, forces them into a strict moralistic pattern or, as in Ross Macdonald, into a psychoanalytic parable with complicated yet resolvable turns.

Since man does not live on tragedy alone, and since the crime story could be considered a folk genre, this may seem no condemnation. There is, however, an exploitative element in all this: our eyes ache to read more, to see more, to know that the one just man (the detective) will succeed—yet when all is finished, nothing is rereadable. Instead of a Jamesian reticence that, at best, chastens the detective urge—our urge to know or penetrate intimately another person's world—the crime novel incites it artificially by a continuous, self-cancelling series of overstatements, drawing us into one false hypothesis or flashy scene after another.

Thus the trouble with the detective novel is not that it is moral but that it is moralistic; not that it is popular but that it is stylized; not that it lacks realism but that it picks up the latest realism and exploits it. A voracious formalism dooms it to seem unreal, however "real" the world it describes. In fact, as in a B movie, we value less the driving plot than moments of lyricism and grotesquerie that creep into it: moments that detach themselves from the machined narrative. Macdonald's California fire affects us less because of its damage to the ecology than because it brings characters into the open. It has no necessary relation to the plot, and assumes a life of its own. The fire mocks the ambitions of this kind of novel: it seems to defy manipulation.

Crime fiction today seems to be trying to change its skin and transform itself (on the Chandler pattern) into picaresque American morality tales. But its second skin is like the first. It cannot get over its love-hate for the mechanical and the manipulative. Even mysteries that do not have a Frankensteinian monster or superintelligent criminal radiate a pretechnological chill. The form trusts too much in reason; its very success opens to us the glimpse of a mechanized world, whether controlled by God or Dr. No or the Angel of the Odd.

When we read a popular crimi we do not think of it as great art but rather as "interesting" art. And our interest, especially in the hard-boiled tale of American vintage, has to do more with its social, or sociological, than with its realistic implications. I don't believe for a moment that Chandler and Macdonald tell it like it is, but perhaps they reveal in an important way why they can't tell it like it is. The American "realist in murder," says Chandler, has purged the guilty vicarage, exiled the amateurs, thrown out Lord Peter Wimsey *cum* chicken-wing-gnawing debutantes. We therefore go to the American tale expecting a naked realism. What do we find, however? A vision that remains as before, a mixture of sophisticated and puerile elements.

The American hero-detective is not what Chandler claims he is, "a complete man." He starts with death, it is true; he seems to stand beyond desire and regret. Yet the one thing the hard-boiled detective fears, with a gambler-like fascination, is being played for a *sucker*. In Hammett's *Maltese Falcon* the murder of Miles, who trusted Miss Wonderly, begins the action; Spade's rejection of Brigid O'Shaugnessy completes it. To gamble on Brigid is like gambling that love exists, or that there is, somewhere, a genuine Falcon. Spade draws back: "I won't play the sap for you."

No wonder this type of story is full of tough baby-talk. So Archer in *The Chill*:

> "No more guns for you," I said.
> No more anything, Letitia.

Taking the gun from Letitia, at the end of *The Chill*, is like denying a baby its candy. It seems a "castration" of the woman, which turns her into a child once more.

In Ross Macdonald's novels the chief victim is usually a child who needs protection from the father or society and gets it from Momma as overprotection—which is equally fatal. Enter the dick who tries to save the child and purge the Momma. Children are always shown as so imprisoned by the grown-up world that they can't deal with things as they are; and so the child remains a "sucker." There is often little difference between family and police in this respect. The psychiatrist is another overprotector. "They brought me to Dr. Smitheram,"

Nick says bitterly in *The Goodbye Look*, "and . . . I've been with him ever since. I wish I'd gone to the police in the first place." The detective alone is exempt from ties of blood or vested interest, and so can expose what must be exposed.

Both the arrested development of the detective story and its popularity seem to me related to its image of the way people live in "civilized" society—a just image on the whole. For we all know something is badly wrong with the way society or the family protects people. The world of the detective novel is full of vulnerable characters on the one hand, and of overprotected ones on the other. Macdonald complicates the issue by emphasizing the wrong done to children, and especially to their psyches. Dolly in *The Chill*, Nick Chalmers in *The Goodbye Look*, and Susan Crandall in *The Underground Man* are as much victims of what Freud calls family romance (that is, family nightmare) as of society. We don't know what to protest, and sympathize with the adolescents in *The Underground Man* who kidnap a young boy to prevent him from being sacrificed to the grown-up world.

Yet "protective custody" doesn't work. In *The Chill*, relations between Roy and Letitia Bradshaw are a classic and terrible instance of the man being forced to remain a man-boy as the price of making it. Roy, the social climber, marries a rich woman who can send him to Harvard and free him from class bondage. But the woman is old enough to be his mother and they live together officially as mother and son while she kills off younger women to whom her "child" is attracted.

Protection, such novels seem to imply, is always bought; and much of the price one pays for it is hidden. Macdonald tends to give a psychological and Chandler a sociological interpretation of this. Chandler is strongly concerned with the need for a just system of protection and the inadequacy of modern institutions to provide it. He indulges, like so many other crime writers, in conventional woman hating, but suggests at the same time that women become bitches because they are overprotected. Helen Grayle, in *Farewell, My Lovely*, is the exemplary victim who (like the Sternwood sisters in *The Big Sleep*) is allowed to get some revenge on her "protectors" before she is caught. Yet

Chandler often lets his women criminals escape, knowing sadly or bitterly that they'll be trapped by the system in the end.

To avoid being a sucker and to expose a crisis in the protective institutions of society are psychological and social themes that are not peculiar to the American detective novel. They have prevailed since chivalric Romance invented the distressed damsel and her wandering knight. But the precise kinds of family breakup, together with new and menacing groups (similar to crime syndicates) which the detective is pitted against, give crime novels a modern American tone. That the detective is a *private* sleuth defines, moreover, his character as well as his profession, and makes him the heir to a popular American myth—he is the latest of the uncooptable heroes.

Yet detective stories remain schizophrenic. Their rhythm of surprising reversals—from casual to crucial or from laconic detail to essential clue—is a factor. The deepest reversals involve, of course, feelings about the blood tie. As in Greek tragedy *pathos* is strongest when there is death in the family. The thrill of a "thriller" is surely akin to the fear that the murderer will prove to be not an outsider but someone there all the time, someone we know only too well—perhaps a blood relation.[12]

In Macdonald's fiction human relations tend to polarize: they are either quasi-incestuous (Roy and Letitia Bradshaw in *The Chill*) or markedly exogamous, exhibiting that inclination to strangers so characteristic of the hero-detective. It is as if our kinship system had suffered a crazy split. There seems to be no mean between the oppressive family ("I felt . . . as if everything in the room was still going on, using up space and air. I was struck by the thought that Chalmers, with family history breathing down his neck, may have felt smothered and cramped most of the time") and the freewheeling detective. Nothing lies between the family and the loner but a no man's land of dangerous communes: virile fraternities, like criminal mobs or the police, which are literally based on blood.

It is, then, an exceptional moment when we find Lew Archer lingering with Stanley Broadhurst's widow and her young son, at the end of *The Underground Man*. For one moment the family exists and the detective is the father. The woman touches him lightly, intimately. It ends there, on that caress, which already has distance and regret in it. We must soon return, like the detective, to a world of false fathers and disabled mothers, to children as exposed as Oedipus or Billy Budd, and to a continuing search for manifest justice. “O city, city!” (*Oedipus Rex*).

Valéry's Fable of the Bee

L'Abeille (1919)

Quelle, et si fine, et si mortelle,
Que soit ta pointe, blonde abeille,
Je n'ai, sur ma tendre corbeille,
Jeté qu'un songe de dentelle.

Pique du sein la gourde belle,
Sur qui l'Amour meurt ou sommeille,
Qu'un peu de moi-même vermeille
Vienne à la chair ronde et rebelle!

J'ai grand besoin d'un prompt tourment:
Un mal vif et bien terminé
Vaut mieux qu'un supplice dormant!

Soit donc mon sens illuminé
Par cette infime alerte d'or
Sans qui l'Amour meurt ou s'endort!

1

Et que dit la piqûre?

Eupalinos

It is hard to determine whether Valéry's "L'Abeille" is cute or acute. One can describe it, not unjustly, as a bit of erotic fantasy in a traditional form, with picturesque symbols that assuage what trouble the verbal wit might cause. The situation of the girl who wants to be "awakened" is not really different from that of the speaker in *La Jeune Parque*, but this does not of itself redeem the poem, for the strict critic might remark that "L'Abeille" has relapsed into an erotic symbolism and a neo-Greek modishness which are a recurrent French *faible*. Pierre Louÿs is still too near. We bring to this lyric a reluctant admiration for its mastery of a very minor genre: the Greek idyll, or little picture.[1] Mastery, not only because the poet respects the limits of the genre, affording us a Greek peek at this sleeper, one both sensuous and naive; but also because he chooses so well a picturable moment.

This moment Lessing called fruitful: that is, charged with potentiality. It echoes a story that we know. The entire action is held fast by this moment and resonates there. Yet what is the story in Valéry's poem? The fruitful moment here is simply the as-yet-unfruitful one; and the situation is not charged with potentiality but rather with virtuality. In brief: no story is made picturable, only a desire for story, or else for a visible, realized subject ("un peu de moi-même") of consciousness. This psyche-figure—dare we call her that?—wants to waken into love, sight or fable, but she also wants to remain herself: the "sens illuminé" of it all.

The bee, a "souhait" of the fabling senses, is a curiously apt if abstract machine. Its gold-blond coloring associates it with light: with the desired illumination, even if that should be a "lueur de la douleur." Its sole other feature is its sting. The bee is nothing, in fact, but a sting or luminous "point" from which (toward which) the self is projected. The form of this device of desire is totally subordinated to its function of illuminating the self through the senses, of making the girl visibly present to herself. I see myself, therefore I am. But this is less a *cogito* than an imaginative *coup*, with the risk implied by that aleatory word. As Valéry said of Descartes:

> Il n'y a point de syllogisme dans le *Cogito*, il n'y a même point de signification littérale. Il y a un coup de force, un acte réflexe de l'intellect, un vivant et pensant qui crie: *J'en ai assez!*[2]

Descartes has had enough of hyperbolic doubt, of a purely negative labor. Valéry presents only the reflex or counter-hyperbole to it. More precisely, he shows that both are hyperboles of desire. For are they not equally in the service of a perpetual effort to awaken—to see more clearly—exemplified by the Jeune Parque as well as by the girl of "L'Abeille"?

un poids d'abeille,
Plongeant toujours plus ivre au baiser plus aigu,
Le point délicieux de mon jour ambigu . . .
Lumière! . . . Ou toi, la Mort!

Philosopher or poet, Psyche or Narcissus: it does not seem possible for us to enter the "kingdom of our eyes."

2

Ce point sonore atome le très pur
Chargé de foudre et follement
futile

"Abeille Spirituelle"

That Valéry should reflect on the condition of his art is a condition of his art. "Je n'ai jamais pu depuis 1891 considérer l'art de littérature qu'en lui comparant et opposant un idéal de travail—un travail qui serait assez comparable à celui du compositeur de musique savante, ou du constructeur d'une théorie physico-mathématique."[3] *Eupalinos* (1922), nearly contemporaneous with *Charmes*, is only the longest and most consequent of these reflections. "Un beau corps," we read, "se fait regarder en soi-même, et nous offre un admirable moment: c'est un détail de la nature, que l'artiste a arrêté par miracle. . . . Mais la Musique et l'Architecture nous font penser à tout autre chose qu'elles-mêmes." Whereas poetry and painting make us remember our eyes, music makes us forget our ears, and even ourselves. The arts of *figure* as distinguished from those of *nombre* cannot totally transform "l'être dans son ouvrage." They are limited to a particular story or representation.

Valéry's pin-up "se fait regarder en soi-même." That is her aspiration, at least. She wants to be not only more alive but also more of a picture ("un peu de moi-même *vermeille*," "mon sens illuminé"). Whether we regard her as an animated (speaking) picture or as a sleeping beauty whose interior speech is made audible, the theme of transformation is "arrested" into the theme of form—the somnolent figure, that is, aspires not toward a total awakening but toward a "point" which promises closure ("bien terminé") and enclosure ("sois [4] mon sens"). The veiled transparence of her language, moreover, and the ambiguous shimmer of the symbols create a poetic *clair-obscur* which prevents, on the level of meaning, easy passage from surface to depth. There is depth here but no myth of depth: the language skin (skein) is so taut that meaning remains epidermic. Whatever the "oeuvre profonde," a reader can only say, as Valéry of another sleeper, "Ta forme veille."

Art, the poet knew, is not that purer "work" which makes all things into substitutes through mathematical-musical or economic operations. Poetry and painting move in a realm where a sense of limits is especially strong. These arts, while aspiring to the condition of music, remain in need of figure or fable. Representation persists as a limit; it is at once heightened by the *touche* or *piqure* of art ("Pique du sein la gourde belle") and drawn to a form "non formé de fruits." The reader's real problem begins here: he feels the coexistence of an empirical with a purer psychology—of the sensuous cliché and a cool hermetic core—yet he is tempted to see it as a deception rather than a relation. That Valéry's art is doubled by a reflection on art only helps him to constitute the latter as the allegorical or deeper meaning.[5]

As is the case with every interesting use of language, the problem is part of the subject, even the subject itself. Valéry insists on figure and fable—on the charms of representation—because his effort is precisely their reduction: that "reduction of sense" which the philosophic tradition has always engaged in, from Plato's dialectic to Descartes, Kant, and Husserl, but which, in France at least, seems to have moved even to stage-center of artistic reflection in the hundred years that join Mallarmé and Jacques Derrida.

"Reduction" and "sense" are not univocal terms. Sense incorporates "meaning," "sensory organ," and (in French) "direction." Reduction suggests an ascetic or logical purification, but also through its Latin root a leading back: especially in philosophy where it rhymes, as it were, with deduction. (So Husserl's "transcendental reduction" is formulated in the context of Kant's "transcendental deduction.") It is necessary to keep the philosophical context in mind, for while "reduction of sense" is usable English, it may not convey that what is reduced is referential (representational) meaning, or the fact that the reduction is not an actual taking away or denial of sense-experience but an affirmative return to it through an understanding of the structure of signification, "l'essence caché de l'empirie."[6]

The concept of a reduction of sense has, therefore, some play in it. It allows us to talk quite sensibly of the non-sense of poetry, or of "purity," "decreation," and "loss of story." When Wallace Stevens, who appreciated Valéry, formulates as part of his poetics the demand "It must be Abstract"; when abstract art challenges the dominance of the subject ("le sujet est ce à quoi se réduit un mauvais ouvrage," Valéry remarked); when a programmatic Symbolism under the slogan "Tout le reste est littérature" subtracts, as it were, the *signifié* from the *signifiant* to gain its own "musical" purity; and when, in every current of philosophical investigation, the question of language in its relation to muter meanings is raised—then we are facing something of more than local literary importance. Compare a naively propagandistic statement of some fifty years ago with the comprehensive terminology and ambition of a recent theorist:

Le vers, après avoir voulu s'incorporer la philosophie et l'histoire, tente de ne plus briller que de son intime cristal, de ne plus exprimer, d'isoler la poésie . . . de tout autre essence qu'elle-même.[7]

Cette puissance révélatrice du vrai langage littéraire comme poésie, c'est bien l'accès à la libre parole, celle que le mot "être" (et peut-être ce que nous visons sous la notion de "mot primitif" ou de "mot-principe" [Buber]) délivre de ses *fonctions* signalisatrices. C'est quand l'écrit est *défunt* comme signe-signal qu'il naît comme langage; alors il dit ce qui est, par là même ne renvoyant qu'à soi, signe sans signification, jeu ou pur fonctionnement, car il cesse d'être utilisé comme information naturelle, biologique ou technique, comme passage d'un étant à l'autre ou d'un signifiant à un signifié. Or, paradoxalement, l'inscription—bien qu'elle soit loin de le faire toujours—a seule puissance de poésie, c'est-à-dire d'évoquer la parole hors de son sommeil de signe. En consignant la parole, elle a pour intention essentielle et elle prend le risque mortel d'émanciper le sens à l'égard de tout champ de perception actuel, de cet engagement naturel dans lequel tout se réfère à l'affect d'une situation contingente. C'est pourquoi l'écriture ne sera jamais la simple "peinture de la voix" (Voltaire).[8]

Yet "L'Abeille," it must be added, is less than decisive in its liberation of the word from the dream of meaning. Its musicality remains a mixed affair, partly abstract, pure sound against sense, and partly generic, the lyricism of song or sonnet ("J'ai grand besoin d'un prompt tourment" is as conventional as any love-pang set to music). If not "peinture de la voix" it is "voix de la peinture:"

Ô seule et sage voix
Qui chantes pour les yeux![9]

The voice that sounds itself in "L'Abeille," even should it seek to reduce meaning to "nombre d'or," is unmistakably a voice, essence of voice. If, as Descartes said, a blind man "voit des mains," then a poet "voit de la voix." Through the luminosity of poetic speech Valéry reaffirms the illusion of action at a distance.[10]

3

dans l'or simple un vol ivre d'insecte

Baignée (1892)

Petit feu naturel d'un sidéral insecte
Né sur le souffle d'or dont le songe s'humecte

Baignée (earlier version)[11]

The genre of the idyll helps, of course, reduction of sense. A phrase like "infime alerte d'or" is at once representational and nonrepresentational. It evokes the "blonde abeille" yet also suggests something as abstract as action at a distance or as fabulous as a Jovian shower of gold. We do not pass beyond fable or reference, yet neither do we pass into them. The image reduces rather than annuls these values. "Il faut . . . des mots avec lesquels on n'en puisse jamais finir—et qui ne soient jamais identiquement annulés par une représentation quelconque: *des mots Musique.*"[12]

Elegant miniaturization does not in itself satisfy the idea of reduction. The turn from large to small, however, in the idyll or similar kinds of *féerie*, runs parallel to the turn from sense to non-sense. It evokes a feeling which can only be called *semiotic*, and which in the present poem connects with the *semeiotic* image of a fine yet fatal sting: of the infinitely small ("infime"), and so, in terms of sense-experience, almost imperceptible, being crucially effective. The "infime alerte d'or" describes the virtual power of signals, their micromegas quality, their capacity of insinuating great matters by a smallest or least perceptible token. It is like a wink or nod immediately understood, like the mystique of veil or dress,[13] or like a glitter alerting the dormant attention. The perfect signal (semeiotic) and the perfect sign (semiotic) seem to merge, as we approach a "pointe" without a "point." O poem, where is thy sting?

The sting is in the tail of the bee, as they used to say of epigrammatic sonnets.[14] Despite our analyses, however, the sonnet's "sens illuminé" has not been made clear. We are still uncertain what the poem is about. Perhaps the condition of aboutness itself? The conversion of semeiotic into semiotic seems to create a point that is not localizable in single images, metaphors, or meanings. It can be discerned only as an affective periphrasis.

If we insist on point in the old sense—on concentered reality or concentrated verbal meaning—we can still import it, since the poem reduces rather than rejects meanings. The sting has a sexual innuendo, for example;[15] yet to take it as a veiled symbol for what might satisfy sexual desire only heightens the contrast between desire and its instrument (complement) to an absurd degree. The sexual "point" is only, as a point in geometry, the means to a construction. It is not the "bien terminé" of the semiotic "desire" aroused.

The reader's liberty of construction, so often affirmed by Valéry, could start equally well from another "point," belonging to art more than nature. The beautiful phrase "alerte d'or" enters the world of *Hermès, Lanvin, Dior*—our modern *précieuses.* (Mallarmé's fascination with this world is well known.) Is not that which "illumines" the girl, and awakens love, a charm: a brooch, a gold pin perhaps? Not that the "blond bee" is in fact a brooch. Rather, from the point of view of voice (if that mixed metaphor can be forgiven) it does not matter whether we consider it as a natural or as an art object. Valéry's poem, which delights in the language of invocation, in that animating magic, finds a focus for itself and gives it a virtual kind of life. A middle life, to be precise, between nature and art, like a woman's tears which are also stars or "diamants extrêmes" in *La Jeune Parque.* So strong is the sense of voice here, or so ideal its imagined effect.

The invoked charm, then, like that "Amour" whose legendary sting is transferred to the bee,[16] is an idol created by desire for self-reflection and self-consumption. Desire is strong (awake) only when fashioning out of its very élan these precious if vain idols. "Tendre corbeille," which conflates basket, breast, and hive—so that the bee is a nurtured enemy—also suggests this intimate genesis. Desire conspires with, if it does not actually inspire, these nothings.

Consumption is not yet consummation; and a comparison of the girl's wish, so impatient for fruitfulness ("corbeille . . . gourde belle"), with the patience evoked in "Palme," shows how far we are in "L'Abeille" from a "figure . . . accomplie." These charms have their use, however. They are relatively transparent, and so do not clothe, or close off, desire (except, perhaps, like a "songe de dentelle").[17] The finer or more ductile they are, the more they appear made of language. Sylphid, and almost interchangeable, they lead to their own "presque disparition vibratoire." They exist, it seems, only for the sake of the voice whose medium they are.

To reduce the conventional, supernumerary figures of poetry, its showy or passionate personifications, to their true status as acts of voice, is an achievement in itself. Yet the ensuing vibrancy is linguistic as well as vocal. It hovers undefinably between an algebra and an abracadabra of virtual acts. By a passage *à la limite*, like that of mathematical formulae projecting a series, Valéry's poetical figures are curiously diminished—detached from all other origin or purpose than to-be-seen and to-be-spoken. They are there "for effect" and not "for cause." So the bee symbol, already a reduction, is metonymically concentrated into an effect (its sting) which is then depicted as sheer affect; so "alert" disappears into an "alertness" almost pure of external cause. We can still refer it to the bee, but we know it tends to a "ravissement sans référence."[18] All the more so as the love theme makes the small appear the intimate: a "bosom" event. We divine a vanishing point rather than a real "pointe."

Valéry often hints at "discours . . . qui ne répondent à aucun besoin, si ce n'est au besoin qu'ils doivent créer eux-mêmes."[19] The girl's "discours" in 'L'Abeille" is at once pure and impure in this regard: impure, as it evokes impatiently its stimulus or satisfaction; pure, as it becomes *causa sui*. Through the reductions already described, we sense that her affective state, when pure, is an *attente*, an alertness independent of what the poet names variably sting, bite, prick. Yet *attente* is always toward a virtual focus. It creates, like a reflex, intentional or correlative objects. One might say that it yearns for event as poetry does for fable. The poem becomes, therefore, a self-purifying prolepsis, a would-be fable or melodic line. Valéry explains his compositional method in a *Cahier* note on *La Jeune Parque*: "J'ai supposé une mélodie, essayé d'attarder, de ritardare, d'enchaîner, de couper, d'*intervenir*—de conclure, de résoudre—et ceci dans le sens comme dans le son."[20]

The most brilliant thing in Valéry is indeed this melodic élan, never quite determined by a content it half-creates. It purifies its own movement toward closure, rendering all figures figures of speech, all terms charms of language. The author will not close the sense for us, by insisting on sense. He would like to be dreamed by language. "C'est la faculté de parler qui parle." His "moi pure" is simply this "divinité du langage."

Hence a counterpoint between the girl's haste and the hesitation of words. The "et si fine, et si mortelle" is proleptic, an anticipation of the worst with the best, to show that no intervention can check her desire. But it is just as clearly the *ritardare* of a supervening "divinité du langage." Her *faux naif* deconstructs itself by the sheer virtue of poetic language, as if language itself were saying to the girl: "Ne hâte pas cet acte tendre."[21]

Poetic speech can insert virtually endless steps between the "vide" and "l'événement pur." This *between* also belongs to "L'Abeille." Its first word is stopped: isolated by a *coupure* that delays *clôture*; and the gap in sense created by such syntactical *espacement* is emblematic of the way the whole poem is spaced out. By halting the precipitation of "quelle," a false term (end) is momentarily suggested; one throw establishes both the idea of a pure source and the danger of staying too near it, of making this beginning an end. This first hesitation, then, models the lyric's "tense" as it creates and consumes terms (ends) which are revealed to be merely the "fins éclairs" of the "pur travail" of language.

Thus poetry, which proceeds by postponing sense, point, or closure, is almost as cruel as Zeno who postponed the very possibility of movement. Poetry's language is at once eleatic and aleatic. We touch here that complex and variable meditation which occupies Valéry from the time of his essay on Leonardo da Vinci (1894). He seeks to reunite the "esprit de géométrie" and the "esprit de finesse." Their Pascalian separation is mocked, gently enough, by his spiritual cubism, his parasemiotic maneuvering of sense or point. "Point," in Valéry's sonnet, is both very fine and abstract. Poetry and abstract thought are not in opposition. Though his poems risk degrading art from an opus into an operation, they absorb the desire for definite (erotic) closure into a rigorously indefinite (poetic) mediation.

The theme of *pointe*, however, in its obviousness, shows how impure, compared to music, poetry remains. In Valéry there is a playful irony concerning the project of reduction or (in post-

Mallarmean terms) purification. The askesis of style is made to exert itself on a recognizably sensuous content which survives it. The reduction meets something irreducible, so that the final impression is of a residual impurity or a welcome defeat. So much less tragic than in Mallarmé, this defeat can even be said to charm Valéry, and so to make him, as an intellectual presence, at once attractive and self-limiting. His poetry, like the touch of sight itself, is tender rather than cruel, a distant or merely virtual possession.

4

"Certains vont au plus loin de l'*origine*—qui est coincidence de la *présence* et de l'événement initiale—et essaient dans cet écart trouver l'*or* et le *diamant*."[22]

If the initial event, textually, is a word or a phrase, "L'Abeille" breaks with it and opens onto an "écart" in which a different value appears, belonging as much to art as to nature. This movement is, as we shall see, repeated in the body of the poem. There are, then, two kinds of value: one arises from a spontaneity (pure or impure) of speech, the other from a disciplined attention that may turn the hazard of words into the poet's luck.

Even supposing poetry could only be a source for the second, artifactual kind of value, it is still a source; and however we distinguish "source" from "origin," Valéry's verse is full of carefully exploited *trouvailles*. A *trouvaille* is a verbal felicity whose origin cannot be clearly determined. Does it proceed from art or nature, from genius or ingeniousness?[23] I read Valéry with divided feelings; each poem is, at the same time, a "fleuve sans coupure," and as lapidary as if it issued from a "source suspendue."[24] Poe's "Philosophy of Composition," a doctrine Valéry acknowledged from the start of his career, fits very well his calculated arrangement of poeticisms, of golden if elaborated points of intensity.

Poésie as Poe-sie. Yet if the theme of water (tears, and so forth) evokes the presence of a source, it is never quite displaced by the theme of gold (diamond, and so forth) which denotes the presence of art. Valéry's poetry retains its character of "eau sourcilleuse." The very conflation, in this *trouvaille*, of "sourcil" and "source," strengthens our sense of verbal hazard—of the "écart" between sound and sense, surface and depth, which the poet must enter to strike it rich. The "infime alerte d'or" manifests its gold through the very remove of a periphrasis; even as the "comble d'or" of the "Cimetière Marin" (st. 3) is only the *tuilerie* of a "visible reserve."

These questions of "source," "écart," and "closure," do not belong primarily to poetics. They are notions revalued by a philosophical criticism (associated eminently with Jacques Derrida) trying to keep philosophy alive in the face of great and contrary pressures coming from objectivist science, on the one hand, and from the sphere of practical life or politics on the other. The terms in which the questions are cast enjoy presently a cool pathos and the functional consistency of variables able to enter any field of the "sciences humaines." How long before they lose their cool, their neutral yet affective status? But whatever replaces them will have to show the same critical and synoptic range, the same detached yet excursive energy. The "essay" which puts them into play must temper likewise positive or practical thought by a "self-determined indetermination" (Coleridge, describing the methodical doubt of Descartes). But this "essaying" is not inherently different from what poetry does. Guided by language itself, poetry—at least Valéry's kind—resists too quick a closing of the sense of words. It maintains itself between speech "source" and logical or grammatical "closure."

Some further consideration of this on the basis of Valéry's sonnet. The "quelle," isolated from its grammatical complement, becomes momentarily a pure speech movement, a projection beyond the bounds (and bonds) of signification. It exhibits "le pouvoir d'évoquer la parole hors de son sommeil de signe." The device that separates "quelle" from "que" is formally a *tmesis*; and in the next couplet we find a secondary tmesis, which distances "jeté" from "je n'ai," creating not merely a rhyme effect but the illusion that these complementary parts of one verbal phrase could be separate entities in a paradigm running "je n'ai," "je t'ai" (jeté), and so on. This secondary tmesis shows a more subliminal use of sound against sense than the first, foregrounded one; and the stanza as a whole is "bien terminé," of course: its last word ("dentelle") roundly rhymes with its first ("quelle").

The interposed "et si fine et si mortelle" is also, in its absoluteness, like a speech gesture, but distinctly signifying. It resembles, though not perfectly, the *mot* of a *devise*, so that the fluidity of the sonnet's opening is halted by a lapidary phrase. While both "hyperboles" arrest meaning, the first does so by a subsemantic, the second by a supersemantic effect. Together they make us think of a purer word-project, whether flowing from the source of speech or from that of signification. As in Mallarmé, "la Syntaxe, qui est calcul, repren[d] rang de Muse." [25]

Less striking perhaps are other devices of retardation: the inversion which opens the second stanza (also a kind of tmesis), the interfering closeness of certain sounds (sein, sens, sans), the convergence of "soit" (line 2) and "soit" (line 12), and the refraining of the last line. Some of this it is possible to understand as constructing rather than reducing sense: as a creative semantics. The echoing of "corbeille" as "*corps*beille,"[26] for instance, mutes the sense of the word only to reinterpret it. Yet even when we recognize a correspondence between device and theme, this does not simply reenforce the theme. It establishes rather a balance between them—an equilibrium of sound and sense, formal and referential values—so that we can entertain the notion that a device is being motivated instead of a motif shaped into words. The relation of symbol (device) and referent (theme) is made to appear reversible.

A poetics of reversibility? Something in time, or linguistic time, is not reversible. Yet the illusion of reversibility, or, more precisely, the poet's effort to reverse the "sens" (direction) of "sens" (meaning), brings our consciousness of language to a heightened level. Valéry never tires of insisting that poets need the constraint of form, and that language, reenforced by convention, provides a formal system they must *reinvent* in order to master. Poets "reverse" language only to understand better its temporal nature, and so to elaborate it as a technique of finitude. Poetry is no more (no less) than language raised to a new power of constraint through this self-awareness: instead of a chaos of arbitrary impositions it becomes a Mallarmean page of sky, "l'hydre inhérente au héros." And, by a reduction of scale which may imply a value judgment, the miniature monster in our poem is the hydra inherent to eros.

In actual poetic practice, reversibility tends to mean inversion. This well known rhetorical device is the crude, though refinable, limit of Valéry's effort. Functioning as a tmesis, for instance, it perplexes closure as efficiently as the rhetorical movement of a language in which it is a much more common, even intrinsic, feature. The freedom of Latin in this respect was a model Valéry admired. His inversions are more, therefore, than elegant archaisms: they are the exponential emblem for a reverse induction. Their purpose is to lead sense back (re-duce it) to the *poésie abstraite*[27] of its language source. Sense is merely one form of closure; to realize this is to understand the domain of virtual signification, the negative capability, as it were, of linguistic process.

Inversions in a relatively uninflected language produce, of course, more disturbance than in Latin. If, on reading "Quelle, et si fine et si mortelle . . . ," one tries to refer the interjection to "[la]quelle" as if that were a subject to be qualified, we get something like the beginning of a riddle. But a riddle, of all literary forms, is the one that makes us most aware of a linguistic asymmetry: of the noncorrespondence between puzzle and solution, form and sense, periphrasis and point. There is consequently a temptation to wish the answer had been lost; you would then approach a hermeneutic situation where there is no "authorized" meaning or point, and where the struggle for a theory of meaning turns on this absence which seems to give literary form its very presence.

The conspiracy to retard induction—by reducing the overt *line of sense*—creates a phantom form, a specious presence, a perplexing and intangible literary effect.[28] What point to this modern kind of riddle (not exclusive to poetry) which continually chastens point?

5

Laure, très beau regard qui ne regarde pas.

Valéry, "La Distraite"

The sonnet is the most sophisticated of the simple forms of verse. Valéry's sonnet, though not a riddle, continues a development (Maurice Scève's *dixain,* Mallarmé) which encouraged its riddling potential. We can call the sonnet, historically considered, a *tender* riddle. The element of cruelty it modifies is that of the lady—her rigor, whether or not interpreted as a divine ploy. Originally, then, the riddling quality of the sonnet is inspired by an amatory theme, the absence-presence character of "Petrarchan" love; yet may it not arise equally from the experience of form itself: from a new awareness of the absence-presence structure of allegory, periphrasis, and figurality?

The meaning of a love that is allegorical is not complete here and now: its closure is postponed. The artist has, therefore, a choice between respecting the asymmetry of riddle and solution, of what is said and what is meant, or seeking to assuage it by a form that is "mixed equally" ("Whatever dies," writes Donne, "was not mixed equally"). By a form, in short, whose inner alchemy or fusion defers the need for a transcendent justification, becoming itself the image of an ideal and a symbol of art's immortalizing power.

There is a type of form, then, foregrounded because of its allegorical or riddling nature; and an obverse type that arrests attention because of its aesthetic charm: it has a purity of design that resists allegorizing kinds of interpretation. Yet it incites them of course, like Leonardo's *Gioconda* or Giorgione's *Tempest.* Painting, indeed, is a privileged area for the experience of purely formal closure; and Valéry's "sleepers" are as much painterly as poetic subjects.

Ut pictura poesis. Valéry gives the formula a surprising twist. The subjects of such poems as "L'Abeille," "La Dormeuse," and *La Jeune Parque* are models, almost in the sense in which painters use the term. They are ideal bodies that can only see (know) themselves through an imagined—"outer"—agency. Thus if the bee of "L'Abeille" is an *eidolon*, so is the body itself which the girl is trying to illumine by that device. This body-phantom must invent (waken) eyes to see itself with: it participates in a "mystique . . . de la Vie Extérieure"[29] through which it becomes formally self-enclosing. "Un beau corps se fait regarder en soi-même . . ."[30]

The sonnet as a genre plays a special role in this reduction of all meanings to form. Traditionally the sonnet's *pointe* combined closure of form with climax of sense; and the earliest experiments of Valéry show him essaying to undo this combination and construct a purely formal high point. The young poet tries to surpass Heredia with sonnets whose verses are justified only as preparatives for a final verse. The idea of this final verse so haunted Valéry that the fact it had to be led up to, obtained through a respect of poetic *durée* however brief, seemed an imposition. The sonnet at least assured the brevity of serial process. Valéry's first letter to Mallarmé reiterates a sentiment already expressed publicly a year before:

> Je suis partisan d'un poème court et concentré, une brève évocation close par un vers sonore et plein.
>
> . . . il [Valéry] doit affirmer qu'il préfère les poèmes courts, concentrés pour un éclat final, où les rythmes sont comme les marches marmoréennes de l'autel que couronne le dernier vers![31]

Such final "splendors" from these early years as:

Car d'invisibles doigts l'élevaient vers les Cieux! . . .
La nuit mystérieuse avec ses yeux sans nombre.
Les Salutaires Voix d'or lointain . . .

and

N'es-tu pas le Calice adorable de Chair
Où l'artiste—blanc prêtre à la magique phrase—
Boit à longs traits le vin suprême de l'Extase?[32]

already evoke, like the *symbole* itself after Nerval and Verlaine, a transcendence that perhaps leads nowhere, that resonates into pure form. The point stings itself into lapidariness; the epiphany into a "finalité sans fin." By the time of "La Dormeuse" (1920), Valéry's use of *pointe* is purified of religiosity and totally formal. There is probably no finer instance of form becoming the very point of a sonnet than the ending of "La Dormeuse." The Petrarchan motif of the strong absence of the beloved, one that incites a lustful or spiritual insomnia, reappears now as a ghostly immediacy, an eye-opening "action at a distance":

> *malgré l'âme absente, occupée aux enfers,*
> *Ta forme au ventre pur qu'un bras fluide drape,*
> *Veille; ta forme veille, et mes yeux sont ouverts.*[33]

Yet precisely in respect of point "L'Abeille" is a surprise. It is not the ending of this sonnet which is remarkable but the beginning. The ending is not weak; it is certainly adequate; yet the feeling of *pointe* is, as we suggested playfully, "refrained." Again, it is the beginning rather than the end which thematizes the problem of form, though the "infime alerte d'or" repeats the theme of point in a more abstract, less literal, way. Why this reversal, or shift from tail to head?

It confirms, I suspect, Valéry's discomfort with time as poetic *durée.* Reversing the sonnet pattern and placing the (literal) point at the beginning shows that the problem of closure is there from the start. In some of the early sonnets Valéry's impatience for a final verse is already so great that the preparatory lines subvert point by proleptically tending to it themselves. Delaying the point means that the form remains open, that each verse, however marmoreal, is merely a step; yet the brevity and concentration of the sonnet form make the stopped character of each line only too obvious. Valéry actually increases the tension between time and reversibility.

It is not my intent to make of "L'Abeille" a "Philosophy of Composition." One should remember, however, Valéry's own estimate of philosophical thinking. "La pensée pure et la recherche de la vérité en soi ne peuvent jamais aspirer qu'à la découverte ou la construction de quelque forme."[34] The thought of this lyric, then, is almost purely formal. How formal may be suggested by diagramming it as a sonnet whose sting is in its mouth:

origin source beginning mouth sting (point)
sonnet écart sonnet
end closure ending tail sting (point)

Consider also that the opening lines resonate, however subtly, with the homophony of *que* and *queue*. It is impossible not to become aware, at some level, of the sequence *quelle, que, qu'un, pique, sur qui.*

How far may one carry this formal speculation? Placing the point at both head and tail, if it were a "figure accomplie," could suggest the emblem for eternity or the problematic issue of "time without end." For Valéry a fall into time (finitude, selfconsciousness, visibility) is inevitable. If the serpent did not exist, it would have to be invented. The girl of "L'Abeille," like the speaker of *La Jeune Parque*, wakes into imagining this enemy-friend now called a bee. "Piqûre" rhymes even conceptually with "morsure." "L'Abeille" is another "ébauche d'un serpent," an extension of *La Jeune Parque*. "Au plus traître de mon âme, une pointe me naît."

One might also seek in the head-tail design a reflection of Valéry's problematic attitude to writing. The pattern could then be viewed as a "Heads or Tails?" alluding to the chanciness of composition, its dependence on the arbitrary character of language or inspiration. These interpretations remain, more or less, in the sphere of formal thought; the witty inversion, however, which makes head and tail, beginning and end, converging terms, could lead to a psychoanalytic query. Is ambivalence being sublimated as equivalence?

I shall stop this side of psychoanalysis. *Qual Quelle*: the words "implexed" by Derrida, to deepen our understanding of the torment (Qual) of the source (Quelle) in Valéry, are still too fluid, or imbued with Teutonic pathos. If we must have an inscription, let it be: *Quelle Que(ue).*

6

"J'ai essayé de tout. Géométrie, rhétorique, mais tout est sans aiguillon."

Letter to Pierre Louÿs (1917)

Inversion as a formal principle is already an aspect of the theme varied by Valéry: that of *Amour piqué*. Amour, having been stung by an insect he defines uncertainly as a "mouche à miel," complains to mamma Venus who shows him no sympathy but points out that usually it is he who does the stinging. An associated motif is that of the poet wishing to become a bee so as to gather honey from the lips of his lady. As in Ronsard's "Aux mouches à miel, pour cueillir les fleurs sur la bouche de Cassandre."[35]

Both themes are highly variable. That Cupid cannot define his aggressor by name,

Il est comme un papillon,
Mais il porte un aiguillon, etc.[36]

or that the poet can wish to be other things than a bee to come near his lady, abet this possible variation. Even richer is the division of Amour into active and passive; now stinger, now stung; now the bee, now its victim. It is not difficult to vary ("enchaîner") till we reach Valéry's poem in which Amour is asked, as it were, to sting himself.

A less subtle variant, but which continues to enmesh the theme in a "grammar" of its own, is making the breast the object to be stung—a breast, of course, on which Amour is sleeping. Here the chain of variation approaches inversion once more, if we consider that these "beaux fruits d'amour" have points of their own. As in the Bee-Cupid merger, we cannot tell whose attribute the sting is. It doubles, so that victim and aggressor, cause and effect, converge. The sting is too much like the thing stung; the "point" here and there at once.

The variations, then, are based on the possibility of inversion; yet inversion is simply another variant. Through the elaboration of this code or cycle you approach a kind of reversibility, a code without a coda; yet you also dull the point of it all by imitability. A *reserve* of forms becomes a mere *repertory*. The sting which according to one version of "Abeille Spirituelle" is "Chargé de foudre et follement fertile," according to a second is "Chargé de foudre et follement futile."[37]

The experience of a variability which approaches reversibility—encouraged by the competitive epigrams of the Greek anthology—leads therefore to conflicting feelings: one delightful, when a medium is envisaged more like music than literature, which subverts its own limits of representation; the other despairing of those limits, and of the fact that formalism, however melodic, deprives poetry of its sting and makes it a sterile game. Valéry's letter to Pierre Louÿs after publishing *La Jeune Parque* is full of a repeated complaint: his "Jeune Chose," as he calls her, has made him old. To elaborate his poem was a sin against its goddess, Eternal Youth, and may have brought her into the shadow of the fatalities of time and love she was to replace. "Oh! rester dans le reversible!" As he remarks of another work in the same letter: "Ce beau projet m'avait enflammé pendant vingt-cinq minutes. J'ai noté *dans le frais* les éléments excitants qui ont brillé pendant cette courte durée. Puis, dodo."[38]

Triumph of form leads to acedia—and perhaps aphasia—as surely as triumph of sense. The poet is doomed to go from dada to dodo. Valéry's career, in fact, seems to turn on this "sleep" which comes in the wake of Mallarmean attempts at essentializing art and reducing it to a "comble d'artifice"—the pure obverse of love's sting. He publishes almost no verse between 1900 and 1917. And in the poems written between 1889 and 1899 there is much evidence to suggest that the myth of Sleeping Beauty took hold of him.

In this *féerie* sleep overcomes the princess at a time of life (15 or 16, according to Perrault) associated with nubility; and it is caused by the prick of a spinning wheel's needle. In Valéry's case the *piqûre* of love is reduced to an artificial *pointe* to disarm it—to keep the poet's mind from having to depend for its "peine bien-aimée" on love. (How much lyric verse, from Petrarch on, is love-complaint.) Nevertheless, like his own "fileuse," whose mysterious sleep ("Sie schlief die Welt"[39]) suggests a desired or necessary process, as if the myth of the spinning Fates had merged with that of "la Belle au Bois Dormant," the poet falls silent. It is a recuperative rather than fatal silence: as in the original story, a sort of moratorium substitutes sleep for death, and allows the poetic impulse to persist somewhere between "la rose et l'épingle." Instead of being guillotined (the phrase is Valéry's) by sensuality *or* its reduction,[40] poetry permits the soul to hover between dream and disenchantment. To hover, rather, in a dream of disenchantment that remains distinctly Mallarmean:

La chair confuse des molles roses commence
A frémir, si d'un cri le diamant fatal
Fêle d'un fil de jour toute la fable immense.[41]

Mallarmé's verse tends to refract *pointe* without dissolving it: phrases, like crystal facets, extend the sensuous highlight ("La chevelure, vol d'une flamme à l'extrême") into apposed *gestes* of speech, until the poem is a broken yet diamondlike surface of lights. The first *geste* is as strong as the last; and the middle a mobile tmesis. In the sonnets, particularly, one sensuous image dominates; but now this sym-bole is composed of hyper-boles. The *condition verbale* here is far more extreme in its doubt of naming the brilliant (fugacious) object than when Amour seeks to word the insect that hurt him: it is a hyperbolic doubt, in fact, similar to that of Descartes, but making defeat its feat. Valéry understood only too well Mallarmé's "exploit": how the moth of words is drawn endlessly to its "Occident de désirs," dying *against* a sensuous light:

Sens-tu, tel un vil astre indifférent, la mouche
Transparente tourner autour du mot très pur

Que tu ne diras pas—fleur, diamant ou pierre
Ou rose jeune encore dans un vierge jardin
Une nudité fraîche sous une paupière
Balancée, amusée hors du chaos mondain.

Cette minute ailée éparpille un sonore
Vol d'étincelles au vent solaire pour briller
Sur tes dents, sur tes hauts fruits de chair, sur l'aurore
Des cheveux où j'eus peur à la voir scintiller.[42]

It is no accident, then, that "L'Abeille" varies a theme associated with the topic of *remedia amoris.* This is the only subject as inexhaustible as form, there being no remedy for love except death. As Venus tells complaining Amour:

cesse de tant ferir,
Mesmes nous qui des Dieux sommes:
Car la Mort guerit les hommes,
Mais ell' ne nous peult guerir.[43]

Yet form remains the only charm against the charm of love. It is a counter-Cupid, an ambrosia of "or fauve et sucré"[44] appeasing an insatiable bee. The "Cantique des Colonnes" even suggests it may be better to let love sleep; that is, to drug the god with the honey of form:

Filles des nombres d'or,
Fortes des lois du ciel,
Sur nous tombe et s'endort
Un dieu couleur de miel.

"Do not wake my love until it please," says the beloved in the *Song of Songs.*

Why then in "L'Abeille" the express wish to have love awakened? Is this another inversion, another twist of the wheel of form against the very drowse it fosters? The poem flows to that imagined sting or restituted point as toward a source.

The lyric wishes to become, one might say, pure melody: the poet, that is, by a subtle and interior variation, draws an analogy between the desire of the bee for *melos* and his own desire for *melody.* This analogy remains so formal that it can be developed only by a reader familiar with the code and its transformations. As in the Anacreontic motif, it is the mouth which is to be culled. The poet's very desire for poetic speech—

for melos/melody—engenders that bee image. Where there is a bee, is there not honey? His mouth needs that virtual sting to waken it into verse.

"O mon silence!" There is little more to say. A version of "Abeille Spirituelle" (composed circa 1920) is entitled "Ambroisie," another carries Valéry's middle name, "Ambroise." Among the many poems not published by him from the crucial years after the encounter with Mallarmé, there are those that suggest clearly, sometimes crudely, the conflict between the *melos* of poetry and the *miel* of sensuality. Love's mead becomes the poet's muteness.

Sur tes lèvres souvent des lèvres de Bacchantes
Nous dérobent tes vers[45]

Le poète sourit, Bathylle, dans ton ombre
Et dévore à mi-mot des grappes dans ton ombre
Sa lyre, en noble bois d'ébène pur, se tait.[46]

How formal, or reduced, that "ombre" and those "grappes" when they recur in:

Dormeuse, amas dorée d'ombres et d'abandons . . .
O biche avec langueur longue auprès d'une grappe!

Though, by the time of "L'Abeille," Valéry's silence is over, his poems tend to be a justification of art in the light of a difficulty never entirely removed. Mallarmé's example remains present as a speech that gives the lie to speech. "Vous mentez, ô fleur nue / De mes lèvres" ("Hérodiade"). The demands of imagination lie rigorously beyond the satisfactions of Amour. Valéry is able to break his silence only when this "désir du désir," so strong in "L'Abeille," is valorized as the founding character of art: what he will call "l'infini esthétique."[47] Whereas practical acts, he suggests, end when they attain what they seek, acts of an aesthetic nature find ends that renew them: so hunger seeks food to satisfy it, but if the food is delicious, hunger is prolonged. What is true of hunger is true of love, and all modes of sensibility, as sight, touch, speech, etc. Hence, while the ordinary verbal sign is deprived of interest by the very act it motivates, or a statement by the point it makes, in poetry the point remains virtual and generates the poem itself as a "prolonged hesitation" between sound and sense, or formal and referential values.

"L'Abeille" hovers therefore over certain accidents of language; and in particular one we have not mentioned. "Pointe" is etymologically related to "poindre," as in the phrase "pointe du jour." The desired waking is to be effected by the "pointe" of the bee; it is, moreover, a passage toward light (illumination, visibility). "L'infime alerte d'or" may evoke, in this context, "pointe du jour," break of day. But this desire for dawn, the characteristic of one kind of *alba*, is countervailed by a second "poetic" *alba* which prolongs time by inserting between converging terms (time-*pointe* and word-*pointe*) an indeterminacy allowing the poem to evolve. The verbal pun joining time and language remains virtual because of the "hesitation" of Valéry's art; and this in itself points to art's precarious status in a world of *praxis*, a world where hasty ends and proleptic words prevail.

Valéry has shifted his interest, by 1919, from the fatality of love ("Orphée antique mort par tes mains furibondes"[48]) to that of time—to problems of *durée* and rhythm. The first World War had made the escalating, even manic, rhythm of civilized life quite clear, but not the inner fatality of it, how the very idea of "event" was deeply involved in inflationary mental habits. The hesitation characterizing the poetics of "L'Abeille" (it includes the idyllic or "Mediterranean" imagery) is directed not against imaginative desire but against something far more haste-ridden and literal—which, in fact, was threatening to annul that desire. The sting, in real life, is a massive need for intoxicants, raising perpetually the threshold of stimulation, and so shortening, and perhaps injuring, the very *durée* of thought:

As for the most central of our senses, our inner sense of the interval between desire and possession, which is no other than the sense of duration, that feeling of time which was formerly satisfied by the speed of horses, now finds that the fastest trains are too slow, and we fret with impatience between telegrams. We crave events themselves like food that can never be highly seasoned enough. If every morning there is no great disaster in the world we feel a certain emptiness: "There is nothing in the papers today," we say. We are caught red-handed. We are all poisoned. So I have grounds for saying that there is such a thing as our being intoxicated by energy, just as we are intoxicated by haste, or by size. . . . We are losing that essential peace in the depths of our being, that priceless absence in which the most delicate elements of life are refreshed and comforted, while the inner creature is in some way cleansed of past and future, of present awareness, of obligations pending and expectations lying in wait.[49]

"L'Abeille" is an economical poem. Its very delicacy, however, makes it a frail instrument when accumulation and waste, memory and mind-blowing, verbal debauch and illiteracy, move in a vicious circle. Though half a century has passed, can we say that a new "économie poïétique,"[50] or Fable of the Bee has emerged?

The Fate of Reading

All that remained of the mystery
was the tale.

Gershom Scholem

The Romance of the Letter. Reading is a modest word, and to defend reading may give the impression of venturing on the minimal. Much reading is indeed, like girl-watching, a simple expense of spirit. Yet the romance of reading has not faded entirely, even today. Milton's words in *Areopagitica* still move some of us: "Books . . . contain a potencie of life in them to be as active as that soule was whose progenie they are; nay they do preserve as in a violl the purest efficacie and extraction of the living intellect that bred them . . . a good Booke is the pretious life-blood of a master-spirit, imbalmed and treasured up on purpose to a life beyond life." On a more basic level, the shock of seeing a "dangerous" or "unspoken" thought in print, the shock also of graffiti, can be linked even to the most genteel theory of artistic expression yet evolved, and found at the turn of the last century in Walter Pater's fragmentary romance, *Gaston de Latour*:

> that was no dubious or generalized form it gave to flower or bird, but the exact pressure of the jay at the window; you could count the petals,—of the exact number; no expression could be too faithful to the precise texture of things; words, too, must embroider, be twisted and spun, like silk or golden hair . . . the visible was more visible than ever before, just because soul had come to its surface. The juice in the flowers . . . was like wine or blood. It was such a colored thing; though the grey things also, the cool things, all the fresher for the contrast—with a freshness, again, that seemed

to touch and cool the soul—found their account there. . . . Here, was a discovery, a new faculty, a privileged apprehension, to be conveyed in turn to one and to another, to be propagated for the imaginative regeneration of the world. It was a manner, a habit of thought, which would invade ordinary life, and mould that to its intention.

Pater chose the period of Ronsard—of liberated clerks and of the "Renascence of Wonder"—to dramatize the way culture refreshed perception, and potentially new-created it in individuals. How strange yet appropriate that Pater has Latour die, with his *chateau* unfinished, in 1594, three centuries to the year before his own death in 1894. Those three centuries both develop and frustrate our belief in the *thaumaturgic* impact of literacy which invests the mere words "reading" and "writing" even today.

I won't try to pinpoint where the Romance of the Letter, still active in television's *Sesame Street*, began; whether in the age of Ronsard or Erasmus or Comenius; nor is the precise date important. For only with the spreading doctrine of universal education in the nineteenth century does "culture" become, as in the hands of Inspector Matthew Arnold, the mighty opposite of "anarchy"; and the proper, unviolent agent to mitigate and even erode class difference.

And it is in the nineteenth even more than eighteenth century that prose flourishes. Matthew Arnold's style is itself less than a grand manner: it polishes, in fact, the rough edges of a "middle" style which had entered the literary scene with Addison and Steele and then blossomed into the familiar essay. Neither the judicious roughness of Ruskin nor the attenuated precision of Pater alters the nature of this prose intensely conscious of its reasonable eloquence. The limpid pedagogy of Arnold, Ruskin, and Pater assumes, prematurely, a society born a second time, of the world of letters. The world of art and letters, of culture, is now seen as a *commonwealth* accessible to all through the key of literacy, and spreading therefore into the homes and consciousnesses of ordinary people.

The Dream of Communication. Looking at the urban wasteland, it is hard to think without pain of Le Corbusier's vision of the Radiant City. So it is with pain that one acknowledges the continuing strength of this ideal of radiant literacy. It has not been disproved, any more than the radiant city has: such visions are transient and eternal as rainbows. Spenglerian epigones who predict the death of the word are fashionable realists afraid of being accused of nostalgia. Secretly they remain utopians who think that words are not thaumaturgic enough. They believe in bigger and better modes of communication: in what I have called the Dream of Communication. One paradox which besets this newest dream is that reading and writing are now actually taught by devices (television, computerized techniques) which may be contaminating the word and contributing to its demise. Another paradox is that the more communications media we have, the less communication, in terms of personal understanding, seems to be going on. Media are not mediations.

A third problem is that the activist potential of articulated or publicized thought, in whatever form, can be doubted: expression may not lead even to catharsis; for where there is so much talk or print or image-mania, the threshold at which people are strongly affected is raised to so high a point that almost all communication falls below it. That which was meant to convert passive knowledge into active, or bring neglected states of mind to light, becomes subliminal once more—and this time without hope of rising up. The desire to know remains, but what is known is no longer desired, and becomes indifferent.

A New Mal du Siècle. This indifference, an apathy or arbitrariness of emotional reaction, or an orgasmic shuttle of both together, remains a complex phenomenon. At its most dangerous it imbues reader and viewer with an invulnerability to the explosive sight and the expletive word, an invulnerability which is probably a psycho-magical defense against stimulus-flooding. The child, as Freud discovered, experiences fantasies about invulnerability or "omnipotence of thought"; and these are also nourished, even in later years, by typical popular fiction with its unscathed heroes and super-persons who somehow get on top of everything thrown at them.

What of reading, in this ambiance? Reading, old-style, elicits large-scale resonances from detail and nuance. It presupposes a "minimalist" art even where the subject matter is as maximalist as in the Bible. Where a visuality more triumphant than Pater ever conceived brings us daily *guernicas* via the screen, it still desires, like Wallace Stevens, to make the visible a little harder to see. In fact, as the demand for visual or sensory evidence inflates, our distrust of it deepens. But this is bound to lead to a perceptual schizophrenia (as in Pynchon's Oedipa, her attempt to "decode" American reality) or similar hermeneutic disorders. We seek to de-realize, by any gnostic device available, the overkill realism of the new master-media.

One mode of de-realization is academic, and directly related to reading habits. While our potentially creative, personal memory is being replaced by libraries with good retrieval systems, our potentially creative or explosive subconscious turns into limbo: an irritable underconsciousness of influences degraded to the status of inputs. We now experience and read scanningly, as if our "reading matter"—perhaps the world itself—had no immediate value but was meant simply to be known and stored. People, who should be sources, become "resource-people"; books, which should be sources, items in a "resource-center." De Quincey's distinction between the literature of knowledge and the literature of power breaks down, for all is "secondary literature" to this new, proleptic reader. His mental life is a voracious parody of the sober if solipsist revels of Hegel's Philosopher, who no longer needs the detour of actual experience. If in the beginning was the Word, in the end shall be the Megafiche.

The result is restlessness our own *mal du siècle* and a curse like that weighing on the Wandering Jew. We seem unable to close off a subject, or any inquiry. Closure is death Though "The Tree of Knowledge is not that of Life" (Byron), we continue to turn life into knowledge. We step bravely over totally unguarded thresholds or try with comic desperation to find a threshold sacred enough so that crossing it would count as a trespass. Unable to summon the energies which could repress what we know (because they are exclusively bent on accumulating knowledge), we become the irritable prey of influences that are there rather than not there, neither quite absent nor quite present, in a printout limbo of restless yet random motion. So the allusiveness of modern art—its touted connotativity or ambiguity—is often only a kind of static, the interference of signals which cannot be cleared from the language system.

Beyond Modernity. The very concept, moreover, of modernity (however old it actually may be) is now in danger. It was based on the idea of periodization, or on that attractive idea of transition which still had Pater in its grip. *Gaston de Latour* is haunted by the possibility of transition, or of breaking into a new world of perception; and Pater's novel remains as unfinished as Latour's own architectural project, a "work to remain untouched for future ages precisely at this point in its growth." Pater draws back from the finished into the fragmentary: he wants to stay in transition, as if the illusion of the new—the glow caught and crystallized, the threshold sanctified once more—were itself renovative. Is it possible for us to give up this now antiquated idea of the Modern? Is Nietzsche's vision of the Eternal Return of the Same, formulated at the very time Pater was flirting so intensely with the notion of re-naissance, an alternative?[1]

Pater or Nietzsche: a strange choice the good God of History would be providing us with. On the one hand, transition, or the promise of entering a truly new ("modern") era; on the other, pure transitivity; on the one hand, perpetual adolescence, a moratorium which keeps the future open; on the other, the pleasures of presenescence, or of a proleptic consciousness for which there is nothing new under the sun except the renewal of that thought. The baroquely elaborated asceticism of the School of Derrida, in particular, confronts life as a Nietzschean vista of repetitions or postponements. How queer that the spermatic and vernal Word becomes, in such word-inspired philosophy, the model for an anti-renaissance, a de-nascence of wonder. Prepare for the end . . . of Modernity.

Disenchantment. There has always been tension between wonder, or scandal, and the philosophic mind. One thinker claims that philosophizing begins in wonder, another that wonder is simply the effect of novelty on ignorance. A third chants, "You must become an ignorant man again / And see the sun again with an ignorant eye / And see it clearly in the idea of it."

The tension between wonder and enlightenment may be analogous to that between literal and figurative meanings. The letter reacts on the spirit with deadening or enlightening effect. Yet so great is the manipulative force of the modern media that this tension or perplexity (how real, say, is Christ's divinity? how literal is all that redemptive blood? is it more than spiritual ketchup?) no longer leads to a sustained wonderment or to that purification of the mind which may attend an elegant solution. Perplexity reduces to sheer manipulative design. What is real and what is fake change places as insidiously as in George Roy Hill's *The Sting*. Indeed, the copy or fake may now be sharper than the original. So the image on the screen, undimmed by memory or the confusion of life, revives a simulacrum of the past brighter in photographic brilliance than the actual happening could have been. How innocent is this nostalgia which turns the badlands of the 1930s into supernaturally clean, doll-like settings? The cool translucence of such movie resurrections shines so strongly through the depredations of mental and historical time that whatever blood stains their costume drama into reality remains curiously abstract—washed clean in the lymph of the medium.

There is good reason, then, why French grammatologists and poeticians seek to modify realistic theories of signification and establish meaning on a basis beyond "organized wonder." The realism of each medium must be disenchanted in advance. It is not so much that the world is older now than it was, but rather that language is what it always was.

A Parable. I can imagine a parable about these foes of afflatus. It should be written in the mode of Chaucer's *Pardoner's Tale.* Chaucer's three rogues, drunk, and surrounded by the ravages of the Plague, set out to kill that "villeyne Death." In a parody of quest-romance, the three find the Death they seek by dying off in very mundane, anti-romance fashion.

My version features mortality-imbued philosophers who set out to kill that ancient villain Wonder. The story idea is not new (how could it be?), since the Oriental Tale had already been used for the purpose of disintoxication by Voltaire (*Candide*) and Dr. Johnson (*Rasselas*); and so one could say that the School of Derrida is engaged in a *Candide*—or *Zarathustra*—against the thaumaturgic Word. But in order to achieve the wonder of disenchantment these "last philosophers" find they must first kill off the human voice or even the human face (poets seek "no wonder but the human face," said Keats). As in traditional quest-romance, they cannot achieve their purpose directly but have to postpone it for an indefinite series of intermediate actions which then constitute the life of their quest. They remain caught in the meshes of a structure which romance wonder-wandering has always expressed.

To Kill the Voice? To make it recede, at least into a "presque disparition vibratoire," a Mallarmean or diacritical poetics. Or to have the notion of the author—and with it, possibly, of authority—disappear. No wonder that obverse simplifications assert themselves: on the one hand, the insistence that there is no meaning without a certifiable authorial intention; and, on the other, that there is no authority except by imposition. There is also the device of shifting much of the burden onto a reader who now becomes co-author, as in the recent revival of *Rezeptionsgeschichte* on a structural basis. I am myself guilty of simplifying here, but I wish to suggest how troubled the contemporary spectrum of aesthetic theories is by the often unacknowledged issue of literary or spiritual authority.

Daemon-author and Daemon-interpreter. It took philosophy some time to divest itself of the notion of simples; and contemporary semiotics has rightly destroyed residual ideas concerning the simple location of meaning or even of the author. But though a text is discontinuously woven of many strands or codes, there is magic in the web. The sense of an informing spirit, however limited or conditioned, or outwitting those limits and conditions, is what holds us. To exorcise that spirit is to make the web inefficacious. Can anything be said about the relation of spirit to web without relapsing into the notion of simples?

When a philosopher, or any generalizing intellect, uses texts as *examples*, he subverts their *exemplary* character. Yet it is hard to conceive of a literary reader who is not immersed in the search for an exemplary text: a text to be used against the wastefulness of living without concentration, or a text to support by one's life, given the need. So at the end of Ray Bradbury's *Fahrenheit 451* (as filmed by Truffaut) each exile from the book-burning state adopts the name of a text he has learnt by heart and which he represents: one person is now called *David Copperfield*, another *Emile*, or even *Paradise Lost*. . . . The extinction in this symbolic situation of the personal names of *both* author and reader shows what ideally happens in the act of reading: if there is a sacrifice to the exemplary, it involves the aggrandizement neither of author nor of reader but leads into the recognition that something worthy of perpetuation has occurred.

As Bradbury's fable suggests, the great work of art is more than a text. It is the "life-blood of a master-spirit" Don Quixote and Mme Bovary are readers without defenses; and if they still move us deeply it is because we are readers with too many defenses. These people in the book are people of the book: parody versions of our own desire for an identification with exemplary acts and lives. So our effort to domesticate the powerful work of art by interpretation bespeaks its sublime presence—if not our own quasi-daemonic drive for an erotic or envious possession of other lives. That darkling appropriation of works of art we call interpretation is surely as much a blind drive as an objective interest. We are forced to predicate a narrative or interpretive will, the will to be an author oneself, or even the author of oneself (and others). Let me try to clarify the nature of this empathic "will" by reflecting on its link to the issue of, specifically, literary authority.

Five Meditations on Will and Literary Authority.

1. We are accustomed to thinking of the artist as having a blind spot that contributes to creative power. He has an ability to

feed on what nourishes his talent and to forget or subdue other realities. It is his extraordinary associations or idiosyncratic vision or the apotheosis of some minute particular which keeps us fascinated. Horace called it art's "peculiar felicity." Often, therefore, a critical discourse based on the criterion of adequation (of vehicle to tenor, for example), even when as complex as that of organic form, disappoints. We feel that structures, norms, techniques, and so forth, are important, but only as they are broken or breaking does the spirit leap forth. Or even as they are suddenly forgotten in a shift of persons or episodes, and a new plot or line of vision comes into being. This curious tension between formal ideas of order and art's betrayal of them from within is well known. But no general theory of such reversals or revisions has been formulated, for to methodize them would be to create a technique once again, or the illusion of a technique.

We are moved by Rousseau, and what we are moved by is the will veiling itself or breaking through its veils, the ornaments of language which are solicited, the wish to complete or complement the will in some way until it enters a realm of human reciprocity, of mutual recognition. If the—call it—feminine respect for "pleasing" is in subtle agreement with a—call it—"masculine persuasive force," the result is not seduction or rhetoric, but style. Yet the sublime or arbitrary will remains a presence in Rousseau always slightly apart from what is being said.

2. Lionel Trilling distrusts both ideological criticism with its exploitative interpretation ("unmasking") of literary works, and its opposite, the formalistic type of criticism which pretends literature is a "structure of words" rather than the complex expression of a personal will. He suggests in a moving essay on Tolstoi's *Anna Karenina* that anterior to any literary skill there is a "moral quality" or "quality of affection" suffusing the words. He approaches the view, therefore, that art is an objectification of will—not its suppression as much as its fullest, most elaborate expression. "What is called the objectivity of Homer or of Tolstoi," he writes, "is not objectivity at all. Quite the contrary, it is the most lavish and prodigal subjectivity possible, for

every object in the *Iliad* or in *Anna Karenina* exists in the medium of what we must call the author's love." If Trilling avoids dealing with literary texts as if they were manipulated words it is not simply because he stands in the tradition of moral rather than formalistic criticism but also because he suspects the formalists of masking *their* will, of bending the text to their moral or ideological views without acknowledging this.

Now it is hard to talk about this "will" because there is no philosophical apparatus in Trilling. Yet we understand Laskell's statement in *The Middle of the Journey* (1947) that "It was not their wills that worried him but the necessity they shared to make their wills harmless." The intransigence of the will, even in the relatively pastoral form of art, provides a reason for the existence of the critic—who, however, has his own will to contend with. To put it another way: whether or not there is a God can be left to the Church, but there is always some "god that failed," and the will is that which remains in the wake of a great personal or political failure. For Trilling's generation, the god that failed was a communism that had degenerated into Stalinism. A god of this sort is not likely to settle down as a gentleman who cultivates the "liberal imagination." Nor as a New Critic. The will, that Prince of Darkness, is no gentleman. It remains in crisis, seeking a political or objective outlet; trying to bring together personal and social worlds; trying to find peace in unselfishness or in a compelling vision of community.

3. Why do Dr. Johnson's magisterial growls still move us today? Not, surely, because they are based on valid judgments (he is a rigid and fallible judge) but because art is dignified rather than diminished by the moral will of his criticism. When he thunders against the "puerilities of obsolete mythology" (pagan allusions) in the poetry of Gray and Milton, the passionateness of his utterance suggests how difficult it was *for him* to put away that kind of childishness. The ecstatic or learned Boy is not extinct in the Doctor. More impersonally, we understand that all art, indeed all culture, tested against an absolute standard or "scripture," could be made to appear puerile. What one responds to in a great critic is this lover's quarrel with art, an

attack so memorable that even if the particular target is demolished, art itself is purified and strengthened.

That quarrel continues today as the lifegiving element in criticism. Yet to attack art in the name of art is one thing; to attack it in the name of religion, social policy, or science, quite another. The bad demystifier of art does not see the mote (or metaphor) in his own eye. What is worse is that, when he does, it may not bother him. He drives before him, like a speckled drove, epistemology, ontology, phenomenology, semiotics—everything to avert raising the issue of the authority of art, or of his own authority as writer or critic.

4. In previous essays I have talked not of will (and its problematic relation to authority) but of a *vis representativa* or "representation-compulsion." It may be objected that will and compulsion are contraries; and, more cogently, that to posit a representation-compulsion is just a fancy way of saying that we have language and tend to use it. It is perfectly true that we distinguish between will and compulsion in some contexts; but any acquaintance with legal philosophy can show how difficult a distinction this may be. I was myself previously speaking in a philosophical and psychoanalytic context; and when we think of Schopenhauer and Nietzsche, and how Freud may be indebted to their concept of the will (the word *libido* itself, central to Freud, has meanings in Latin ranging from caprice to appetite to violent, unrestrained desire), the idea emerges that the one thing we may not be able to will away is will itself. "I am that I am," says the will, sacred or profane. There is, of course, a will not to will; but this produces situations as complex as the Freudian defense mechanisms or such depressed self-assertions as Melville's Bartleby exhibits. What I mean by representation-compulsion is not different from what Keats meant when he called every great artist's life a "life of allegory," or what is structurally achieved by the *Arabian Nights* which link, through Scheherezade, a story-line and a life-line.

My feelings about the inevitability of self-assertion are as pessimistic as those expressed by the doctrine of Original Sin. "If it be Sin," Coleridge writes, "it must be *original*," so that the phrase Original Sin seems a pleonasm. "A State or Act, that has not its origin in the will, may be calamity, deformity, disease, or mischief; but a *Sin* it cannot be." And more dramatically still: "No *Natural* thing or act can be called an originant, or be truly said to have an *origin* in any other. The moment we assume an Origin in Nature, a true *Beginning*, an actual First—that moment we rise *above* Nature and are compelled to assume a *supernatural* Power (Gen. 1.1.)."[2] But I may be more pessimistic than Coleridge who considered art as an authentic purgation or ensnaring of self-will, though I too recognize that art is the most conscious form of anti-selfconsciousness yet devised, and that language raised to the power of art mediates what Coleridge names the self-originating tendency, or spirit. It operates in the same area as religious or social tradition, which it must join or fight to gain a measure of authority.

Yet Coleridge's Mariner, whose act in shooting the albatross is willy-nilly spiritual, finds himself in a "darkness of mediations." He awakes through the consequences of his act to his own spirituality, conveyed by the supernatural symbolism of the poem. And the "punctual agony" of the Mariner does not bode well for the artist whose prototype he may be: his narrative, deeply compulsive, is a catharsis which may be as interminable as Freudian analysis or the libido itself. We do not get beyond purgatory. There is never a point at which we can say: "In Art is our Peace."

5. Not so long ago Allen Tate distinguished Dante's "symbolic" from Poe's "angelic" imagination. The distinction intended to deepen the traditional one between symbol and allegory, or imagination and fancy. Symbolic poetry is concrete, analogical, and capable of "literal metaphors." The literal or sensuous level of understanding is not jettisoned, however high or deep the poet's vision ranges. Angelic poetry, in contrast, is a product of the dissociated or hypertrophied will, which cannot subdue itself to traditional perspectives based on the "ladder of analogy," but, like Milton's Satan impatient to enter Eden, with one bound overleaps all bounds. Tate's distinction is as interesting as it is invidious. He knew that imaginative empathy

is related to passion, and in particular to such dubious manifestations of it as envy, erotic jealousy, self-assertion, and hydroptic curiosity. It is linked, in short, to the psychic area of the will, or sublimated compulsion; and when, according to Tate, that will, joining itself once more to intellect and feeling, struggles through to a peace based on concrete religious (that is, Christian) affiliation, the result is genuinely imaginative. "In His Will is our Peace."

The will remains, however, whether we call it, honorifically, imagination, or deplore it as "the self whose worm dieth not, and whose fire is not quenched" (Kierkegaard). Against critics like Tate one could argue that poetry and divinity are always at odds: the one must be a scandal for the other, whatever temporary accommodations may occur. Yet Tate's powerful if contrite description of a modern poetry of the will had the important effect of making us aware of the will of the critic. Instinctively, I think, Tate understood that poetry no longer scandalized us, unless so recent as to defy assimilation. He tried therefore to foster critical judgments leading to intellectual war.

Literature is today so easily assimilated or coopted that the function of criticism must often be to defamiliarize it. Cooptation, in this "post-classical" age, overtakes both the new and the canonized work of art; which is one reason why so many are struggling to keep the notion of a "classic" from being reduced to that of a "paradigm." A pluralism verging on indifference accommodates the most extreme fiction by means of genetic explanation, grammatical analysis or ideological exploitation—in short, by "coming to terms" with it. Perhaps the simple fact of allowing everything into the classroom already breaks down the "threshold" distinction between curricular and extracurricular, canonic and apocryphal, classic and nonclassic, *mishnah* (the teaching) and *baraitah* (the marginal).

A Saving Scandal. In this situation, what *can* scandalize? Yet the critic knows that despite all the reasonableness that has poured down on art in the last century, despite all attempts to consider figurative speech (or its equivalent in other arts) as a natural thing, something escapes which, while it cannot be called irrational, is deeply disturbing to the notion of both ordinary speech and scientific discourse. It is disturbing to scientific discourse because, as I.A. Richards noted, the referent of figures is not clear or not verifiable. We don't know exactly what Keats's Saturn or Hyperion represent; we don't even know how to locate the field of reference—it is not divinity or astrology, yet also not (or not simply) the poet's mood—so that we fall back, usually, on the statement that a figure refers to other figures, to an entire symbolic field created by the poet in conjunction with other poets. There is no guarantee, however, as there is in science, that this field of figures will rationalize itself in a progressive way; in fact, there is no guarantee that it is, despite appearances, the same field for each significant writer or national (vernacular) literature.

When we turn to the disturbance wrought by figures in ordinary or functional speech the problem is even more complex. There is the distaste if not disgust of your eighteenth century reader, of Voltaire affronted by Shakespeare's "blanket of the night," or of Mrs. Barbault and Dr. Johnson fending off overextended, hence indecent or promiscuous, figures of speech. There is the more contemporary objection to critical or academic prose being punctuated by "dives into the stunningly metaphoric," which may bring criticism too close to poetry, or privatize inquiry.[3] These objections presuppose a decorum, or classical norm, that is breached by a showiness which endangers commonality.

Above all, we have the phenomenon of the sublime, which goes even beyond the emotive power of heightened speech. Poets in the plain style or the Wordsworthian tradition may be as suspicious of this afflatus as any scientific proser. Wallace Stevens tends to put his poetic highs ("The Stars are putting on their glittering belts,/ They throw around their shoulders cloaks that flash . . .") in a kind of recantatory brackets, always hoping that the sublime "may come tomorrow in the simplest word." Extended, and consciously attenuated, allusion in eighteenth century poetry also suggests, like the wintry bareness that Stevens foresees while standing in the auroral glow of figuration, a Negative Poetics. And Milton, too, in his winter scene, tries to chasten Nature, and make her a little less baroque:

It was the Winter wilde,
While the Heav'n-born-childe,
All meanly wrapt in the rude manger lies;
Nature in aw to him
Had doff't her gawdy trim . . .

Yet poetry never really doffs its trim. What the Christ child of the Nativity Hymn is to Milton, "the simplest word" is to Stevens: it motivates the poem. But this is precisely what the Russian formalists say about the literal or social referent insofar as it can be determined: it "motivates" the figure. But is this not truly scandalous, that the referent of all this trooping of ghosts and troping of speech is itself a word, "the simplest word," whatever that may be? The only thing it can be, I am afraid, and it increases the scandal, is abracadabra, or a formula like it: in short, the magical idea of speech, literacy as thaumaturgic, the word able to transform or clarify our lives. "Let there be Light." But to explain magic by magic leaves us where we began. Perhaps a bit further along, for nothing is so disturbing as the idea that all, not just figurative, language is magical.

Time! The magical idea of immediacy is always accompanied by the inveterate mediacy of the word. No magician can do without his abracadabra. Or without that gestural baton which, like the written mark, is the metonymically condensed representative of a source of power. Word and stick; word-stave and magic staff; the one is already the two-in-one. What is required is a slightly deferred gesture, a one-two sequence for the magic to be wrought. Even the spirits must be alerted; and all our trouble, of course, and all our power of development, flows through that necessitous time gap. It allows us to be watchful and perhaps to affect the interval.

The replicating tic-toc of mechanical time is a mere shadow or stutter-form of this magical sequence. Frank Kermode has shown how apocalyptic expectation expands that stuttering tic-toc into a richer but still self-repeating rhythm.[4] If we hear meanings in the wind, we hear them in the passage of time. Each syllable of recorded time, for the religious watcher, disconfirms the expected end of time, so that a sentence runs on toward infinity.

I have argued in "The Voice of the Shuttle" (*Beyond Formalism*) that interpretation is in league with "the mercy of time" and mediates such strong beginnings and endings (tics or tocs) by the elaboration of middle terms. Figures of speech are "characterized by overspecified ends and indeterminate middles" and "the very elision or subsuming of middle terms allows, if it not actually compels, interpretation." Yet the danger is that interpretation may interpose itself too much and relativize all terms as middle terms. The experienced reader soon fights a growing sense that "The originals are not original" (Emerson), that everything tends, after a while, to become echo or quotation, until we fall into what Thomas Gray calls *Leucocholy*: the white melancholy. "The only fault of it is insipidity; which is apt now and then to give a sort of Ennui, which makes one form certain little wishes that signify nothing." An insipidity which seems to have been caused, in Gray, by overdoses of reading. "My life is like Harry the Fourth's supper of hens. 'Poulets à la broche, Poulets en Ragout, Poulets en Hâchis, Poulets en Fricasées.' Reading here, Reading there; nothing but books with different sauces." [5]

Against this insipidity one can proceed only by overvaluing drives and impossible wishes and so risking that black choler which Burton in his famous *Anatomy* tried to purge by exhaustively cataloguing it. Is not Freud's work a similar *Anatomy*? He develops a technique for reading dreams which may blacken them to make them interpretable. The darkness of his mind sets the dream off and intelligibly explains its inarticulateness. By a maieutic "alliance" with the patient he shapes the stuttering dream into an articulate, recountable presence.

Against insipidity, then, we have only this remedy. You take responsibility for the darkness you see. To see the dark ("le soleil noir de la mélancolie") the eyes must themselves be pupiled by darkness. Freud was a kaka-angelist rather than an euangelist. Yet the Pauline interpretation of the Old Testament is, in its way, equally scandalous. We go from one scandalously evangelic or kaka-angelic simplification to another.

Against Insipidity (1): Freud. Dumas's *dame aux camélias* wears a fresh white camellia daily for twenty-five days of the month. The rest of the time she wears a red one.[6] A mystery, a private ritual? A public mystery, perhaps. (Goethe called Nature "das offentliche Geheimniss.") The camellia is a professional sign, an identity badge or heraldry as blatant as Hester's "A" (Hawthorne's *The Scarlet Letter*) yet totally discreet. What kind of intentionality does any flower's color have? How do we interpret that sexual aesthetics?

Dumas's courtesan, by flaunting the public image of woman as "flower," accepts it so totally as to transform it. Her symbol triumphantly, freely, *inscribes* its intention. In that change from white to red the flower-idealism and its materialist aim coexist. The color change splits her, or our image of her, as if blood were drawn directly from her skin. What gets to us is this split in the person so immediately translated into symbol. The public sign pointing to a private condition. The open, unmistakable signal of a prostitute and her sophisticated maintenance of decorum. Though the symbol is based on an association (of the flower and those colors with femininity) it is the dissociated use of the symbol which allows the play of meaning.

Is it so with all sign language that becomes symbolic? Are symbols not, at once, obscure and clear, as direct as sexual or social need and as mediated as the body by—whatever the body is mediated by?

The face is the body trying to be more naked than the body. That is, more directly expressive. Symbols then are language trying to be more naked (unmediated) than language. Yet they cannot be more, ever, than flowers of language. Carnations incarnate.

Since the naked is never naked enough we try yet another way of denuding. Another idealism, another in-vestment, another—exciting?—strip. O Isis! O anything! Why this craze for the naked truth?

"Beauty is the erection of the whole body. Symbols are the erections of language." Here I go again. Down, libido. Or, up lipstick—a psychoanalytic friend tells me that lipstick is menstrual blood beautified, that is, displaced upward. What can we do with such blasé unblushingness? Must we burn Freud?

The point is . . . that sexuality is simply a pointing. If you don't get the point, there is little one can do. You fear castration, and you hover compulsively, emptily, near that point. "Omne tulit punctum" said horny Horace. A promiscuous metaphor is better than a faceless literalism. So Freud moves on, winning his point.

The Freudian reduction, like the Christian, builds communities. *In hoc signo vinces.* Interpretation is part of the feast as the therapeutic community acknowledges its new blood-consciousness. Everyone is slain, daily, on the stem of generation. Everyone is regenerated, daily, on the stem of interpretation.

Against Insipidity (2): Melville's Pun. When Shakespeare's Mercutio, having been mortally wounded, proclaims himself a "grave man," we admire his jest. His spirit is not subdued even now; and the extravagant yet trivial pun expresses well enough the sad waste of a good man's life. Melville is Shakespearean in the energies of his prose, and in him too there is strange fire in the form of pun and wordplay. But what if an entire story, and one as moving as *Billy Budd*, were basically derived from a pun or quibble? Would our astonishment survive our distaste?

Billy Budd is, probably, so entrenched as a modern classic that the extreme interpretation can only honor it. Vilest things become themselves in it. Yet so much remains unresolved, or hinges on what seems like an accident, that the whole thing quizzes us in an uncomfortable way. Thomas Rymer averred that too much depended on Othello's loss of a handkerchief; and too much, it can be argued, turns on Billy's tendency to stutter.

But the relation of trivial to important is always problematized in fiction. The Biblical drama revolves around "An Apple," as Milton's Satan disdainfully points out. The Rape of Troy seems very different from the Rape of a Lock; but did not both "mighty contests," as Pope suggested, spring from "trivial things," that is, "amorous causes"? And what is smaller yet more charged than verbal signs, so that, as the Talmud says, "Life and Death are in the hands of the tongue"?

It may be strangely appropriate if *Billy Budd* were punbegotten. The fact that the hero stutters points to either a pathological or a sacred condition; and his name (quite apart from possible mythic allusions) seems to collapse on itself, as if alliteration and stuttering blended to suggest a sacred pathology. It does not give the impression of being a real name: rather, it is something still wanting to utter itself.

Like Melville himself as narrator, I feel myself delaying, hesitating to come to the point. In the beginning was the Word, and the Word was with God. But there is no such Word here. It is the absence of the word which dooms Billy Budd: his word, or that of a father-advocate, or divine representative. What is the condition of the word in Melville's tale?

"Handsomely done, my lad! And handsome is as handsome did it, too!" Claggart says to Billy. A casual yet condensed statement, which betrays his sense of the beauty of the lad, but leaves everything else unsaid. It is proverbial; and also because of that no one expects it to be very meaningful in a personal or prophetic way. Yet when Billy strikes Claggart he fulfills, literally, that passing phrase. He is that Hand. In consequence he dies at the "main-yard arm."

Hidden wordplay is common enough in fiction and easily overvalued. It shows the condensing power or contaminating energy of the creative mind. Yet, however common, is it not also a fearful feature, a matter for woe and wonder? All at once, in *Billy Budd*, a casual phrase takes on prophetic status. A passing remark becomes part of a fatal series. A figure puts on literal truth and words are dangerous again.

Billy Budd is not presented as eyewitness truth. The author claims to use documents perhaps falsified by fantasy, as ballad stories often are. He is at a distance from the source and among reports as unreliable as time. The thrust of the narrative goes, in fact, beyond the possibility of direct testimony. When Billy Budd kills Claggart he puts himself beyond all evidence except the evidence of things not seen or the Word of God itself. But who, as Melville remarks, can get "a Voice out of Silence"? Only the gothic novel perhaps, with its counterfeit supernaturalism. In Charles Brockden Brown's *Wieland*, supernatural voices, later unmasked as ventriloquistic phenomena, bring false testimony. Perhaps it is better, after all, to let a pun be the God of the Machine. Not only Claggart's prophetic pun. Billy Budd's *mutiny* is nothing else but a rising up of his *muteness*: a protest against the condition of the word.

Epitaph for a Cricket. Literary criticism is a sublunar activity. The "ever-whirling wheel of Change" affects it even more than art works whose "being" it "dilates." One reason criticism does not age well is that though it may aspire to something more than fugitive prose or hit-and-run reviewing, it suffers from an inbuilt kind of parochialism. It becomes coterie criticism despite itself. Let a generation or two pass and the "cruel sports" of mutability turn the most ambitious commentary into a period piece. For if the critic is polemical without knowing it, he cannot bring to the issues a universalizing scrutiny; and if he is polemically self-aware, he rarely outlives his usefulness to topic or time. Who remembers Ramon Fernandez except as an allusion in a Wallace Stevens poem? Is Walter Bagehot more than an entry in René Wellek's *History of Criticism*?

The mortality rate of criticism is what it is. But that is no reason to treat those whose avowed aim is to remind us to read as second-class citizens of the Republic of Letters—by reading them carelessly, if at all. The mortality rate of fiction is at least as high. A great interpreter like Erich Auerbach, a great critic-scholar like E.R. Curtius, a prodigal son like Kenneth Burke, or men of letters like Paul Valéry and Edmund Wilson, who practiced the minor mode of prophecy we call criticism, are not annulled by the fact that they may be explicitly writing about the writing of others. It may be a weakness in them to prefer, at times, the indirectness of commentary to the creation of their own news, but it may also be a conviction that their identity is bound up with the writings of others—that the mind is laid waste by the false Unas of literature even as it is renewed by faith in the classic or neglected text.

Style and the Critic. Reading, then, includes reading criticism. But if prose fiction is not allowed to be poetry, criticism labors under a further restriction: it is not allowed to be prose—that is, what Wallace Stevens called "essential prose." It is expected to be "functional." Any attempt to write intensely falls under the suspicion of mandarin purposes. Yet what is a critic supposed to write if not prose?

There are modes of prose as of poetry. Criticism is such a mode. It would not be very fruitful to define this mode too sharply except to suggest that it always involves, directly or obliquely, the reading of specific texts. Criticism has to decide what "presence" to give to the text, from the simple question of how much of it to quote to the complex one of how to decide where a text ends or begins—since "textuality" may lead us indefinitely on to other texts.

Additionally, a critic has to decide what *his* language is supposed to be doing; and in general he has two options. He may construct a *metalanguage*, analogous to the "poetic diction" of Pope or Mallarmé in its abstract reordering of terms; or he may construct a *paralanguage*, which subordinates abstract concepts by playing them off against the specificity of texts. The creation of metalanguage ("epidiction" might be a better word) has the advantage of consistency, purity, and seeming logic; its disadvantage, however, is that it remains an unhistorical "grammar," a mental Latin rather than a lingua franca. The advantage of the more playful, indeed carefully promiscuous testing of terms in paralanguage, is that it reminds us that language is fate. The practice may degenerate, however, into paraphrase or intellectual glossolalia. (I admit to a variable style, which consists mainly of a playful dissolving of terms and abstractions, but one that seeks to bring out their creative force as unrecognized "poetic dictions.")

However expert literary critics may be in discussing the play of language in art, they remain uneasy with it in critical prose. There they prefer a "solid without fluctuation." But is criticism a yea yea, nay nay affair, best conducted in as dry a prose as possible? This admirable ideal has its shortcomings. It establishes too often a schizoid rather than useful distance between art and criticism. Under the pressure of such an ideal writers divide into a class of artists and a class of adjudicators, each with its own prerogatives. Surely a bureaucratic or managerial, rather than a human and persuasive solution. Why shouldn't the critic be "divers et ondoyant," in the essay form at least? (Perhaps we need a distinction between literary review and literary essay, though this too should hardly be absolute.) In any case, to prescribe the separateness of literary and literary-critical genres, and put down all mixed criticism as bad art, does not resolve the contradiction faced by those who want criticism to be a rigorous testing of interpretive hypotheses or clarifying of the artist's intention. How will they reconcile the notion of essay—tentative, continuously self-reflective, structured, yet informal—with the rigor that evaluative or historical criticism should ideally bring to its subject? Having no solution, *Beyond Formalism* opened by admitting that it "combine[d] literary history—the discerning of large, continuous and highly speculative patterns—with literary criticism—a daily, discontinuous, and very pragmatic effort."

Past and Present. For about fifty years now we have experienced a backlash to Ruskin and Pater: to the so-called "impressionistic criticism" with which I.A. Richards broke in his *Principles of Literary Criticism* (1924). On the Continent, following English example, Anatole France had created a personalist mode of art appreciation despite the scientism of Brunetière and others. No doubt there was, and is, a danger to this mode. Not so much the potential chaos of impressionism, subjectivism, relativism, and so forth, but rather that what matters for these writers is chiefly the development of *prose* as a modern medium. An ideology of prose arises which tends to reduce genre differences to musical variations of a basic medium; and this can make the text described too much a pretext. Just as the romantics often value "poesy" more than the individual poem, so there emerges now a "proesy."

Can we not, however, fifty years after the new chastity of Eliot and Richards, and a hundred after Pater and Ruskin, afford a détente? The more "creative writing" runs amuck in fiction, the more we find ourselves indecisive before it: now stupidly admiring, now donnishly supercilious. The literary essay can avoid that split; it knows itself as both creative and receptive, a part of literature as well as about literature. True, we can't go back to Pater or Ruskin, or the best Hazlitt and Coleridge; the amount of positive historical knowledge we are expected to carry along is too great. But they gave the essay a dignity which it need not lose in its more specialized and burdened form.

A Difference of Function. The question persists, however, whether there is a specific function that differentiates literary criticism from literature. There is one, at least, and Richards described it well in his book on Coleridge. *Practical Criticism* had shown how accultured an even minimally correct reading of poetry has to be, and now Richards asserts: "Intellectual tradition tells us, among other things, how *literally* to read a passage. It guides us in our metaphorical, allegorical, symbolical, modes of interpretation. The hierarchy of these modes is elaborate and variable; and to read aright we need to shift with an at present indescribable adroitness and celerity from one mode to another."

It seems that literature itself is not a sufficient guide to its "philosophy of rhetoric." The intrinsic study of texts must be reenforced by "intellectual tradition": clearly enough a synonym for the history of critical or hermeneutic techniques applied also to other than "literary" objects, and leading to some kind of consensus. (Today, for example, semiotics would count as part of "intellectual tradition.") Literary understanding, then, has two components: literary tradition proper, or an expansible canon of texts; and criticism, which helps to form this canon and guide its interpretation—which prepares us, at least, for the complexities of literary expression.

We are, then, as critics, part of that "intellectual tradition." We reflect on the relation of literal and symbolic in the context of an "elaborate and variable" sign system. There is something in literary understanding which corresponds to the division between "letter" and "spirit," except that it is impossible to say that literature is on the side of the letter and criticism on the side of the spirit. The reverse may be the case, but this too is unlikely, because these "sides" must be seen together in some kind of binary relation. Yet if the structure of this complementarity is not clear, our analysis suggests that literary hermeneutics is still, like its religious counterpart, shaped by the problem of belief. It is this problem which worries Richards ("how *literally* to read a passage . . ."). What kind of statement does literature make? And, more immediately, what credence (or authority) should we give here and now to this work before us? English critics seem to resent "soteriological" theories of the function of art, but their emphasis on belief, engagement, evaluation, is by no means purely epistemological.

The pragmatic conclusions that follow from this are modest ones. Criticism should be reflective vis-à-vis itself as well as vis-à-vis its immediate object, the work of art. It should reflect on its historical debts (that it may not be as distinct from religious hermeneutics as it might wish to be) and on the possibility that it is, after all, an art form—more of a *mythologie blanche* (Derrida) than it realizes. That is also why those who insist on reading critical prose only literally are betraying the function of criticism vis-à-vis . . . criticism. All we can be certain of is that literary understanding is bipartite, requiring both literary discourse (texts) and literary-critical discourse (commentary, or associated texts), and that too strong a privileging of fictional over nonfictional texts (of "primary" over "secondary" literature) reifies literature still further and disorders our ability to read. Whether we want to follow Richards in seeking a systematics, a "theory by which the skill [of reading] may be regained—this time as a less vulnerable and more deeply grounded, because more consciously recognized endowment," is another matter.

Reading: Alive or Dead? I wonder, finally, whether the very concept of reading is not in jeopardy. Pedagogically, of course, we still respond to those who call for improved reading skills; but to describe most semiological or structural analyses of poetry as a "reading" extends the term almost beyond recognition.

Reading and writing, moreover, associated for so long in our culture, may be drifting apart. It is not possible to "read" some kinds of writing—concrete poetry or extreme experimental prose, for example—though it is quite possible to analyze them and construct by that means something readable: a metanarrative. One can foresee, however, an era where writing will be as semi-automatic as casual reading is now. In that era writing and reading would be competitive rather than mutually reenforcing activities. Those who read merely to find a starter for their own performance are already close to that productive (or is it exploitative) state.

The condition I point to has been recognized. But the threat to reading is usually viewed as coming primarily from the media, or trivialized art. Richards had already drawn the moral consequences of that. "The extent to which second-hand experience of a crass and inchoate type [as in the popular movie or novel] is replacing ordinary life offers a threat which has not yet been realized." Max Frisch generalizes wittily: "Technology . . . the knack of so arranging the world that we don't have to experience it." [7] In the present situation the horizon of reading is being limited still further by the learned techniques that should liberate it, as well as by various ideologies of performance and production.

Compare the 1970s with the 1920s. Richards turned to communications theory to improve the writer-reader (text-response) relation. He wanted an ideal reciprocity, or at least the technical basis for it. But writing has now won the initiative so thoroughly that reading seems to have fallen behind. Writing appears as productive, activist, material; reading as passive, accumulative, retrograde—the most recalcitrant of bourgeois idealisms! I exaggerate, of course; yet something of that bias is found not only in countercultural students but also in such theorists as Kristéva, Sollers, and Deleuze. To what can we turn now to restore reading, or that conscious and scrupulous form of it we call literary criticism?

I hate to end on a question that sounds like a dignified whimper. But modern "rithmatics"—semiotics, linguistics, and technical structuralism—are not the solution. They widen, if anything, the rift between reading and writing. They convert all expression into generative codes needing operators rather than readers.

A sophisticated technique is accompanied too often by a barbarous or parochial narrowness of culture. When, as in the work of Roman Jakobson, this is not true, one is not sufficiently convinced that the technique is more than a style. In this Age of Irony there are still a lot of iron men around.

The advance that has occurred is mainly in the area of theory of convention, as it rules both reading and writing. The movement sparked by Jakobson, for example, though based on modern psychology and linguistics, can still be linked to the prescriptive criticism of the rhetorical schools from Antiquity on, which established a store of "devices" to regulate the character, and assure the success, of the work of art. These rules or devices served to build a community of literate people, where all were potentially writers or orators. That this historical rhetoric has its productive as well as prescriptive side is clear when we think, for example, of Erasmus's *copia* method, or Lessing's *Essay on Fables*, with their literary formulae that could motivate new narratives as well as analyze existing ones. Those who are presently expanding and rationalizing the historical study of rhetoric in the hope of evolving a scientific "grammar" on the level of poetics, are fulfilling, in my view, more of a communitarian than a scientific function: this grammar of forms, more systematic than Northrop Frye's, and as eminently teachable should enable reading to gain back its anticipatory (but not necessarily prescriptive) vigor.

A Happy Ending. "All that remained of the mystery was the tale." One wonders how long it will be before the tale itself disappears because we do not—are unable to—read it any more. My epigraph is taken from Scholem's *Major Trends in Jewish Mysticism.* Scholem's commentary summarizes a story by the Hebrew novelist S.J. Agnon: "When the Baal Shem had a difficult task before him, he would go to a certain place in the woods, light a fire and meditate in prayer—and what he had set out to perform was done. When a generation later the 'Maggid' of Meseritz was faced with the same task he would go to the same place in the woods and say: We can no longer light the fire, but we can still speak the prayers—and what he wanted done became reality. Again a generation later Rabbi Moshe Leib of Sassov had to perform this task. And he too went to the woods and said: We can no longer light a fire, nor do we know the secret meditations belonging to the prayer, but we do know the place in the woods to which it all belongs—and that must be sufficient; and sufficient it was. But when another generation had passed and Rabbi Israel of Rishin was called upon to perform the task, he sat down on his golden chair in the castle and said: We cannot light the fire, we cannot speak the prayers, we do not know the place, but we can tell the story of how it was done."

Agnon is not satisfied with the naive, desperate humor of the "golden chair in the [Rabbi's] castle." He wants a Happy Ending to outdo Happy Endings. So he concludes: "The story which the Rabbi told had the same effect as the actions of the other three." Agnon, coming still later in the tradition, tells a story about this story. He has enough strength left to add an ending which asserts the power of the rememorative word in the absence of other powers. He mourns a fading gift, but he mourns it on a golden footstool made of its radiant words. His sublimely positive extension of a negative series is more effective than simple irony: like so many Jewish jokes, in which something is saved from nothing, it keeps the faith. Scholem the reader understood Agnon the writer: "The story is not ended . . . the secret life it holds can break out tomorrow in you or me." Stories do not end as long as there are such reader-interpreters to augment them.

Part Four
Position Papers

On the Theory of Romanticism

Every Jack will have his Jill. This utopian and "romantic" proverb makes me think it is unnecessary to mention in detail what scholar-critics of the coming decade should be concerned with. If book V of the *Faerie Queene* can attract, after years of benign neglect, notable studies, there is hope for book VIII of *The Prelude* or for Wordsworth's later poems. The accelerating growth of scholarship is such, that, even without computerized dating, Robert Bloomfield can expect to find his interpreter in the 1970s. Let me confine myself, therefore, to the *theory* of romanticism, to worrying a period term we have been unable to exorcize. All the more so since there are topics of study which deeply affect the theory.

1. We still need an answer to Lovejoy's scepticism concerning the usefulness of the concept or term romanticism. Wellek began answering some twenty years ago, but one sometimes feels that if Lovejoy had written Wellek's article Wellek would have countered with Lovejoy's. The debate is a twenty-year standoff.[1]

2. Perhaps the debate finds its solution elsewhere, in a "Discrimination of Enlightenments." [2] Romanticism seems to me a viable *poetic* form of enlightenment (or post-enlightenment) thought. Several essays and books have already challenged the idea that romanticism and modernism are discontinuous,[3] while W. J. Bate has shown that the burden of the past weighed on the romantic with at least the same intensity as on the neoclassical writer.[4] A great specific advance, in this respect, has been

made in the area of Blake studies. Harold Bloom remarks that after Damon, Frye, Erdman, and others, we cannot say that Blake was opposed to rationality, only that he opposed certain rationalisms. That marvelous conclusion to *The Four Zoas*, "The dark Religions are departed and sweet Science reigns," is an enlightenment topos. But the case of Shelley and of Keats has not been completely argued. Matthew Arnold's feeling that the romantics were children when they thought or Yeats's that in Keats "intellectual curiosity was at its weakest" still prevails in high places. Two recent books of distinction, Thomas Whitaker's on Yeats and Dwight Culler's on Arnold,[5] implicitly support the Arnoldian view. It is true, of course, that the romantics did not, on the whole, commit their thoughts to any systematic or existing framework, and that what thinking they did was limited by a certain faithfulness to romance modes. But this simply raises the question of their relation to Romance—their perplexed or purified use of the strange fire from that source. Even Wordsworth, for whom myth and figure had to justify themselves by being grounded in real emotion, admits in the Great Ode that we are all born into Romance. Here, despite Earl Wasserman's emphasis on the Romantics' "subtler language," there is not enough close reading: if we make every allowance for the use of the persona in neoclassical and modern poetry, we should also for the seductive presence of romance motifs in Shelley and Keats.

It would be unfair to leave this theme without paying a tribute to Northrop Frye, whose general theory of literature is based on romance modes or their survival. Yet precisely because it is a general theory, it is also what might be called "superductive"—too good a conductor of the individual poem out of itself into some larger spiritual form. It takes a lot to convince us that Frye's observation that the romantic prefers "within" metaphors to "up there" metaphors is significant, or that Wordsworth's central poems are *Peter Bell*, the *Idiot Boy*, and *The Waggoner* because they drive us along by a "propelling metrical energy" which expresses the poet's identification with a larger, vehicular form of creative power.[6]

3. Can we ever convey the kind of thinking art is without being reductive or superductive? It is a question best left for another forum. But one enchantment that the romantic scholar will continue to face in the 1970s—like a knight in romance coming upon an attractive pastoral spot—Henry Adams named, surprisingly, "the mental indolence of history." He meant that he read poets for their obvious historical relations which comforted him with known types, ideas or (to use a modern locution) recognizable deviations from the norm. His temptation, in short, was history of ideas. And without wishing to be polemical I must report that Adams felt eighteenth-century poets to be light on the mind compared to Wordsworth. "He . . . read shelves of eighteenth century poetry, but when his father offered his own set of Wordsworth as a gift on condition of reading it through, he declined. Pope and Gray called for no mental effort; they were easy reading; but the boy was thirty years old before his education reached Wordsworth" (*The Education of Henry Adams*, chapter 2).

4. But let me damp my superciliousness and insist that we cannot appreciate the Romantics as thinkers if we do not also understand them as cultural or, in the broadest sense, political thinkers. Here David Erdman and also Carl Woodring have done work of note.[7] They have helped to restore our sense for a local, rather than vehicular, body of thought. That the two bodies are not inimical was shown by M. H. Abrams' classic paper on "The Spirit of the Age" [8]; and I am sure the 1970s will see interesting scholarship on such apparently local issues as debating and revolutionary societies, the emerging class of readers called women, the role of the newspapers and magazines, the effects of industrialization, and so on. I have sometimes encouraged the idea of a thesis with the title *1791*, or any (relatively) noncataclysmic year in the period considered romantic; this is not the direct province of the literary historian but it could be a propaedeutic for an authentic larger-scaled literary history. Local issues, as I have suggested, connect often with more literary or exemplary ones: the magazines of the time, for example, print anonymous or pseudonymous poems, many of them by

women readers, which leads to the feeling that a submerged class is struggling for its *voice*. As soon as we realize that "voice" contains both the idea of expression and that of representation, both a literary and a political element, we have joined two types of history.

5. I have tried not to let personal interests intrude too much in the above suggestions but now wish to mention two areas which seem to me essential for both the study of romanticism and modern literature. One is the literary consciousness as such, the consciousness a poet has of his vocation, not the programmatic statements only, in letters and manifestoes, but principally the opus operatum, the poem as recapitulating a vision of literary destiny or constitutive of it.[9] The notion of literary influence must, in other words, be put on a broader and deeper basis. Whether history is biography, as Emerson thought, or biography history, few of us live or write without making contact, often through the pressure of the work itself, with psychohistorical notions—attitudes, mediated by specific poems and authors, about the role of the arts in society. It may be that new insights will come from the side of Marxism—Christopher Caudwell's work has remained without sequel, and we lack in this country a developing sociology of literature—or from the side of psychoanalysis—Harold Bloom's extension of the idea of family romance into the relation between *literary* fathers and sons is a fascinating, revisionist use of Freudian theory.[10] Yet in Jonathan Wordsworth's scrupulous study of "The Ruined Cottage" there is an almost principled refusal to consider those great father-figures Spenser and Milton. It will not do to see a Wordsworth jousting chiefly with lexical echoes or local literary influences, even when they presume to include a Taylorized Goethe.[11] The need to nurture an emergent national tradition and to separate it from incumbent Englishness makes the American scholar especially sensitive to what the past means: he knows that every great spirit is subject to that glorified bully, tradition. If American criticism overstates the psychic drama which occurs when a poet tries to free himself of influence, of an incumbent past or a missionary future, then English criticism seriously understates it.

6. Yet the history of consciousness is one thing, that of forms another. A writer is situated not directly in time and place but in print, images, types and forms. He must work with competing or contrary mediations in order to gain something unmediated; at least more deeply mediated.[12] Can the study of forms be enlarged to contribute to the study of consciousness? Most of us agree that the problem of how perception (or nature) stands to imagination becomes acute in the romantic era. Blake, for example, describes the relation as an antagonism; Wordsworth as a mutuality. The matter is complicated by the fact that what we perceive is, today, increasingly artificial (nature plus art), that not only do we see more art around us through the spread of museums and reproductions but our impressions are themselves processed by the ubiquity of radio, television, cinema, the papers—by noisemakers and newsmakers.[13] The student of romanticism in the 1970s cannot but pay attention to art's interaction with the habitat of art.[14] One can isolate two main aspects of this interaction: how art (especially high art) maintains itself against outside influences, and how it sustains itself on them. Imagination, Stevens said, presses against the pressure of reality: it has something to do with our self-preservation. A deepened theory of literary influence connects here with the problematics of environmental influence. When Father Ong reinterprets the thesis of a romantic "shift of sensibility" as a McLuhanite shift in the sensorium, he is exploring this area.[15] Every good study of the dangerous liaisons of high art with popular art also explores it: we have only begun, for example, to take seriously the persistence of gothic romance though our most sophisticated fiction is still indebted to it. And the development of a modern prose style, furthered by the essays of Lamb, Hazlitt, and Coleridge, and related to Wordsworth's championing of a natural diction, is one of those major shifts toward a new public medium which we neglect because it is so much with us.

7. It may be objected that I have left out "literary criticism" in busying myself so completely with "literary studies." There is a difference between scholar and critic; yet criticism, as it comes down from Arnold, is engaged in assessing the relation

of art to life in a context that obliges us to consider the relation of art to culture. Life, for Arnold, was life in a culture, and the broadest possible one. Life called for "criticism" by means of art because it was increasingly involved with art-forms: in Arnold's day the phrase "overcultured" or "overconscious" became current (without provincialism disappearing) while taste sunk as well as spread.[16] Criticism today is still caught in the Arnoldian bind: it strives to maintain some distinction between art and popular culture while characterizing art as a type of knowledge which is not against life, which can be conscious yet not overconscious, aware *and* organic, reasoned *and* strongly rooted in national or communal values. The literary scholar is a literary critic, therefore, as long as he overvalues neither the intellect nor its apparent opposite, life; as long as he approaches "ideas" with the discretion of a Leavis or a Trilling, understanding that what lies beyond ideas is not life (as in vitalistic philosophies) but simply more ideas, or . . . art.

Perhaps this does imply that the critic stumbles necessarily into an art ideology. Yet there seems to be no consensus as to whether art is always, by its nature, disestablishing itself, passing into some other form or activity (popular culture, politics, prose thought) or whether it remains attached, against all odds, to a self-renewing and even hieratic tradition. Nor is it clear, if we choose the latter view, which is more strictly that of "art ideology," whether its sanction lies in a religious or secularist sphere. Here we touch of course on a most sensitive area in romantic and modernist scholarship: the role of art in the conflict between secularism and the religious sensibility.[17]

8. Finally, a plea for being aware in the 1970s of the history of scholarship. The accumulation of knowledge, like that of capital, makes us deceptively secure. We forget the scarcity that was and the precarious growth of guiding ideas. Donald Wesling's recent book on Wordsworth [18] fails because it does not know, or eschews, the long ideological struggle to define the romantic mode against the very notion of "adequacy" it takes over from Arnold, and which Arnold himself still associated with a view of classicism influential from Winckelmann on. Mr. Wesling's book, though attractive in itself—in style, and in matters

of detail—deals with the notion as if it had no roots in the history of interpretation. How intriguing that the distinguishing mark of classicism in its maturity should now be applied, so disingenuously, to a Romantic poet! Only in the author's last pages does something new and problematic emerge, and this has to do with the "inadequacy" of landscape—where "inadequacy" is not only an aesthetic but also an ethical or historical concept, as in Schiller's "On naive and reflective poetry," which defines the modern, reflective style as one for which nature description cannot suffice. Some comparative literature is useful, after all.[19]

Self, Time, and History

I find it difficult to take a position without recourse to a venerable metaphor, that of the *theatrum mundi.* I stand in what is roughly defined as contemporaneity, but the backdrop against which my words echo is much older, and may be defined as a controversy between progressivist and antiprogressivist philosophies of history. The issue of historical progress is left moot by Herder, who makes no ultimate distinction between culture and enlightenment, pointing out that both words are metaphors from different areas of experience,[1] yet insisting that some cultures are more enlightened than others, and anticipating therefore the vast Hegelian design of a movement from East to West which does not end in decadence but rather in a fulfillment of "Humanität." The controversy is brought to sharper focus by, first, Kierkegaard's attacks on Hegel, with Kierkegaard making subtle and subversive use of the concept of repetition; then by Nietzsche's formulation of the concept of an "eternal return" but also by his relentless critique of the notion that "Weltgeschichte ist Weltgericht," a slogan which seems to go back to Schiller. As we enter the present century, we know the controversy best through an appreciation, now general, of Vico's principle of "ricorso"; through such figures as Yeats and Spengler, who try to build the "ricorso" into their conjectural histories of the human spirit;

Delivered in 1974 at a conference on "Romanticism and Historicism" sponsored by the Programme in Comparative Literature at the University of Toronto.

through Karl Popper's attack on "Geistesgeschichte," that is, on Hegel's "totalitarian" version of historicism; and through Walter Benjamin's moving struggle to purify dialectical materialism of its progressivist or utopian bias—a struggle in which, for Benjamin, Nietzsche and especially Baudelaire play a crucial role. "Den Weltlauf zu unterbrechen—das war der tiefste Wille in Baudelaire." [2]

Yet what I contemplate, as I stand under that vast philosophical sky, that backdrop which already seems somewhat unreal and scenic, is a set of purely formal problems, which, though distinctly literary, are also unreal. The reason for this further unreality is that these problems, being formal, cannot be made culture-specific, or materially historical, unless we already have a philosophy of history in mind with which—more forcibly than cogently—we associate them. These formal problems have to do with the conduct of narrative rather than with the conduct of world history ("Weltlauf"): they deal with such literary features as digression and allusion; with such themes as the labyrinth; with such myths as the Orient as Origin and the Westward Course of the Spirit; with such questions of poetics as the mimetic dimension of character, point of view, persona, metaphor; and through all these, with the relevance of art to our function in time and history.

That I hesitated before writing "function" rather than "role" or "place" or "situation"—that I chose the neutral or scientific word—says something about the intellectual bias of our time, which is against pathos; and the same bias makes one feel uneasy about such large verbal concepts as "self" and "time." Yet we cannot do without them, any more than without historical speculation. Even in the purest discourse there remains what Anatole France and Derrida have named a "mythologie blanche." The inertia of language is part of the force of language, and is a power to be reckoned with; not everything in it is slag; and if artists like James Joyce complain of the language-jam, they still exploit its facticity, its accidental sonorities, its etymological depth, its paradigmatic and syntagmatic qualities.

In the same way we cannot shrug off the inertial force of historical poetics; we are stuck, for a time, with such terms as "self" and "time"; and the relatively slow rate of change in our conceptual system, what we have called its inertial force, actually furnishes us with constants of a remarkable degree of universality. Take, for example, the notion of self as it emerges from the retarding, inertial concept of character; consider that Wordsworth, one of the poets in whom the term "self" emerges as distinct from "character," and who had his difficulty with that historically transmitted notion,[3] is also the one who founded the "character of the poet"—that is, who claimed for the poet a special sensibility, independent of class or social circumstance, indeed a "great birthright" which lodges in all as an "infant sensibility" but is unfortunately not developed in all, but repressed or broken off.[4] Then apply this conceptual disharmony between self and character to the Boy of Winander episode, which images a break in self-development, by evoking a great divide with the Boy on one side and the Man on the other. There is no easy progression; the structure, in fact, is that of an interrupted pastoral; and it is impossible to say where the poetic self lodges, whether in the dead boy, or the living, meditative man conscious of mortality.* The two parts don't fit together, despite the progressivist argument of a poem subtitled the "Growth of a Poet's Mind."[5] "Dust as we are, the immortal spirit grows/ Like harmony in music," Wordsworth exclaims near the beginning of his memorials; but one is constantly made to feel the precariousness of the harmony, of this "self-building" spirit which the Victorian poets, developing the musical analogy, and influenced by the German idea of "Bildung," consolidated into doctrine.

When Keats writes, "A Poet has no Identity," he means the same as "A Poet has no Character"—his self-image is perpetually dissolved by the dream element or the self-emptying power of empathy in him.[6] It is proper to recall here Pope's wittily sexist observation that "Women have no character at all." That is the curse, or odium, weighing on the line going from Wordsworth to Keats. The modern poets, of course, aided by the findings of mythologists and psychoanalysts, will become aggressively insistent that the feminine or Marian or matriarchal element has been repressed and must be reintegrated into human culture;

*See end of chapter for the text of "The Boy of Winander."

poets will now be rediscovered, and simplified in this light; but though Tennyson, Swinburne, and Hopkins are on the horizon, Yeats's *Vision*, with its stylized historical gyration of self and anti-self, is still a century away.

Since we are in a kind of theater and have already travelled forward to Yeats, let me now invite you to turn back two centuries or more to Milton. To one of the really magical moments in literature, not uninspired by theater and masque for it presents a transformation scene, such as changed a poor man's hut into a palace, or hell into paradise, and vice versa. I allude to the ending of the first book of *Paradise Lost* (ll. 761ff.), in which Satan's pompous host, assembled in Pandemonium, is changed before our eyes into a fairy circle which a belated Peasant "sees/ Or dreams he sees" in the moonlight.[7] Formally considered, this sequence is an elaborate digression from the apparent line of action; it creates in the narrative not only a moment of rich, conspicuous, even irrelevant foregrounding of the poetical texture but also a ghostly, dimensional shift from action to observation, one which slows the narrative flow even as it quickens the reader's mind by the sounded wealth of allusions.

Here, then, is a strange turn, or troping, or deviousness—whatever you wish to call it. The result, in any case, is that all kinds of time feelings reenter, which had been allayed by the regular, even triumphant course of the narrative. If we take stock, during this ghostly pause, of the illusions imposed on us, we realize that even an unobvious phrase can prove to be enchanted ground. Exploring the literary etymology of "sees/ Or dreams he sees"—a phrase which thematizes, however passingly, the illusionist atmosphere of the entire epic—we are whisked back seventeen centuries to a glimpse of Virgil's Dido, seen through the surprised yet uncertain eyes of a guilty Aeneas, and in a moonlight not unsimilar to that which illuminated her first appearance in Virgil's epic.[8] So time—the literary-historical time separating Virgil and Milton, as well as the mortal time in which Aeneas sacrificed Dido—becomes at once curiously weightless and decisive, innocent and guilty. Our hearts, like the peasant's, rebound with joy and fear. The moon itself, of course, that changeable mother of the months, is a time symbol; while even the temporal dimension of genre is evoked, if we recall that pastoral, as Puttenham noted, displays a prophetic reserve by glancing at greater things under the semblance of lesser.

The most interesting feature, however, in this transformation scene is the figure of the peasant. A pastoral needs a peasant; in that respect his appearance is innocent; but the recursive pattern of the formal transformation places him in a spot previously occupied by Satan/Soldan, Sun-and-Taurus, Moon, and (implicitly) Aeneas. The only thematic link between these oddly consorted observers is, possibly, that of *labor* in its precarious relation to *grace*. In the light of the laboring moon we understand that the peasant too is a laborer; that his harvest is as uncertain as that of Virgil's *agricola* in the *Georgics*, or as that of Mammon-Mulciber, whose "high towers" and "engines" availed him nothing (*Paradise Lost* I. 748–50).[9] Indeed, they are being transformed even now into this unpretentious moment by the *mirabile dictu* of Milton. But this artisanal magic evokes in turn the figure of the artist as laborer and his relation to grace. It is, after all, his "engines" which are at work here, ransacking (*inter alia*) pagan literature for allusions or "treasures better hid" (I. 685ff.). Will there be grace for his work, for the "precious bane" of literature? Can the justifier be justified? We return thus to the central issue of the "character" of the poet in a Puritan age, or any age. *Wozu Dichter in dürftiger Zeit?*

A poet in search of a theme, and so of his poetic identity, is how the *Prelude* opens. The Miltonic brooding has become overt, but directs itself at inactivity and vacillation, as Wordsworth fears he is "a false stewart who hath much received/ And renders nothing back." "Was it for this . . ." he asks (*Prelude* I. 269), that Derwent sent a voice flowing along his dreams even in infancy? That the "winding" river, like the immortal mother of a mortal hero, began to manifest his destiny? The Boy of Winander is also river- or lake-born; and how "winding" the hero's fate may be is quietly conveyed by the flow of Wordsworth's last paragraph. It suggests not only the "wandering steps and slow" of belated, post-Edenic man, but also how broken or devious the path is that leads from the "marvelous Boy," whose portrait has been drawn, to the mature person, the fully "cultivated" poet. We are presented at once with the image of a split self and with that of a split sound, in the form of a curiously awkward syntax. For, in Wordsworth, it is always a sound or voice that must "grow with thought," as well as a person. As if when voice broke, identity itself were in danger of breaking: the "break" after "There was a Boy"[10] is eloquent, and both Lucy and Matthew poems are characterized by cries or "fits" of speech which leave an echoing hiatus in the mind.

There is a special sort of split or broken sound which is Wordsworth's "natural" model for the way experience elaborates itself by growing into thought or fading into redundance. It is associated with one of the oldest motifs of pastoral poetry. I mean the sound we call an *echo*, which is as important to Wordsworth as afterimage or reflection. His experiences tend to divide into an event and its repercussions. The one act characterizing the Boy of Winander is that he makes nature—its hidden life—echo responsively. The reflective man standing over the boy's grave does a similar thing, for the logic of the episode as a whole imposes the thought that he, just like the boy, is calling a voice out of silence. We find ourselves before a tragic ode to Echo. There is no *imago* here (to borrow the psychoanalytic term), only an *imago vocis*: a "wandering utterance" that cannot be unified or localized.

Ye wandering Utterances, has earth no scheme,
No scale of moral music—to unite
Powers that survive but in the faintest dream
Of memory?

("Ode on the Power of Sound")

It is interesting that the boy's first trial of the voice, his hallooing, raises uncontrollable echoes; while nature's indirect or imperceptible action moves so quickly inward that it too overwhelms. There is either no response or too much of it. Voice, in short, does not find its voice. "O Rocky Voice," Man cries to Echo in a late poem by Yeats, "Shall we in that great night rejoice?/ What do we know but that we face/ One another in this place?" The poet's muteness expresses, in this context, an unimaginable sound, a crying too inward for tears—

for such Tears of the Muses, I mean, as echoing streams, hills, rocks, or similar pastoral and elegiac tropes.[11]

I have called this echo structure a tragic one, because echo and afterimage are progressively internalized until the possibility of response is buried on the bourne from which no traveller returns. So deeply if providentially split are childhood and manhood, or poetic self and character. It is hard to conceive them as dwelling in one person, still in touch with each other, mutually responsive. Hence, when Wordsworth says, "A full half-hour together I have stood," one is tempted to detach "together" from "half-hour" and read it with "I have stood." The "I," in this mute reflection, has gathered to itself a remembered mode of being and "stood together" in unity for a space of time which, significantly, divides time to make us aware of it.[12]

In Milton's *Comus* (ll. 230–43) there is an actual ode to Echo. The Lady, wishing to call a voice out of silence—the voice of her brothers, but in any case a saving voice—asks the help of Echo, alluding to her as a kind of universal presence, at once water nymph and "Daughter of the Sphere," while climaxing in the classical vow that Echo be "translated to the skies,/ And give resounding grace to all Heav'n's Harmonies." Milton's elaborately airy sonnet—as airy and wandering as echo itself—is a lyric tour de force woven out of the substantial nothingness of sound effects and the redundant harmonics of literary allusion. Though it anticipates the "adjuring verse" addressed by the Attendant Spirit to Sabrina, it is not crowned with success, for the next voice we hear is that of Comus. Music is labor lost at this point, not because it lacks charm but because the relation between vocal charm and grace is an uncertain one.

Now the one kind of echo missing from Wordsworth's poetry, or very carefully used when used at all, is the echo we call a literary allusion. The literary echo, in Wordsworth, is "reduced" to experience by a "cure of the ground"; and when it does occur it is so internalized that it points to the *phenomenology* of literary allusion.[13] This grounding of allusion in experience—in the personal and mortal experience of time—has an unexpected result. Take away the play of allusion, the comforting ground of literary-historical texture, and you place the burden of responsiveness directly on the reader. He must echo in himself a verse which he can only develop by the recognition that *de te fabula narratur.* The verse adjures him; demands grace of him; and no poet who reads so easily at first puts as resolute and lasting a demand on the reader. We are asked to read in ourselves.

Thus Wordsworth's echo structure extends itself until we feel a relation between the poet looking "mutely" at the Boy of Winander's grave and the Stranger or Traveller—that is, Reader —on the horizon who will ponder this verse, the poet's inscription. Time stretches through this reader into a potentially infinite series of echoes. It is the reader who makes the verse responsive, however inward or buried its sounds: he also calls a voice out of silence. Alone, or as part of a family which includes Dorothy and Coleridge, he redeems the poet's voice from solitariness. In the ultimate pastoral, voice remains ghostly until it makes even the mute rock respond. "All things shall speak of Man."[14]

Such a transformation, of course, is never shown by Wordsworth. There is no "resounding grace," no ultimate pastoral. The path that leads, in "The Boy of Winander," from invocation to echo to mute reflection is the only one. Yet this path is not lost to us because, however inward, it remains temporal, and so may be recalled through "the turnings intricate of verse." This power of recall, as the *Prelude* shows, is no simple imitation, but a creative response, a venture which extends and renews time.

I have slipped from my initial metaphor of the theater of life to that of pathfinding, and culture in its link to cultivation. One reason Lucy lives "unseen" and among "untrodden ways" is that there is no path to her which is not an illusion. It is the path as well as voice which "breaks" in "Strange fits of passion." On the level of poetic speech, moreover, this means she cannot be "addressed": her mode of being has not emerged into culture, she is as unrealized as Echo ("Sweet Echo, sweetest

Nymph that liv'st unseen . . ."). [15] If we had a masculine equivalent for "nymph," we could apply it to the Boy of Winander, who also remains *in* nature, never far from "the bosom of the steady lake." It is as if the path from nature to culture were lost and had to be found once more by an action which is the opposite of "blazing." So the influence of nature on the Boy of Winander, by which she seeds images "for immortality" in his mind, [16] subtly "plants" this path towards a steadier, more eternal "character."

Yet Wordsworth's "for immortality" has a sinister aspect, considering the early demise of the Boy. We are left with a sense of disjunction in personal development curiously similar to that which, according to Wordsworth, had overtaken history —the historical flow of time—with the French Revolution. The thinkers of his day were tempted by the para-apocalyptic idea that there was a radical schism between past and future, *ancien régime* and the new politics: "The man to come, parted, as by a gulph,/ From him who had been" (*Prelude* XII. 59ff.). This threatened to undo the lesson of the English Revolution of the seventeenth century, which had maintained legal forms and imaged itself as a reform, rather than revolutionary, movement. Wordsworth's radicalism was now displaced, as it were, into a poetry that took literally the concept of *culture* as *cultivation*: he returned from revolutionary schism to the idea of a ground out of which things grew slowly, precariously; where accident was important, some grew and some didn't, but where there were, for humanity generically considered, infinite chances of birth and rebirth. The literalism of "Fair seed-time had my soul" (*Prelude* I. 301) shocks us into a view of culture as nature. But in the Boy of Winander episode the figure of "growing" in the "cultured Vale" breaks, and reveals what it was never intended to hide, the winding or "eccentric path" (Hölderlin) of individuation, leading from nature to death, or through the consciousness of death to the counterbalancing vision of a self uninjured by time.

Boy of Winander Episode

(Version in the 1805 *Lyrical Ballads*)

There was a Boy, ye knew him well, ye Cliffs
And Islands of Winander! many a time,
At evening, when the stars had just begun
To move along the edges of the hills,
Rising or setting, would he stand alone,
Beneath the trees, or by the glimmering lake;
And there, with fingers interwoven, both hands
Pressed closely palm to palm and to his mouth
Uplifted, he, as through an instrument,
Blew mimic hootings to the silent owls
That they might answer him. And they would shout
Across the watery vale, and shout again
Responsive to his call, with quivering peals,
And long halloos, and screams, and echoes loud
Redoubled and redoubled; concourse wild
Of mirth and jocund din! And, when it chanced
That pauses of deep silence mocked his skill,
Then, sometimes, in that silence, while he hung
Listening, a gentle shock of mild surprise
Has carried far into his heart the voice
Of mountain torrents; or the visible scene
Would enter unawares into his mind
With all its solemn imagery, its rocks,
Its woods, and that uncertain heaven, received
Into the bosom of the steady lake.

This Boy was taken from his Mates, and died
In childhood, ere he was ten years old.
Fair are the woods, and beauteous is the spot,
The Vale where he was born: the Church-yard hangs
Upon a slope above the Village School,
And there, along that bank, when I have passed
At evening, I believe, that oftentimes
A full half-hour together I have stood
Mute—looking at the grave in which he lies.

Lionel Trilling as Man in the Middle

For more than thirty years, starting with a book on Matthew Arnold (1939) and a brief work on E. M. Forster (1943), and via several well-known collections of essays, *The Liberal Imagination* (1950), *The Opposing Self* (1955), *A Gathering of Fugitives* (1956), and *Beyond Culture* (1965), Lionel Trilling has seen literature as a "criticism of life." The phrase comes from Matthew Arnold, and Trilling rightly interprets it to mean that literature is moral rather than moralistic in character, that it always makes its comment on the individual caught up in society or culture. Every person's freedom is affected by the habits and presuppositions of his time, which often sustain him unconsciously; and our culture could not exist for long without the antagonism of what Trilling calls, drawing among others on Hegel, an "opposing self."

Yet Trilling, of course, has no grand philosophy or overview of the conflict between the two powers he isolates: the self and culture. It is here as in morals generally: the good and the evil grow up together, inseparably. A critic's soul is made, like any other man's, by recognizing that life *in* society—civilized, cultured life—is an irreversible necessity: what Keats called a "world of Circumstances" is the only school or testing place for a self always in search of its identity.

By defining Trilling as a moral critic one says the obvious, but it is not easy to describe further the at once subtle and strenuous nature of his enterprise. Morals, as R. P. Blackmur suggested, are the quarrel we have with behavior, which evades strict ideals or categories. Yet they are also, surely, a quarrel we have with art itself. For art also evades morality, being on the one hand too playful or esthetic, and on the other surreal and even daemonic—in either direction, art reaches beyond accepted definitions of good and evil. What is remarkable about Trilling is that he has remained, despite pressures, a man in the middle, trying to value art's thrust beyond morality while maintaining a belief in its humanizing and acculturating virtues.

His task has not become easier with the years. The critical spirit, in its modern exacerbated form, not only aspires, like Socrates, to examine everything, but conspires to alienate us from whatever was previously accepted as truth. Having forsaken nature for culture, it now treats culture as a second nature, and is equally suspicious of it. Traditions, customs, institutions—the "rich horn" and the "spreading laurel tree" in Yeats's pastoral and nostalgic view—all these have to pass like guilty things before the bar of consciousness.

Our powers of indignant perception, as Trilling so elegantly calls them, are now directed not only against prisons of stone but also against "mind-forged manacles." The fear grows strong that it is we who commit ourselves to prison by accepting the ideals and subtle coercions emanating from bourgeois society. The *new* coercion, writes Trilling in *The Opposing Self*, requires of each of us that he sign his own liberty away and be benevolently locked up "in the family life, in the professions, in the image of respectability, in the ideas of faith and duty, in (so the poets said) the very language itself."

Trilling's diagnosis of the modern sensibility is interesting, but it is not what is most important in his work. It is doubtful, first of all, that we can so clearly characterize anything as "modern." When Calypso, on some enchanted isle, offers Odysseus immortality on condition that he live with her, he refuses politely yet firmly. Now Odysseus is not exactly a representative of the critical spirit characterizing modern times, yet he shares what André Malraux called its "lucid horror of seduction." Trilling is not deeply concerned with doing history as an exact science or with evolving precise definitions. He is pointing out—unmethodically, even gropingly—that all our attention these days is devoted to resisting terms and circumstances we have *not* freely chosen, whereas we have already been unconsciously seduced by the terms we *have* chosen—by the very rhetoric in which we make our claim for freedom and autonomy.

For if anything is modern it is the labor of self-definition, which absorbs so much of our energy and is accompanied by so much pathos and self-pity. While we are chaste and scrupulous enough that even the gifts offered by culture or society are seen as constraints in disguise, we all too readily change every social or educational structure in the name of greater "sincerity" or "authenticity." Literary and moral criticism come together in Trilling when he uncovers, as in the first of his two new books (*Sincerity and Authenticity* [1972]), the power of these words and relates them to a movement "beyond culture" (especially beyond high culture) strangely blind to its own history.

With teachers like Hegel, Freud, and Matthew Arnold it did not need the turmoil of the 1960s to draw Trilling's attention to the modern attack on culture. To Arnold he owes perhaps his greatest debt because Arnold foresaw in so cool and judicious a manner the increasing malaise of civilized life. Arnold did not, like Hegel, attribute to it world-historical implications. "Modern times," Arnold wrote in 1863, "find themselves with an immense system of institutions, established facts, accredited dogmas, customs, rules, which have come to them from times not modern. In this system . . . life has to be carried forward, yet [modern people] have a sense that this system is not of their own creation, that it by no means corresponds exactly with the wants of their actual life."

This sense of not being "with it" fosters today a rhetoric of victimage. Even sexual identity can be viewed as mere custom or socially imposed. "The inculpation of society," says Trilling, "has become with us virtually a category of thought." Trilling's aim has been to acknowledge the discontents or psychic difficulties of modern life yet to prevent their becoming a blind—that is, a politically reckless—ideology.

Trilling's debt to Matthew Arnold makes him one of the few American critics the English tolerate. The English have never gotten over Arnold, and Trilling's biography of the latter suggests the reason. Arnold reconceived literary criticism as an English type of intellectual life—casual, eclectic, undogmatic—opposed to the French disease of turning out instant ideologies. He kept the English "clerk"—academic, journalist, middle-class intellectual—from wanting to be a little Robespierre. By his distrust of what he called the "Hebraic" or "Puritan" strain in English life, Arnold filtered out moral radicalism; and by his attack on French intellectuality, he impeded political radicalism. Literary criticism was to accept the new reality of ideas in the age following the French Revolution but to insist on their "disinterested" play and circulation. Thus the English way of doing things would be maintained; culture would continue to grow organically, without political shocks; and by diffusing itself gently would eventually atrophy the class structure and bring sweetness and light to all.

Trilling is especially wary of ideological criticism (be it religious, feminist, Marxist, or whatever) and its willful bending of works of art to its own purpose. His urbane and crafted essays—so casual yet so woven, digressive yet powerfully recursive—have a decided touch of Arnoldian "sweetness" or of that flexibility, that "belief in the relaxed will" he once attributed to E. M. Forster. The only place in his work where a text is used in an ideological and transformative way is in his novel *The Middle of the Journey* (1947). There Gifford Maxim, a lapsed Communist, by turning Melville's "Billy Budd" into a semi-Hegelian, semi-Christian parable, reveals that Communism was indeed a "God that failed"—a religion masking as a political program.

A deliberately relaxed style has its problems, of course. One often yearns for that more forceful and trenchant kind of comment found in Trilling's contemporaries, Philip Rahv and Irving Howe. *Sincerity and Authenticity* can read like a Commonplace Book, where thoughts remain *pensées*—though by one of the truly cultured scholars of our time. We come to value mainly the quality of the mind from which they issue: a mind that carries with it, and balances, so much of the literary past, that embraces without envious distortion the spiritual form of each author.

Yet Trilling knows that our scrutiny of the human will, either masked (as in art) or naked (as in politics), should remain subject to the oldest question: Is it good or is it evil? It is precisely the difficulty of this question in the modern period (though Trilling conceives of modern widely, as including many figures of the eighteenth and nineteenth century) that leads to the writing of *Sincerity and Authenticity*. A powerful diagram of the moral life from Shakespeare to the present, it shows the force as well as fallibility of two substitute questions: Is it sincere, and, is it authentic?

According to Trilling "sincerity" was a new concept when Shakespeare's Polonius instructed his son, "To thine own self be true . . . Thou canst not then be false to any man." What is this "own self," however? Is it the "best self," or something which, because it violates public morality, is thereby more authentic? Without going deeply into Shakespeare's subversions of the new ideal, Trilling traces its history: how it held out the promise of reconciling self with society, or desire with duty; how it disintegrated under the categorical pressure of moral reflection and the dialectical pressure of modern philosophy (Rousseau, Jane Austen, Hegel, and Diderot's *Rameau's Nephew* are prime witnesses); and how a further ideal of "authenticity" emerged. Of Wordsworth's Michael (in the poem of that name) who has lost his only child, Trilling says: "It is not the case with him, as it is with Hamlet, that he has 'that within which passeth show.' There is no within and without: he and his grief are one. We may not, then, speak of sincerity. But our sense of Michael's being, of—so to speak—being-in-grief, comes to us as a surprise." The need arises for a new word to describe Michael's mode of being, and this is "authenticity."

"We cannot think modernly in ancient words; we betray either the one or the other time." So Trilling had written in 1939 in his book on Arnold. His present study tries to find modern words to think in. Even if we are skeptical of its approach (to trace the history of the self, he admits, is to "deal with shadows in a dark land"), it is a book crowded with insights. The value of *Sincerity and Authenticity* does not lie in its being an "authentic narrative" but in the kind of attention it bestows on texts like "Michael" or *Rameau's Nephew*.

There is a danger, of course, that having found his modern words Trilling will not think modernly in them. We may discover the old in the arms of the new, after all. It is strange that, in comparing Wordsworth's Michael with Abraham, he does not raise the question of how the modern idea of authenticity is related to the ancient. Also strange is that he nowhere mentions Kierkegaard, who *had* raised that question.

The reason for the omission of Kierkegaard is perhaps that Trilling refuses to define authentic moral experience in terms of a transcendent religious perspective. For Kierkegaard, no conventional moral thought can explain either God's command that Abraham should kill his son or the patriarch's dumb obedience. This episode, terrible in its implications, defines a limit of Trilling's sensibility. He acknowledges but does not explore deeply the demonic side of the psyche. For him the "terror" in ordinary cultural situations is enough.

Trilling points out, and it may be his deepest insight, that a relentless exposure to others in society, especially urban society, turns us all into people who want to be sincere or true to a single self, yet are forced to become manic producers (as well as consumers) of roles, shades of Rameau's Nephew. Society demands with an intensity that is spiritual, yet totally secular, that we display "personality," and this demand cannot be met except through impersonation. Here is part of Diderot's description of Rameau's Nephew, who seemed to both Goethe and Hegel a fateful type of the modern spirit:

> He jumbled together thirty different operatic melodies, French, Italian, comic, tragic—in every style. Now in a baritone voice he sank to the pit; then straining in falsetto he tore to shreds the upper notes of some tunes, while imitating the stance, walk and gesture of the several characters. . . . [He was] being himself both dancer and ballerina, singer and prima donna, all of them together and the whole orchestra, the whole theatre; then he redivided himself into twenty separate roles.

Is this not a parody of the modern artist in search of his own voice by means of different voices (personae) which end up cannibalizing him?

It is hard to avoid Trilling's conclusion that role playing, which expands culture by strengthening the sympathetic imagination, also subverts stability of self and even the social fabric. The histrionic antics of Rameau's Nephew prove seductive to the bemused yet bourgeois Diderot. (Norman Mailer, as Richard Poirier has described him, is another such "performing self.") In Jane Austen's novels, likewise, many characters are attracted to the slightly shady rather than the archaic and noble suitor. The lady, in short, wants to run off with the raggle-taggle gypsy-o.

Sincerity and Authenticity is a synthesizing rather than original effort, anticipated by exemplary essays on Dickens, Freud, and Austen's *Mansfield Park* in *The Opposing Self* and *Beyond Culture*. While its range of allusions is great, the number of texts actually discussed, and the generative ideas put forward are limited. Its taste, depth, and penetration are classical, rather than pioneering, qualities. Yet whatever doubts arise from the synthesizing or condensed nature of this brief for the modern, Trilling does not shirk the task of conveying his own feelings while studying "the moral life in process of revising itself."

He shares the "appalled elation" of Milton and Freud at the spectacle of man's defeat by life. He recognizes its "beautiful Necessity" (Emerson), even "historical necessity," yet is unwilling either to praise or condone. Taught by Hegel, he knows that the self must subvert and be subverted; that its "alienation" is the spiritual dynamics which bring us to a higher level of awareness; yet taught by Milton, he accepts his obligation to discern the good from the evil in this process. The final pages of his book eloquently upbraid those like R. D. Laing for whom mental illness is a seductive image of "upward psychopathic mobility." At such moments Trilling becomes another last Puritan, or displaced Hebraic consciousness, roused from his Arnoldian flirtation with modern Hellenism.

Few lay sermons are entirely successful, and Trilling's second new book, *Mind in the Modern World*, is no exception. Others have disserted on Mind in this generic way (H. G. Wells, whom Trilling mentions; more significantly, Valéry and Husserl); yet mind on Mind produces a risky selfconsciousness. Trilling, imbued by his sense of crisis, takes that risk, but the simplifications he falls into, and the unremitting solemnity of the style, suggest a cartoon à la Beerbohm: "Mr. Trilling as Mind, venturing to examine a course it has taken and to correct it."

This ungenerous comment should not hide my admiration for the way the critic confronts a "dark portent" though speaking under the "bright aegis" of the Jefferson lectureship instituted by the National Endowment for the Humanities. He summarizes cogently not only the tradition of anti-intellectualism in American life, but the more general causes for it due to the very success of science, technology, and specialization. These have indeed wounded the self esteem of the average intellectual, and brought about his disaffection with or even radical protest against "mind." What Trilling calls the "growing intellectual recessiveness" of college and university faculties, their inability to defend themselves against governmental edicts or to produce an articulate theory of higher education, is demoralizing, and his strictures help to break a silence he rightly deprecates.

Yet he overidealizes the historical sense whose decay, he feels, is part of the crisis. It is true that the study of history has a diminished place in the school curriculum; that the contemporary is too much with us. Yet to claim that "Voltaire, Diderot, Rousseau, Goethe, Hegel, Darwin, Marx, Freud—all were rooted in their sense of the past, from which derived the force with which they addressed themselves to the present" is too easy. In fact it evades the issue because it is historical knowledge as much as science that has brought us to (yet another) crisis of mind.

What Voltaire called "The Philosophy of History" is no more than a corrosive bundle of human absurdities culled from his study of other cultures. To rationalize them was, he thought, to methodize madness, *mettre de la raison dans la folie*. For Nietzsche, who stands closer to us, culture is a burden and inseparable from feelings of guilt. We too perceive that our trouble with historical knowledge is not only intellectual ("how is understanding possible, given so many facts or reports") but also moral ("after such knowledge, how is life to be faced"). Both types of trouble, surely, are part of the dilemma we are in; and what has helped to wound us cannot be so simply offered as its remedy. Trilling's achievement elsewhere is precisely that he exemplifies rather than prescribes a "sense of the past" which intervenes between us and the easy solution.

Signs of the Times
A Review of Three Books

The Performing Self: Compositions and Decompositions in the Languages of Contemporary Life. By Richard Poirier. (1972)

Blindness and Insight: Essays in the Rhetoric of Contemporary Criticism. By Paul de Man. (1972).

The Modern Spirit: Essays on the Continuity of Nineteenth and Twentieth-Century Literature. By Robert Langbaum. (1972).

"Nobody . . . knew for sure . . . in what kind of performance he was involved." Richard Poirier makes this remark on the Rolling Stones' festival at Altamont, which turned into a bloody fray. Criticism is no Altamont, and critics no Rolling Stones, but the one thing these three books have in common is their uncertainty about what kind of "performance" criticism may be. We feel how difficult it is for them to insist on themselves, on their own function.

The literary critic has always worried about being faithful to the great, the revelatory, text, but today he worries also about being there at all, in the classroom, or as the mediator of a genuine discipline. There are many reasons for this. Criticism is, by nature, a problematic activity. Even the best essays are secondary products, stimulated by the literature on which they comment. We read them to remain in the shadow of something that is greater and that we don't wish to face all the time. But a new reason, in the case of Poirier's *The Performing Self*, is the claim to recognition made by popular culture.

Great art reduces us to silence or banality but popular art wants to be noised about and to achieve the widest currency. It has no discernible gold standard. How can we study it without overintellectualizing—imposing standards or attitudes from so-called high culture? Indeed, is not the danger of intellectualizing even greater when touchstones from high culture cannot be applied? For then art of any kind becomes simply an "object" with an analyzable "structure."

"The study of popular culture must start with analyses that are as close, disciplined and detailed as one can make them." Let us agree with Poirier that we can learn from the Beatles as well as from Blake, but where do we go for our terms if we don't want merely a self-advertising puff or "a bad dream of Brooks and Warren"? Is it to structuralism, is it to sociology?

Ten years ago Poirier coedited a book called *In Defense of Reading*. His new work is in good part a defense of what is coming to be known as "cultural reading." Yet "reading" a culture may be as perverse an activity as westernizing China. Reading is not a neutral technique; it is shaped by classics it in turn supports. To "read" boxing matches or pop festivals yields, therefore, predictable results. Modern popular art is seen to be a "bad dream" of high art, a gay nightmare, so to speak. Parody, energy, and role playing move to the fore. But the cultural reader will not assume that popular art wants to waken from the nightmare, or into something else. He lets it be. It is what it is: the demonic shadow of high culture, accusing, self-indulgent, self-wasting, exuberant.

A malaise affects, however, even those critics who do not accept the challenge of popular culture. They can argue, after all, that the distinction between popular and high art is exaggerated. Each has its own realm, to be sure, but it is virtually a cliché of literary history since Herder and the Romantics that the comprehensive vision of great artists—Chaucer, Rabelais, Cervantes, Shakespeare—is related to their respect for popular traditions. "Popular culture" and "youth culture" are not the same, in any historical perspective. The new element is not folk art but youth's self-identification as its source and champion. No need, therefore, to accept this new myth uncritically.

Then why are scholar-critics like Poirier so uneasy? Because, first of all, there is still a historical debt to be paid in America to the "vernacular matrix" (W. J. Ong) of literature. In England F. R. Leavis and the Scrutiny group emphasized English as a living, idiomatic tongue—verbal making, what Poirier characterizes as "the mere turning of a sentence this way or that," became more important than other literary accomplishments (satisfying genre specifications, for example) precisely because it played against "the accumulations of culture." But recovering the English vernacular matrix meant reviving a literate tradition (ballads, dialects, spoken idiom) while in America the recovered matrix never seemed to reach further down than to the naive myths and horny humor of the white settlers. The expressive potential of the subcultures was too submerged; in any case, less literate, more bound up with semiverbal forms like Negro spirituals or contemporary rock. To recover the vernacular matrix in America involves a sharper clash between literate and nonliterate.

From this point of view Poirier's interest in the performing arts is justified. One might say that these arts too have been a mere subculture for the literate critic, and are only now being brought into the main stream of articulate thought. Poirier's adjustment of literature to the other arts through the concept of "performance" may be of real value in redirecting our attention and honoring the affinity of folk art to theater, song, and bodily energies. Whether it is of value to literature itself is more doubtful.

There is a final reason for the pop perplexity of some modern critics. Even if we explode the myth of youth culture, youth remains. We are not critics to society, at present, but to collegiate youth. We have been trapped into a reduced role or social identity: into a client relation opposite to (but no better than) that of high-class retainers at "elitist" universities. The sheer numbers involved in mass education and the weight of expectation on the critic-teacher are turning him into a literary disc jockey. The pressure to *conform* has given way to the pressure to *perform*. The rapping needed to counter the counterculture will end by reviving the preacher we have been trying to kill off in ourselves these last hundred years.

There is, consequently, a lot of very explicit and dramatic language in *The Performing Self*. The book is fraught with agonistic terms and it tries to achieve coherence by means of the concept of "performance." The word is a rich one, stressing engagement, energy, play, productivity, and form-giving. But the concept itself is not a significant advance over the idea popularized by the New Critics that there must be a commitment of the artist to his art, to his medium. One shapes a self, says Poirier, out of the materials in which it is immersed. He does not define those materials, however. They are simply that which opposes or challenges the self. Any "self-discovering, self-watching, finally self-pleasuring response" to pressures and difficulties could fall under the concept. The resultant perspective is at once intensely materialistic (valuing social or physical determinants) and intensely idealistic (valuing the self-shaping self). Instead of genuine theoretical essays we have a lively but mixed book of criticism, confession, and literary apologetics. One can argue for impurity in art, but an impure theory is merely a confused theory.

The idea of performance is useful, at best, to modify our obsession with "technique." Poirier is surely right in identifying technique as something the artist performs against. The artist faces a chaos of forms, of possible structures, and what was once an effective idea of order may now be part of the chaos, part of what is to be overcome. "One must fight through the glitter and rubbish to express anything worthwhile, to express even the rubbish." Poirier's best essays are on the subject of waste, self-parody, and accumulation: on the experience of being "heaped" (Ahab's word in *Moby Dick* for the pressure on him of the great whale). The concept of performance is counter-assertive to this pressure, as the concept of style was in his earlier *A World Elsewhere*. Poirier now thinks of literary technique as a false mastery of the contemporary situation, or as part of a general embarrassment of riches that besets the individual artist.

Our "waste land," in other words, is not a desert but a dump: we suffer from too much rather than from too little, from that rate of change and inexorable accumulation of cultural detritus that Henry Adams noted toward the end of his *Education*. Actually there are two heaps between which we live: that of the signifiers, the outmoded signs, myths, allusions, and styles, and what the signifiers supposedly signify: reality, the Vietnam war, the war in our cities, all such immediate pressures that disable the signifiers from another angle. Our sense of existence, of being-in-the-world, is at once heightened and undermined by an endlessly inflowing contemporaneity.

There is no easy solution to this dilemma. "Performance," as a term and concept, seems all too light for it, too Pateresque. Is it aestheticism's last defense? Beyond it one glimpses clown or messiah, rather than Michelangelo's "Captive" depicted on the dust jacket, and described as "emerging from stone . . . straining up as from the elements . . . trying to push off the imposing weight which imprisons the head." The real hero of this book is Norman Mailer, who, says Poirier, "at his best . . . seeks contamination." One thinks sadly of the ending of Cavafy's famous poem, "Awaiting the Barbarians": "Those men were a kind of solution."

Poirier is too cool a critic to deify Mailer. His admiration is nuanced; and he also stops short of announcing the manifest destiny of youth culture. His last essay, in fact, comments on our inevitable failures of sympathy as the demand on those sympathies escalates. "It must be recognized that the feeling of sympathy is altogether more circumscribed and selective than we have allowed ourselves, under the stimulation of the classics of literature, to believe." Yet how perverse to put the blame on "the classics of literature," which is code for works admired in the academic curriculum, works of the "liberal imagination."

The classics, surely, by the very notion of convention, admit the need to anchor imagination in the ground of some common interest: national, racial, religious, social. We cannot hold them responsible for the academic bull market that developed after World War II, and its speculation in literature as "world-community" stock. The great works of the Romantic period, moreover, which first expressed that doctrine of the sympathetic imagination that still has us in thrall, show clearly enough the tragic conflict between it and life. "The good die first / And those whose hearts are dry as summer dust / Burn to the socket." (Wordsworth)

Poirier is a brilliant critic as long as he remains critical. He scores palpable hits on precise targets that include young as well as old, relevance seekers as well as academics. Yet his power to construct an effective literary theory lags behind his brilliance as a critic. The reason for this is that he does not trust literature enough. He does not trust it to throw off theories that idealize it wrongly. He is so concerned with the academy and its imprisonment of art in exalted "liberal" ideas that through him the voice of the teacher rather than that of the work itself is heard. Fine moments of immediate engagement with literature (his analyses of Eliot, Mailer, Frost, and Borges, among others) fall back into the polemical context and become part of the history of pedagogy rather than that of criticism.

In *Beyond Culture* Lionel Trilling also acknowledged the challenge of modern literature to the teacher and to the "liberal imagination" generally. The path from this literature to the humanistic study of it seemed to Trilling complex and precarious because its passions strained against any known political or cultural framework. Yet Trilling was able to suggest what in the older framework helped the radical impulse to survive. Through the Greek and Latin classics, for instance, Freud acquired the notion of an ideal type of culture with deep human interest yet no very contemporary relevance. This helped to prevent the nation-state from appropriating his thoughts. It fostered a power of what might be called *dissimilation.* Trilling saw, of course, the negative side of this "useless passion" for the classics, but what is important is that he looked at social conventions as a whole and was unafraid to speculate on the functional aspects of idealism.

Poirier restricts his interest, however, to the fallacious or destructive idealism. Take his objection—valuable in itself—to our identifying the young as a new "virgin land." "Current attacks on the young . . . depend on a prior idealization, a separation of them from history. To treat them as if they alone, of all the elements of society, are so exonerated as to represent some saving remnant is ultimately murderous." Criticism of idealistic residues is not enough, however. What is equally imperative is to think about the idealism that *any* creative or structural concept implies. The idea of a "saving remnant" can be misapplied, but its survival value is too great to be demystified.

The challenge to literary studies of the de-idealizing or demystifying critics is taken up by Paul de Man in his collection of nine essays on major figures in European criticism. *Blindness and Insight* is the most subtly argued book of its kind I have read: the product of a continuously alive intelligence. It has in it what Wallace Stevens calls "The hum of thoughts evaded in the mind." De Man's argument begins, in a sense, with his own style, an antirhetorical "rhetoricity" more insidious and powerful than the theory supported by it.

Poirier, for instance, is rhetorical in the common sense of the word, strident, associative, full of what might be called offsights—those strong, partly analyzed ideas that are spun off his passion for literature and its relevance. A vocabulary of crisis predominates. But criticism is the opposite of crisisism for de Man. It does not respond counterassertively to pressures from without, and is not afraid to amount to very little that is positive (or positivistic). Because de Man combines a religious sense of the vanity of human understanding with a philosophical irony that insists on understanding as the only good, he can detach himself from the immediacies (both pedagogical and political) we feel so overwhelmingly in Poirier's book. This detachment is not unawareness but a response at a different level, a more reflective and intrinsically critical position.

To move now from de Man's style to his theory of critical style. His counterattack on those who see literary language as idealistic involves a view that lessens the distinction between literary and literary-critical discourse. Modern art, as Friedrich Schlegel remarked, is distinguished by its deeply self-critical aspect. De Man adds that critical writing in turn has a literary component, and he means by that not blowsy or purple-poetic but something that remains "in the difficulty of what is to be":

> A literary text is not a phenomenal event that can be granted any form of positive existence, whether as a fact of nature or as an act of the mind. It leads to no transcendental perception . . . but merely solicits an understanding that has to remain immanent.

De Man's opening essay ("Criticism and Crisis") shows what happens when a critic becomes too positive and resorts to the language of crisis. The language of crisis like that of love is always the same, and it is blind. It arrogates to itself that very "privilege" it seeks to destroy in others. It remains rhetorical or literary but without knowing that it is. So Edmund Husserl, pursuing a universalistic thesis in "The Crisis of European Humanity and Philosophy" (1935), fails to question the privileged point of view from which he writes: the European, post-Hellenic conception of philosophizing that he promulgates at a moment catastrophic for it.

It is this very question of a privileged mode of language or point of view—under attack in Continental thought from the side of structuralism, anthropology, linguistics, and Marxism—that de Man's book scrupulously examines. Literary idealism, generally defined, is a belief in the possibility of unmediated expression or in a constitutive self with the power to break through social veils and similar determinants. De Man says quite simply that these "privileges" are never claimed by art in any literal or unequivocal way. The mistake of would-be demystifiers is to *literalize* the idealism of art, and so to claim more by asserting something about fiction than it claimed by not asserting—by remaining fiction. Although literature means what it says (de Man excludes psychologism or other modes of depth analysis) it never totally says its meaning because sign and meaning cannot coincide. To think they can is the greatest naïveté; to think art believes they can, the next greatest. It makes of art a nostalgic semantic, a vicarious or compensatory fullness that deprives it of authenticity vis-à-vis both life and signification. There is a "constitutive discrepancy" of word and self in all genuine writing, whether literary or literary-critical:

> That sign and meaning can never coincide, is what is precisely taken for granted in the kind of language we call literary. Literature, unlike everyday language, begins on the far side of this knowledge; it is the only form of language free from the fallacy of unmediated expression. All of us know this, although we know it in the misleading way of a wishful assertion of the opposite. Yet the truth emerges in the foreknowledge we possess of the true nature of literature when we refer to it as *fiction* . . . . Here the human self has experienced the void within itself . . . . (pp. 17–19)

Blindness and Insight does not develop de Man's theories in any systematic way. This is unfortunate because too many questions remain unsettled, or are lost in the sinuous prose. We still need from de Man a clear theory of reading (or misreading) and a clear concept of textuality that would allow us to distinguish literary from literary-critical. He goes too deviously from the semiotic to the hermeneutic, from the discrepancy between sign and meaning to that between the assertive critical model and the interpretive insight seemingly based on it. Despite all his subtly eloquent variations on this discrepancy—despite all the difficult and deceptive interplay of blindness and insight or text and reader—a stubborn sense remains in us that there is an accountable difference between literary and literary-critical texts. The implied monism of de Man's theory of textuality pairs strangely with a semiotic that is binary or dualistic. One must ask whether the distinction so peculiar to literary studies between primary and secondary texts is fallacious, or whether some notion of privilege or ontological priority does not accrue to the work of art over against that of critic.

De Man's refusal to expose his insights in a systematic manner is puzzling, and may be owing to the accident of collecting this book before his more literary studies on the Romantic and post-Romantic tradition. It may also be a matter of temperament erected into theory. He likes exegesis: he treats critics like Blanchot, Poulet, and Lukács as if they were primary texts and not commentary—as if they had the texture and strength of Mallarmé's *La Musique et les Lettres* (de Man considers it "more than equal in verbal and thematic complexity . . . to a page of *Un coup de dés*"). Reading de Man on Derrida on Rousseau—which could have produced sterile metacriticism—fosters instead a "fourth" dimension that is like the *generalized conscience* of the act of reading. There is intellectual accrual but there is also a negative movement that swerves from every new and possessive insight.

This is not to say that *Blindness and Insight* makes no tangible contributions. Its "deconstructions" can be disarming but it analyzes with precision writers who have provided European thought with new conceptual models and who are gradually becoming known in America. The essays on Maurice Blanchot and Jacques Derrida in particular seem to me definitive; that on Georges Poulet is both more and less than a critique—it penetrates to the man's own sense of fragility. The article on the Swiss psychoanalyst Ludwig Binswanger contains a distinction between the empirical (personal) and ontological (aesthetic) self profounder than that provided in American persona theories. An important continuity in de Man's book is the recurrent and highly critical analysis of the basic notions of intentionality, hermeneutic circle, modernity, and genetic historiography. This could restore to American criticism the philosophical bases it has either ignored or employed eclectically. De Man, at the same time, by the centrality he accords to poets as thinkers, suggests the usefulness rather than necessity of these sources: philosophical currents are not privileged at the expense of literary ones but acknowledged because they were (and are) present. Finally, his skepticism toward the organicist assumption in critical theories—it asserts in protean ways Coleridge's view of art as reconciliation—can emancipate us from an attractive superstition that has held sway at least since I. A. Richards. It is the more necessary, therefore, that de Man displace by a systematic effort of his own Richards' *Principles of Literary Criticism*, which is the fountainhead of contemporary theories of reading and threatens even now to beget powerful imps at Berkeley.

Matthew Arnold, not Richards, is the problem for Robert Langbaum. Or rather he is no problem. Langbaum's essays and addresses of the last five years, collected under the title *The Modern Spirit*, are still Arnold-intoxicated in theory and style. They are unashamedly pedagogic in their total respect for the student: every reference is made clear, the pacing is perfect, and they are, despite deep learning, totally free of pedantry. Like Arnold, too, Langbaum thinks that the bloodiness of ideas will cease, that ideas can circulate easily in a free market of discourse, and that religion in particular has already yielded its sting and become poetic myth. "Value" here is a contemplative rather than a fighting word; poetry's "roleplaying" and "strategy" seem to be a kind of war game at best; and the most general premise of his first, explicitly Arnoldian essay, "The Function of Criticism Once More," that "it is [the critic's] job to turn the work of art into a cultural acquisition" allows him to face even Norman Mailer with clearsightedness and relative pedagogic serenity. Each of these various essays—on Wordsworth, on the Victorian idea of culture, on Tennyson, Browning, E. M. Forster, on Shakespeare, and on modern nature poetry—uses familiar critical concepts in an urbane and lively manner: organic form, historical evolution, dynamic unity, projection, the quest for identity. I find myself in the embarrassing position of agreeing with Langbaum on most points yet feeling too much the ease of his formulations. In the face of his mastery I become a kind of Satan, muttering to myself, "Difficulty, be Thou my good."

In a sense, then, Langbaum is an exception to what I said about these critics being deeply apologetic. *The Modern Spirit* could have been published twenty years ago: its language is very much that of Eliot and Trilling, although the applications are always interesting and one feels its indebtedness as a *classic* instance of continuity. Indeed, the book reveals continuity whenever it can: the point, for instance, in Wallace Stevens where "nature poetry comes full circle from the rejection of the old religion of nature to the discovery of an inevitably re-emerging religion of nature at the source of things." De Manian blindness is not emphasized; insight is, and on the whole this critic (as was already clear in his book on Isak Dinesen) prefers those whose eyes are darkly gay, like the mandarins in Yeats's "Lapis Lazuli." While we do not hear in his essays a naïve "O brave new world," we do constantly hear something equivalent to the astronaut's "Contact!" The essay on Mailer, for example, is probably the best single introduction to his literary career, and far more detailed and dispassionate than that in Poirier's *Performing Self*, but Poirier keeps the scandal of such writing more vividly before us, and resists making the man into a "cultural acquisition."

Yet appearances deceive, or perhaps I want them to deceive and to find behind Langbaum's acculturations symptoms of what Freud called "Unbehagen"—unease. The idea of culture is the book's hero: it (or a complex of associated ideas) is said to give coherence to the main body of modern literature. The Victorian writers, in Langbaum's revaluation, have taught us that culture "can and should be antithetical to the prevailing ideology." He suggests, in fact, that we should henceforth classify societies into open and closed, into those respecting the autonomy of culture and those that use it for propaganda purposes—to reinforce, that is, the dominant ideology. There is culture and there is *Kultur*.

Yet the objection—so much a motivation for Poirier—that all culture is a covert form of culture-politics is not taken up. Moreover, Langbaum's wish for a "complete criticism" that will make the literary work transitive, and allow its energies to commute back and forth in the context of the human sciences, and so teach our dangerously technological age the importance of the literary mind—this surely runs the risk of making literature too serviceable. The cry for social relevance is strong enough to determine the polemical shape, at least, of Langbaum's essays. They are crafted to keep the wolf from the door: they try to reform the methodological base of literary studies by returning to the very distinction (between culture and *Kultur*) that radicals decry as a liberal fallacy. One reads with pleasure Langbaum's essay on Tennyson—one savors its close analysis and psychological finesse—but one is nevertheless conscious of it as an ideological drama. It reenacts the speaker's spiritual recovery in *In Memoriam* (after his failure to reconcile science and faith) as *our* recovery. Tennyson, through art, its "dynamic unity," and "epistemological sophistication," becomes an exemplary poet.

Even de Man cannot escape searching for an exemplary text—or perhaps an exemplary textuality. Not to have a text would mean to have to discover oneself as the text, to read oneself perpetually, with the empirical world the mere occasion or held in a kind of suspense. Something is needed to set a bottom for inwardness, to limit an endless and corrosive self-concern. The modern spirit seems strangely medieval in its continual search for role models and *exempla*. The more critical we get the greater our commitment to this "textual materialism." It is time, therefore, to stress the scandal of literary study: our obstinate bookishness or text-centeredness. Honest literary theory will insist that texts ingest as well as liberate us: not because we are McLuhanite Children of the Book but because the critical reader is always questing for his bible, or some wholly secular meditation.

Notes

The Interpreter: A Self-Analysis

1. Rilke, *Malte Laurids Brigge* (Leipzig, 1910).
2. Balzac, describing the antiquary's shop in *Peau de Chagrin* (1831).
3. "Prelude," *Fear and Trembling* (1843).
4. Freud, "Psychogenic Visual Disturbance" (1910) and "Notes on a Case of Obsessional Neurosis" (1909); Karl Abraham, "Restrictions and Transformations of Scoptophilia" (1913), in *Selected Papers on Psychoanalysis*, tr. D. Bryan and A. Strachey (London, 1927), pp. 169–234; Alfred Winsterstein, "Psycho-analytic Notes on the History of Philosophy," *Imago* 2 (1913); G. H. Hartman, *The Unmediated Vision* (New Haven, 1954), pp. 129, 152–54.
5. Christopher Smart, *Jubilate Agno*, ed. W. H. Bond (London, 1954).
6. "Those who create images of animate men and thereby violate divine prerogatives are punished, like Prometheus, Daedalus or Hephaestus. Interdicts of imagery to protect the divine from magical practice prevail over centuries in many cultures. . . . Painters conclude pacts with the devil in order to compete with God, while builders, heirs to the builder of the tower of Babel, commit suicide. . . . The sculptor Messerschmidt believed that the Gods were jealous of his secret knowledge and therefore persecuted him." (E. Kris, *Psychoanalytic Explorations in Art* [New York, 1962], chap. 5.)
7. Goethe, *Faust II*, describing Wagner.
8. The *hypnothetic* function of some interpretative hypotheses does not, by any means, put our realistic perceptions to sleep or absorb them psychotically into imaginative vision. It simply allows art to survive when so much in the type of thought ordinarily called awake is against it. Interpretation, in this sense, literally "preserves" art by allowing it to persist like a separate stream or vortex in what surrounds it.

9. The distinction is made by Gilles Deleuze in *Proust et les signes* (Paris, 1964, 1970). On the *déjà lu*, see Roland Barthes, S/Z, and also the phenomenological model discussed in Wolfgang Iser's "The Reading Process," *New Literary History* 3 (1972).

10. See Husserl, *L'origine de la géométrie*, ed. and trans. J. Derrida (Paris, 1962), p. 182: "C'est seulement grâce au langage et à l'immense étendue de ses consignations, comme communications virtuelles, que l'horizon d'humanité peut être celui d'une infinité ouverte."

11. On the Hermes myth, see N. O. Brown, *Hermes the Thief* (Madison, Wisc., 1947). Though a more dignified Hermes appears in Martianus Capella's *De Nuptiis Philologiae et Mercurii* (fifth century), his functional identity as the embodiment of a mediating or accommodating eloquence is maintained.

12. See the Homeric "Hymn to Hermes."

13. See especially W. J. Bate, *The Burden of the Past and the English Poet* (Cambridge, Mass., 1970).

14. Kris, *Psychoanalytic Explorations in Art*, chap. 2; Harold Bloom's *The Anxiety of Influence: A Theory of Poetry* (New York, 1973).

15. The source of this kind of speculation is probably in Freud's "A Note on the 'Mystic Writing Pad' " (1925).

I.A. Richards and the Dream of Communication

1. *Principles of Literary Criticism* (London and New York, 1924), p. 237.

2. Published as a pamphlet in 1930 and included in *For Continuity* (Cambridge, 1933).

3. *Principles*, p. 231.

4. Preface (1800) to *Lyrical Ballads*. Compare Richard Bernheimer, in his important book *The Nature of Representation* (New York, 1961): "How disastrous the effect can be when secondary diversions take the place of reality need hardly be emphasized, for we see all about us the loss of inner wealth, the inability to taste the savor of things that comes from acceptance of experience in terms of manufactured substitute capsules. Nor can it be denied that there is a specific substitutional art, created with the weary city-dweller in mind and distinguished not only by the predominance of certain media such as those of television and of the cinema but also by specific artistic attitudes." (p. 204)

5. *Principles*, p. 248. The remark comes at the end of a beautiful description of tragic catharsis.

6. *Principles*, p. 195–96. Hume's essay "Of the Standard of Taste" (1757) is also relevant.

7. *Principles*, pp. 25–27 and 192–93.

8. In "Why Literary Criticism Is Not an Exact Science" (1967), now in *Grounds for Criticism* (Cambridge, Mass., 1972).

9. *Principles*, chapters 34–35; and *Science and Poetry* (New York, 1926).

10. *Science and Poetry*, chap. 6. See also additional remarks in the reissue of the book as *Poetries and Sciences* (New York, 1970).

11. One should add, perhaps, related and important work in the area of the "sociology of knowledge," from Karl Mannheim to T. S. Kuhn.

12. See, especially, John R. Searle, *Speech Acts: An Essay in the Philosophy of Language* (Cambridge, Mass., 1969).

13. "Every object is best viewed when that which is not separate is posited in separation. . . ." Aristotle, as quoted by Richards.

14. *Coleridge on Imagination* (New York, 1935), Preface.

15. *Coleridge*, pp. 193 and 195.

16. *Coleridge*, pp. 220–21.

17. *Coleridge*, p. 232.

18. Preface (1800 and 1802) to *Lyrical Ballads*.

19. *Biographia Literaria* (1817), chap. 8. For the intellectual background of the *vis representativa* concept, and Coleridge's search for a self-active mental principle, see Thomas McFarland, "The Origin and Significance of Coleridge's Theory of Secondary Imagination," in *New Perspectives on Coleridge and Wordsworth*, ed. G. H. Hartman (New York, 1972).

20. *Principles*, p. 237.

21. *The Prelude* (version of 1850), I. 341–44. The wording of this passage is very suggestive. "Cling" evokes early tactile dependency as well as, perhaps, that bee-clustering which served as a microcosmic analogy for society; while the "dark . . . workmanship" is like the "mighty working, whereby he is able to subdue all things to himself" (even the corruption of the flesh) in *The Book of Common Prayer* (Order for the Burial of the Dead).

22. *Principles*, p. 29.

23. *Principles*, p. 252.

24. Milton, *Paradise Lost*, XII. 521.

25. See *The Meaning of Despair*, ed. Willard Gaylin (New York, 1968), Preface.

26. For example, *Principles*, p. 246: "The joy which is so strangely the heart of the tragic experience is not an indication that 'All's right with the world' or that 'somewhere, somehow, there is Justice'; it is an indication that all is right here and now in the nervous system."

27. From "Psychoanalysis and the History of Art," in *Freud and the Twentieth Century*, ed. B. Nelson (New York, 1957), p. 201.

28. I see a movement toward it, however, in N. O. Brown's *Love's Body* (New York, 1966), in the chapter entitled "Representative," which makes strong use of Ferenczi's speculations in *Thalassa*.

29. "Freud—and the Analysis of Poetry" (1939), as in *Psychoanalysis and Literature*, ed. H. M. Ruitenbeck (New York, 1964).

30. The significant poetical precursor here is Shelley, whose Platonism (viz. idealism) is deeply skeptical. See, for the prior

tradition, C. E. Pulos, "Scepticism and Platonism," in *The Deep Truth* (Lincoln, Neb., 1954).

31. The then currency of Anatole France may be gauged by the fact that Ludwig Lewisohn's *A Modern Book of Criticism* (1919) leads off with this extract, among others, from the Preface to the *Vie littéraire.* Eliot somewhere remarks on France's influence on the intellectual life of Paris during his stay there in 1910–11.

32. Title of section D in the chapter on "The Dream-Work."

33. See, for example, Freud's discussion in "Vergänglichkeit" (1916): "Warum . . . diese Ablösung der Libido von ihren Objekten ein so schmerzhafter Vorgang sein sollte, das verstehen wir nicht und können es derzeit aus keiner Annahme ableiten. Wir sehen nur, dass sich die Libido an ihre Objekte klammert und die verlorenen auch dann nicht aufgeben will wenn der Ersatz bereit liegt. Das also ist die Trauer." Freud's important essay on "Mourning and Melancholy" was published in 1917.

34. This provides, perhaps, a point of connection with Kant's important formulation, in the "Analytic of the Sublime" of *The Critique of Judgment* (section 49), that the aesthetic idea "induces much thought, yet without the possibility of any definite thought whatever, i.e., concept, being adequate to it."

35. "Negation" (1925).

36. Arnold H. Modell, *Object Love and Reality* (New York, 1968), p. 22. Needless to say, the depletion anxiety also takes the form of fearing that one's *self* is "all gone"—that it can no longer respond feelingly or creatively to influences. Compare Harold Bloom's psychoanalytically oriented work on the relation of poets to great precursors, *The Anxiety of Influence: A Theory of Poetry* (New York, 1973).

37. *The Prelude*, ed. E. de Sélincourt and H. Darbishire (Oxford, 1959), p. 576.

38. *The Prelude*, V. 65–68. Wordsworth's statement, which refers in context to "Poetry and Geometric Truth," is part of his own Dream of Communication. As regards geometry the thought is commonplace. "Except in geometry," Coleridge writes in the *Biographia*, "all symbols of necessity involve an apparent contradiction." Wordsworth is saying, by a strong metaphor, that the symbolic language of poetry heals or subsumes contradiction. Compare, for the metaphor of invulnerability, Richards' praise of Tragedy: "It can take anything into its organization, modifying it so that it finds a place. It is invulnerable . . ." (*Principles*, p. 247).

39. See the "Recluse" fragment, quoted in Wordsworth's Prospectus to *The Excursion* (1814).

War in Heaven

1. Bloom, I believe, does not raise the question as to whether the increasing stature of prose-fiction is related in any way to the decline of poetry.

2. See Harold Rosenberg's fine essay, "The Resurrected Romans," in *The Tradition of the New* (New York, 1959).
3. See Philip Rieff on Freud's analogical method, in *General Psychological Theory* (New York, 1963), pp. 8–9.
4. "Beiträge zur Psychologie des Liebesleben" (1910), in *Gesammelte Werke*, vol. 8 (London, 1943), pp. 70–76. See also Karl Abraham, "The Rescue and Murder of the Father in Neurotic Phantasy-Formations" in *International Journal of Psychoanalysis* 3 (1922):467–74.
5. Harold Bloom, *Yeats* (New York: Oxford University Press, 1970), p. 5. And see also *The Anxiety of Influence*, p. 63.
6. The full title in English of Newton's *Principia* is *Mathematical Principles of Natural Philosophy.* Blake's earliest contrast of the "Poetic or Prophetic character" with the "Philosophic & Experimental" is in the two versions of "There is no Natural Religion," both of which contain interesting uses of "ratio."
7. See Blake's *Milton*, plate 17, where the precursor is shown falling starlike from the sky and entering Blake's left foot. The complex relation of this image to the conventional figure of synecdoche or metonymy could open a path from Bloom's psychopoetics back to a theory of rhetoric, especially as Kenneth Burke conceived of it.
8. The history of the term "revisionism" is still to be written. The term begins in socialist thought (Eduard Bernstein) and continues to be used in Communist polemic to characterize "heresies" in the political sphere.
9. *Fearful Symmetry*, chap. 1, sec. 2.

Spectral Symbolism and Authorial Self in Keats's *Hyperion*

1. I accept W. J. Bate and Robert Gittings rather than Aileen Ward on dating *The Fall of Hyperion.*
2. Wallace Stevens, "The Auroras of Autumn."
3. Wallace Stevens, "The Owl in the Sarcophagus."
4. My text is H. W. Garrod's edition of *Keats' Poetical Works*, 2d ed. (Oxford, 1958), except for some punctuation.
5. Wallace Stevens, "The Auroras of Autumn."
6. On the relation of specter to parents, see especially Karl Abraham, *Selected Papers*, trans. D. Bryan and A. Strachey (London, 1927), pp. 224ff.
7. The focus of the *Eddas* is also, of course, mainly on the gods (or their "twilight"); and Keats seems to have wished to blend Pre-Olympian or Titanic with Celtic or "Northern" mythology. Note his remarks on Fingal's Cave in a letter to Thomas Keats of July 1818: "The finest thing [on the island of Staffa] is Fingal's Cave—it is entirely a hollowing out of Basalt Pillars. Suppose now the Giants who rebelled against Jove had taken a whole Mass of black Columns and bound them together like bundles of matches —and then with immense axes had made a cavern in the body of

these columns—of course the roof and floor must be composed of the broken end of the Columns—such is Fingal's Cave except that the sea has done the work. . . ."

8. Letter of 3 February, 1818 to John Hamilton Reynolds.

9. Letter of 27 October, 1818 to Richard Woodhouse.

10. Letter of 21 or 22 September, 1818 to John Hamilton Reynolds.

11. Primal scene imagery is not excluded by this interpretation, but it strikes me as childishly narrow.

12. Verse "Prospectus" to the *Excursion* (1814), 97–98.

13. Ibid.

14. Psyche, in the ode, is addressed as "latest-born and loveliest vision far/ Of all Olympus' faded hierarchy." The grammar of this is just sufficiently ambiguous to suggest that the Olympians themselves saw her afar as their visionary child.

15. What happens in the *Hyperion* sequence may be capable of generalization. The authorial self, even if "assumed" by the artist, is always in question. In a sense the whole struggle for authority turns around whether it can be "assumed"; and this struggle is not likely to cease, since the artist's quest remains equivocal. For, on the one hand, to "assume" a self (its rights of speech, its *Mündigkeit*) means to subsume rather than to "show" it; yet, on the other hand, to "assume" a self is also *the* creative or legitimating act, so that some clear epiphany or emergence is called for. Hence a deep ambivalence between revealing and concealing the authorial self. It is always the precious and yet the accused (accursed) object. "My selfhood—Satan arm'd in gold" (Blake).

16. *Philosophy of History*, trans. J. Sibree (New York, 1901), pp. 317–19.

17. These are Yeats's terms in "Ego Dominus Tuus," a more complex poem than my allusion to it here suggests.

18. A point developed somewhat differently by Aileen Ward in *John Keats: The Making of a Poet* (New York, 1963), especially p. 340. Direct biographical speculation should probably include the fact that nursing Tom might have woken in Keats memories of nursing his mother in the winter of 1809–1810.

19. There is no evidence that Keats read the (at that time) untranslated *Convito* or anything of Dante's except the *Divine Comedy* in Cary's version. But through other sources (Hazlitt? Coleridge?) he could easily have learned of Dante's encomiums on the mother-tongue.

20. It is well known how central the vampire motif is to the gothic novel. The theme is also mediated by the ballad revival (Goethe's "Die Braut von Korinth" and related "belles dames sans merci"). It is not irrelevant that both Shelley and Byron flirted with gothic motifs; see also Mary Shelley's *Frankenstein*, in which a creator is haunted, if not vampirized, by his creation.

Christopher Smart's *Magnificat*: Toward a Theory of Representation

1. In this discussion I occasionally rely on sections 6 and 7 of "I. A. Richards and The Dream of Communication" in this volume, pp. 32ff. On self-presence, see also E. Goffman, *The Presentation of the Self in Everyday Life* (New York, 1959); on shame (and embarrassment), O. F. Bollnow, *Die Ehrfurcht* (Frankfurt a/M., 1947), and H. M. Lynd, *On Shame and the Search for Identity* (New York, 1958); and on the relation of theatricality to presence of self, the studies of Jonas A. Barish on "Antitheatrical Prejudice," *Critical Quarterly* 8 (1966): 329–48, and *ELH* 36 (1969): 1–29, as well as Lionel Trilling, *Sincerity and Authenticity* (New York, 1972), passim.

2. See Coleridge, "On Original Sin," in *Aids to Reflection* (London, 1831): "Where there is no discontinuity there can be no origination, and every appearance of origination in nature is but a shadow of our own casting. It is a reflection from our own will or spirit. Herein, indeed, the will consists. This is the essential character by which Will is opposed to Nature, as spirit, and raised above Nature as self-determining spirit."

3. Fragment B 1, 43. My references throughout are to W. H. Bond's edition of the *Jubilate Agno* (London, 1954).

4. See "I. A. Richards and the Dream of Communication," this volume, pp. 39–40. Since the first demands of the child focus on the mother, there may be a tendency later on to imagine a less used up, that is, *male*, source of comfort.

5. Coleridge, a century after Swift, is still deeply worried by enthusiasm, and makes this analysis in the "Conclusion" to *Aids to Reflection*.

6. "Le sot projet qu'il a de se peindre et cela non pas en passant et contre ses maximes, comme il arrive à tout le monde de faillir, mais par ses propres maximes et par un dessein premier et principal. Car de dire des sottises par hasard et par faiblesse, c'est un mal ordinaire; mais d'en dire par dessein, c'est ce qui n'est pas supportable, et d'en dire de telles que celles-ci." (Blaise Pascal, *L'Apologie de la religion chrétienne* in *Oeuvres Complètes*, vol. 3, ed. Fortunat Strowski [Paris, 1931].)

7. I have considerably abridged Pascal's *Mémorial* as found in his *Penseés*, trans. A. J. Krailsheimer (Baltimore, 1964), pp. 309–10.

8. W. K. Wimsatt, Jr., "The Augustan Mode in English Poetry," in *Hateful Contraries* (Lexington, Ky., 1966), pp. 158–62.

9. Part of Coleridge's attack on Enthusiasm in *Aids to Reflection*.

10. From Hervey's "Contemplations on the Starry Heavens."

11. " 'Clapperclaw' is an archaic verb, meaning to scratch and claw, to attack with tooth and nail. Smart seems to be implying

that the words in a poem should be associated as violently and powerfully as cats in a fight claw and bite one another." (Moira Dearnley, *The Poetry of Christopher Smart* [London, 1969], pp. 163–64). But "clapperclaw" was also theater-slang for applause (a topic dear to Smart) so that an ambivalent and complex relation is suggested between various drives: the sexual-aggressive, the verbal-expressive, the applause-seeking (theatrical and exhibitionist), and the applause-seeking (antiphonal and divine). For the slang term, see the printer's address to the reader in the first quarto of Shakespeare's *Troilus and Cressida: "A never writer to an ever reader. News.* Eternal reader, you have here a new play, never staled with the stage, never clapper-clawed with the palms of the vulgar, and yet passing full of the palm comical."

12. See his "Life of Milton" and "Life of Waller" in *The Lives of the English Poets* (London, 1779–81).

13. Consider how many aspects of this poetry reflect a concern with generation: the Biblical genealogies, from which Smart borrows many names; the generic emphasis of the names themselves; the personal allusions to family; and puns that range from the simple and innocuous to the complex and atrocious. Of the first kind is "Let Gibeon rejoice with the Puttock, who will shift for himself to the last extremity" (B 1, 81), and of the second, perhaps, "For the power of the Shears is direct as the life" (B 1, 179). Stead and Bond give a tenuous explanation of this line by referring to ancient methods of divination and so on, but a cruder and more powerful one emerges if "Shears" is read as "She-ars."

14. One reason David fascinated Smart was that this "cunning player on an harp" drove away "the evil spirit" from Saul (1 Samuel 16:14–23).

15. See W. M. Merchant, "Patterns of Reference in Smart's *Jubilate Agno*," *Harvard Library Bulletin* 14 (1960), p. 23; and Moira Dearnley, *The Poetry of Christopher Smart*, pp. 156 ff.

16. "Ro-ach," in fact, moves close to "Ru-ach," Hebrew for breath or spirit. See *Jubilate Agno*, B 2, 626.

17. Dearnley, *The Poetry of Christopher Smart*, p. 164.

18. Even representation by the personal name is not so simple a matter, then. Smart's enumerative evocation of names (taken from obituaries as well as genealogies) is analogous to invoking saints or intermediaries, yet he so expands the roster that representation, while verging on mediation, insists on the *proprium* of each proper noun.

19. I do not know how Derrida would interpret Smart's use of names and proper nouns. Or his ritually insistent, repetitive, affirmations. Would he compare all this with Nietzsche's "affirmation en jeu" or Heidegger's risky "espérance"? See his crucial essay on "La différance" in *Marges de la Philosophie* (Paris, 1972), especially pp. 25–29.

20. Much of Ruskin's work in the 1860s and early 1870s was secretly aimed at weaning young Rose La Touche from a religious enthusiasm (not unlike Smart's, though morbid and distinctly

Evangelical in origin) which was to end in her mental derangement, symptoms of which Ruskin also carried within himself. *Love's Meinie* (parts I and II on robin and swallow were published in 1873; part III on the chough in 1881) ministers to a mind diseased by giving glory back to life. It has its private as well as public dimension: Ruskin weaves, for example, the *Roman de la Rose* into his book because it must have seemed an equally troubled yet saner version of the "Romance" he was experiencing in his own courtship of Rose.

21. The problem of taxonomy is at the center of Michel Foucault's work, which views "science" and "madness" as obverse modes of representation. Linnaeus, founder of the Latin terminology to which Ruskin objects, was of Smart's era.

History Writing as Answerable Style

1. Saul Bellow, *Mr. Sammler's Planet* (New York, 1970), pp. 3–4.
2. Letter to B. R. Haydon, 21 March 1818, and to George Keats, 17 December 1818.
3. See "The Storyteller," in *Illuminations* (New York, 1968).
4. See W. J. Ong on the "synchronic present" in *American Quarterly* 14 (1962): 239–59; but especially Valéry's first letter on "La Crise de l'Esprit" (Paris, 1919), its follow-up "La Politique de l'Esprit" (Paris, 1932), and "Le Problème des Musées," in *Pièces sur l'Art* (1931).
5. See David Jones, "Preface" to *Anathemata* (London, 1952); T. S. Eliot, "Ash Wednesday," and Alain Robbe-Grillet, preface to the ciné-roman *L'Immortelle* (Paris, 1963).
6. "Art," in *Essays* [First Series] (Boston, 1841).
7. Saul Bellow, *Mr. Sammler's Planet*, p. 149.
8. Emerson, "Art," in *Essays* [First Series].
9. See the conclusion to the *Phenomenology of Mind* (1807).
10. A. Van Gennep, *Les rites de passage* (Paris, 1907); also Mary Douglas, *Purity and Danger* (London, 1960).
11. Victor Turner, *The Ritual Process* (Chicago, 1968). Turner uses the phrase "chaos of roles" which led to my "chaos of forms." In Europe the image of what Lionel Trilling calls *the other culture*, "the idealized past of some other nation, Greece, or Rome or England" (*Beyond Culture* [New York, 1965], pp. 112–14) strengthened the marginality of art, but from above, as it were.
12. See Douglas, *Purity and Danger*, p. 116, on the "hoax aspect" of ritual dangers.
13. William Blake, *Jerusalem*, last plate (99).
14. A Nyakusa saying, quoted in Douglas, *Purity and Danger*, p. 208. Hamlet's madness, if more than strategic, is part of his trouble with the dead—and, perhaps, with dying conventions.
15. See W. J. Bate, *The Burden of the Past and the English Poet* (Cambridge, Mass., 1970); Harold Bloom, *Yeats* (New York, 1970); and Ann Wordsworth's review of the latter, "Wrestling with the Dead," *The Spectator*, 25 July 1970.

From the Sublime to the Hermeneutic

1. From "Eleusis" (addressed to Hölderlin in 1796), reprinted in G.W. Fr. Hegel, *Recht, Staat, Geschichte*, ed. F. Bülow (Stuttgart, 1955), pp. 86–89.

2. "Stanzas from the Grande Chartreuse."

3. See the essay on Georges Poulet in *Blindness and Insight* (New York, 1971).

4. *Letters on Chivalry and Romance* (1762).

5. See the concluding paragraphs of Hegel's *Phenomenology*.

Poem and Ideology: A Study of Keats's "To Autumn"

1. Jonathan Wordsworth, *Cornell Library Journal* 11 (1970): 22. Compare Allen Tate, *Collected Essays* (Denver, 1959), p. 168: " 'Ode to Autumn' is a very nearly perfect piece of style but it has little to say."

2. *John Keats* (Cambridge, Mass., 1963), pp. 581 ff.

3. Theodor Adorno, "Rede über Lyrik und Gesellschaft," in *Noten zur Literatur I* (Frankfort, 1958). The debate that took place in the thirties and forties, under the influence of T. S. Eliot, concerned literature and belief—where "belief" referred primarily to religious dogma, or political and moral positions inspired by it.

4. See Kurt Schlüter, *Die Englische Ode* (Bonn, 1964), chap. 2.

5. On "climate" theory in Milton, see Zera Fink, *The Classical Republicans*, 2d ed. (Evanston, 1962), pp. 91–94.

6. Wallace Stevens, "The Westwardness of Everything."

7. W. J. Bate, *John Keats*, pp. 581 ff.

8. My italics. "Dying" is qualified by "soft" but also perhaps by the pictorial sense of the word continued in "rosy hue."

9. On *templum* and its suggestive context in Renaissance poetry, see Angus Fletcher, *The Prophetic Moment* (Chicago, 1971), pp. 14 ff. See also Northrop Frye on *tenemos* in Keats, in *A Study of English Romanticism* (New York, 1969).

10. *Wordsworth's Poetry* (New Haven, 1964), pp. 9–13.

11. See John Hollander, "The Metrical Emblem," *Kenyon Review* 21 (1959): 290.

12. "Always the goal is his mastery of infelt space." See John Jones, *Keats's Dream of Truth* (London, 1969), p. 11 and passim.

13. Wallace Stevens, "The Course of a Particular."

14. John Jones, *Keats's Dream of Truth*, p. 269. Jones has fine and inward remarks on the ode's "antiphonal whisper," on "gathering" as "the last of the poem's harvesting and perfecting words" and on the poem's objectivity.

15. The presence of nonmigrating robins as well as migrating swallows increases the tension between staying and departure. Some have felt that the swallows are not gathering, at this point, for longer flight; but if the impression is, as I think, that night comes before

winter, the precise nature of the gathering is not that important. The word "bourn" (1.30) is from the French only if it means "boundary"; if "stream" it comes from an Anglo-Saxon root.

16. Hesperia belongs to what Vico calls "poetical geography" (*Scienza Nuova*, bk. 2, sec. 11, chap. 1). It referred originally to the western part of Greece, and extended into Italy (Hesperia magna) and Spain (Hesperia ultima). England seems excluded except from a visionary point of view. And although the extension is partly of my own making (a visionary concept of this kind being needed to clarify the geospiritual sense of writers like Milton and Collins), the Tudor myth encouraged it by its linking of James and Elizabeth to the Hesperus-Hesperides-Atlas complex. See, for example, Ben Johnson, *Pleasure Reconciled to Virtue* (1619). Hesperia, as Lemprière also defines it, is basically the region of the setting sun.

17. Letter to Benjamin Bailey, 22 November 1817.

18. Wordsworth was highly impressed by Milton's "Union of Tenderness and Imagination." See *Wordsworth's Poetry*, p. 266, and pp. 51–53 (on *Paradise Lost* VIII).

19. See Charles I. Patterson, Jr., *The Daemonic in the Poetry of John Keats* (Chicago, 1970), for an interesting but very different approach. His chap. 7 on "The Triumph of the Anti-Daemonic" emphasizes the distinctiveness of the Autumn ode in Keats's work, and anticipates the tenor of the interpretation given here.

20. *Die Englische Ode*, chap. 2.

21. On the development of "Hesperianism," see G. H. Hartman, "Romantic Poetry and the Genius Loci" in *Beyond Formalism* (New Haven, 1970). See also pp. 287–89, for remarks on the ideology of temperateness. There is no study of the relation between poetics and politics (or national ethos) centering on the "frame of Temperance," but important indications can be found passim in Angus Fletcher's book on Spenser, *The Prophetic Moment* (Chicago, 1971). Fletcher's interest in the encyclopedic (and cyropedic) qualities of *The Faerie Queene* led him to weigh the interactions of law, culture, national ideals, and poetry. Leo Spitzer's study, *Classical and Christian Ideas of World Harmony* (Baltimore, 1963), contains information and speculation galore on the semantic field of *temperare*

22. Marx and Engels would doubtless interpret Hesperianism, as I have described it, as the penetration of a mystifying ideology into the poetical domain. "We do not set out from what men say, imagine, conceive, nor from men as narrated, thought of, imagined, conceived, in order to arrive at men in the flesh. We set out from real, active men, and on the basis of their real life-process we demonstrate the development of the ideological reflexes and echos of this life-process. The phantoms formed in the human brain are also, necessarily, sublimates of their material life-process, which is empirically verifiable and bound to material premises. . . . Life is not determined by consciousness, but consciousness by life" (*The German Ideology*, trans. by Roy Pascal [New York, 1947], pp. 14–15). It is important to acknowledge, therefore, that I do indeed set out from "what men say, imagine, conceive . . . from men as narrated"—in short,

from literature. The question is whether this starting point is as inauthentic as the authors of *The German Ideology* believe. Is literature, as treated here, the *English* ideology, or is it in its own way a "material premise"?

23. Letter to J. H. Reynolds, 21 September 1819. I have inserted the sentence in brackets, which comes from a journal-letter of the same date to George and Georgiana Keats, and which goes on to the famous statement that "Life to him [Milton] would be death to me."

24. See what W. K. Wimsatt says about latent design in "The Structure of Romantic Nature Imagery," in *The Verbal Icon* (New York, 1958), p. 110. He refers, inter alia, to Keats's ode.

25. See Schlüter, *Die Englische Ode*, chap. 2. His important, specific analysis of the Autumn ode (pp. 218–35) recognizes the muting of epiphanic structure but fails to understand its structural or ideological context.

26. *Philosophy of History*, trans. J. Sibree (New York, 1901), pp. 317–19. This book was compiled posthumously from a series of lectures given by Hegel between 1822 and 1831. Sibree's translation is not always very literal but it catches well enough the spirit of the original. "Individuality conditioned by beauty" renders a conception of the Greek aesthetic character introduced by Winckelmann but which Lessing associated specifically with Classicism's understanding of the limits of the picturesque.

27. See Peter Szondi, "Überwindung des Klassizismus. Der Brief an Böhlendorff vom 4. Dezember 1801," in *Hölderlin-Studien* (Frankfurt, 1967). It is interesting that, as Szondi points out, Hölderlin should use the word "Geschik" to suggest both "destiny" and "(poetic) skill." To be a poet, yet a national poet, is always a complex fate. See also Hölderlin's remarks on Weather, Light, and the natural scenery of his native country in the second letter to Böhlendorff (2 December 1802): "das Licht in seinem Wirken, nationell und als Prinzip und Schicksalsweise bildend . . . das philosophische Licht um mein Fenster."

28. "History and Criticism: A Problematic Relationship," in *The Verbal Icon* (Lexington, Ky., 1954).

29. The best treatment is in Schlüter, *Die Englische Ode*, pp. 223–35.

30. For Keats's "Imitatio Apollinis," see especially Walter H. Evert, *Aesthetic and Myth in the Poetry of Keats* (Princeton, 1965).

31. Letter to B. J. Haydon, 23 January 1818.

32. "Temper my lonely hours / And let me see thy bow'rs / More unalarm'd," Keats wrote in his poem to Apollo ("God of the Meridian") of January 1818. The poem breaks off at that point and in the letter to J. H. Reynolds which quotes it, is followed by "When I have fears that I may cease to be."

To emphasize Apollo is not to discount Demeter but to suggest a transmythologic merging in the poem of "conspiring" (foreseeing) and "maturing" functions. The poem to Apollo breaks off, like *Hyperion*, when "bearing" becomes "overbearing," when maturing, instead of strengthening the prophetic or foreseeing character, leads to an overload destructive of it.

33. Horace, *Epistle* 2.2.187.
34. The first quotation comes from Keats's sonnet of late January 1818; the second is the opening line of Rilke's sonnet "Herbsttag."

Evening Star and Evening Land

1. This is the accepted date, though it is speculative. The poem first appeared in the posthumous edition of Akenside's *Poems* (1772).
2. See *The Greek Bucolic Poets*, ed. J. M. Edmonds, Loeb Classical Library (New York, 1928), pp. 410–13.
3. See *The Poems of Samuel Taylor Coleridge*, ed. E. H. Coleridge (Oxford, 1962), p. 16. In the 2d (1797) edition of his *Poems on Various Subjects* Coleridge surmised that "if the Sonnet were comprized in less than fourteen lines, it would become a serious epigram."
4. The preposition "to" in st. 1 foregrounds itself so strongly that, to subordinate it, one is tempted to read it on the pattern of "to-night" (i.e., proclitically) and so bring it closer to the bonded preposition "sub" in *supply, suppliant* (a near pun, anticipating the reversal mentioned above) and even *suffer*. Compare the syntax of st. 6; also the "prefer" of l. 19 which makes "vows" both its direct and indirect object. It draws attention once more not only to the prepositional but also to the syntactical bonding of one verse-line with another. All this fosters a sense of the discontinuous or precarious path followed by the verses' "feet." It is interesting that in Christopher Smart's *Song to David* (1763) the problem of hierarchy, subordination (hypotaxis), and prepositional-syntactical bonding reaches an acute stage.
5. Compare Tennyson, *In Memoriam*, 121, "Sweet Hesper-Phosphor, double name . . ."
6. See Blake, *Milton*, and Collins, "Ode on the Poetical Character."
7. Spenser, "Epithalamium," l. 290.
8. Blake, "To the Evening Star." "Full soon" could mean both "very soon" and "soon full" (having reached its ripest or intensest point).
9. Shelley, "To a Skylark," ll. 21–25. This describes the morning star; Shelley wrote an expressively bad poem to the evening star in 1811 (see *The Complete Works*, ed. T. Hutchinson [London, 1960], p. 870) and uses Plato's verses (cited above, p. 151) as an epigraph for "Adonais." His most famous evocation of Hesperus-Lucifer is in "The Triumph of Life," ll. 412–20. On the importance to Shelley of the evening-morning star theme, see W. B. Yeats, "The Philosophy of Shelley's Poetry," in *Ideas of Good and Evil* (1903). To gain a complete "phenomenological thematics" it would be necessary, of course, to consider the evening star theme in relation to that of the moon, the night, other stars, birds (nightingale / lark), star flowers, the hymeneal theme (compare Catullus, "Vesper adest"), etc.
10. See the ending of "Night the Ninth" in the *Four Zoas*.
11. Like "golden," these lines were added in 1815. Compare "She Was a Phantom of Delight," whose first stanza is clearly indebted to the evening star motif, and whose rhythm is similar. For a

large-scale speculation on sky-earth imagery in "Daffodils," see Frederick Garber, *Wordsworth and the Poetry of Encounter* (Urbana, Ill., 1971), pp. 152 ff.

12. For an interpretation of Wordsworth's "middle-ground" parallel to mine, and to which I am indebted, see Paul de Man, "Symbolic Landscape in Wordsworth and Yeats," in *In Defense of Reading*, eds. R. A. Brower and R. Poirier (New York, 1963).

13. "It Is No Spirit," ll. 7–8.

14. Also perhaps Wordsworth's marital situation. He had gone to France to see Annette Vallon and his daughter prior to marrying Mary (in October 1802). There is also the poet's general sensitivity to "floating," or images of suspended animation, or even the word "hung."

15. For "race," a probable pun, see Psalms 19:5.

16. This and the following quotation are from *The Complete Poems of Emily Dickinson*, ed. T. H. Johnson (Boston, 1960), poems 1135 and 1616. See also Eleanor Wilner, "The Poetics of Emily Dickinson," *ELH* 38 (1971): 138–40.

17. Compare T. S. Eliot, *The Waste Land*, ll. 97 ff.

18. I am indebted for this insight to my student Frances Ferguson.

19. Coleridge, "The Aeolian Harp" (1795), l. 28. The line was not in the original published version, but entered the text in 1828.

20. For the role Milton as Voice played in Wordsworth, and the Romantics generally, see Leslie Brisman, *Milton's Poetry of Choice and Its Romantic Heirs* (Ithaca, N.Y., 1973), chap. 5. For "Voice" after Wordsworth, cf. Thomas Whitaker's "Voices in the Open" (lecture at the 1970 English Institute) and John Hollander's *Images of Voice* (Cambridge, 1970), as well as his essay "Wordsworth and the Music of Sound," in *New Perspectives on Coleridge and Wordsworth*, ed. Geoffrey Hartman (New York, 1972), pp. 41–84.

21. See Angus Fletcher, *The Prophetic Moment* (Chicago, 1971).

22. "Fingal," in James Macpherson, *The Poems of Ossian*. Compare the role of voice (the wind's and that of—originally—Lucy Gray) in Coleridge's "Dejection: An Ode."

23. Macpherson, *Songs of Selma*.

24. Last lines of *Songs of Selma*.

25. Wallace Stevens, "Our Stars Come from Ireland," in *The Auroras of Autumn*.

26. Michael Bruce, "Lochleven," in *Poems on Several Occasions* (Edinburgh, 1782).

27. For the general thesis see Harold Bloom, "Coleridge: The Anxiety of Influence," in *New Perspectives on Coleridge and Wordsworth*, pp. 247–67; W. J. Bate, *The Burden of the Past and the English Poet* (Cambridge, Mass., 1970); and G. H. Hartman, *Beyond Formalism* (New Haven, 1970), pp. 270 ff. and 367 ff.

28. Numbers 11:29, and plate 1 of Blake's *Milton*.

29. Norman Fruman, in chap. 6 of *Coleridge, the Damaged Archangel* (New York, 1971), shows the young poet systematically "vamping" the mediocre poetry of his time. On this "substitution of conventionality for originality" and the closeness in Coleridge of

"self-construction" and "self-annihilation," see M. G. Cooke, "Quisque Sui Faber: Coleridge in the *Biographia Literaria*," *Philological Quarterly* 50 (1971): 208–29.

30. The psychological background is extremely complex: he was deeply identified, by this time, with Wordsworth and indeed the entire Wordsworth "family," as the Verse Letter to Sara Hutchinson (later "Dejection") of the previous April shows. His Scafell experience was also recorded in (prose) letters to Sara. Bowles's "Coombe Ellen" and "Saint Michael's Mount" may have been in his mind, but in a negative way—his letter to Sotheby of September 10, 1802, leads into a mention of the Scafell-Chamouny Hymn via criticisms of Bowles's "second Volume" (*Poems*, by the Reverend Wm. Lisle Bowles, vol. 2, 1801) which contained these poems.

31. Fruman has interesting remarks on Coleridge's use of "hope" in an implicitly sexual sense (*Coleridge*, pp. 425 ff.). Sara Hutchinson is always in his thought at this time (see note 30 above), and the attempt to "rise" out of a nightmare moment of trance or passivity could have involved sensual "Hopes & Fears."

32. "Stay" in "Hast thou a charm to stay the morning star / In his steep course" could be ambiguous and reflect the double image of the mountain-darkness as (1) preventing and (2) supporting the star.

33. See the letter quoted on p. 173.

34. See Angus Fletcher on "liminal anxiety" in Coleridge, " 'Positive Negation': Threshold, Sequence, and Personification in Coleridge," in *New Perspectives on Coleridge and Wordsworth*, pp. 133–64.

35. G. M. Hopkins "Carrion Comfort," l. 13.

36. Compare Harold Bloom, *Shelley's Mythmaking* (New Haven, 1959), pp. 15–19.

37. Compare "To the Nightingale," ll. 12–14; "This Lime-Tree Bower My Prison," ll. 38 ff.; and passages mainly from the *Notebooks* which tell how gazing produced a "phantom-feeling" by abstracting or "unrealizing" objects. See *The Notebooks of Samuel Taylor Coleridge* (New York, 1961), 2: 2495, 2546; also the letter quoted above, pp. 173–74.

38. *Collected Letters of Samuel Taylor Coleridge*, ed. E. L. Griggs (Oxford, 1956–), 4: 974–75.

39. There seems to have been two Scafell letters, now extant only in Sara Hutchinson's transcript (Griggs, *Collected Letters*, 2: 834–45). The second one (no. 451 in Griggs) begins strangely with Coleridge mentioning his "criminal" (for a family man) addiction to recklessness when descending mountains, then describing a narrow escape. "I lay in a state of almost prophetic Trance & Delight—& blessed God aloud, for the powers of Reason & the Will, which remaining no Danger can overpower us! O God, I exclaimed aloud—how calm, how blessed am I now / I know not how to proceed, how to return / but I am calm & fearless & confident / if this Reality were a Dream, if I were asleep, what agonies had I suffered! what screams! —When the Reason & the Will are away, what remains to us but Darkness & Dimness & a bewildering Shame, and Pain that is utterly Lord over us, or fantastic Pleasure." This experience of mingled

fear and exaltation may have something of the conventional "sublime" in it; but it confirms that there was a *trance* and a deep moment of wakeful, rather than sleep-bound, passivity. It also suggests that, however exalted the trance, Coleridge feared it could lead (by the "streamy nature" of consciousness?) into painful sexual thoughts. The only explicit trace, in the Hymn, of this shame at passivity is its formal turn: "Awake my soul! not only passive praise/Thou owest . . ."

40. "On a Cataract. Improved from Stolberg" (1799?). Both of the F. L. Stolberg lyrics translated by Coleridge—"Der Felsenstrom" and "Bei William Tell's Geburtsstätte"—are about places of origin.

41. The quotations in this paragraph come from "To the Rev. W. L. Bowles," "The Aeolian Harp," "Hymn before Sunrise, in the Vale of Chamouni," and "Kubla Khan."

42. That there may be a subjective or pseudohistorical element in the thesis does not disqualify it, unless we erect it into actual history: all art, it can be argued, seen from the point of view of "imagination," is a *second* rather than a *first*—haunted, that is, by being mere copy, re-creation, or afterglow. If poetry since the Renaissance (and at times in the Renaissance) felt itself approaching an evening stage, it could mean that poets judged their work more absolutely: either as coinciding with, or failing, Imagination. For the thesis, see W. J. Bate, *The Burden of the Past and the English Poet*; Harold Bloom, *Yeats* (New York, 1970), and *The Anxiety of Influence: A Theory of Poetry* (New York, 1973); also G. H. Hartman, "Blake and the Progress of Poesy" and "Romantic Poetry and the Genius Loci," in *Beyond Formalism.*

43. Wallace Stevens, "Autumn Refrain." Compare "Man on the Dump."

44. On the relation between vision and representation in the masque, see Angus Fletcher, *The Transcendental Masque: An Essay on Milton's Comus* (Ithaca, 1972), pp. 8–18.

45. Tudor myth, which exalted Elizabeth as "that bright *Occidental* star" (Dedicatory Epistle to the King James Bible) and compared James to "the radiant Cymbeline/Which shines here in the west" (*Cymbeline*, V.v. 474–77), helped to convert the theme of a *translatio imperii* into that of a *translatio artis.*

46. Milton, "Arcades," ll. 18–19. This queen-moon, it may be added, is also a "western star," since "Arcades" is based on the conceit of finding a new Arcady in the West—that is, in England. Keats's "Endymion" stands to the theme of the moon as Shelley's "Adonais" to that of the evening star: my essay breaks off before those luxurious revivals.

47. Wordsworth, "Ode: Intimations of Immortality," st. 2.

Wordsworth and Goethe in Literary History

1. The quotations that follow are from "Über Ossian und die Lieder alter Völker," in *Von Deutscher Art und Kunst* (Hamburg, 1773). I have translated freely.

2. Herder is referring, at one and the same time, to a mental experience and to his actual journey from Riga to France in 1769.

3. J.P. Eckermann, *Gespräche mit Goethe* (1823–32).

4. *Northern Antiquities*, by Bishop Percy. New Edition, revised throughout, and considerably enlarged . . . by I.A. Blackwell (London, 1847), p. 243. I have been unable to trace these sentences to Mallet's original French edition (1755–56) or to Percy's original version (1770). The history of the German translations of Mallet is somewhat unclear: a section was translated into Danish in 1756, and the complete work was put into German in 1765–69 as *Geschichte von Dänemark.* Mit einer Vorrede von Gottfried Schütze. 3 bde. (Rostock, Greifswald bei A.F. Röse). The first part of this translation was reviewed by Herder in the *Königsbergsche Gelehrten und Politischen Zeitung* of 12 August 1765. "Es kann dies Buch eine Rüstkammer eines neuen Deutschen Genies seyn, das sich auf den Flügeln der Celtischen Einbildungskraft in neue Wolken erhebt und Gedichte schaffet, die uns angemessner wären, als die Mythologie der Römer." (I am grateful to Beth Gaskins for pointing out Herder's review.) Concerning the metaphor of a Northern Sun, see Frank Sayre, *Dramatic Sketches of Northern Mythology* (Norwich, 1790) which quotes on the title page Milton's "Fallor? an et radios hinc quoque Phoebus habet" (Elegy VII. 56).

5. The North/South or Celtic/Classic (etc.) dichotomy appears in standard form in Percy's preface to this volume which was delayed till 1763. Percy singles out an exceptional feature of the ancient Danes: "It will be thought a paradox, that the same people, whose furious ravage destroyed the last poor remains of expiring genius among the Romans, should cherish it [poetry] with all possible care among their own countrymen: yet so it was. At least this was the case among the ancient Danes."

6. "Though founded on a Danish tradition, this Ballad was originally written in German, and is the production of the celebrated Goethe, author of Werter, etc." (Lewis's note). Lewis was collecting materials for his "hobgoblin repast" as early as 1798; he had been to Weimar and seen Goethe in 1792; and he inserted translations of the "Erl-king's Daughter" and Goethe's "Erl-king" into the fourth edition (1798) of *The Monk.* Both of these poems had appeared in *The Monthly Mirror* for October 1796. Chapter eight of the third volume of the original edition (1796) of *The Monk* already included "The Water-king—A Danish Ballad."

7. Compare "The Two April Mornings," also composed at this time, in which Emma's singing comes at a specific moment and is followed by death. The disconcerting contrast of numerals in "Nine summers" (the age at which Emma sang and died), "Six feet in earth," and even "Two April Mornings," seems to subvert the concept of "timely utterance" on which *lyrical* or *natural* poetry depends.

8. E. de Selincourt, ed., *The Poetical Works of William Wordsworth* (Oxford, 2d ed., 1952), 2: 493. That Wordsworth could be inspired to write as late as 1842 "The Norman Boy" (and its sequel) shows how deep the imaginative scene of a legendary child in a border-region or dreary Wild lay in him. This "Southern" (yet

English) version of "The Danish Boy" has its own charms and climaxes in the vision of a "Chapel Oak" which seems to reconcile the orders of Nature, Religion, and Poetry (human artifice).

9. If one were to analyze the verbal style minutely one would find in it a shifty series of self-weakening affirmations, corresponding to the decremental or declining plot-series in "We Are Seven" or "The Last of the Flock." Compare also the subversive interplay in "The Danish Boy" between "is" and "seems" or the reversal of the weak "there" ("There is") in "There sits he . . ."

10. See especially "The Ruined Cottage" (1798), later revised as *The Excursion*, bk. I; also *The Excursion*, bks. VI-VII, entitled "The Churchyard among the Mountains," where the "silence" of the "characters" is of course the death of persons with universal or at least "type" features.

11. The kinship theme in these ballads or stories is remarkable. "With a brother's love/I blessed her . . ." restitutes a broken "bond of brotherhood" the pedlar had noticed at the beginning.

12. Friederich Gundolf, *Goethe* (Berlin, 1925), p. 507.

13. De Selincourt, *The Poetical Works of William Wordsworth*, 2: 511.

14. Emil Staiger suggests that "anmutig" should be understood as "anmutend" (*Goethe* [Zürich, 1952], 1: 342). The repeated rime "Wind"/"Kind" helps us travel back to childhood where such sensations had a durée which did not need the artificial support of poetry or story; it may even clarify the nature of the particular sensation by suggesting that this wind, like the child affected by it, is of more than natural origin. "Der Wind, der Wind, das Himmlische Kind." Goethe's comment on "Der Fischer," cited above, comes from remarks on the ballad in *Über Kunst und Altertum* (dritten Bandes erstes Heft, 1821).

15. What we know of Goethe's *Singspiel* suggests that its theme was that of the Lost Girl (Dortchen, who recites "The Erl-King"); and that its main theatrical effect was to have been that of an outdoors illumination provided by the torchlight of the search party. The theme of the Lost Girl (as in the Lucy poems) is at least indirectly related to the Persephone myth and so to an Orphic katabasis.

16. Eckermann, *Gespräche mit Goethe* (1823–32).

17. "Dies Werden der Wissenschaft überhaupt oder des Wissens ist es, was diese Phänomenologie des Geistes darstellt. Das Wissen, wie es zuerst ist, oder der unmittelbare Geist ist das Geistlose, das sinnliche Bewusstsein. Um zum eigentlichen Wissen zu werden, oder das Element der Wissenschaft, das ihr reiner Begriff selbst ist, zu erzeugen, hat es durch einen langen Weg sich hindurchzuarbeiten.—Dieses Werden, wie es in seinem Inhalte und den Gestalten, die sich in ihm zeigen, sich aufstellen wird, wird nicht das sein, was man zunächst unter einer Anleitung des unwissenschaftlichen Bewusstseins zur Wissenschaft sich vorstellt; auch etwas anderes, als die Begründung der Wissenschaft;—so

ohnehin als die Begeisterung, die wie aus der Pistole mit dem absoluten Wissen unmittelbar anfängt und mit anderen Standpunkten dadurch schon fertig ist, dass sie keine Notiz davon zu nehmen erklärt." From Hegel's "Vorrede," *Die Phänomenologie des Geistes* (1807).

18. "Everything is hateful to me that intends only to instruct without at the same time increasing or directly stimulating my creative powers," are the words of Goethe with which Nietzsche introduces his *Vom Nutzen und Nachtheil der Historie für das Leben* (1874).

19. Moneta's accusation against Keats, or the figure of the Poet, in *The Fall of Hyperion: A Dream* (composed 1819).

20. The notion of the "characteristic" (raised by Goethe as early as his "Von Deutscher Baukunst" included in Herder's *Von Deutscher Art und Kunst*) is, of course, a very complex one, especially in conjunction with nationalistic music-metaphysics that involved Rousseau, Gluck, Diderot, and others.

21. It is no accident that Richard Onorato's psychoanalytic study of Wordsworth is entitled *The Character of the Poet* (Princeton, 1971). On the concept of character in traditional poetics, and its relation to Wordsworth, see also Robert Langbaum, *The Poetry of Experience* (London and New York, 1957); and Herbert Lindenberger, *On Wordsworth's Prelude* (Princeton, 1963), pp. 15–40.

22. Goethe's Helena is, it seems to me, the culmination of all these frigid ghostly beauties.

Literature High and Low: The Case of the Mystery Story

1. S. H. Butcher, ed. and trans., *Aristotle's Theory of Poetry and Fine Art*, 4th ed., XI.6 (1452b 9–13). There is a second brief mention at XIV.4 (1453b 17–22).

2. See Gerald Else, *Aristotle's Poetics* (Cambridge, Mass., 1967), pp. 356–58).

3. See Jacques Barzun, "The Novel Turns Tale," *Mosaic* 4 (1971): 33–40.

4. The elliptical "cuts" of Eliot's *The Wasteland* often produce a similar effect. Ellipsis joined to the technical principle of montage (in Eisenstein's conception) consolidate the international style we are describing.

5. *Maidstone* is a blatantly eclectic script-tease: it flirts with crime, sexploitation, politics, and film about film. Its plot consists of a wager by Norman T. Kingsley that the actors in the film will invent that scene of passion, he, the director, cannot or will not invent—that they will kill the King, that is, the director, that is, Norman.

6. For a straight psychoanalytic interpretation, see Marie Buonoparte, "The Murder in the Rue Morgue," *Psychoanalytic Quarterly* 4 (1935): 259–93; G. Pederson-Krag, "Detective Stories and the

Primal Scene," *Psychoanalytic Quarterly* 18 (1949): 207–14; and, especially, Charles Rycroft, "The Analysis of a Detective Story" (1957) reprinted in his *Imagination and Reality* (London, 1968). I emphasize in what follows the eye rather than the cry; but, as in Wordsworth's ballad, there is often something ejaculative or quasi-inarticulate (a "tongue-tie," to use Melville's phrase in *Billy Budd*) accompanying.

7. See Freud's "The 'Uncanny'" (1919). His analysis of repetition, in relation to (ambivalent) reanimation may prove essential to any psychoesthetic theory of narrative. This may also be the point to introduce thematics, especially the thematics of the genius loci: animism, ghosts, ancestor consciousness, quasi-supernatural hauntings of particular places. Freud connects them either with memories of an intra-uterine (oceanic) state or with the later illusion of "omnipotence of consciousness." In Poe, one might speculate, the mystery story is intra-uterine gothic while the detective story is omnipotence-of-consciousness modern. See also note 8.

8. This almost inverts the sense of the gothic novel which Poe transformed into a modern tale of detection by dividing its mystery part from its rationalizing part. The mystery story, as he develops it, deals mainly with *vestiges* that intimate someone's *life-in-death*, and he exploits the horror of that thought. His detective stories tend to sublimate this theme of the "living dead" by demystifying vestiges as clues: signs of (and for) a persistent or mad or "omnipotent" consciousness. Frederic Jameson's "On Raymond Chandler," *Southern Review* 6 (1970): 624–50, gives an interesting account of how the "formal distraction" of the detective quest leads into genuine revelations of death-in-life.

9. Sterne's *Tristram Shandy* may be the original of this comic anamnesis which cannot begin (find the true starting point) and so cannot end.

10. See my "The Voice of the Shuttle" in *Beyond Formalism* (New Haven, 1970).

11. Andersch is a distinguished German journalist and man of letters who has written several novels and was one of the original members of the famous post-war association of writers called "Group '47."

12. Charles Brockden Brown's *Wieland* (1797) remains the classic instance of a pattern which recalls Freud's understanding of family ambivalences.

Valéry's Fable of the Bee

1. On the "idyll," ("little picture" may be a false etymology) the "naive" epigram, and "the success of the Greeks in inventing, for the West, and perfecting the small poetical idea," see James Hutton, *The Greek Anthology in France* (Ithaca, 1946), Intro-

duction. "Blonde Abeille" is not uncommon in Greek Anthology epigrams. See *Anthologie Grecque* (Paris: Librairie Hachette, 1863), vol. 1, epigram 562, and vol. 2, epigram 210. I quote from the latter, attributed to Plato and entitled *Sur un Amour endormi*: "[il] dormait, le sourire sur les lèvres, tandis que de blondes abeilles venaient voltiger sur sa bouche charmante pour y recueillir leur miel."

2. "Descartes" (1937).

3. 1891 is the date (stylized) of his discovery of Mallarmé and Rimbaud.

4. Variant found in *Charmes* (1922) and *Vers et Prose* (1926).

5. "Le sujet concret s'efface et fait place au sujet abstrait." (Berne-Joffroy, *Présence de Valéry* [Paris, 1945], p. 181, on *La Jeune Parque*). "La déception est vive, lorsque l'allégorie nous oblige à ne voir là que l'image figurée d'un esprit d'écrivain à la recherche de l'inspiration." (Hubert Fabureau, on "Les Pas," cited by Berne-Joffroy, *Présence de Valéry*, p. 189.)

6. See, especially, Jacques Derrida, *La Voix et le Phénomène* (Paris, 1967); and his essay on Valéry "Qual Quelle," in *Marges* (Paris, 1972).

7. From the introduction to the anthology, *La Pléiade*, eds. La Contesse de Noailles and others (Paris, 1921). For the importance of Valéry to it, and especially his essay on Lucien Fabre's *Connaissance de la déesse*, see Kenneth Cornell, *The Post-Symbolist Period* (New Haven, 1958), pp. 142–44.

8. Jacques Derrida, "Force et signification," in *L'Écriture et la différence* (Paris, 1967), pp. 23–24.

9. "Cantique des Colonnes" (1919).

10. For Valéry's early interest in this concept, see his *Essai sur la méthode de Léonard de Vinci* (1894).

11. See the Pléiade edition of the *Oeuvres de Paul Valéry*, ed. Jean Hytier (Paris, 1957–60), 1: 1544–46 (henceforth referred to as *Oeuvres*). On the importance of *or* in Valéry, both as concept and quasi-morpheme, see also my *The Unmediated Vision* (New Haven, 1954), pp. 110–12.

12. *Analecta* (The Hague, 1926).

13. Charles Maurron's chapter "Valéry: la Dormeuse" in his *Des métaphores obsédantes au mythe personnel* (Paris, 1963) gives a biased if powerful account of Valéry's distant encounter with Mme. R, expressed in such feelings as: "Ah! savez-vous ce que c'est qu'une robe—même en dehors—surtout en dehors, de tout désir simpliste de chair? Mais seule la robe et l'oeil L'idéaliste agonise" (letter to Gide of 4 July 1891, cited by Maurron on pp. 176–77). See also the ending of a sonnet of late 1891, printed in *Oeuvres* 1: 1591, which alludes to "échos des étoffes profondes."

14. James Hutton, *The Greek Anthology in Italy to 1800* (Ithaca, 1935), quotes the following couplet of unknown origin: "Omne epigramma sit instar apis; sit aculeus illi; / Sint sua mella; sit et corporis exigui" (p. 60 note 3).

15. See the version of "Abeille Spirituelle" dating from 1920, in *Oeuvres*, 1: 1680–81; see also pp. 241 ff.

16. Love-poetry and the Greek Epigram play, of course, with the theme of the stinger stung (see section six, below).

17. On this matter of veils, and so on, Valéry is close to Shelley.

18. *Analecta.*

19. "Poésie et Pensée Abstraite" (1939).

20. *Oeuvres*, 2: 1615.

21. "Les Pas" (1921).

22. *Cahiers*, vol. 8 (1922) (Paris, 1958), p. 895. Compare Derrida, "Qual Quelle," *Marges*, pp. 344–45.

23. See the discussion of the seashell in Valéry's *Eupalinos*, and Hans Blumenberg, "Socrates und das 'Objet Ambigu,'" in *Epimeleia*, ed. F. Wiedmann (Munich, 1954).

24. "Poésie" (1921).

25. "Je disais quelquefois à Stephane Mallarmé" (1931).

26. Compare the effect of the hidden "dent" in "songe de dentelle," which links the "songe" once more with "piqure" and the desire for a "mal vif."

27. Essentially different from "concrete poetry," which also aims at this reduction, but differs in its extreme selectivity, or suspicion of the poet's *coup de dés*, his "lucky strike." For poetry's resistance to sense, see also my *The Unmediated Vision* (New Haven, 1954), pp. 99ff. (where reduction is called retroduction); and Derrida's "Qual Quelle."

28. Mallarmé's *Igitur*, with its purified gothic ambiance, is important here; so is the entire (unpurified) line of gothic fiction. It popularized the formula of riddling scenes followed by an explanation (*le surnaturel expliqué*). The structural principle of *hesitation* used by Tzvetan Todorov to classify types of fantastic fiction could provide a bridge to this (Mallarmean) kind of poetry.

29. See "Berthe Morisot" and "Autour de Corot" in *Pièces sur l'Art* (Paris, 1934).

30. What is *La Jeune Parque* but an extended *blazon*, a lighting up of the body by a will to form which reveals it as the basis of all painterly-poetic construction, of all "temples" or works of art? The "burning," consequently, which emblazons this body is not erotic but rather a sacrifice of the erotic motive ("Quels secrets dans son coeur brûle ma jeune amie") to the formal. There is a conflict, of course, between these motives, as there is between the sensuous cliché and its reduction in "L'Abeille." The two poems, in fact, are linked most evidently by the icon of the illuminated or burning breast, the clearest focus of erotic, maternal, mystical and painterly (formal) solicitations. As mediterranean art gilded or haloed parts of a saint's body (Valéry in his essay on Nerval quotes "Sainte Napolitaine aux mains pleines de feux"), so this belated neopagan goddess aspires to a condition of total visibility "sous les espèces d'or d'un sein reconnaissant."

31. *Oeuvres*, 1: 1574 and 1579. See Valéry's unpublished article of November 1889 "Sur la technique littéraire": ". . . un sonnet . . . sera un véritable quintessence, un osmazôme, un suc concentré, et cohobé, réduit à quatorze vers, soigneusement *composé* en vue d'un effet final et foudroyant." (*Oeuvres*, 1: 1786ff.) How close this is to what Hutton tells us about sixteenth century verse: "the word epigram inevitably suggested 'point' and a chief effect of the epigram-sonnet was to make the sonneteer strive for an 'illustre conclusion.' " (*The Greek Anthology in France*, p. 44.)

32. *Oeuvres*, 1: 1574–86. The poems date from 1889 to 1891.

33. The "et" of the last line, simple as it is, refuses to convert contiguity into causality.

34. Letter to Souday, May 1923.

35. Compare the Greek epigram cited in note 1 Here are two related translations by A. Ferdinand Herold from the Greek anthology, in *La Guirlande d'Aphrodite* (Paris, 1923). "*L'Abeille.* Ton nom, Mélitta, est le nom de l'abeille, et tu m'aimes comme l'abeille aime les fleurs. Ton baiser sur mes lèvres laisse la douceur du miel, et pourtant tu me piques au coeur d'un injuste aiguillon" (pp. 50–51). "*Erôs piqué.* Dans une rose s'était cachée une abeille. Erôs s'approcha de la fleur; il voulait la cueillir; brusquement s'échappa l'abeille, et elle pique le doigt du petit Dieu. La main douloureuse il vola vers la belle Cythérée. Il criait: 'Mère, je suis perdu, je suis mort. Un serpent ailé m'a mordu: il était, je crois, de ceux que les laboureurs nomment abeilles.' Et Cythérée se mit à rire, et répondit: 'Si l'aiguillon de l'abeille est d'une telle cruauté, que diras-tu des souffrances qu'inflige la piqûre de tes flèches?' " (pp. 72–73). See also, in the Renaissance, Joannis Secundus, *Basia* (1539) no. XIX; and Olivier de Magny, "Quant je te vois au matin," in *Les Odes Amoureuses* (1559). James Hutton discusses variation, reversal, and so on, in the use of sources in *MLN* 58 (1943).

36. Olivier de Magny, "Plaincte d'Amour à Venus," in *Les Odes Amoureuses* (1559). The clearest source of the *Amour piqué* theme is an Anacreontic ode (translated by Belleau under that title). There is also an "idyll" of Theocritus on the subject.

37. *Oeuvres* 1: 1681, and 2: 1618.

38. *Oeuvres*, 1: 1618.

39. R. M. Rilke, *Sonnette an Orpheus* 1: 2; and Valéry, "La Fileuse," the first poem in *Album des Vers Anciens* (Paris, 1920).

40. The encounter with Mallarmé and the experience with Mme. R. are almost contemporaneous: everything critical, point and counterpoint, occurs between 1889 and 1892.

41. "Féerie," in *Album des Vers Anciens.* For the complicated publishing history, see *Oeuvres*, 1: 1543–1544. See also the poem entitled "Au Bois Dormant" (1891).

42. "Ballet," *Oeuvres*, 1: 1592.

43. The ending of de Magny's "Plaincte" in the *Odes Amoureuses.*

44. From "Conseil d'Ami," *Oeuvres*, 1: 1590.

45. "A Alcide Blavet" (1890), *Oeuvres*, 1: 1588. The bee-ambrosia theme is also there.

46. From a sonnet of 1891, "Bathylle de Lesbos," in *Oeuvres*, 1: 1591. The "dans ton ombre" may contain a subtle allusion to the Anacreontic odes on Bathylle, reenforced by a reference to Anacreon's famous first ode on his lyre which will only intone themes of love.

47. See "L'Infini esthétique, in *Pièces sur l'Art* (Paris, 1934).

48. *Oeuvres*, 1: 1591.

49. "Le Bilan de l'Intelligence" (1935), as translated in *The Collected Works of Paul Valéry*, ed. Jackson Mathews, vol. 10, *History and Politics*, trans. Denise Folliot and Jackson Mathews (New York, 1962), pp. 141–42. The essay develops ideas broached as early as the famous "La Crise de l'Esprit" of 1919, the year "L'Abeille" was composed. (In *Regards sur le Monde Actuel* Valéry claims that the ideas go back still further, even to the period of his own crisis: "La Crise de l'Esprit . . . ne contient que le développement de ces pensées qui m'étaient venues plus de vingt ans auparavant.")

50. The idea of an "Economie poétique ou poïétique, qui joue dans 'l'Univers d'Esprit' le même rôle que la notion d'Economie politique dans le monde des choses pratiques" is explicitly developed by the poet in the last decade of his life, and especially in lectures he gives as holder of the Chair of Poetics at the Collège de France. See *Oeuvres*, 2: 1605, and many pieces published in *Regards sur le Monde Actuel* (Paris, 1931, 1938).

The Fate of Reading

1. Nietzsche first formulated the thought in aphorism 341 at the end of the fourth book of his *Die Fröhliche Wissenschaft* (composed in the early 1880s), and it is hinted at in the opening aphorism (276). The context of the thought is a complex one: it includes that "Hang und Drang zum Wahren" which Nietzsche (a step beyond Goethe's Faust) resents because it will not let him rest despite his wish to do so ("Wie Vieles verführt mich nicht, zu verweilen!"). Hannah Arendt's comment on Augustine's vision of history, "Secular history repeats itself, and the only story in which unique and unrepeatable events take place begins with Adam and ends with the birth and death of Christ" (*Between Past and Future*), suggests how radical a secularization Nietzsche aimed at. The "restlessness" I have previously mentioned (see *Die Fröhliche Wissenschaft*, aphorism 309), also therefore points to a residual drive for authority: we still seek but fail to discover events that augment history by the foundation of new or exemplary (renascent) works.

2. *Aids to Reflection* (1831), "Aphorisms on Spiritual Religion, X." Coleridge in this appears like a strange middle term between Fichte and Derrida.

3. See for example Nancy Struever, "Classical Investigations," *New Literary History*, 5 (1974): 515–26. On style and the critic, see pp. 268–70 in this volume.

4. *The Sense of an Ending* (New York, 1967).

5. Letter to Richard West, May 27, 1742.

6. See *The Interpretation of Dreams*, chap. 6, "The Dream-Work," sections "C" and "D."

7. Daniel Boorstin uses this quote as an epigraph for his *The Image: A Guide to Pseudo-Events in America* (1962). Boorstin's remarks on the marketing of illusions, the reduction of all works to commodities, the substitution of celebrity for fame, and the fading of the original in the "Graphic Revolution," may be compared with previous critiques of modern culture: Walter Rathenau, *Zur Mechanik des Geistes* (1913); Walter Benjamin, *The Work of Art in the Era of its Mechanical Reproduction* (1936); and Hannah Arendt, *Between Past and Future* (1961), passim. Another interesting analysis is found in Valéry's *La Crise de l'esprit* (1919) and *Le Bilan de l'intelligence* (1935).

On the Theory of Romanticism

1. A. O. Lovejoy, "On the Discrimination of Romanticisms," *PMLA* 39 (1924); R. Wellek, "The Concept of Romanticism in Literary History" (1949) and "Romanticism Re-Examined," in *Concepts of Criticism* (New Haven, 1963).

2. Compare G. H. Hartman, *Beyond Formalism* (New Haven, 1970), pp. 330–36.

3. Robert Langbaum, *The Poetry of Experience* (London, 1957); Harold Bloom, *Yeats* (New York, 1970); G. H. Hartman, *The Unmediated Vision* (New Haven, 1954). Paul de Man, in various essays, also posits a similarity, but chiefly to break false models of historiography which suppose that the new (modern) differentiates itself from the old (romantic) by historical gradualism, by a filial and benevolent progress. He shows that everything claimed for the "moderns" is already found in the romantics, and that the proper—perhaps only?—distinction is that between great poetry and lesser. The archaism of "blindness" attributed to romantic writers is not caused by a failure of intellectual or moral light (as in Bostetter's *The Romantic Ventriloquists* [Seattle, 1963]) but by their very commitment to the basically mediatory, if enigmatic, character of poetic language.

4. *The Burden of the Past and the English Poet* (Cambridge, Mass., 1970). The "Classical Romantics" is a topic remaining largely undeveloped despite Kurt Schlüter's *Die Englische Ode* (Bonn,

1964) and literary-iconographical studies beginning with Harry Levin's *The Broken Column* (Cambridge, Mass., 1931).

5. T. R. Whitaker, *Swan and Shadow* (Chapel Hill, 1964); A. D. Culler, *Imaginative Reason* (New Haven, 1966).

6. See "The Drunken Boat . . .," in *Romanticism Reconsidered: Selected Papers from the English Institute*, ed. N. Frye (New York, 1963).

7. D. Erdman, *Prophet Against Empire* (Princeton, 1954); C. Woodring, *Politics in English Romantic Poetry* (New York, 1970); also D. P. Calleo, *Coleridge and the Idea of the Modern State* (New Haven, 1966).

8. In *Romanticism Reconsidered.*

9. See "Toward Literary History," in *Beyond Formalism.*

10. C. Caudwell, *Illusion and Reality* (New York, 1936); H. Bloom, *Yeats* (New York, 1970), especially Introduction.

11. J. Wordsworth, *The Music of Humanity* (London and New York, 1969).

12. See *The Unmediated Vision*, pp. 127ff.

13. Günter Anders, in *Die Antiquiertheit des Menschen* (Munich, 1956), says that we suffer from Promethean *shame*: an anxiety about what has not been processed, shame for the work of our hands in contrast to what is more perfectly machined.

14. See, for an early analysis of this kind, Wordsworth on the social and political causes blunting "the discriminating powers of the mind," and to counter which *Lyrical Ballads* is written (Preface to *Lyrical Ballads*).

15. W. J. Ong, *The Presence of the Word* (New Haven, 1967). See also John Hollander's more detailed studies of the representation of sound, as in *Images of Voice: Music and Sound in Romantic Poetry* (Cambridge, England, 1970).

16. See Raymond Williams, *Culture and Society, 1780–1850* (New York, 1958).

17. Positions range widely. Harold Bloom talks of an "apocalyptic humanism" (to some a contradiction in terms); M. H. Abrams is tracing the secularization of religious forms but in a way that evinces their traditionary life. Kenneth Burke is interested in desubliming the subliminations (*ecclesia super cloacam*) and Murray Roston in a neglected book, *Prophet and Poet* (Evanston, 1965), sees romanticism growing out of a renewed understanding of Biblical style and the Hebraism/Hellenism opposition.

18. *Wordsworth and the Adequacy of Landscape* (London, 1970).

19. Besides René Wellek the following have recently placed English romanticism in a European context: M. H. Abrams, *Natural Supernaturalism* (New York, 1971) and *The Mirror and the Lamp* (New York, 1953); Thomas McFarland, *Coleridge and the Pantheist Tradition* (Oxford, 1969); Karl Kroeber, *The Artifice of Reality* (Madison, 1964); E. D. Hirsch, *Wordsworth and Schelling* (New Haven, 1960); Paul de Man, "Wordsworth and Hölderlin," *Schweitzer Monatsheft* 45 (March 1966); and Harvey Gross,

"Hegel, Beethoven, Wordsworth: 1770–1970," *The American Scholar* 40 (Winter 1970–71). Also, John Jones, "Postscript on Romantic Feeling," in *John Keats' Dream of Truth* (London, 1969). Among older books the reissue in 1966 of Owen Barfield's *Romanticism Comes of Age* (London, 1944) should be mentioned.

Self, Time, and History

1. In eloquent remarks on the "second genesis" of man, *Ideen zur Geschichte der Menschheit* (1784–87), book 9, part 1.

2. "To interrupt the course of the world—that was Baudelaire's deepest intent." See especially Benjamin's "Theses on the Philosophy of History." He also tells the story of Parisians shooting at clock-faces during the 1830 Revolution as if, like Joshua, to stop the time.

3. See *The Letters of S. T. Coleridge*, ed. E. L. Griggs, 1, 566. ". . . at last we [Coleridge and Wordsworth] ended in metaphysical disquisitions on the nature of character, etc. etc." See also the essay on "Wordsworth and Goethe in Literary History" in this collection.

4. *Prelude* (1850), II, 232–72.

5. The Boy of Winander episode, first published in the second (1800) volume of *Lyrical Ballads*, was incorporated into Book V of the (1805) *Prelude*.

6. Keats, letter to Richard Woodhouse, 27 October 1818.

7. John Hollander remarks in *The Oxford Anthology of English Literature* (I: 1271) that the "exhalation" of Pandemonium already suggests a masque transformation scene.

8. *Aeneid* VI and I.

9. *Georgics* I, passim. See also my essay, "Milton's Counterplot" in *Beyond Formalism* (New Haven, 1970).

10. A break is also felt, of course, after the apostrophe, and after the "Mute" of the final line of the original poem.

11. Compare *The Excursion* (1814) I, 475–84, a passage already found in "The Ruined Cottage" of 1797. On "echo" in Wordsworth cf. John Hollander, "Wordsworth and the Music of Sound" in *New Perspectives on Coleridge and Wordsworth*, ed. G. H. Hartman (New York, 1972), and Frances C. Ferguson, "The Lucy Poems: Wordsworth's Quest for a Poetic Object," *ELH* 40 (1973): 532ff. On echo in Milton see Angus Fletcher, *The Transcendental Masque: An Essay on Milton's Comus* (Ithaca, 1971), pp. 198ff.

12. The indeterminacy here is equivalent to that in echo itself which is both a broken sound (1/2) and a doubled one (2). As I have previously said, the temporal structure of the episode suggests non-fulfillment by showing something too early or premature (first paragraph) and something belated (second paragraph). If we add Wordsworth's notorious thought "The Child is Father of

the Man" then the "touch of time" becomes more "unimaginable" still. On the difficult relation of rhetoric and temporality see Paul de Man's essay "The Rhetoric of Temporality" in *Interpretation: Theory and Practice*, ed. C. S. Singleton (Baltimore, 1969).

13. I am not arguing Wordsworth succeeds in this project. Should we compare "The Boy of Winander" with "Lycidas"—on the basis of their personal or elegiac echo-invocation, and on the additional feeling that Wordsworth's Boy is, potentially, a *genius loci* like the lost poet lamented by Milton—then it could be argued that Wordsworth's poem still "reflects" or "echoes" Milton's. The resemblance of the latter to the former is an "echo of thought in sight"—which is how Wittgenstein, at one point in the *Philosophical Investigations*, defines the experience of "seeing an aspect."

14. A variant belonging to "The Ruined Cottage."

15. Milton's *Comus*, l. 230. That Lucy is "unseen" makes her, like Echo, an antitype of Narcissus; and while Wordsworth is obviously open to the charge of narcissism, this charge must always be modified in the light of his respect for the breaking or unimageable image.

16. See Wordsworth's remarks on "There was a Boy" in the Preface to the 1815 volume, where it heads the "Poems of the Imagination."

Index of Names and Works

Index of Topics